£2.00

THIS SUN OF YORK

Mary Clive

THIS
SUN OF
YORK

A biography of Edward IV

MACMILLAN

SBN 333 14752 9

First published 1973 by

MACMILLAN LONDON LTD

London and Basingstoke
Associated companies in New York Dublin
Melbourne Johannesburg and Madras

Printed in Great Britain by

A. WHEATON & CO.

Exeter

CONTENTS

ILLUSTRATIONS

Between pages 190 and 191.

MAPS

Drawn by K. C. Jordan

The plans of Tewkesbury are based on the maps in *The Battlefields of England* by Lt.-Col. A. H. Burne (Methuen, 1950).

AUTHOR'S NOTE

ALL my sources are in print and I have not checked with the original manuscripts. Stories which are flagrantly untrue have been omitted and no notice has been taken of writers whose evidence would be considered worthless by normal standards. Spelling, punctuation and the inflections of verbs have nearly always been modernized, and if the meaning of a word has altered this is indicated by inverted commas. Personages are called by whichever of their names or titles is most distinctive, regardless of consistency. Occasionally I have taken the liberty of rendering a translation less stilted by altering a word or two. Distances are approximate and based on the A.A. Book.

I am extremely grateful to the many experts, both professional and amateur, who have been so kind as to write me letters on various aspects of fifteenth-century life and to help me in other ways; in particular I should like to thank Mrs M. Whitehead, Mr Cecil Price, Mr G. Naish, Mr K. F. Plummer, Mr Roy Read, Mr R. Shaw Kennedy, Sir Dennis Stucley, and Miss Cecily Hacon. Miss Helen Rogers made many useful criticisms when she was typing the manuscript, and the London Library was indispensable.

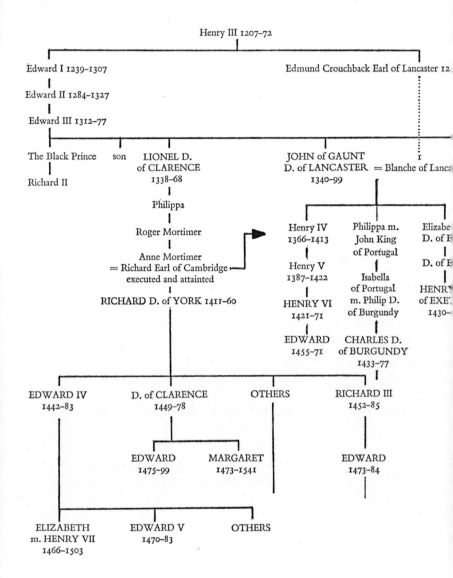

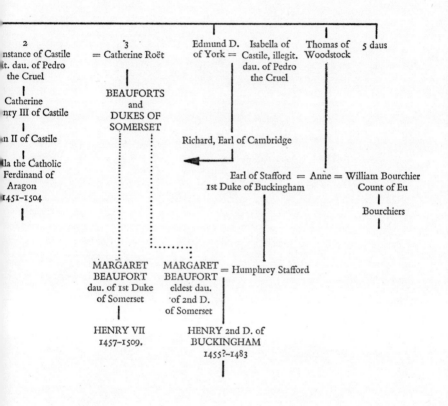

2
nstance of Castile
t. dau. of Pedro
the Cruel
|
Catherine
nry III of Castile
|
n II of Castile
|
lla the Catholic
Ferdinand of
Aragon
1451-1504
|

3
= Catherine Roët
|
BEAUFORTS
and
DUKES OF
SOMERSET

Edmund D. Isabella of Thomas of 5 daus
of York = Castile, illegit. Woodstock
dau. of Pedro
the Cruel

Richard, Earl of Cambridge

Earl of Stafford = Anne = William Bourchier
1st Duke of Buckingham   Count of Eu
|
Bourchiers
|

MARGARET
BEAUFORT
dau. of 1st Duke
of Somerset
|
HENRY VII
1457-1509.

MARGARET
BEAUFORT = Humphrey Stafford
eldest dau.
of 2nd D.
of Somerset

HENRY 2nd D. of
BUCKINGHAM
1455?-1483

Claimants to the English throne in the Second
Half of the Fifteenth Century

All claimants were descended from either Lionel Duke of Clarence or John of Gaunt, but
it is a false simplification to divide them into two parties, Yorkists and Lancastrians.

Brothers and Sisters of Edward IV

Children of Richard Duke of York (1411–60). He married in 1424 Cecily Neville (1415–95) youngest child of Ralph Earl of Westmorland and his second wife, Joan Beaufort.

ANNE; b. 10 Aug 1439 at Fotheringhay; m. 1447 Henry Holland Duke of Exeter (1430–75). Their daughter Anne Holland m. Thomas Grey, son of Elizabeth Woodville by her first husband, and died about 1473. Duchess Anne divorced Exeter in 1472 and m. Sir Thomas St Leger (executed 1483). Their daughter Anne St Leger m. Sir George Manners of Belvoir and was the ancestress of the Dukes of Rutland. Duchess Anne died in 1482.

Henry; b. 10 Feb 1441 at Hatfield; d. young.

EDWARD IV; b. 28 Apr 1442 at Rouen; Earl of March; King, 4 Mar 1461; m. 1 May 1464 Elizabeth Woodville (1438?–1492), widow of Sir John Grey. Ten children. Died in the Palace of Westminster 9 Apr 1483.

EDMUND; b. 17 May 1443 at Rouen; Earl of Rutland. Killed at Wakefield, 30 Dec 1460.

ELIZABETH; b. 22 Apr 1444 at Rouen; m. about 1460 John de la Pole 2nd Duke of Suffolk. Their eldest son, John Earl of Lincoln, was named by Richard III as his heir. Lincoln was killed at the Battle of Stoke, 1487. Elizabeth had six other sons and many daughters. She died 1503/4. Tomb in Wingfield Church, Suffolk.

MARGARET; b. 3 May 1446 at Fotheringhay; m. 1468 Charles the Bold Duke of Burgundy; d. at Malines 1503.

William; b. 1447; d. young.

John; b. 1448; d. young.

GEORGE; b. 21 Oct 1449 in Dublin Castle; Duke of Clarence; m. 1467 Isobel Neville (1451–76), dau. of the Earl of Warwick. Their son Edward Earl of Warwick (1475–99) was executed by Henry VII. Their daughter Margaret Countess of Salisbury (1473–1541) m. Sir Richard Pole and among her children was Cardinal Pole. She was executed by Henry VIII and was the last of the Plantagenets. Clarence was put to death in the Tower on 18 Feb 1478.

Thomas; b. 145?; d. young.

RICHARD III; b. 2 Oct 1452 at Fotheringhay; Duke of Gloucester; m. 1472 Anne Neville (1456–85), younger dau. of the Earl of Warwick. They had one son, Edward Prince of Wales (1473–84). Killed at the Battle of Bosworth 1485.

Ursula; b. 1455; d. young.

Children of Edward IV and Elizabeth Woodville

Elizabeth Woodville was the daughter of Lord Rivers and widow of Sir John Grey, the son and heir of Lady Ferrers of Groby. Grey had been killed at St Albans in 1461 and by him Elizabeth had two sons—Thomas Grey, afterwards Marquis of Dorset and Lord Ferrers of Groby (1455–1501), and Richard Grey (executed by Richard III in 1483).

Elizabeth; b. 11 Feb 1466 at Westminster; m. Henry VII 18 Jan 1486; d. 1503 soon after the birth of her seventh child. Her children were: Arthur 1486, Margaret 1489, Henry VIII 1491, (Elizabeth, died young), Mary 1496, (Edmund and Catherine, died young).

Mary; b. 11 Aug 1467 at Windsor; d. 23 May 1482 at Greenwich. Bur. Windsor.

Cecily; b. 20 Mar 1469 at Westminster; m. 1487 John Viscount Welles (1451?–1499), son of Lionel Lord Welles by his second wife, Margaret, widow of John, 1st Duke of Somerset, and thus half-brother to the King's mother. Cecily married about 1502 an obscure William Kyme, possibly a Lincolnshire neighbour of Ld Welles, and is said to have lived at East Standen in the Isle of Wight and to be buried at Quarr Abbey near Ryde. She died 1507, and left no children.

Edward V; b. 2 Nov 1470 in Westminster Sanctuary; King, 9 Apr 1483; d. in the Tower, June? 1483.

Margaret; b. 10 Apr 1472 at Windsor; d. Dec 1472. Bur. Westminster Abbey.

Richard; b. 17 Aug 1473 at Shrewsbury; Duke of York, Duke of Norfolk and Earl of Nottingham; m. Anne Mowbray, heiress of John 4th D. of Norfolk, 15 Jan 1478; d. in the Tower, June? 1483.

Anne; b. Nov 1475 at Westminster; m. Thomas Howard 3rd D. of Norfolk. Her four children died young. She died 1511.

George; b. 1477 at Windsor; Lieutenant of Ireland, 1478; d. 1479. Bur. Windsor.

Catherine; b. 1479 at Eltham; m. 1495 William Courtenay, son of the Earl of Devon. She died 1527. Her one son was executed in 1539.

Bridget; b. 10 Nov 1480 at Eltham. Became a nun at Dartford, Kent; d. about 1517.

The Woodvilles

Sir Richard Woodville (1405?–1469), afterwards Earl Rivers, of Grafton in Northamptonshire, married secretly in 1436 Jacquetta (1416?–1472), daughter of Pierre Count of St Pol of Luxemburg and widow of John Duke of Bedford. Thirteen of their children lived to grow up but it is not known when they were born or in what order.

Anthony, Lord Scales and 2nd Earl Rivers; m.(1) Elizabeth dau. of Lord Scales and widow of Henry Bourchier; (2) Mary dau. of Sir Henry Fitzlewis. Executed at Pontefract by Richard III in 1483.

John; m. (as her fourth husband) Catherine Neville, Dowager Duchess of Norfolk. Executed by the Earl of Warwick, 1469.

Richard, 3rd and last Earl Rivers; d. 1491. He left Grafton to his nephew, the Marquis of Dorset, and the 2nd Marquis exchanged it with his cousin, Henry VIII—hence its present name of Grafton Regis.

Lionel; Bishop of Salisbury, 1482; d. 1484.

Edward; killed fighting for the Bretons 1488.

Elizabeth; m.(1) Sir John Grey; (2) Edward IV. Died 7 or 8 June 1492.

Margaret; m. Lord Maltravers, heir to the Earl of Arundel.

Anne; m.(1) William Bourchier (d. 1483) eldest son of the Earl of Essex; (2) George Grey, 2nd son of Lord Grey of Ruthin, Earl of Kent. She died 1489.

Jacquetta; m. Lord Strange. Their daughter married the eldest son of Lord Stanley who took the name of Lord Strange and was held hostage by Richard III.

Catherine; m.(1) Henry 2nd Duke of Buckingham; (2) Jasper Tudor, Duke of Bedford; (3) Sir Richard Wingfield (1469?–1525) a young diplomat.

Mary; m. William Herbert, son of Lord Herbert Earl of Pembroke. He exchanged his earldom for that of Huntingdon. In 1484 he m. Catherine Plantagenet, illegitimate dau. of Richard III. Mary Woodville's dau. Elizabeth was sole heir to Raglan castle and the Herbert lands and was Baroness Herbert in her own right. She m. Charles Somerset, illegitimate son of Henry Duke of Somerset, afterwards Earl of Worcester.

Eleanor; m. Anthony Grey, eldest son of Lord Grey of Ruthin, Earl of Kent.

Martha; m. Sir John Bromley.

It is said that there were also two sons, Lewis and John, who died young.

Prologue 1400—1459

BEFORE 1689 THERE WERE NO WRITTEN LAWS GOVERNING THE succession to the English crown and precedents were conflicting. Was England the personal property of the King to be bequeathed to whom he chose like a manor or a farm? (William the Conqueror bequeathed it to his second son and Queen Elizabeth was implored on her death-bed to name a successor.) Should the people elect their king and, if so, what assembly would represent 'the people'? The laws of God and of Nature were often invoked but what exactly were these famous laws? (In the Bible it is the cunning man who wins and that would also appear to be the law of Nature.) What was the custom of England in the good old days? (Local customs varied and in some districts primogeniture was not recognized.) Did an attainted ancestor disqualify a claimant? (Attainders were reversible and in the fifteenth century eighty-four per cent were in fact reversed.) Did two weak claims equal one strong claim? Would a foreigner be acceptable? How should bastards, acknowledged or suspected, be assessed? Should personality and ability be taken into account? (In the case of a disputed succession the answer was emphatically yes; it was useless to put on the throne a man who could not hold it.) How many generations must pass before the descendants of an usurper could be accepted as the true heirs?

The argument that a man was descended in the male line carried little weight in fifteenth-century England. Not only did the English claims to France depend on the rejection of the Salic law, but the property of nearly everyone, from the greatest nobleman to the industrious apprentice who had married his master's daughter, had been built up on the dowries of heiresses. But, if a king left any descendants at all, one of them must certainly be his heir, and it was the failure of Richard II to beget even a daughter which was the fundamental cause of the dissensions in the royal family which flared up intermittently from the Battle of Shrewsbury in 1403 to the Battle of Stoke in 1487.

In 1385, when Richard II was still a youth, Parliament had attempted to forestall trouble by declaring that his heir was his young cousin, Roger Mortimer, Earl of March. In 1398 Roger Mortimer was killed fighting in Ireland and in 1399–1400 another cousin, Henry Bolingbroke, son of John of Gaunt, took advantage of the disturbed political situation to bring off a skilful military coup; Richard was deposed and afterwards murdered, and Henry Bolingbroke ascended the throne.

Henry IV was accepted for the reason that he was the strong man who had seized power, but it was necessary to produce some theoretical proof that he was morally and legally in the right. Specious arguments were not lacking but Roger Mortimer had left children, and so Henry resorted to faking his pedigree, and it was announced that Henry's mother's great-grandfather, Edmund Crouchback, Earl of Lancaster, who had been dead for over a hundred years, was in reality the *elder* brother of Edward I and not, as hitherto supposed, six years his junior; and, as the man in the street could not produce evidence to the contrary, the lie served its turn. Henry Bolingbroke duly became king, and the only fundamental weakness of his position lay in the existence of Mortimer's heirs who had been cheated out of their birthright. In later years it was said that the misfortunes of Henry VI were God's punishment for Henry IV's murder of Richard II, but even if Richard had passed away from natural causes the descendants of Roger Mortimer were bound to be a perpetual menace to the descendants of John of Gaunt. Time did nothing to obliterate resentment and forty years later Richard Duke of York[1] was well aware that his family had been defrauded of the crown.

---

[1] Richard Plantagenet, Duke of York (1411–60). His mother was the daughter of Roger Mortimer and his father was the son of one of the younger sons of Edward III.

Richard Duke of York was the highest-ranking cousin of Henry VI and his social importance was enhanced by the fact that he possessed enormous estates in England, Wales and Ireland. He was not on good terms with the Court clique which ruled the country in the name of the young king and his considerable abilities were hampered by chronic tactlessness, but his right to high military command was indisputable and during the 1430s he took part in several campaigns in France where the English were struggling to retain their possessions. In May 1441 the Duke of York arrived in Rouen, the capital of Normandy, at the head of an expeditionary force. His wife, Cecily,[2] accompanied him, and in the following spring, on 28 April 1442, she gave birth to a son in the castle of Rouen. This was the future Edward IV.

Edward was the Yorks' third child but only surviving son and so he was an important baby. He was the heir of the greatest landowner in England and, if Henry VI failed to have children, he might one day inherit the throne. With characteristic lack of timing, the Duke tried to obtain for his son the hand of one of the daughters of the French king, but his advances were rebuffed. In the autumn of 1445 the York family returned to England and memories of Rouen must soon have become very dim to Edward. However, his nurse, Anne of Caux, came from Normandy, and after her retirement received a pension of twenty pounds a year, and it is possible that Edward's first language was French; certainly throughout his life he was conspicuously friendly towards foreigners. A less happy consequence of his birth in Rouen was that, later, opponents would be able to say that he was not a true-born Englishman.

The Duke of York had managed his forlorn expedition competently if not brilliantly, and he returned from Normandy very much against his will. Supplies which should have been sent to him had been deflected to an expedition which was led by his rival, John Beaufort, Duke of Somerset;[3] and, though Somerset's expedition was a fiasco, that was

[2] Cecily Neville (1415–95) m. Richard Duke of York in 1424. For a list of their twelve children see page xii. Cecily was the 23rd and youngest child of the Earl of Westmorland. Her mother, Joan Beaufort, was Westmorland's second wife and she persuaded her husband to disinherit, as far as was legally possible, the progeny of his first wife in favour of herself and her fourteen children.

[3] John Beaufort, Duke of Somerset (1404?–1444). Grandson of John of Gaunt by his mistress Catherine Roët (whom he afterwards married as his third wife). The Beauforts

small consolation to the Duke of York, who remained convinced that if he had been properly supported with men and money he would have made a success of his campaign, and that if he were permitted to return to Normandy he would recoup the expenses which he had incurred. That the Exchequer owed him £38,666 15s. 4d. was his claim and this was not disputed; however, royal debts far outweighed royal resources, and he accepted tallies for £30,000. In the current state of national bankruptcy it was not unusual to accept reduced payment and, as was also not unusual, few of York's tallies were honoured.

Great landowner though he was, from then on York lived in ignominious debt, and as Edward grew up he must have realized that his father, theoretically so rich, could not pay his bills, had pawned his plate and jewels, and owed money to friends and dependants. Edward must also have listened to endless complaints about the expense of the expedition to Normandy, and it would not be surprising if he drew the moral that it would be very pleasant to possess hard cash and that war with France was a futile pursuit. All the same, in spite of irksome economies, Edward lived in surroundings which many boys would have envied.

English peers had never entrenched themselves in solid duchies as did the grandees on the Continent; instead, their estates took the form of an archipelago of scattered properties and the Duke of York owned land in twenty or more counties. His main residence was Fotheringhay Castle near Peterborough, which was conveniently situated in the middle of England, some eighty miles north of London.[4] Luxuries could be brought to it up the river Nene; mild, flat, well-watered meadows surrounded it; and there was excellent hunting nearby in Rockingham Forest. His second home was Ludlow Castle which he had inherited

---

were legitimized by the Pope in 1396 and by Parliament in 1397, and Henry IV confirmed their legitimacy but debarred them from the throne. These various pronouncements may or may not have been valid, but the Beauforts always behaved as though they were genuine members of the royal family and for all practical purposes their original illegitimacy was cancelled. John Duke of Somerset was the grandfather of Henry VII. His tomb is in Wimborne Minster.

[4] Fotheringhay Castle attained notoriety in 1587 when Mary Queen of Scots was executed in the great hall. Soon afterwards it fell into decay and it was pulled down in 1627. The remains, a grassy mound reflected in still water, leave everything to the imagination and are none the worse for that.

from the Mortimers and which was a Marcher stronghold on the Welsh Border; and in the same district he owned another large castle, Wigmore. He also owned Sandal Castle, near Wakefield in the south of Yorkshire.

IN VIEW OF THE FACT that for nearly half a century Henry VI[5] occupied a very prominent position in English public life, it is necessary to be absolutely honest and to enquire what sort of a person he really was. From the very first he was the victim of circumstances. He became king of England when he was less than a year old and a few months later he received the title of King of France, and it is not surprising that one of his first guardians[6] made the complaint that Henry was disobedient and unmanageable, that he was only too aware of his royal status and that he had been got hold of by the wrong people; fairly soon it must have been apparent to the inner Court circle that the real trouble was that his brain was not equal to the tasks that would be required of it and that he would always be a puppet in the hands of someone or other.

Physically Henry appears to have been perfectly healthy and it is only the use of the euphemistic word 'illness' to describe his mental breakdown which has given rise to the notion that he was delicate. Nor is there any reason to think that he inherited his intellectual disabilities from his grandfather, the mad king of France, who was quite normal in his youth and whose numerous other descendants seem to have been of average intelligence. In the absence of precise details it may be tentatively suggested that Henry VI was merely a very slow-witted boy such as may be born into any family, one who is capable of earning his living as a manual worker but who gets called 'retarded' if any great intellectual prowess is expected of him. He disliked soldiers and war and all the things for which his father had been famous, and he countered the roughness of his courtiers by surrounding himself with priests and by carrying piety to such extremes that it verged on religious mania.

[5] Henry VI (6 December 1421–23 May 1471). Son of Henry V and Catherine, daughter of Charles VI 'the Mad' of France.
[6] Richard Beauchamp Earl of Warwick (1382–1439). Father-in-law of the 'Kingmaker'. His gilded effigy is in St Mary's, Warwick.

After Henry's death a short account of him was written in Latin by an elderly cleric who had formerly been one of his chaplains.[7] For the most part he appears to have been drawing on his personal recollections, but memories are fallible, and one of the few statements which can be checked (a reference to the will of Cardinal Beaufort) is not accurate.

Henry, says the chaplain, was a simple man, without crook or craft of untruth. He was so humble and pious that even when he was wearing his kingly crown he would bow before the Lord as devoutly as any young monk. When praying on horseback he rode with bared head so that his royal cap would often have fallen to the ground if it had not been caught by his servants. His meals always began with a dish which represented the five wounds of Christ as it were red with blood. He would arrive at the very beginning of divine office and he did not weary however long it continued, and he would not allow hawks, swords and daggers to be brought into church, nor business discussions to be carried on there, even daring to reprove great men and nobles. He also restrained swearers, whatever their rank, his own expression being 'Forsothe and Forsothe'.[8]

His chastity was quite remarkable. He avoided licentiousness when he was young and after he married the Lady Margaret (by whom he begot one son, Prince Edward) he was entirely faithful to her, even during her absences which were often very long; and when they were together he did not approach his wife violently or in the manner of lewd people, but with propriety and as their circumstances required; there being preserved between them conjugal respectability and the greatest dignity.

Of nudity he had a particular horror. One Christmas a nobleman sent in a troop of dancing-girls with naked breasts and he very angrily averted his eyes and turned his back upon them and went to his chamber saying: 'Fy, Fy, for shame, forsothe ye be to blame.'[9] On another occasion at Bath, he saw some men bathing naked and he hurried away,

---

[7] *Henry the Sixth*. A reprint of John Blacman's memoir, with translation and notes by M. R. James, Provost of Eton (1919).

[8] These words are in English in the original.

[9] These words are in English in the original.

much displeased. In his room he had hidden windows through which he could watch unseen lest foolish women coming to his house should cause the fall of any of his household, and if he met Eton boys who had wandered up to Windsor Castle he would give them money and warn them against the wickedness of the Court.

Henry refused to dress like a king. It is well known that from his youth up he always wore round-toed shoes and boots like a farm-worker, and a long gown with a rolled hood like an ordinary citizen's. At festivals he wore a hair shirt.

Henry complained when he had to exchange his devotions for affairs of state. Once, when he and his chaplain were together at Eltham, a certain mighty Duke knocked on the door and the King said: 'They do so interrupt me that by day or night I can hardly snatch a moment to be refreshed by reading of any holy teaching without disturbance.' The same thing happened when they were together at Windsor.

He forgave all injuries and affronts and once, when he noticed the quarter of a traitor on a stake, he ordered that it should be removed.[1] 'He that saw it bears witness.'

The chaplain also mentions a few miracles performed by the king. He was able to turn a small quantity of wheat into enough bread to feed his army; he divined that a church which he was passing did not contain the Sacrament; before his final capture he was warned of it for seventeen days by the voices of saints; when he was in the Tower he saw a woman about to drown a child and he sent a messenger to her and she desisted. The sketch ends with a reasonable little speech supposed to have been spoken by Henry during his imprisonment, pointing out that his father and grandfather had been kings before him and that he had been acknowledged king when he was a child in the cradle.

From this artless hagiography it emerges that Henry could not prevent his courtiers from teasing him, and that they could not induce him to behave in a dignified manner nor to dress in a way that would earn

---

[1] Henry's subjects knew so little about him that a London chronicler wrote of the year 1450–1: 'And at Rochester nine men were beheaded . . . and their heads were sent unto London by the King's commandment and set upon London Bridge . . . and twelve heads at another time were brought unto London and set up . . . as was commanded by the King. Men called it in Kent the harvest of heads.'

him the respect of his subjects; and a few cases from the records of the King's Bench hint at the bad impression he made when he appeared in public.

In 1442 a yeoman of Kent bought a pardon after remarking, 'The King is a lunatic as his father [sic] was', while two years later a gentleman narrowly escaped being hanged for comparing Henry unfavourably to the Dauphin. A few years later a London draper was in trouble for disparaging the King's face and 'wit'; and a German of Ely who said that he looked more like a child than a man, and a farmworker of Cley in Norfolk who called him a fool, were also brought up for trial. In 1450 a Sussex yeoman was indicted for saying in the market-place at Brightling that 'the King was a natural fool and would oft-times hold a staff in his hands with a bird on the end, playing therewith as a fool, and that another king must be ordained to rule the land'.²

When Henry was a baby, affairs of state were managed by his uncles but when he became adolescent an outsider, William de la Pole, Earl of Suffolk,³ the Steward of the Royal Household, won his confidence and eventually obtained supreme political power. It was Suffolk who arranged Henry's marriage. The bride was a niece of the French king and the alliance was one of the conditions of a peace treaty by which the French gained many advantages and the English none.

Margaret of Anjou⁴ belonged to the international royal family which was so cosmopolitan in outlook that any member of it was ready to undertake the rule of any country at any moment. Her father, Count René of Anjou,⁵ inherited the widely separated provinces of Anjou and Provence and the small Duchy of Bar, and acquired Lorraine through

---

² R. L. Storey, *The End of the House of Lancaster*.

³ William de la Pole, 4th Earl and 1st Duke of Suffolk (1396–1450). He was one of the few people whose family had originally been merchants and not landed gentry, and so little did the worlds of town and country mingle that it was still remembered that his grandfather had been a merchant of Hull. He married Alice Chaucer, granddaughter of the poet Chaucer and Philippa Roët (sister of John of Gaunt's mistress).

⁴ Margaret of Anjou (23 March 1429–25 Aug 1482) Daughter of René Count of Anjou and Isabella of Lorraine. Her wedding festivities lasted a year, beginning with her betrothal in Tours and ending with her coronation in Westminster Abbey on 30 May 1445.

⁵ René Count of Anjou (1409–80). 'Good King René'. He looked like a pug-dog but by temperament he was an aesthete and he painted and wrote, and spent recklessly on buildings, gardens, zoos, and *fêtes champêtres*. By the time he was twenty-one he had four children of which Margaret was the youngest.

his wife; he also inherited claims to be king of Naples, Sicily, Hungary and Jerusalem. In his early years he was much occupied by unsuccessful wars and he was for some time prisoner of the Duke of Burgundy in Dijon; then he joined his wife who had managed to establish herself temporarily in Naples. Owing to her parents' adventures, Margaret saw little of them, and was brought up by her grandmother, Yolande of Aragon, a powerful matriarch who acted as regent in Anjou. Yolande's daughter Marie had married Charles VII of France and the courts of Anjou and France—both centred on the Loire—were hand in glove; Margaret thus grew up in a tradition of courageous female rulers and friendship with France and war with Burgundy. She had a good understanding of international intrigue but none at all of national prejudices.

When Margaret was about thirteen her grandmother Yolande died and her parents, ejected from Naples, returned to Anjou and set to work to find her a husband. Without a dowry beyond nominal rights in Majorca and Minorca, her prospects were not very bright, and it was a great coup for the whole family—and particularly for her uncle Charles VII—when she married the King of England. She was well coached in the part she was expected to play and she had not been married very long before she was writing to tell her uncle that she had persuaded her husband to hand over the disputed province of Maine. Soon afterwards Henry VI himself corroborated the offer, but these irresponsible promises were not honoured by the English government and when Maine did eventually change hands it was taken by force of arms.

Margaret's conception of the role of a queen consort might have been appropriate in a Mediterranean or oriental country, but it was bound to be resented in England where harem intriguers have never been encouraged. The popular queen consort is quite a new phenomenon and in the fifteenth century there were very few ways by which a queen could endear herself to her people except by mitigating the harshness of a stern husband. The last two queens had been disgraced and Margaret's sponsors, the Earl and Countess of Suffolk, were disliked by all factions except their own. As for her husband, he was dimwitted, religious to an absurd degree, had a morbid horror of sex, took no interest in the government of the realm and provoked the contempt of his subjects by insisting on dressing like a member of the lower classes.

To make matters worse, the country was drifting into a state of anarchy; Suffolk's government was corrupt; law and order had broken down; in the provinces violence was a commonplace. At the Court money was squandered and embezzled and the Exchequer sank deeper and deeper into debt.[6] The usual committees of important nobles ceased to meet and the Royal Signet, which Suffolk could absolutely control, was constantly used instead of the Great Seal or the Privy Seal. Henry would sign anything or grant anything and, as he had no idea of the value of money, give anything away. Among his fixed ideas was the amiable conviction that a king should be merciful, and he was ready to pardon any petitioner, however atrocious his crime. Very naturally, access to him was restricted and at first Margaret also was easily by-passed; her function was to produce children and not to meddle in affairs of state.

Margaret did not meekly acquiesce in this passive role. There has survived a book containing copies of letters written by her secretary;[7] they begin shortly after her arrival in England and they are very bustling and business-like. She recommends protégés, arranges marriages, settles quarrels, bestows offices and rewards. Now her messengers are to bring goods through the customs without paying dues, now she supports the safe-conduct already given by the King to a fifty-ton ship importing wine from Brittany. She wants deer ready to hunt; she wants two bloodhounds trained. She wants the Duchess of Somerset to ask the Duke of Somerset to pay the money which Henry had promised to Margaret's squire. The voice is authoritative but the impression of queenly power is considerably modified by the editor's disclosure that her commands were generally disregarded, especially when she attempted to dispense patronage which did not belong to her and to reward friends with offices which were in the gift of other people.

Time passed, and Margaret showed no signs of performing her all-important duty: she bore no children and it was openly suggested

[6] Paradoxically, throughout the fifteenth century wages were higher in relation to prices then ever before, so that, whether they knew it or not, the working classes were enjoying a boom.
[7] *Letters of Margaret of Anjou* (Camden Society, 1863).

that the ostentatious piety of the King might be responsible, and that when he wished 'to have his sport' with her his confessor, the Bishop of Salisbury, advised him 'not to come nigh her'.[8] Be that as it may, Henry was without a child and the question who would become king if he died remained of great interest.

IN 1447 THE DUKE OF YORK was given the office of Lieutenant of Ireland. It was a very suitable appointment as he had inherited the title of Earl of Ulster and enormous Irish estates, but he let two years elapse before he could bring himself to go into exile, and he did not arrive in Ireland till 6 July 1449. It is not known whether Edward and his other children accompanied him but Duchess Cecily was as usual at his side, and on 21 October 1449 she gave birth in Dublin Castle to her ninth child, George, afterwards Duke of Clarence. The Irish were already suffering from absentee landlords and they hailed the baby with delight, pathetically hoping that he would grow up to be a prince who would live among them and rule them wisely and justly.

Broadly speaking, there were three groups with which the Duke of York had to reckon; the native Irish chieftains, the Norman-Irish nobles, and the English government in Dublin, and there was always the fear that the Irish and the Normans would sink their differences and combine to eject the English. Occasionally a Parliament was called and representatives from the eastern counties and a few towns assembled, but for most of the time he had a very free hand and, surprisingly, was a popular Lieutenant. However, this limited success did not satiate his ambitions, and he continued to brood over his hereditary wrongs.

In England disturbances were increasing and in 1450 there were a series of explosions. Suffolk was impeached and assassinated and his two closest collaborators, the Bishop of Chichester and the Bishop of Salisbury, were lynched—the former at Portsmouth by infuriated soldiers whose wages were in arrears and the latter as he was conducting mass in a village church in Wiltshire. Shortly afterwards the Men of Kent marched on London under a mysterious leader known as Jack Cade.

[8] R. L. Storey, *The End of the House of Lancaster.*

But the death of Suffolk and the two bishops had given Queen Margaret her chance. Although she was still only twenty-one she adroitly joined forces with Edmund Beaufort, Duke of Somerset[9] and became the leader of the Court party.

In the autumn of this troubled year the Duke of York came over from Ireland and attempted to obtain official recognition of his claim that he was the heir to the throne, but he made no headway; tactless, pushing York with his string of righteous grievances and his empty pockets was not a man his fellow peers would accept as a leader. Two years later he made another effort to assert his rights. He did not suggest deposing Henry who was the crowned and anointed king; all York demanded was that he should be the power behind the throne. It was, however, asking too much. Edmund Duke of Somerset had no intention of taking second place and, frustrated, York retired again to Ireland.

1453 was another eventful year. The fall of Constantinople in June may have aroused little interest but the loss in July of the district round Bordeaux was a shattering blow; it had happily belonged to the kings of England for three hundred years and now all that was left of England's continental possessions and the conquests of Henry V was the port of Calais and a few miles of land behind it. Meanwhile a new twist was given to home politics by the announcement that the Queen was pregnant.[1]

On 15 October 1453, Queen Margaret gave birth to a son in the Palace of Westminster. He was christened Edward and later was officially known as Edward Prince of Wales although the opposition chose to refer to him as 'the Queen's son'. Eight years had passed since Henry's marriage and his notorious horror of sex made it inevitable that there should be suspicions that the child was not his; among sug-

---

[9] Edmund Beaufort, Duke of Somerset (1406?–1455). Brother of John Duke of Somerset, who had died leaving his fortune to his baby daughter, Margaret Beaufort. The Dukedom was created afresh for Edmund, but it is convenient (though incorrect) to refer to him as the 2nd Duke. He married Eleanor Beauchamp, one of the many daughters of Richard Beauchamp, Earl of Warwick, and they had three sons and five daughters.

[1] A palace official, Richard Tunstall, secured an annuity of £40 for informing the King of the Queen's pregnancy. In 1454 this was cancelled by the Duke of York but restored (reduced to 50 marks) in 1456. Tunstall appears to have been a man of great ability, and he was trusted by Edward IV and Henry VII. He died 1491/2.

gested fathers were Edmund Duke of Somerset and the Earl of Wilt-shire,[2] who were only suspected because they were the most prominent members of the Court party. Queen Margaret certainly had no accepted lover, and the Earl of Warwick told a Burgundian chronicler[3] that the Prince's father was a *baveur* or *baladin*, a low nobody.

To cast doubts on a child's paternity is extremely easy and a good scandal, however impossible to prove, is impossible to kill. In days when lawsuits over property were incessant and there were no birth certificates[4] and much depended on the credibility of a manuscript pedigree, slander was very tempting, and when the inheritance of a kingdom was in dispute allegations of bastardy were quite usual. The truth about Margaret's baby can never now be known and it was not known at the time. If he was illegitimate perhaps only two people, herself and her lover, knew the secret; if he were legitimate only one person, herself, could be absolutely sure of the fact; consequently, though everyone chose to believe what he found most convenient, there would always be a tiny speck of doubt.

Assuming that Henry was not the father of the baby, excuses can be made for Queen Margaret. Here was a bright, lively girl tied for over seven years to a slovenly recluse who failed to give her a child; she was surrounded by normal young men and without being exceptionally depraved she might have fallen in love with one of them and have desperately decided that an heir would be welcome however she came by him. It may well have been that Henry was horrified when it was announced to him that Margaret was pregnant; he had either to accuse his alarming wife of adultery or allow the holy office of king to descend to a bastard.

Early in August 1453, about two months before Margaret's baby was born, Henry had a complete mental breakdown which rendered him unable to appear in public. The attack came on him at Clarendon, a royal hunting-lodge in Wiltshire, and he habitually lived in such

[2] James Butler, Earl of Wiltshire (1420–61). He was the eldest son of an Irish peer, the 4th Earl of Ormonde, and his second wife was a daughter of Edmund Duke of Somerset.

[3] Chastellain. *Baveur* is literally a dribbler; *baladin* an itinerant dancer.

[4] Parish registers were not started until 1538 when Thomas Cromwell issued the order that every incumbent should keep a record of the christenings, marriages and burials in his parish.

seclusion that it was possible to conceal his condition for six months. Parliament, which had been called for November, was postponed on the pretext that there was an outbreak of plague, and it was hoped that he would be better by the New Year; in fact he remained hors de combat for sixteen months and did not recover until December 1454.

In February 1454 the postponed Parliament met and the Duke of York came to London bringing with him his eldest son, Edward, now nearly twelve years old and able to ride with the men. Life was so uncertain that a hefty-looking son and heir helped to bolster up credit. The political situation was highly dangerous and many peers, not wishing to become involved, stayed away, and for the only time in medieval history there were fines for non-attendance. Queen Margaret, remembering that her grandmother had successfully ruled Anjou, demanded to be appointed regent. She was female, French, had shown no particular signs of wisdom, and she was brushed aside. The Duke of York also offered his services; more capable than the Queen, he was scarcely more trusted and like her he carried the stigma of being short of money. His patriotic pose did not carry conviction and Parliament, at a loss, sent a deputation to Windsor to interview the King and to decide whether a regent was essential. The report they brought back was that he was entirely blank and silent and unable to move without assistance and so, grudgingly, the Duke of York was made Protector with very limited powers and with a council of magnates to act as a check.

The Queen's party now included the King's two half-brothers, Edmund and Jasper Tudor,[5] the sons of Catherine of France, who had secretly married one of her household officials, a Welshman named Owen Tudor. This unorthodox idyll had not been discovered till 1436 by which time Catherine had given birth to several children. She then retired to the state apartments at Bermondsey Abbey and died a few months later, while Owen Tudor, a slippery character and possibly a pleasant change after the inflexible Henry V, dodged in and out of prison and finally established himself in north Wales, his native country.

[5] Edmund Tudor (1430?–1456). Cr. (1453) Earl of Richmond; m. (1455) Margaret Beaufort.

Jasper Tudor (1431?–1495). Cr. (1453) Earl of Pembroke and (1485) Duke of Bedford; m. (1485) Catherine Woodville, widow of the Duke of Buckingham.

Edmund and Jasper were suitably educated and in due course appeared at Henry's court where they behaved with great circumspection. Welshmen were not permitted to contract marriages in England without royal permission but in 1452 Parliament pronounced their parents' marriage to be valid, and their social position, though curious, was assured. They had, of course, no English royal blood in their veins and were not in the line of succession.

By this time the Duke of York was beginning to build up a faction and had become the head of the anti-Court, anti-Somerset peers. In debt he might be, but he was still owner of enormous estates where dwelt potential soldiers, and allies snowballed round him, impelled more by their own quarrels and ambitions than by the rights and wrongs of the Duke.

The peerage numbered about fifty men, give or take a dozen, who were tied together by their social position for the whole of their lives. They were all landowners and they bickered over rights and duties, honours and perquisites, boundaries and buildings, poaching and local politics, and as they were much intermarried there were wills and dowries and inheritances about which they could disagree. How they would align themselves could not be calculated in advance; next-door neighbours might be friends or foes, a son might not keep up his father's feuds, and a quarrel of long standing might be suddenly healed by a marriage alliance.

The landowners' quarrel which had the most far-reaching consequences was the rivalry between the Earl of Northumberland[6] and the Earl of Salisbury.[7] The lands of the Percies and the Nevilles were interlocked and stretched in patches from the Scottish Border to the Humber, and the minor landowners of the north were sucked in as

[6] Henry Percy, 2nd Earl of Northumberland (1394–1455). Son of Harry Hotspur. He married Eleanor, sister of his rival, the Earl of Salisbury.

[7] Richard Neville, 1st Earl of Salisbury (1400–60). He was the eldest son of the Earl of Westmorland by his second wife, Joan Beaufort, and as his eldest half-brother inherited the Westmorland title he had been granted the title of his wife's father. Three of his brothers married heiresses and became Lord Fauconberg, Lord Latimer and Lord Abergavenny, and a fourth procured the bishopric of Durham. His sisters included the Duchess of Buckingham, the Duchess of Norfolk and Cecily Duchess of York. The Nevilles and their relations by marriage did not all act together, but enough of them co-operated to make them the strongest family complex in England.

associates on one side or the other. The Percies had the advantage that they were genuine local chieftains of long standing, but the Nevilles had been gaining strength ever since John of Gaunt married his daughter Joan Beaufort to the Earl of Westmorland with the deliberate intention that the Nevilles should keep down the power of the Percies while assisting them to fight off the Scots. The Nevilles, moreover, had among them one truly masterful personality, Salisbury's eldest son, the young Earl of Warwick.[8]

As a child of six Warwick had been married to the nine-year-old Anne Beauchamp, and this marriage, which when it was made was no more than a reasonable bargain, by chance turned out to be fantastically advantageous. The vast Beauchamp fortune was inherited by Anne's only brother but in 1446 he died, and when in 1449 his only daughter also died Anne scooped the pool to the exclusion of her four half-sisters; this was legally correct though naturally resented by the husbands of her half-sisters, one of whom was Edmund Duke of Somerset. At the age of twenty Warwick obtained the title which his father-in-law had rendered famous, as well as the wealth which made possible his subsequent career.

Unfortunately there is no contemporary portrait of Warwick nor a description of his appearance nor even an intelligent assessment of his character. He was evidently a man of abounding energy, equally at home on sea as on land, and so adaptable that he could in a moment scrap one plan and invent another. He entirely understood the importance of appearing successful and display came naturally to him. His retainers swarmed in the streets; his badge, the ragged staff, became the best known of all badges; and his housekeeping was so extravagant that it was said that any friend of his servants could walk in and take away a chunk of meat on the end of his dagger and that all the taverns near his London house were supplied with meat from his kitchens. Everyone could see that he was both rich and generous, and a leader whom it would be shrewd to follow.

---

[8] Richard Neville, Earl of Warwick (1428–71). 'The Kingmaker'. In 1434 he married Anne Beauchamp, daughter of Richard Beauchamp Earl of Warwick, and in 1449 he was created Earl of Warwick. A man who married the heiress of a peer did not automatically succeed to his father-in-law's title, but it was often given to him.

In view of the inter-marriages of the magnates, the great families might have grouped themselves in any way; as things were, Warwick's quarrel with Somerset drove him away from the Court Party and into the camp of the Duke of York and other Nevilles followed, while the Percies automatically joined the Queen.

During the Duke of York's protectorate, which lasted from the spring of 1454 to the end of the year, he acted with energy and good sense. Even if he were not so public-spirited as he made out, even if his motives were selfish and his methods severe, he did at least know how a kingdom ought to be governed which is more than could be said for either Edmund Duke of Somerset or the late Duke of Suffolk. The suppression of lawlessness was the most urgent problem, and one of the first tasks which confronted him was to deal with a rising in Yorkshire which was headed by two wild young men, Lord Egremont[9] and the Duke of Exeter.[1] Egremont was a Percy, a landless Hotspur who dashed hither and thither harrying the Nevilles, while Exeter was a descendant of John of Gaunt by his first wife, Blanche of Lancaster, and incidentally married to York's eldest daughter Anne. On paper he was heir-presumptive to Henry VI, but there must have been something obviously futile about him for he was never able to attract a faction and he was not taken seriously by either side. He may have been a spendthrift or a drunkard, or just blatantly absurd. On this occasion, Exeter announced that he wished to govern the kingdom and he also claimed the estates of the Duchy of Lancaster which were without question the private property of Henry VI.

At York's approach the rebellion petered out and Exeter fled to Westminster Sanctuary, from which he was removed with questionable legality; the next few years he spent in various prisons. Egremont escaped capture till the autumn, when he and his brother were rounded up by the Nevilles who astutely sued them for damages and arranged that they should be fined a sum which was too large for them to pay; convicted in this manner they could not buy themselves off with a

---

[9] Thomas Percy Lord Egremont (1422–60). Second son of 2nd Earl of Northumberland.

[1] Henry Holland Duke of Exeter (1430–75). His grandmother was full sister to Henry IV. He married Anne, daughter of Richard Duke of York in 1447; they were separated by 1464, and she obtained a divorce in 1472.

royal pardon and they were confined as debtors in Newgate, their imprisonment ending two years later when they bribed a warder, smuggled in arms, and escaped on horses while the other prisoners fought on the roof.

While the Duke of York was making his successful foray into Yorkshire he received two letters from his sons, Edward and Rutland, whom he had left behind in Ludlow Castle and these are the only private letters of Edward's which have come down to us. Actually they were penned by a secretary and they are a mixture of stilted compliments and the usual boyish 'Thank you . . . Please send . . .' And, as was the case with so many letters, the really important part was left for the messenger to convey by word of mouth.

The first was written on 27 April 1454. After some formal filial greetings, congratulations and thanks for sending news, it goes on:

> Also we thank your noblesse and good fatherhood of our green gowns now late sent unto us to our great comfort. Beseeching your good lordship to remember our porteux [prayer-books]. And that we might have some fine bonnets sent unto us by the next sure messenger, for necessity so requireth. Our thus right noble lord and father please it your highness to wit that we have charged your servant William Smith bearer of these for to declare unto your nobility certain things on our behalf, namely concerning and touching the odious rule and demeaning of Richard Croft and of his brother. Wherefore we beseech your gracious lordship and full noble fatherhood to hear him in exposition of the same and to his relation to give full faith and credence.[2]

It is signed in bold, wobbly letters, E. Marche and E. Rutlonde.

The other letter, dated 3 June, appears to have been mostly composed by the secretary, but the boys' voices are heard at the end. 'Also we beseech your good lordship that it may please you to send us Harry Lovedeyne, groom of your kitchen, whose service is to us right agreeable; and we will send you John Boyce to wait on your good lordship.'

It sometimes happens that at our first meeting with a person he does or says something which afterwards turns out to be typical of him, and Edward's letter is comically characteristic. He is polite in a jaunty sort of way, he regards fine clothes as a necessity, he wants a handsome prayer book, he expects that his younger brother will sign on the line, he is confident that the messenger will carry out his wishes, he has

---

[2] British Museum, Cotton MS., Vespasian F. iii.f.16.

strong ideas as to who is suitable for what job, he refuses to put up with bullying and he is not in the least afraid of his father.

Richard and Thomas Croft, incidentally, were the brothers of a neighbour, Sir Richard Croft of Croft Castle, near Ludlow. They were then about twenty, and were evidently following the usual custom and finishing their education in the castle of the local great man. This tiff with the young sons of the house did their careers no harm and during the reign of Edward IV the Croft brothers received many small government appointments and grants of land.[3]

BY CHRISTMAS 1454 HENRY VI had sufficiently recovered from his trance or stupour again to go through the motions of being a king. He could walk and talk and appear in processions, but it is probable that his mind had deteriorated and that, from having been merely rather slow-witted and eccentric, he was thenceforward a harmless lunatic who could be pushed around without his having any clear idea of what was happening. The official version issued from the Palace was that he recovered his senses quite suddenly and that when the Queen showed him the Prince of Wales he expressed great pleasure, but according to the story which reached the Continent—and which was considered so amusing that it was forwarded to the Duke of Milan—when Henry saw the baby he exclaimed that it must be the child of the Holy Ghost.

As it was never admitted that Henry was mad, from then on he was the equivalent of an inanimate object with the singular quality that whoever held his person could use him as a cover behind which they could be, in effect, the ruler of England. At the beginning of 1455 Henry was in the custody of the Queen and, by March, she and Somerset were again all powerful and York and his faction had retreated to their castles in the north, and had set about mobilizing their supporters.

In the spring Somerset summoned a Great Council to meet at Leicester, himself nominating the commoners who were to attend, and

[3] O. G. S. Croft, *The House of Croft of Croft Castle* (Privately printed 1949). Croft Castle is still inhabited by members of the same family.

in May the Court Party began moving from London towards the rendezvous, escorted by a large guard, and taking Henry with them as a symbol of authority. They had got no further than St Albans before they were brought up short; York and Warwick, ignoring the order to go to Leicester, had made a lightning dash south with an army said to number three thousand men.[4]

The town of St Albans had only rudimentary defences and the Court Party had not expected to have to fight a battle, but they did what they could to protect themselves. The morning of 22 May found them barricaded into the market-place, which was a long wide street with many openings, and from there they attempted to parley with the enemy. Warwick and York and their army were just outside the town on its eastern side, and they demanded that Somerset should be handed over to them; Somerset naturally refused to give himself up and Warwick attacked. At first his men were nonplussed by the barricaded side-streets, but they found ways to creep through the flimsy houses and strips of garden and soon they had burst into the market-place and the defenders, confused and overwhelmed, were fleeing in all directions. Edmund Duke of Somerset,[5] the Earl of Northumberland and Lord Clifford[6]—all particular enemies of the Neville family—were caught and killed, and the affray known as the First Battle of St Albans was over.

The victors at once expressed great loyalty to Henry, who had been slightly wounded in the neck by an arrow; then, triumphantly, with the King, passive as ever, in their midst, they proceeded to London. Public opinion was shocked by what had happened, and the victors themselves were somewhat apologetic and offered to pay for masses for the souls of the deceased. However, Edmund Duke of Somerset was dead and his offices were divided among them, Warwick obtaining the much coveted and extremely responsible post of Captain of Calais. It seemed as if the Court Party was broken for ever.

[4] Medieval estimates of armies are generally too large and often quite wild; on the other hand estimates of distance are apt to be too small.

[5] The spot where the Duke of Somerset was killed is marked by a plaque on the National Provincial Bank, which stands on the site of the Castle Inn.

[6] Thomas, 8th Lord Clifford (1414–55). Hereditary Sheriff of Westmorland. Buried in St Albans Abbey.

This was far from being the case. The King could not be held a prisoner indefinitely and the Queen, gaining confidence, rallied round her the many peers who did not like either the Duke of York or the Nevilles. There was a new Earl of Northumberland[7] who naturally joined the anti-Neville faction, a new Lord Clifford,[8] and Edmund Duke of Somerset had left three sons, the eldest of whom stepped forward to take his father's place. Henry Beaufort, 3rd Duke of Somerset,[9] was only nineteen, but he quickly rose to be Margaret's right-hand man and commander of her fighting forces. Her opponents, of course, were also gathering strength, but they suffered from having divided aims; the objective of the Nevilles was to obtain permanent possession of the puppet king, while the Duke of York was determined to be recognized as the heir to the throne.

FOR FOUR YEARS AFTER the First Battle of St Albans an uneasy peace was maintained, but animosity increased and, in the late summer of 1459, both sides began to collect armies. The Queen, who was now in complete control of the Court Party, went up to Cheshire to raise troops from the Duchy of Lancaster, while the Duke of York mustered his forces at Ludlow Castle in south Shropshire. For him and his friends the outlook was not unpromising. The active Herbert family were coming from Monmouthshire with their retainers, Warwick was bringing over some of his professional soldiers from Calais, and the Earl of Salisbury was recruiting on his Yorkshire estates.

On 23 September 1459, the Earl of Salisbury with his sons Thomas and John Neville[1] was proceeding along the road from Newcastle-under-Lyme to Shrewsbury with an army which a hostile Parliament said was 5000 strong but which was probably much smaller, when their way was barred on Blore Heath by a force sent by the Queen and led

[7] Henry Percy, 3rd Earl of Northumberland (1421–61), son of the 2nd Earl. Killed at Towton.

[8] John, 9th Lord Clifford (1435–61). Killed at Ferrybridge.

[9] Henry Beaufort, 3rd Duke of Somerset (1436–64). Eldest son of Edmund, 2nd Duke of Somerset. Executed after Hexham.

[1] Thomas Neville, killed at Wakefield, 30 December 1460. John Neville, Lord Montagu, 1461, Earl of Northumberland, 1464, Marquis of Montagu, 1470 (*c.* 1431–71).

by Lord Audley.[2] There was a head-on encounter with many casualties on both sides and a good deal of confusion. Thomas and John Neville were taken prisoner but Lord Audley was killed, and the Earl of Salisbury was able to cut his way through and continue with what was left of his army along the road towards Ludlow.[3]

[2] James Tuchet, 5th Lord Audley (1398–1459).
[3] Blore Heath is on the A53 at a point a little short of Market Drayton. A monument marks the spot where Lord Audley fell.

England and Southern Scotland

xli

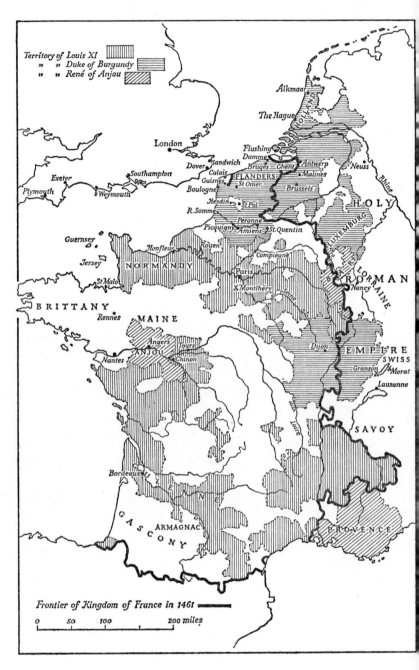

Map of France c. 1461

I

Ludlow Castle Autumn 1459

L
UDLOW CASTLE STOOD ON THE SUMMIT OF A SMALL HILL ABOVE A
market town and round the base of the hill wound the River
Teme. Today the castle is a ruin, the rooms open to the sky, but
in 1459 it was very dark inside. Every scene was a Rembrandt. Shafts
of light slanted through narrow windows set in thick walls and as dusk
fell the gloom deepened till candles and tapers were lit here and there.
Compared to Norman barons who had existed like refugees camping
in farm buildings, the Duke of York lived in luxury; he had glass in
his windows and tapestries on his walls, but his castle was not smart or
fashionable. The elegancies of life came from abroad, and Ludlow was
far from the sea and boats could not get up the river. In the hall there
was little furniture except trestle tables and benches, a stool or two, and
a chair for the Duke; and the great status symbol, the altar-like side-
board known as the cupboard, was somewhat bare because the Duke
had pawned his plate. In the bedrooms there was practically nothing
except big beds with testers from which bunched-up curtains hung out
into the middle of the room like enormous pears. People sat on the beds,
on cushions on the floor, or on the rushes. The rooms led into each
other;[1] hangings, screens and curtains made alcoves, recesses and

---

[1] Corridors did not begin to appear in English country houses until the end of the next
century.

cubicles, but there was no more privacy than in a school. People were everywhere; groping up and down the spiral staircases, sleeping on the ground, crouched in the window-seats trying to get light for some ploy. The noise was unceasing and there was a strong smell of horses and dogs.

Our ancestors have left behind them a very misleading impression of their appearance by contriving for themselves beautiful stylized effigies with smooth faces and regular features, and bodies of the right size and shape; all are dignified, pious and serene, and any true portrait looks like an unkind caricature. All knights are brave and dressed in armour (which in fact they only wore on the rare occasions when fighting was expected); all ladies are pure and good; all merchants are worthy and philanthropic; all bishops are learned and ascetic; it is only peasants who are ugly and comic, who play the bagpipe, steal pigs and beat their husbands.

Posterity has added two myths of its own. One is that medieval men were all very small, which is disproved by the comfortable proportions of choir-stalls and also by the fact that suits of armour are found in every size. The other myth is that people aged very fast, that boys were precocious and fifty was considered old. Nothing corroborates this. Young men did not make their mark particularly early. The baby kings did not really rule; the child marriages were not consummated; and the regular army call-up was 'for all men between the ages of sixteen and sixty'. Elizabeth Woodville was over forty when she gave birth to her twelfth child; Caxton was over fifty when he set up his printing-press; and the Battle of Flodden was won by a man of seventy. It would rather seem that the veterans who had managed to keep alive were greatly respected; their names had gradually become well known and, in a period when books were mines of misinformation and everything had to be learnt the hard way, first-hand experience was extremely valuable.

Among the nobles and knights assembled in Ludlow Castle were some of the future rulers of England. Like the majority of their compatriots they were countrymen who drew their incomes from the land; a tough, weather-beaten, outdoor crowd, accustomed to ride all day, in all weathers, summer and winter. They had teeth missing, skin eruptions, scars and blemishes. They talked with local accents and aitches were optional. Some were almost illiterate. Lawyers, merchants, businessmen, land agents and certain kinds of cleric had to read and write in the course of their daily work, but noblemen could dictate to secretaries and their learning grew rusty from lack of practice.[2] The older men had seen fighting in France, and they knew a good deal about England from visiting the outlying portions of their property. They had a rough working knowledge of law, farming and estate management, and the young picked up what they could as they went along.

The women were also tough, and a woman who was worth her salt could do business for her husband in his absence. She grew up with the knowledge that her marriage would be arranged by her parents, and that if her husband died she would probably marry again immediately and that her original dowry would revert to her, and that she would also receive a large portion of her late husband's estates. On the other hand she might die in childbed and then it would be her husband who would marry again.

Beside the Duke of York and the Earls of Salisbury and Warwick, the notable men inside the castle included Lord Clinton,[3] a minor peer; Sir John Wenlock,[4] who had been in public life for forty years and had had great experience both of war and politics; and William Hastings[5] from Leicestershire whose father had been a personal friend of the Duke of York. There were also two young Bourchier nephews, sons of the Duke of York's sister.

Duchess Cecily was in Ludlow Castle too. The chroniclers do not mention her daughters, but her four sons were present; Edward and Rutland, now seventeen and sixteen respectively, were rated as men,

---

[2] Editors of printed letters seldom reveal whether or not a letter is dictated.

[3] John, 5th Lord Clinton (1410–64).

[4] Sir John Wenlock (d.1471), Lord Wenlock, 1461. He was already active in 1421 when he received a grant of lands in Normandy. Six times M.P. for Bedfordshire. Speaker of the Parliament of 1445. Chamberlain to Queen Margaret and wounded fighting on her side at St Albans, 1455. He had no useful relations and there are indications that he was not liked or trusted, so his rise must have been entirely due to hard work and brains. J. S. Roskell, 'John Lord Wenlock of Someries,' in *Bedfordshire Hist. Record Society*, Vol. 38 (1958).

[5] William Hastings (1430–83). Lord Hastings, 1461. He became Edward's best friend and most trusted general. Besides his properties in Leicestershire, he had inherited land in Yorkshire, Northamptonshire and Warwickshire.

while George (Clarence) was not quite ten and Richard (Gloucester) was just seven.

All that can be said about the number of soldiers in the town is that there were not as many of them as the Duke of York would have liked. Salisbury's contingent had been depleted at Blore Heath, and although supporters had trickled in with their retainers the large army which the Herbert brothers were supposed to be mustering in south Wales had not arrived.[6] However, Warwick's contingent had got through safely. The Calais garrison were the only professional soldiers which England possessed and they were commanded by the famous Andrew Trollope, a soldier of fortune who had risen from obscure beginnings and was noted for his daring deeds and his swashbuckling personality. He had marched his men up from Kent and they were now camped in the flat fields just outside the town and across the river, where they could block the road from the south and guard the bridge. Here they fortified their position, placed some guns on carts, and awaited the worst.

The royal army which was moving towards Ludlow is said to have been large. Henry was in its midst, carried along unseen like a fetish which is too sacred to be gazed on by the vulgar. Proceeding slowly through Worcester, they reach Leominster eleven miles south of Ludlow, and halted in a last attempt to avoid a battle. Courteous messages were exchanged with the Duke of York, one side condescendingly promising pardon, the other declaring personal devotion to the King, but no compromise could be reached and on 12 October the royal army left Leominster and started moving along the road to Ludlow. They were delayed by bad roads and 'let of waters' and as they drew near the town the day was closing in; it was too late for an attack, but a few shots were fired from the guns of the defenders and then the Duke of York and his friends perceived to their horror that Andrew Trollope and the Calais garrison had come out from behind their fortifications and had joined the enemy.

[6] The head of the Herbert family was Sir William Herbert (c.1423–69); Lord Herbert, 1461; Earl of Pembroke, 1468. His father had been Sir William ap Thomas of Raglan in Monmouthshire, who had adopted an English surname. The Herberts backed the English against the Welsh and were efficient, loyal, hard-working and unpopular. The badge they chose was a cart-horse.

Trollope afterwards explained that his men had had no idea that they would be required to fight against their anointed king—a pious excuse which need not be taken very seriously. The ordinary amateur levies were quite indifferent to such fine points of honour, and it is not likely that professional soldiers in an age of mercenary armies would be more squeamish than civilians, particularly as their pay was always in arrears and what they received was advanced by the Calais merchants. Soldiers fought on whichever side their officers thought would win. There had been ample opportunity for Margaret and Somerset to come to an arrangement with Trollope and the hard fact was that York had lost the best part of his army.

It was now impossible for the rebel peers to fight a pitched battle and Ludlow could not withstand a siege; they had no option but to disperse. The royal army would not make any further move till morning; there was a bridge behind the castle by which the river could be crossed without attracting attention and, when dawn broke, York, Edward, Rutland, Salisbury, Warwick, Clinton and Wenlock had disappeared.

Duchess Cecily and her two younger sons, Clarence and Gloucester, were left in the castle. They were in no danger. Women and children of high rank could not, at that particular date, be killed or imprisoned or used as hostages—for one thing, reprisals would have been too easy. That Duchess Cecily would communicate with her husband was obvious, but no worse fate befell her than being sent to live with her eldest sister, the Duchess of Buckingham.

Much the most lively of the fifteenth-century London chroniclers is an unknown, comical cockney who continued a chronicle partly written by a mayor called Gregory.[7] Pseudo-Gregory seems to have had a personal dislike to the Duchess Cecily, and he asserts that when she was with her sister she was 'kept full strait and many a great rebuke', but this was just wishful thinking; very soon Duchess Cecily was at liberty again. She demanded from Parliament the allowance which was usually made to a lady whose husband had been attainted and she obtained the handsome sum of 1000 marks a year.

[7] *The Historical Collections of a Citizen of London in the Fifteenth Century* (Camden Society, 1876). This chronicle ends in mid-sentence in 1469.

The knights and gentlemen who remained in Ludlow surrendered, were fined and ultimately bought themselves pardons. Some unimportant people were hanged, but this excited little interest and as there are no registers of hangings it cannot be known how many victims were sacrificed nor why particular men should have been chosen. Somerset either was not able to control his men or did not try to do so; they ran amuck, got very drunk, raped the women and looted the castle as though they were in a foreign country. However, the town was not burnt and Trollope and the soldiers who were accustomed to wars in France must have been astonished at their own moderation.

The fugitives, meanwhile, had separated. The Duke of York was still Lieutenant of Ireland, and he and his son Rutland and Lord Clinton made their way to Dublin. Warwick had left Calais in the care of his uncle, Lord Fauconberg,[8] and he and his father (Lord Salisbury) and Sir John Wenlock set out to get back there, taking Edward with them. This arrangement was sensible and worked out very well, but they acted on the impulse of the moment and it is very much in character that Edward should choose the whirl of Calais with his successful Neville relations rather than retreat to a backwater with his father.

To reach Calais before Trollope and his soldiers returned and to avoid being recognized on the way required some ingenuity, and accounts differ as to the route they took, but it is certain that their escape was contrived by means of a gentleman from Devonshire named John Dynham.[9] What seems most probable is that they rode to south Wales where the Nevilles owned property and there chartered a coasting boat under the pretext that they wished to sail to Bristol, and that once at sea Warwick forced the crew to take them across Barnstaple Bay and round the redoubtable cliffs of Hartland Point. The Dynham family had long owned the Hartland peninsula, and there were beaches where small boats could put in and where tracks led up the cliffs to their manor-house. At Hartland Manor they rested until horses were procured, and then they rode across Devonshire to the Dynhams' other

---

[8] William Neville, Lord Fauconberg (d.1463). Earl of Kent, 1461. His heiress wife, Joan Fauconberg, is said to have been an imbecile. She had three daughters by him and after his death was soon married by an adventurer. She died in 1490, aged 84. Fauconberg acknowledged two bastard sons.

[9] John Dynham (1433–1501). Lord Dynham, 1467.

house, Nutwell, near Exmouth, where they threw themselves on the mercy of John Dynham's widowed mother, Joan.

Joan Dynham rose to the occasion. She hid her exalted visitors until she had procured them a ship and then they all—including John Dynham—embarked and sailed from Exmouth. After touching at Guernsey, they reached Calais on about 2 November and found, to their relief, that they had arrived in time: Trollope and his men had not yet returned, and it was still held by Fauconberg.

Joan Dynham had to wait for payment but she was not forgotten. When Edward became king he gave her a royal ward, whom she married to one of her daughters, and she was also sent £80 in cash for 'her household and servants and for the mariners, by way of regard and in recompense for their true services, labour and diligence at the last departure of the King that now is from his realm towards his town of Calais and for his safe conveyance to the said town'.[1]

---

[1] R. Pearse Chope, 'The Last of the Dynhams', in *Transactions of the Devonshire Association* (1918).

II

Calais November 1459–June 1460

ALAIS WAS ESSENTIALLY A TRADING POST, A SMALL ENGLISH
colony clinging precariously to the continent of Europe. The
wool, leather, skins, lead and tin that were exported to Burgundy had to pass through Calais to be graded and taxed[1] and the
fortunes of Calais affected producers and labourers all over England. It
was also a useful base from which to attack foreign ships as they came
through the straits, though the professional pirates operated further
down the coast from Devon and Cornwall. Its disadvantage was that
to protect it an expensive garrison was necessary, and soldiers also had
to be maintained in the nearby castles of Guisnes and Hammes. Fortunately Calais was not actually in France, but was a bite taken out of
Burgundy and the French could not reach it without violating Burgundian territory; the Duke of Burgundy much preferred that it should
be held by the English than by the French, and he also knew that the
whole system of Anglo-Burgundian trade depended on it. The possibility that the King of France would suddenly make a pounce had

---

[1] There were exceptions; for instance, coarse wool from the north of England could
be sent direct to Flanders, and dishonest merchants were liable to evade the Calais staple
by pretending that their wool was northern wool.

always to be reckoned with, but only occasionally did an attack seem imminent.

The post of Captain of Calais was said to be the most lucrative of all official appointments and it was usually given to a great magnate who had other duties elsewhere, and he appointed a deputy or lieutenant. The Merchants of the Staple were very rich and the bustle and business, the constant coming and going, made Calais a lively town. In addition it was, in good weather, only two days' journey from London, with Canterbury an agreeable half-way stopping-place, and from Warwick's point of view it was the ideal refuge from which to prepare plans for his return. He had already cultivated many useful friends in Kent; his local reputation had been enhanced by several showy acts of piracy in the Channel, and he had a positive genius for finding frustrated and ambitious men who were willing to risk their all in an attempt to get out of the narrow rut in which they lived.

Edward spent eight months in Calais, from the beginning of November 1459 to 26 June 1460. He, Salisbury and Warwick were known as the Three Earls, Warwick being very much the leading spirit and Edward chiefly valuable as a visible sign that their party included the Duke of York. He was much the youngest and it is not recorded that he took any part in the forays and expeditions in which Warwick and his friends distinguished themselves.

This does not mean that those eight months were wasted; on the contrary, it is likely that they were of great importance in the formation of his tastes and opinions. For the first time Edward was out in the world on his own. He had never even been away to school, and he suddenly found himself loosed from the restraints of home in a very stimulating milieu. He was not a royal prince, he had no position to maintain, he had nothing to do but amuse himself and keep on the right side of the Nevilles. Seldom, if ever, has a future king of England enjoyed a similar period of freedom at an impressionable age.

Writers of all kinds agree that Edward was strikingly good-looking and their unanimity suggests that he approximated to some ideal which was popular but rare: perhaps he was not unlike the alabaster effigies of young knights which old gentlemen placed on their tombs. According to the portrait at Windsor Castle, he had a straight nose, hazel eyes and brown hair; he was about six foot four;[2] he dressed elegantly; and he could be either very charming or very formidable.

Throughout his reign Edward surprised his subjects by consorting with merchants and businessmen, and it would not be unreasonable to suppose that it was at Calais that he acquired these bourgeois tastes. A pleasant boy of seventeen can squeeze through doors that would be closed to an older person and, carefree and emancipated, Edward had a happy time in Calais, closely observing rich men whose wealth, instead of being tied up in manors and farms, consisted of cash, credit and merchandise. Shipping of all nations came into the harbour and sailed through the straits, international finance was a topic of conversation, the transactions of the merchants of Flanders were matters of paramount interest, and in Edward's alert and receptive mind was planted the idea that the thing which really mattered was trade—and, above all, trade with Burgundy. At the same time it was necessary for him to conform with the customs of his aristocratic relations; he not only lived with the Nevilles, he could see that he would always have to live with the Nevilles—he could never do without them or get away from them. Most people find it perfectly easy to lead a double life and to show different faces at home and at work, and Edward can have had no difficulty in adapting himself alternately to the lords and knights in the castle and the businessmen who lived round the harbour. It may well be that he explained away his eccentric behaviour by assuming the role of a gay dog who was always slipping down to the town in pursuit of girls, and doubtless he did pursue girls, and doubtless the resultant chaff was flattering to his vanity, but the great advantage of having the reputation of being a mere play-boy was that it enabled him to associate with whom he chose without arousing jealousy and suspicion, and it gave him a useful mask which hid from friends and foes alike the alarming fact that he had a quick, clever brain and a will of iron.

MEANWHILE THE QUEEN'S PARTY SUMMONED A PARLIAMENT, the members of which they selected themselves. It met at Coventry and was

[2] His skeleton was disinterred in 1789 and measured 6 foot 3½ inches. Some contemporaries mention that he was tall, but nobody calls him gigantic or seems to have thought his height extraordinary.

afterwards known as the Parliament of Devils. As was only natural, all the opposition leaders were attainted, and forfeited lands and offices were shared out among supporters. Wives of rebels were allowed to retain their estates—the only exception being the Countess of Salisbury, Warwick's mother. The address to the King was a grandiloquent harangue of the usual kind, and praised Henry's warlike virtues: 'You of your knightly courage without delay took the field.' It accused York's party, among other things, of pretending that Henry was dead. This is the sort of rumour that easily grows of itself in anxious days, particularly when a leader remains out of sight for a suspicious length of time, and if the Duke of York really had been able to plant the story not only in Ludlow but in the King's own camp it might be considered a rather brilliant piece of psychological warfare. According to the Speaker, Henry himself had countered the disloyal libel by addressing his army 'in so witty, so knightly, so manly, in so comfortable wise, with so princely apport and assured manner' that everyone desired to do battle for his sake. The members of Parliament who listened knew perfectly well that poor, peace-loving Henry never had had a princely apport and assured manner, and that he was now incapable of making a sensible speech, but the fiction that he was a virile ruler keen to fight battles had to be maintained.

It should be added that it is unfair to scrutinize these addresses and manifestoes too closely. They were hurriedly concocted by clerks to be read aloud to semi-literate gatherings and, like election speeches, their object was to sway the audience at the moment. Also, it is doubtful if anyone considered them important; it just happens that documents of this sort get preserved while what was said in discussion has left no trace.

The Queen extracted from all the nobles and bishops present an oath of allegiance to Henry and Prince Edward, and promises to protect them and herself, but this can have afforded her small comfort. The fragility of oaths taken at the sword-point was well known; if oaths of allegiance had really been binding there would have been no rebellions, and rulers would have had carte blanche to behave as abominably as they chose. Everyone swore; there was no option, and among those who took the oath and obviously had not the faintest intention of supporting the Queen was Warwick's brother, George Neville, Bishop of Exeter.[3]

It was the fault of the times in which he lived that George Neville found himself masquerading as a man of God. One of the Earl of Salisbury's sons had to enter the church because it was convenient to have a bishop in the family, and George was slightly bookish. He attended Balliol College, Oxford, and when only twenty-two secured the bishopric of Exeter; he was below the legal age, but such things could be arranged. Energetic and enterprising like the rest of his family, he faithfully backed his eldest brother in all things, and that was about the sum of his political creed.

Margaret, unfortunately for herself, had attracted to her party some of the most foolish and irresponsible peers, and if there were any among them who proffered good advice no attention was paid to them. Typical of her supporters were the Earl of Wiltshire, Lord Scales[4] and Lord Hungerford[5] who, some time in the first half of 1460, swooped down on the town of Newbury (which had been taken from the Duke of York and given to Jasper Tudor), hanged, drew and quartered several prominent citizens, imprisoned others and looted the town. It is arguable that popularity with the general public was unimportant and that the power to raise soldiers depended on quite other factors, but Warwick and Edward certainly thought that frightfulness did not pay and that it was better to be conciliatory than brutal.

Immediately after the capture of Ludlow, Henry Duke of Somerset and Andrew Trollope, now close friends, made a determined effort to regain Calais, but by the time they arrived the Three Earls were already in possession and they were repulsed and forced to retreat to the Castle of Guisnes, to which they obtained entry by promising to pay the garrison their arrears of wages. They were unable to fulfil this promise but they remained in Guisnes hoping that Margaret would send men and money, and presently a relief expedition did set out under the command of the new Lord Audley[6] and Humphrey Stafford of

[3] George Neville (1433?–1476). Bishop of Exeter, 1455. Chancellor, 1460-7. Archbishop of York, 1464.

[4] Thomas, 7th Lord Scales (1399–1460).   [5] Robert, 3rd Lord Hungerford (1431–64).

[6] John Tuchet, 6th Lord Audley (d.1490). Master of the King's Dogs and a Privy Councillor with a salary of £100 a year, 1471.

Southwick.[7] Neither of these young men were clever and they were captured and brought into Calais. Lord Audley's father had been killed at Blore Heath fighting against the Earl of Salisbury, and according to the rules of romance there should have been a dramatic interview between him and the slayer of his father, but vendettas are rare in England; young Audley and young Stafford just changed sides and for the rest of their lives were personal friends of Edward, though never very useful to him. Somerset and Trollope continued to hope for reinforcements, but none got through to them, and they remained until the summer isolated, but impregnable, in the Castle of Guisnes.

At this point a digression must be made to introduce Richard Woodville, Lord Rivers, a professional soldier who stumbled into prominence because of a clandestine marriage, or—more accurately—two clandestine marriages.

This Richard Woodville (born *c.* 1405) came from an old-established Northamptonshire family which owned the manor of Grafton near Stony Stratford. His father was a soldier who had served with some distinction under Henry V and John Duke of Bedford, and Richard followed in his father's steps and served in France and won a place on the Duke of Bedford's staff. In 1433, when the Anglo-Burgundian alliance was breaking down, Bedford[8] married the seventeen-year-old Jacquetta of Luxembourg, daughter of Pierre, Count of St Pol of Luxembourg, whose assistance he very greatly needed. The desire to have a son was an added incentive, but when Bedford died a couple of years later he was still without an heir and his young widow inherited all his estates.[9] Richard Woodville was one of the officers of Jacquetta's household; the force of propinquity was stronger than that of prudence; and before she and her fortune could be disposed of to a suitable bidder she had married him (*c.* 1436).

By the time this misalliance came to light, nothing could be done about it. Jacquetta was repudiated by her extremely aristocratic French

---

[7] Humphrey Stafford of Southwick (1439–69). Earl of Devon, 1469. Executed by Warwick after the Battle of Edgecott.

[8] John Duke of Bedford (1389–1435). Brother of Henry V. His first wife had just died in childbed and, as things then stood, he was heir to Henry VI.

[9] Except for one castle left to a bastard son.

relations and in England she was fined £1000, a sum she raised by selling Bedford lands to the family financier, Cardinal Beaufort, who had probably imposed the fine in the first place. Jacquetta retained the title and rank of Duchess of Bedford and (until the arrival of Margaret of Anjou) this young French girl, married to a mere knight, took precedence over all the ladies of England—a situation which would have caused annoyance at any court at any time, but which was particularly irritating at a period when, in an effort to live in a civilized manner, fantastic attention was paid to ceremony and protocol. To add to the peculiarity of her plight, Jacquetta was not protected by any relations and, having no one to stand up for her, had to fight her own battles. However, Richard Woodville was a useful soldier and he accompanied John Duke of Somerset to France in 1439 and the Duke of York to Rouen in 1441; and Duchess Jacquetta was probably in the castle and may even have been in the room when Edward was born.

When Margaret of Anjou married Henry VI, Duchess Jacquetta found an ally, and in 1448 Richard Woodville was created Lord Rivers; but it was too late, and to the day of his death, and long after the nature of his original offence had been forgotten, Lord Rivers and everyone connected with him bore the stigma of being *low*.

It is possible that the Woodvilles did possess some disagreeable characteristics, but there is no evidence that this was so. Duchess Jacquetta has been called ambitious and scheming but if that had really been her nature she would hardly have married the insignificant Richard Woodville. Judging by what happened to them, the family would appear to have been amiable blunderers who fell into every trap and who were consistently unlucky and sometimes ridiculous. However, there was one way in which they were indeed annoying. Many peers lacked a child to come after them and Duchess Jacquetta, who had failed to produce an heir for the great Duke of Bedford, absurdly presented Richard Woodville with a string of babies of which she actually managed to rear thirteen, five sons and eight daughters.

At the beginning of 1460 Richard Woodville/Lord Rivers was given command of an expedition which was to make a fresh attempt to relieve Somerset and Trollope in Guisnes, and to recapture Calais, and, accompanied by his wife and Anthony Woodville, his eldest son,

he went to Sandwich and began to muster ships and men.[1] His preparations could not be hidden from Warwick and, in the early hours of
15 January 1460, John Dynham made a surprise raid on Sandwich with
a band of amateur commandos which included a gentleman, two
yeomen, a mercer, a merchant, a tailor, an apothecary, a chapman, a
butcher and a servant,[2] and returned to Calais with all Lord Rivers'
ships (except for one which was not ready to sail) and also with Lord
Rivers himself, Duchess Jacquetta[3] and Anthony, whom they had captured in their beds.

Londoners were tremendously amused when they heard the story
and mention of it is made by several writers. One letter[4] describes in
circumstantial detail how Lord Rivers and Anthony were brought
before the Three Earls with eight score torches, and how the Earl of
Salisbury abused Lord Rivers 'calling him knave's son' and asking him
how he dared accuse them of being traitors, for they should be found
to be true liegemen when he was revealed as a traitor. Warwick also
abused Lord Rivers and said that his father was only a squire of Henry VI,
that he had made himself by marriage and became a lord, and actually
it was beneath Warwick, who was of the King's blood, to be insulted
by mere lords. And Edward Earl of March abused him in the same way.
And Anthony was abused by all three Earls because of his offensive
language.

This letter was written nearly a fortnight after the kidnapping; the
details are improbable, and represent what the outside world hoped
had happened inside the Castle of Calais. Salisbury had spent a lifetime
involved in affairs of state, Warwick was adept at ingratiating himself,
and Edward had charming manners and afterwards became deeply
attached to Anthony. They were in great need of friends and it was
most unlikely that they would storm at their prisoners; certainly
nothing was said that was unforgivable and when, fifteen months later,

---

[1] Dover was closer to Calais but the harbour at Sandwich was far better.

[2] Inquisition Miscellaneous, Chancery, file 317. Cora L. Scofield, in the *English Historical Review*, Vol. XXXVII (1922).

[3] It was soon reported that she had returned to Kent, and she may not really have been
taken to Calais.

[4] William Paston in London, writing to his brother John in Norfolk, on 28 January
1460.

the Woodvilles decided that the Queen's cause was lost they found it perfectly easy to change sides. It is even possible that Lord Rivers, seeing that his men had defected and his ships were captured, had come voluntarily to talk to Warwick: Calais, incidentally, was his second home— he had been Lieutenant of Calais and so had his father before him, and he had a married sister living in the town.

The really interesting thing about the story is that it shows that even then the Woodvilles were butts and that any misfortune which happened to them was considered extremely humorous. Peers were usually referred to in very guarded terms[5] but the Woodvilles were helpless and could be laughed at with impunity. It is also noticeable that it is Warwick who is supposed to have said that he is of 'the King's blood'; he was, like a number of other people, descended from Edward III, but it was his money and the way he spent it which made him seem more royal than either Edward or his own father.

WHILE EDWARD WAS IN CALAIS, Richard Duke of York remained in Ireland where he continued to act as Lieutenant although Queen Margaret had dismissed him and assigned the office to her favourite, the Earl of Wiltshire. She sent an envoy with a writ for his arrest but the Dublin Parliament supported his intransigence and the unfortunate envoy, after a perfunctory trial, was hanged, drawn and quartered.

In the spring Warwick, as enterprising on sea as on land, collected a large convoy of ships and sailed to Ireland, reaching Waterford on 16 March 1460. The two leaders discussed plans and the Duke of York agreed to give Warwick a free hand and to stay in Ireland until after the person of Henry VI had been captured.

Meanwhile, Margaret had heard of Warwick's expedition and the Duke of Exeter undertook to intercept him on his return journey and for this purpose joined forces with a Devonshire knight, Sir Baldwin Fulford, who had already mustered some ships. A Venetian carrack

---

[5] A correspondent of the Pastons, having retailed some gossip about the bickering among the peers after the first Battle of St Albans, added: 'And after this is read and understood I pray you burn or break it, for I am loth to write anything of any lord. But I must needs: there is nothing else to write.'
Henry Windsor in London, 19 July 1455. *Paston Letters*.

which happened to be in the Thames was hired for a hundred pounds a month, three Genoese carracks lying at Sandwich were also chartered, and an attempt was made to secure the services of the great Venetian trading fleet known as the Flanders Galleys, which were the fastest ships afloat.[6] The Venetians, however, had no wish to waste their time or become involved in someone else's civil war and they hurriedly set off for home, whereupon the Venetian merchants in London were thrown into prison and to free themselves had to give security for 36,000 ducats.[7]

Towards the end of April Exeter put to sea and began patrolling the Channel, but it was the middle of June before he sighted Warwick's returning convoy, and by that time his men were on the verge of mutiny from lack of food and lack of pay and they refused to attack. Warwick sailed back to Calais unopposed, bringing with him his mother—who had somehow managed to get to Ireland—and probably Irish soldiers from the Duke of York's estates.

As for King Henry, he remained gentle and pious, and during Lent 1460 he spent three days in the Lincolnshire Fens at Croyland Abbey, which had the distinction of possessing the shrine of St Guthlac. The Abbey was on an island and could be approached either by boat or along a narrow causeway, and it was occasionally in request as a fortress, sanctuary, bank, safe-deposit, hospital and hotel, and Henry's visit was duly recorded in the Abbey chronicle. This chronicle had been begun in much earlier times for the purpose of faking deeds, charters and grants, and for providing the Abbey with written evidence for rights that were only traditional and could be disputed, and it turned into a rudimentary history of England. The two portions which concern Edward IV were written in 1469 and 1486 respectively, and are known as the Second and Third Continuations.[8]

[6] They were rowed by highly paid and often well-born oarsmen who were recruited at St Mark's; convicts were not used till the middle of the next century. Galleys were effective but very expensive.

[7] 'Very great caution should be used in this matter,' wrote the Venetian Senate. *Calendar of Venetian Papers.* 16 May 1460.

[8] *Ingulph's Chronicle of the Abbey of Croyland.* Croyland is now called Crowland, the fens have been drained and the abbey ruins rise, strange and beautiful, out of very prosaic, flat fields.

The Second Continuation is the work of the Prior of the Abbey, a simple, unsophisticated, credulous man with considerable talent and a great urge to write history, which inspired him to sort the old letters and documents in the Abbey archives and to weave them into a consecutive narrative.[9] He was almost totally ignorant of the world outside the Fens and believed that Wales was an island, but he could vividly describe his own experiences, and he concluded by saying that he had contemplated signing his name to his work but he had decided against it because he felt that it would be vanity, but that he hoped that God would reward him all the same and write his name in the Book of Life. Inside the medieval monk there was a modern literary man struggling to get out.

The Third Continuator was a very different kind of cleric. As his predecessor had modestly remained anonymous he could not reveal his name, but it appears that he was a doctor of canon law who worked in some government office at Westminster (perhaps the Chancellor's office), and that in the summer of 1471 he carried a letter to Duke Charles of Burgundy at Abbeville. In the first year of the reign of Henry VII (1486) he chanced to find himself buried down in the Fens at Croyland, and he amused himself by bringing the Abbey Chronicle up to date. He was of a sarcastic disposition and he explained: 'We began this description chiefly for the purpose of amending the pious and praiseworthy ignorance manifested by the Prior of this place who compiled the preceding portion, and who, though extremely well versed in Divine matters, was sometimes most reasonably mistaken in those of a secular nature,' and he mentioned with pardonable pride that he had written his chronicle, which covered twenty-six years of English history, in ten days, finishing on the last day of April 1486.

The Third Croyland Continuator is superior to other English fifteenth-century chroniclers because he was an educated and intelligent man living near the centre of power, but he only knew the common gossip of Westminster and he was quite in the dark as to what went on in the inner rooms of the King's palace or the castles of peers. His general attitude was cynical and contemptuous; taxes were iniquitous;

[9] He uses a phrase which is almost identical with one used by Pius II in his autobiography, and so he must have had a circular letter from the Pope in front of him.

wars were costly, unnecessary and badly run; battles were mere scuffles; victories were empty. Sometimes he seems to have his tongue in his cheek and to be making fun of the unsophisticated monks of Croyland and it is difficult to be sure of his real opinions, which he originally expressed in fifteenth-century Latin and which have now been re-expressed in nineteenth-century scholars' English.[1]

The visit of Henry VI to Croyland Abbey in the spring of 1460 was recorded by the Prior, the 'Second Croyland Continuator', with great satisfaction. Henry joined in all the religious observances, requested that he might become an honorary brother and, in return for the three days' hospitality which he had received, he bestowed upon the monks a charter exempting them from taxes for ever. The Prior saw Henry at very close quarters, and a few pages further on he wrote down in black and white the truth which was generally glossed over: 'In consequence of a malady which had been for many years increasing upon him, he had fallen into a weak state of mind and now held the government of the realm in name only.'

BY THE END OF JUNE 1460 Warwick's plans were complete. Friends and agents in Kent were on the alert. A manifesto was distributed in the name of the Duke of York and the Three Earls in which they recapitulated the crimes and follies perpetrated during Henry's reign, not forgetting the alleged murder of good Duke Humphrey;[2] they also complained of the wrongs which they themselves had suffered and expressed an earnest desire to assist King Henry to rule wisely and well.

Political broadsheets were always popular and some doggerel verses celebrated the virtues of the rebel lords. The Duke of York was the 'true-blood'; Edward was an unknown quantity but 'his fame the earth shall spread'; Salisbury was 'named Prudence'; Warwick was 'the shield of our defence' and also 'a noble knight and flower of manhood'; and 'little Fauconberg' was a 'knight of great reverence'.

---

[1] *The Croyland Chronicle* ends with a short unfinished 'Fourth Continuation' which perhaps was written by the same man.

[2] Humphrey Duke of Gloucester (1390–1447). The capricious and irresponsible brother of Henry V. He was arrested by the Court party and died with suspicious suddenness.

John Dynham made another raid on Sandwich during which he was wounded—from then on he walked with a limp. The port of Sandwich was taken and held as a bridge-head by Fauconberg and, on 26 June 1460, Edward once more set foot on English soil. The little party which had fled from Ludlow to Calais were still together and they had been augmented by new friends and an indefinite number of soldiers. Warwick had also attached to himself a papal legate which gave the—quite erroneous—impression that his enterprise enjoyed the blessing of the Pope.

The legate, Coppini,[3] was a small, talkative, plausible Italian bishop, and because many of his letters are preserved among the archives of Milan[4] a good deal is known about him, although his machinations hardly influenced the course of events. Originally he had been sent to collect money for a crusade against the Turks, but finding that the Turkish menace meant nothing to the English—who shrewdly surmised that it would be a long time before the Infidel reached Dover—he turned his attention to English politics. Queen Margaret snubbed him and prevented him from meeting Henry (who of course was in no fit state to give interviews to distinguished foreigners) but Warwick flattered and encouraged him and he was soon an enthusiastic supporter of the Three Earls on the understanding that, in return, Warwick would press the Pope to make him a cardinal. Besides representing the Pope, Coppini was also in secret correspondence with Francesco Sforza, Duke of Milan,[5] who wished to embroil France in war with England. Sforza was interested to receive letters from England, but it bothered him when Coppini wrote between the lines in invisible ink and conjured him to reply in code.

---

[3] Francesco Coppini, Bishop of Terni. Eventually the Pope discovered his double-dealing and, instead of being made a cardinal, he was disgraced and reduced to the rank of monk.

[4] Calendar of Milanese Papers (translated) 1912.

[5] Francesco Sforza (1401–66). He had been a condottiere and he was elected Duke of Milan by popular acclaim. His wife was the (illegitimate) daughter of Filippo Maria Visconti, the previous duke.

III

Capturing the Crown
26 June 1460–28 June 1461

WARWICK'S PREPARATIONS HAD BEEN VERY THOROUGH AND AS soon as the Three Earls landed at Sandwich volunteers flocked to their standard. The Men of Kent were always ready to march on the capital, though who shall say whether this was because of their inborn pugnacity, or because the local laws of land-tenure produced a class of independent free-holders, or because generations of returning soldiers had settled in the district, or because the traffic which passed along the road to London was a constant reminder that just over the horizon there was a city where the streets were paved with gold. Canterbury welcomed the Earls and the whole way along the route sympathizers joined them and they advanced on London with a great show of boldness.

Inside the City was perplexity. Lord Hungerford and Lord Scales and some other members of the Court Party had mustered a few soldiers and intended to try to hold it for the Queen but, after much havering, the City Council decided that the safest course would be to offer no resistance to the approaching army and, on 2 July 1460, Lord Hungerford, Lord Scales and their friends retreated into the Tower; the city gates were opened and Edward made his first triumphal entry into London.

The next step was to obtain possession of the person of King Henry without whom no caucus of peers could claim the right to govern, and so, after a busy couple of days, Warwick, Edward and the greater part of their army set off for the midlands in search of him, while Salisbury and Wenlock stayed behind to besiege the Tower. The number of Warwick's supporters had grown and he now rode with an impressive company which included half a dozen peers, the Prior of St John's,[1] the legate Coppini, six bishops and the Archbishop of Canterbury, Thomas Bourchier.[2] The Bourchiers were mild, likeable people who, in spite of the royal blood in their veins, evinced no presumptious ambitions, and the Archbishop could be trusted to accept whichever party happened to be in the ascendant.

King Henry was at Northampton, some sixty-six miles from London. An army usually progressed from one market town to the next at a rate of from eight to fifteen miles a day; Warwick and Edward covered the distance in six days and by 10 July they were outside Northampton and ready, if need be, to do battle. The Court Party, on their side, were quite prepared to fight it out and their soldiers were drawn up in the meadows south of the town near Delapré Abbey, with their backs to the river Nene; they had dug trenches and placed guns in position. King Henry was in the camp but Queen Margaret was at Coventry, thirty miles away.

Warwick followed the usual custom and spread out his men in a line facing the enemy, the centre and wings commanded by the three most important people present—in this case himself, Edward and Fauconberg. With untrained soldiers morale was all-important, and it was necessary that officers should be conspicuous and should fight on foot among their men; courage rather than science was required and Edward, large and brave, was perfectly able to command a wing. Warwick would have preferred to gain his objective without bloodshed and during the morning delegations of bishops went back and forth between the two camps, but no terms were acceptable and, in the early afternoon, he gave the order to attack.

[1] Robert Botyll. The Priors of St John's were professional soldiers.
[2] Thomas Bourchier (1405?–1486). Archbishop of Canterbury, 1454. Cardinal, 1467. His grandfather was Thomas of Woodstock, the youngest son of Edward III. He crowned Edward IV, Richard III and Henry VII.

The Battle of Northampton was extremely short. It had been raining, the trenches were flooded and Henry's cannon could not be fired. Warwick's men easily broke through the defences. Lord Grey of Ruthin defected from the Court Party. Rout was total. Many fleeing soldiers were drowned in the river. Four peers were killed.[3] Henry was captured in his tent. In half an hour all was over and Edward had learnt that a quick attack led by determined men can carry all before it.

When Queen Margaret heard the result of the battle she realized all its implications and that she must flee to safety, and she at once set out for north Wales taking her little son, Prince Edward, with her. 'And most commonly she rode behind a young poor gentleman of fourteen year age; his name was John Combe, born at Amesbury in Wiltshire.'[4] Perhaps it was on this miserable journey that her celebrated encounter with the robbers occurred, and that she was robbed by her own servants—neither of which stories reflect well on the knights who should have been escorting her. She was, however, indomitable, and eventually she got through to Harlech, an exceptionally strong castle on the coast of Caernarvonshire protected by the wilds of Snowdonia, where she found a temporary refuge and where she was able to make contact with Jasper Tudor. Some women at this point would have taken ship and gone back to Anjou, but Margaret's family did not lightly relinquish a crown and she never wavered in her determination to be Queen of England, cost what it might.

WARWICK AND EDWARD RETURNED triumphantly from Northampton bringing with them Henry, their trophy of war, and they entered London on 16 July. It was to their interest that the mystique of kingship should be maintained, and Henry was treated with outward respect. The peers defending the Tower had now no one to fight for and they were allowed to surrender on easy terms; three of them joined Warwick and the rest were set free to find their way back to Margaret. Unfortunately, they had in their stupidity turned the guns of the Tower onto London

---

[3] The Duke of Buckingham, the Earl of Shrewsbury, Lord Beaumont and Lord Egremont (the maverick brother of the Earl of Northumberland). The bodies were given decent burial.

[4] Pseudo-Gregory.

and had 'cast wildfire into the City and shot in small guns and burned and hurt men, women and children in the streets'[5] and the mob wanted revenge. Seven officers who had formerly been employed by the Duke of Exeter (and perhaps were personally disliked) were tried by jury, found guilty of treason, and hanged, drawn and quartered for the delight of the crowd, and the brutal Lord Scales was recognized by watermen as he was trying to reach the safety of Westminster Sanctuary and was killed on the spot. His corpse was immediately stripped 'and lay there despoiled, naked as a worm',[6] until it was reclaimed by his relations.

Warwick's party could now make their own political appointments. The post of Chancellor was usually, though not always, held by a bishop, and it was inevitably given to Warwick's brother, George Neville, Bishop of Exeter. Protected by his mitre and armed with the Great Seal, he was a useful auxiliary. The Privy Seal was entrusted to Stillington, Dean of St Martin-le-Grand,[7] a man whose adventures appear to be so utterly inconsequent that one can only imagine that there were some factors which have not been recorded but which, if discovered, would explain everything. The Council which assembled to deal with current business was composed of well-known men who had sat on previous Councils, Edward being the only newcomer; not much could be settled until the autumn, when Parliament would meet and the Duke of York—no longer to be kept off the stage—would arrive from Ireland.

For Henry there were ceremonies and processions, and the usual moves from one palace to another. Warwick found time to cross over to Calais and persuade Somerset and Andrew Trollope to leave the Castle of Guisnes, which they were doubtless glad enough to do; they could go where they liked, and they ultimately joined the Queen in Yorkshire. Edward remained in London, still fairly carefree, merely the young Earl of March, his father's son and a cousin of the great Earl of Warwick.

[5] Chronicle, ed. J. S. Davies (Camden Society, 1856).
[6] Pseudo-Gregory.
[7] Robert Stillington (d. 1491), Bishop of Bath and Wells, 1466. Chancellor, 1467–70 and 1471–73. He originally came from Yorkshire.

In September Duchess Cecily arrived in town with her two youngest sons and her unmarried daughter, Margaret; she put up at a fine mansion in Southwark which happened to be standing empty, and which Edward had commandeered for her. The steward wrote to tell his master about it. After a couple of days Duchess Cecily heard that her husband had landed at Chester, and he soon sent for her to join him at Hereford; she then hurried away leaving the children behind. 'And my Lord of March comes every day to see them.'[8]

Edward had strong family feelings and was fond of children, but it is possible that his fraternal attentions were not appreciated by Margaret, Clarence and Gloucester. Large families inevitably split up into groups the outlines of which are never quite lost; the small fry may have thought their big brother unbearably condescending and patronizing, and perhaps the disruptive way in which Clarence and Gloucester behaved in after years was partly caused by the irritations and frustrations of childhood.

The arrival of the Duke of York was awaited with considerable apprehension by his partners and allies who, now that they had the puppet-king once again in their hands, deprecated his claims to the throne. Duchess Cecily had given a hint of what to expect when she left London in an ostentatious conveyance (which Pseudo-Gregory described as a 'chariot covered with blue velvet and four pairs [of] coursers therein') and when the Duke appeared he went even further; he had a sword carried in front of him as though he were already a king, and the banners of his trumpeters were emblazoned with the royal arms. The Houses of Parliament were not only embarrassed but genuinely shocked when he had the effrontery to demand that he should be recognized as the rightful king and produced a pedigree to prove that the three Henrys were usurpers.

If England had been a piece of ordinary property the Duke of York's title to it would have been hard to dispute, and if it were argued that Henry IV had been elected by the nation because the King was unfit to govern and the true heir was a child it could be answered that exactly the same situation had now arisen again. But Parliament would

---

[8] *Paston Letters*. Christopher Hanson to John Paston, 12 October 1460. The house had belonged to a rich old man, the late Sir John Fastolf, and John Paston was his executor.

not accept this argument: for better or worse, Henry had been crowned and once a king had been crowned the matter must be considered closed until he died. With unusual humility, the House of Lords declared that the question of the Duke of York's claims was too hard for them to decide and passed it on to the Judges who, equally modest, confessed that 'it was above their law and passed their learning' and, though the Lords pointed out that they were paid to decide difficult cases, the Judges were adamant and refused to give an opinion. Actually it was the kind of case which everyone present understood only too well. They were all property owners of a kind and held strong views about the rights of heirs and heiresses and orphan children and—changing from the general to the particular—most of them were sure that they did not want the Duke of York to be their king. It was an impasse but guided by the Chancellor, Bishop George Neville, they came to an agreement, which was that they had all sworn allegience to King Henry and therefore he must remain king and it should be forbidden to murder him, but that when he died the Duke of York should succeed him. It was an arrangement very like that which Henry V had made in France, with the difference that the Duke of York was ten years older then Henry VI and, with any luck, would die first.

On 9 November 1460 the Duke of York was officially declared to be the heir to the throne, and Henry was said to have aquiesced. The existence of Margaret's son was ignored, though it may be supposed that his name was not entirely absent from the discussions and that, in private, many coarse jokes were cracked at his expense. If Henry was capable of understanding the arrangements which had been made, it is possible that he considered them to be perfectly satisfactory; there are indications that he tenaciously clung to the crown, but none that he took any interest in the fate of Queen Margaret and Prince Edward.

By this time the peers who were backing the Queen had rallied and were reassembling their forces in the north. The new Earl of Northumberland was determined to get even with the Nevilles; the young Duke of Somerset, still accompanied by Andrew Trollope, had reappeared from Guisnes; and the peers in London were well aware that before they could settle down comfortably with their puppet king they would have to fight another pitched battle.

Edward went home to Ludlow, and set about collecting soldiers from the lands along the Welsh Border; Warwick stayed in London to guard King Henry and to raise an army in the south; and the Duke of York with his son Rutland, and the Earl of Salisbury with his son Thomas Neville went together to Yorkshire, where they spent Christmas in the Duke of York's castle at Sandal near Wakefield. This was a mere ten miles from the great royal castle at Pontefract where Somerset, Northumberland and Andrew Trollope had foregathered.

The Church festivals which made breaks in the long hard grind of daily life were all much appreciated, and of these Christmas was the most conspicuous; for one thing, it was the longest holiday of the year, lasting nearly a fortnight, and even kings relaxed and stayed in one place until the final gala of Twelfth Night of 6 January; great, therefore, was the astonishment when it became known that in the middle of this season of peace and goodwill, feasting and merry-making York, Salisbury, their sons and all the knights who were with them had been attacked and wiped out by Somerset and his friends. The Battle of Wakefield, as this exploit is called, occurred on 30 December 1460, and accounts differ as to what happened, though it seems that the unconventional Trollope thought up some trick or surprise which may or may not have contravened the unwritten laws of war as then understood, but which was so ingenious that it deceived both York and Salisbury 'named Prudence', and the other officers with them. One story has it that Trollope dressed up his men as women; according to another account, he ambushed York's foragers and surrounded the peers when they made a rash sortie to rescue them; a third version asserts that one of the disinherited Nevilles gained entry into Sandal under pretence of bringing in reinforcements and then seized the castle. It is quite possible that Trollope did nothing more recondite that to disregard the truce which it was tacitly assumed would be observed during the twelve days of Christmas; but, however it was contrived, the trap caught them all.

The Duke of York was killed in the fighting, and so was his son Rutland who was seventeen—quite old enough to fight and therefore to be killed, though folklore afterwards turned him into a pathetic little boy, unfairly murdered. Thomas Neville was also killed. The Earl of Salisbury was captured alive, and executed in Pontefract Castle by the Earl of Northumberland and his followers, a score in the Percy-Neville rivalry rather than a blow struck in the cause of Henry VI. A dozen or so heads were sent to York and put up on high over the gates, and the head of the Duke of York was said to be decorated with a paper crown. This was a gratuitous exhibition of spite, as it was not the custom to decapitate the bodies of men killed in battle, though their corpses might be exhibited for a short time to show that they were, in truth, dead. On the other hand, to execute prisoners was almost a necessity; there was no other way of rendering them harmless. A prisoner could not be kept in a dungeon for the rest of his life and, in any case, no castle was safe—even the Tower changed hands; if a man were banished he intrigued with foreign rulers, and if he were released in England he at once began to collect a fresh army.

The news of the Battle of Wakefield would have taken a couple of days to reach Edward and it was probably on New Year's Day 1461, when he was at Shrewsbury, that he heard that his father and his brother had been killed, and that henceforth his fortunes depended on himself alone. He had become the head of his family and the heir to the crown. His surviving brothers were children who would not be of any use for years to come, his mother had no judgement and the only relation to whom he could look for guidance was his cousin Warwick. Warwick, on his part, had had a similar access of power and responsibility, and had lost the restraining influence of his father. To a man of his daring temperament the situation was stimulating, even intoxicating. His enormous wealth was now augmented by most of his father's estates. He was in actual possession of the puppet king. He was on the best of terms with the chief pretender to the throne, a very frivolous young man. The Pope's legate was under his thumb. Anything might happen.[9]

WHILE SOMERSET AND TROLLOPE were establishing themselves in Yorkshire, the intrepid Margaret plunged bravely into the unknown and,

[9] On 11 January 1461, Warwick, writing to the Pope, referred lightly to 'the destruction of some of my kinsmen', and mentioned that the legate Coppini was most useful. (*Cal. Venetian Papers.*) He also praised Coppini to Sforza. On 24 January 1461, a friend

undeterred by the rigours of a northern winter, journeyed up to Scotland for the purpose of enlisting the aid of England's ancient enemies.

At that moment the Scots government was as shaky as the English. The late king James II[1] had died in the preceding August and his son, James III, was only nine years old; there were seven regents but the operative two, the Queen Mother, Mary of Gueldres,[2] and Kennedy, Bishop of St Andrews,[3] did not see eye to eye, and powerful lords were on the alert. Queen Mary of Gueldres was a dashing character, and she came to meet Margaret at Lincluden Abbey (near Dumfries and some thirty-five miles from Carlisle), and here, on 5 January 1461 the young French woman and the young Flemish woman settled the affairs of England and Scotland to their own satisfaction. The natural bias of Mary of Gueldres was pro-Burgundian and anti-French, but she could not resist Margaret's offer of Berwick-on-Tweed, the fortress which controlled to some degree the Border raiders on the east coast, and in return she promised Margaret a Scottish army with which to march on London. To the two queens it was quite simple, and the deal was completed by a marriage alliance—Margaret's son was to marry Mary's daughter when a suitable opportunity arose.

Margaret then returned to York where the leaders of her party had gathered, and the agreement which she had made at Lincluden was ratified by all the peers present, including the Duke of Exeter, Henry Duke of Somerset and the Earl of Devon,[4] three men who were descended from John of Gaunt and who were recognized as being reserve candidates for the throne. Noblemen thronged York, but to pay a large army was beyond their power and Margaret's soldiers were promised that south of the Trent they would be free to loot at will.

---

of Coppini's, Antonio de la Torre, wrote to Sforza from Sandwich: 'The Earl of Warwick, who is like another Caesar in these parts is amazed . . . If they do not quickly send the hat everything will go to ruin.' (*Cal. Milanese Papers.*)

[1] James II (1430–3 August 1460). He was killed by the explosion of one of his own cannons when he was besieging the border town of Roxburgh, then held by the English. His widow continued the siege and won back Roxburgh.

[2] Mary of Gueldres (?–1463). Great-niece of Philip the Good, Duke of Burgundy. She was quickly edged out and had lost power by July 1462.

[3] James Kennedy, Bishop of St Andrews (1406?–1465). First cousin of James II.

[4] Thomas Courtenay, 6th Earl of Devon (1432–61). His mother was Margaret Beaufort, sister of the 1st and 2nd Dukes of Somerset and of Joan Beaufort, Queen of Scotland.

This shortage of money afflicted both sides alike; nobody could afford to keep up a standing army, so troops met at a rendezvous at the last possible moment and were dismissed immediately after the crisis had passed to return to their normal occupations.[5] There was no difficulty in recruiting men in winter; work on farms was slack, stores of food and fodder were at their highest, and people were used to discomfort.

Some soldiers could be collected by royal fiat, but most of them were raised by the great landowners who sent circular letters to the lesser landowners and to the councils of the towns where they had influence. Many examples of such letters survive; the tone is a mixture of lofty command and polite request, there are reminders of favours past and hints of benefits to follow, and the recipients had to work out for themselves the disadvantages of inadvertently fighting on the losing side against the disadvantages of not having fought for the victors. Soldiers expected to be paid in cash and so, though there were big prizes to be won, the stakes were high.

It is easy to imagine the excitement when the quiet of some remote manor-house was disturbed by the arrival of a summons to war. The restless and ambitious man would see it as an opportunity, an adventure, an escape from the constrictions of his humdrum daily life, a trip to London, the beginning of a career at Court, the chance of winning a salaried job, of earning glory and of trying out in real battle the weapons with which he had practised since boyhood; the cautious would argue that nothing would be lost if he lay low; the doubtful would send to find out what his neighbours were doing and what was being said in the local town, he would re-read old letters and consult his wife or his head groom or a passing pedlar who happened to be in the yard. There were, however, several things which the puzzled country gentleman certainly did not do: he did not enquire into the political pre-

---

[5] The old feudal knight's service had been for forty days in a year, and this was still about the maximum time that amateur soldiers were willing to spend away from home so the same army could not be expected to fight two consecutive battles. The French chronicler, Comines, says that the English were of the opinion that for the purpose of one battle raw troops were the best, and he noticed that in the first battle in which he himself fought he felt no fear.

judices of the 'tall fellows' who would accompany him to battle;[6] he did not examine a genealogical table to try to work out who really was king by 'God's law, man's law and the law of Nature'; and he did not leave home unless he thought that his own particular 'good lord' had chosen the side which had the best chance of winning.

What happened when the batches of heterogeneous recruits arrived at the meeting-place is harder to visualize. How did a small town cope with an influx of several thousand horses and men? How were the men-at-arms, foot-soldiers and wagons got into an orderly procession along a mud track? Officers and men talked in local dialects as well as in Welsh, Irish, Breton, French, Scots and Flemish, and how were peers, gentlemen, knights and burghers arranged in a military hierarchy which took into consideration their social importance, martial accomplishments, probable loyalty, friendships and feuds?

There is among the Stonor Papers[7] a list of the fencible men in the Oxfordshire half-hundred of Ewelme; the date would be some time between 1478 and 1494, but it probably gives a fair picture of the armies which Edward, Warwick and their opponents put into the field. Seventeen villages contained eighty-five possible soldiers of which seventeen were archers. Ewelme itself could produce six men. 'Richard Slythurst, a harness[8] and able to do the king service with his bow. Thomas Staunton [the constable], John Holme, whole harness and both able to do the King service with bill. John Tanner, an harness and able to do the King service with a bill. John Pallying, a harness and not able to wear it. Roger Smith, no harness, an able man and a good archer.' Other men are described as 'able with a staff', and there could be no question of making them into tidy units like the French 'lance' which comprised six mounted men—a man-at-arms, a squire, a page, a *valet de guerre* and two archers.[9]

---

[6] The rank and file were apparently completely indifferent when, as occasionally happened, their leader suddenly changed sides.

[7] *Stonor Letters and Papers* (Camden Society, 1919). These family papers are fewer and less interesting than the *Paston Letters*, though superior to any others. They owe their survival to having been impounded on some occasion when the Stonors were in trouble and they are now in the Public Record Office.

[8] Armour.

[9] A hundred 'lances' plus four officers made a company. Sir Charles Oman, *A History of War in the Middle Ages* (1924).

Contemporary estimates of the size of armies vary wildly, and so do the guesses of modern historians. Even the leaders must have been fairly vague about the numbers of their own men and they probably never saw the enemy army in its entirety; there were always bushes, trees and scrub to prevent a panoramic view of the battlefield. One interesting point is that, as far as can be seen from such accounts as exist, all the English amateur battles of this period were won by the side which took the initiative, even if they were attacking uphill. It is also worth remarking that, except in one or two very confused battles[1] nobody of importance on the winning side was killed—men entirely encased in armour were more or less safe until they were surrounded, knocked down and their helmets opened.

Untrained cavalry had been found to be worse than useless and everyone fought on foot;[2] the horses wore no armour and were tied up in the rear with the baggage. Battles generally began with an exchange of arrows which were the most deadly of all weapons, but once the armies had closed the archers could no longer shoot. The commander-in-chief had to remain in the centre, and could see little of what was happening in other parts of the field; but in any case the soldiers were too untrained to respond to fresh orders. If there were a reserve its commander could bring it up on his own initiative, otherwise little could be done to counter an unexpected enemy manœuvre. Once the battle appeared to be lost there was a general *sauve qui peut*, and everyone who had a horse hurried back to it; from all battles there were peers and knights who fled and lived to fight another day but to be killed fleeing was not to one's credit.

BY THE END OF JANUARY 1461, Edward had mustered a fair-sized army on the Welsh Border and just when Margaret and her wild Northmen were beginning their march from York to London he was setting out from the West to join up with Warwick; however, he had gone no further than Gloucester when he received word that Jasper Tudor and

---

[1] The Second Battle of St Albans, and Barnet.
[2] Comines says that in France fashionable young men thought it smart to fight on foot in the English manner.

the Earl of Wiltshire were on the move in Wales with a large force, and he turned back to confront them. The site he chose as a battlefield was a stretch of flat fields not far from Ludlow, near a cross-roads known as Mortimer's Cross.

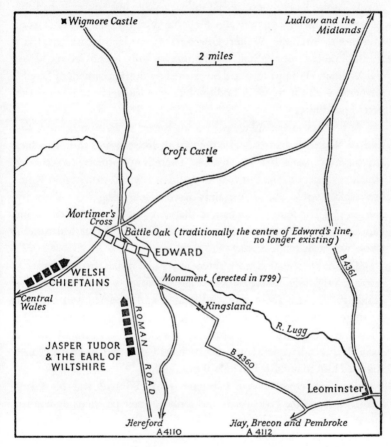

Battle of Mortimer's Cross

In view of the way that Edward conducted his later campaigns, it is safe to assume that he picked the brains of his staff but made it quite clear who was Commander-in-Chief and that, having laid his plans with deliberation, he pursued them with vigour; also that he was kept informed of the enemy's movements by scouts, and exploited to the full the advantages of being on familiar ground while the enemy was travelling through hostile Mortimer country. He had a natural genius for the kind of battle which he had to fight, while neither Jasper Tudor nor Wiltshire had any noticeable military skill; moreover, he had the assistance of men he knew well—Sir John Wenlock, the Herberts from Monmouthshire, Sir Walter Devereux from Herefordshire,[3] Lord Audley and Humphrey Stafford of Southwick (his friends from Calais), and William Hastings who had been fined by the 'Parliament of Devils' for being with the rebels in Ludlow but who had rejoined them at the first opportunity.

Jasper had raised soldiers from his estates in Pembrokeshire, the Earl of Wiltshire had brought men from Ireland, and they also had Breton mercenaries and Welsh allies. There is no evidence to show by which road they came, but as it was mid-winter the army from Pembrokeshire would almost certainly have come along the valleys by Brecon and Hay, and it is possible that some of the Welsh chieftains had come by another road from central Wales and that Mortimer's Cross was their rendezvous.[4]

The battlefield was only three-and-a-half miles from Edward's castle at Wigmore, where there was also an abbey with extensive outbuildings,[5] and his army was well lodged and well fed and had not far to go in the morning. He knew the district intimately from riding over it as a boy, and the ground he had chosen was actually on the estate of his old acquaintance, Sir Richard Croft, whose brothers had annoyed him so much when he was younger.

On Candlemas Day, 2 February 1461, Edward and his army arrived early at the cross-roads and took up their positions at leisure, spreading out across the strip-fields of the village of Kingsland. At

---

[3] Sir Walter Devereux (1432–85). Lord Ferrers of Chartley, 1461. His sister married Sir William Herbert. He was the most important landowner in the central Marches and the enemy probably passed close by his castle at Weobley. He was killed at Bosworth fighting for Richard III.

[4] This is guesswork. Lt.-Col. A. H. Burne, author of *The Battlefields of England*, examined the site and expressed the opinion that a reconstruction of the battle was impossible.

[5] Wigmore Castle is now a ruin and little remains of the Abbey.

about ten o'clock, when they were still waiting for the enemy to arrive, they were startled to perceive three suns in the sky. This pheno-menon, known as a parhelion,[6] is somewhat uncommon, and it would have been regarded as a very sinister omen had not Edward had the pre-sence of mind to announce that it represented the Trinity and that it was a sign that they enjoyed the protection of the heavenly powers; his interpretation was confirmed by the smashing victory which followed, silencing any qualms which might have been felt as to the impropriety of fighting on Candlemas Day. In after years the thing most clearly remembered about the battle was the miracle of the three suns which everyone had seen and which could be described in two words; for the rest, there was just a confused recollection that the Welsh had been completely routed and that the dead strewed the fields—a stroke of luck for the neighbouring peasants who stripped the dead and wounded[7] and acquired riches beyond their wildest dreams.

'King Edward told me', wrote Comines,[8] 'that in all the battles which he had won, as soon as he was on top, he mounted his horse and shouted that they must spare the common soldiers and kill the lords, of which none, or few, escaped.' On this occasion Jasper and the Earl of Wiltshire extricated themselves in time and disappeared into the Welsh hills, but Jasper's father, Owen Tudor, was captured and to-gether with a handful of other prisoners was taken to Hereford. The heads of Edward's father and brother were still on the gates of York, so reprisals were inevitable. Hereford market-place was the scene of the execution, and the crowd watched with interest, especially when it came to the turn of the famous adventurer, Owen Tudor. Pseudo-Gregory described the occasion with gusto, but he cannot have been an eye-witness, as he confused Hereford with Haverfordwest and was muddled about the situation of Wigmore.

[6] Generally caused by ice crystals in the upper air, though it is sometimes seen in summer. The three Brontë sisters saw a parhelion in July or August 1847. Their friend Ellen Nussey, who was with them, accepted it as an omen and exclaimed: 'You are the three suns!'

[7] This made identification difficult and first lists of dead were generally wrong.

[8] Philip de Comines, Lord of Argenton (1447–1511), wrote memoirs which are superior to those of any contemporary. He began his career in the service of the Duke of Burgundy and subsequently worked for Louis XI.

Owen Tudor, he says, was 'weening and trusting all the way that he should not be beheaded till he saw the axe and the block, and when that he was in his doublet he trusted on pardon and grace till the collar of his red velvet doublet was ripped off. Then he said, "That head shall lie on the stock that was wont to lie on Queen Catherine's lap", and put his heart and mind wholly unto God, and full meekly took his death.'

This glimpse of an elderly charmer who cannot believe that his luck has deserted him is very credible, though the reference to Queen Catherine's lap is likely to have been a comment from the crowd, and Owen himself was probably thinking of more recent attachments. His head was set upon the highest point of the market cross 'and a mad woman combed his hair and washed away the blood off his face, and she got candles, and set [them] about him burning more than a hundred'.[9]

BY THE TIME THAT EDWARD HAD ascertained that Jasper's army had totally dispersed, and had reorganized his own army and resumed his interrupted march eastwards, he was a fortnight or more behind schedule; Margaret was well ahead in the race for London, and the Earl of Warwick was under the necessity of defending the City with such men as he had been able to collect in the south.

Queen Margaret and her small son travelled with her army, a performance which has won her more admiration from posterity than it elicited from her contemporaries. To take a child to war was considered rather shocking; the amazon type was not admired; coarse, tough, hard-bitten women were no rarity and the females who usually accompanied armies were the lowest of the low.[1] Margaret knew better than anybody else how hopeless it was to present Henry as an

[9] According to the *Dictionary of National Biography*, Owen Tudor had an illegitimate son called Daffyd or Owen, who was knighted and married to a Bohun heiress.

[1] In 1487 the herald who travelled with the army of Henry VII to the Battle of Stoke (fought against Lambert Simnel) recorded that at Leicester they made an effort to get rid of 'common women and vagabonds, for there were imprisoned great number of both. . . . And at Loughborough the stocks and prisons were reasonably filled with harlots and vagabonds. And after that, there were but few in the host until the field was done.' Richard Brooke, *Battlefields of Britain* (1857).

inspiring leader, and for some time she had been trying to build up her son as the symbol around which her supporters should rally, with the result that in the public mind she had become dissociated from Henry and appeared to be actually fighting against him. Her soldiers had been fitted out with a rudimentary uniform, and Pseudo-Gregory records with interest that every man wore his lord's livery and that every man and lord wore the Prince's badge, a band of crimson and black with ostrich feathers.

These distinguishing symbols were both numerous and confused. A nobleman inherited arms and supporters, a crest, livery, and a badge or badges. He could also invent for himself a personal device. Kings, with their long pedigrees, inherited many badges which they used on different occasions; this added interest to pageants, but must have been bewildering for simple soldiers in the heat of a battle. Contemporary artists rarely depict any badges or liveries, which is curious as even if they had never seen a battle troops of retainers wearing the colours of their lords must have been a familiar sight. As far as is known, the servants of Henry VI did not wear a red rose,[2] but it is true that the favourite badge of Edward IV was a white rose said to have come to the York family by marriage with a Clifford heiress, which had the advantages of being conspicuous, easy to make and genial, as well as holding for some people an erotic *double entente*.

The Midlands were not accustomed to the ravages of an invading army and the conduct of Margaret's undisciplined Northmen, who had been promised loot in lieu of wages, aroused terror and indignation. Their behaviour was mild by continental standards and no towns were destroyed, but they came south on a wide front said to extend for thirty miles, and nothing was held sacred. Local riff-raff joined in. News of their depradations went ahead of them, and the Prior of Croyland vividly remembered the dreadful days when an attack on the Abbey was expected at any moment.

'The Northmen swept onwards like a whirlwind from the North and in their fury attempted to over-run the whole of England. Also at

---

[2] It has been pointed out that in Shakespeare's *Henry VI* it is *Somerset* whose badge is a red rose. The usual Beaufort badge was a portcullis, but if a red rose was sometimes used it would certainly explain the Tudor rose. J. R. Planché, *The Pursuivant of Arms* (1851).

that time paupers and beggars flocked forth in infinite numbers, just like so many mice rushing forth from their holes, and abandoned themselves to plunder and rapine without regard to place or person.' They even looted churches, and broke open pyxes and shook out the sacred contents, and the priests who tried to resist them were slaughtered at their altars. Pack animals were confiscated and loaded with booty, and men were forced to dig up the things which they had buried. 'What do you suppose must have been our fears, dwelling here in this island?' Croyland was almost in the path of the invaders and, to make matters worse, refugees crowded in bringing their valuables with them. The monks hid all the treasures of the abbey, their jewels, vestments, charters and archives, and they walked in procession chanting, and prayed at the tomb of St Guthlac with more fervour than ever before. They also blocked the waterways to the island and barricaded the causeways with trees and branches, and eventually they heard to their great relief that the enemy horde, having come within six miles of them, had passed them by, and 'our Croyland became as another little Zoar[3] in which we might be saved, and by divine grace and clemency it was preserved'.

Such a thing had not happened in England in living memory, and the wealthy citizens of London were as terrified as the monks of Croyland. The defences of the City were in disrepair, the reactions of the populace uncertain, and Warwick decided to go north and fight a pitched battle in the open country. Margaret would not dare to go past him and he could choose the battlefield and fortify his position. By about the middle of February he occupied the town of St Albans, where he had triumphed six years before, and the nominal commander of his army, Henry VI, was brought along and placed in some safe house in the town—at the previous Battle of St Albans he had been wounded. Warwick then spread out his men in an irregular line towards the north-east in such a way as to block two of the roads to London.[4] His brothers Bishop Neville and John Neville, Lord

[3] Zoar was the little city in which Lot took refuge when Sodom and Gomorrah were destroyed. Margaret's army certainly went through Peterborough, which is only nine miles from Croyland.

[4] Lt.-Col. A. H. Burne thought that his line stretched, with breaks, for about four miles. The Queen's army was expected to come from Harpenden, either by the A6 to St Albans or by a diagonal road leading to Hatfield and the A1.

Montagu,[5] were with him, and he also had the assistance of several peers of whom the greatest was the Duke of Norfolk,[6] a very rich magnate of the old pugnacious school.

Pseudo-Gregory, too, was present, in what he regarded as the army of King Harry,[7] and he appears to have served in the infantry. 'As for spearman,' he wrote, 'they be good to ride before the foot men, and eat and drink up their victual, and many more such pretty things they do, hold me excused though I [seem to boast] for in the foot men is all the trust.'

Warwick, enterprising as ever, had bought an assortment of defensive gadgets and novel weapons, but Pseudo-Gregory was very contemptuous of them. The Burgundian mercenaries were armed with guns which were supposed to shoot pellets of lead, enormous arrows, and wildfire, but when the time came they would shoot nothing at all and the fire turned back on the gunners. There were also nets studded with nails, shields with a folding leg and a loophole which could either be stood up and shot through or laid on the ground as obstacles, spiked lattices with which to block gateways, and spiked contraptions called caltraps. But sensible men who 'will not gloss nor curry favour for no partiality' agreed with Pseudo-Gregory that none of these things did any good or harm either—except, possibly, to King Henry's own side.

Queen Margaret was undoubtedly the moving spirit behind the invasion, but there are no signs that she attempted to interfere in military matters. The commander of the army was presumably Somerset, with Trollope as his chief advisor, and now Trollope sprang another of his surprises. Warwick had reckoned that the enemy would attack his carefully prepared defences some time during the daylight hours of 17 February, but Trollope moved faster than Warwick expected and acted differently. Conventional armies did not march at night nor attempt

---

[5] John Neville appears to have been created Lord Montagu by Warwick shortly before this.

[6] John Mowbray, 3rd Duke of Norfolk (1415–61). His mother was a Neville and his wife was a Bourchier. He was in bad health and died later in the year.

[7] Harry was the ordinary English form of Henri. It was sometimes spelt Herry or Hery and the Duke of Milan was expected to recognize it when it appeared as Ari. The form 'Henry' was sometimes used by the upper classes.

night attacks, but Border cattle-raiders were well accustomed to ride great distances in the dark and on 16 February, instead of coming straight down the obvious road, Trollope sent a force westward to seize Dunstable, and under cover of darkness of the night of 16–17 February they rode the twelve miles down Watling Street to St Albans and broke into it from the west at a point where no attack was expected. Surprise was complete; the town was taken, and with it King Henry. Pseudo-Gregory was puzzled and pained by the capture of his leader, which he mistook for defection. 'And in the midst of the battle King Harry went unto his Queen and forsook all his lords, and trusted better to her party than unto his own lords.'

Trollope was now end-on to Warwick's attenuated line; the situation was unusual, and neither side knew how to turn it to advantage. The rest of the Queen's army arrived and spasmodic fighting began and continued all day in chaotic patches. Many years later, after Warwick was dead and disgraced, an Englishman told Comines that Warwick had been a coward and that during battles he would remain on his horse until he was certain of victory, but it seems unlikely that Warwick, so intrepid in other ways, should not have been able to put up a good show on the battlefield, and the origin of this slander may have been that at the Second Battle of St Albans he did spend the day on horseback trying to collect his units and to rearrange them facing the enemy. Late in the afternoon he gave up the attempt and, leaving London to look after itself, he and the remains of his army rode off to the west to join up with Edward.

The Second Battle of St Albans had two far-reaching consequences. One was that, by losing Henry, Warwick was no longer in possession of the puppet king and so he had to abandon all his old plans and quickly invent an entirely new programme. The other was that, fighting for Queen Margaret, a certain Sir John Grey had been killed. Sir John Grey had married Elizabeth Woodville, the eldest daughter of Lord Rivers and Duchess Jacquetta, and she now became a widow; most widows remarried and Elizabeth's second marriage was destined to cause even more of a sensation than her father's had done.

On the face of it Queen Margaret's long march from the north had been triumphantly successful. She had recaptured Henry, defeated

Warwick, and London—only twenty miles down Watling Street—lay helpless in front of her. Pseudo-Gregory, repeating second-hand gossip, wrote that on the evening after the battle King Henry knighted his son, who was wearing a suit of armour covered with purple velvet and ornamented with gold, and who was then able to knight some of his followers beginning with Andrew Trollope. Trollope had injured his foot in one of Warwick's caltraps and said, in his boastful way, 'My lord, I have not deserved if for I slew but fifteen men; for I stood still in one place and they came unto me—but they bode still with me!' Half a dozen very distinguished prisoners had been taken[8] and Lord Bonville[9] and one or two others were executed; it was said that the Prince acted as judge and that he and his mother watched the executions but this story, though widely believed, may merely be a reflection of the general disapproval that they should be there at all. Margaret was determined that her son should not be a feeble creature like her husband, but she overdid the toughening process and the prince acquired the reputation of being a blood-thirsty little brute.

In London the City Council was in a frenzy. They knew how weak were their fortifications and what happened on the Continent when a town was sacked, and they sent to Margaret to inform her that they would open the gates if she would promise to keep her soldiers under control. Their envoys were accompanied by three of the greatest Court ladies (Duchess Jacquetta, and the widow of the Duke of Buckingham, and the widow of Lord Scales),[1] in the hope that they would work on Margaret's softer feelings and persuade her to treat London leniently. Duchess Cecily, shaken by the recent loss of her husband and her son Rutland, determined to take no chances; she put her two youngest sons on a ship and sent them over to Burgundy, where they were given an ostentatiously warm welcome by the Duke of Burgundy. His only

[8] John Neville, Lord Montagu, had been again taken prisoner but his life was spared once more and he was sent up to York.
[9] William, 1st Lord Bonville (1393–1461). His long political career had been full of incident and his execution was perhaps due to personal animosities. He seems to have been in charge of King Henry and was probably captured with him.
[1] The daughter and heiress of Lord Scales had recently married Anthony Woodville, eldest son of Duchess Jacquetta, and he was thenceforward known as Lord Scales. Included in the Scales property was Middleton Castle near King's Lynn, Norfolk.

grandchild, Mary,[2] people noticed, was just the right age to marry one of the boys, either Clarence or Gloucester.

On 19 February 1461, two days after the Battle of St Albans, an Italian merchant in London wrote to a friend in Bruges: 'The shops stay closed and nothing is done either by the trades-people or by the merchants, and men do not stand in the streets or go far away from home. We are all hoping that, as the Queen and Prince have not descended in fury with their troops, the gates may be opened to them on good terms and they may be allowed to enter peacefully ... God be our protector and may He not consider our sins.'[3] The writer added than no one quite knew what had become of the Earl of March, but he was believed to be in the Cotisgualdo.[4]

On 22 February the same Italian wrote again to his friend with the worrying news that just after the authorities had announced that the Queen must be allowed to enter peaceably into the City there was a rumour that the Duke of York[5] was coming with 60,000 Irish and the Earl of March with 40,000 Welsh, and that the populace were demanding the keys of the gates. 'They called for a brewer as their leader and that day the town was in an uproar, so that I was never more frightened that anything might happen. [*la paura che tutto andrasse alla ventura di Dio.*]'

Had they but known it, Margaret was bluffing. Her northern soldiers had been on the road for a long time, they had collected as much booty as they could carry, spring was coming and they were needed at home. Already they were deserting in droves. She could not possibly have besieged London, weak though it was. She had no siege engines, she was short of money and provisions, and Edward's victorious army —reported to be enormous—was bearing down on her from the west. Her followers were behaving badly in and around St Albans and the London crowd, more courageous than the merchants, were determined not to give in without a fight. The Mayor ordered that food and money

[2] Mary of Burgundy (1457–82). Daughter of Charles the Bold and Isabella of Bourbon. Became Duchess of Burgundy in 1477. Married Maximilian of Austria the same year.
[3] Cal. Milanese Papers.
[4] The Cotswold Hills were well known abroad because of the high-quality wool produced in the district.
[5] The Duke of York had been dead for over two months.

should be sent to the Queen, but the mob, incited by the cook of Sir John Wenlock, stopped the carts and shared out the stores among themselves. 'But as for the money', wrote Pseudo-Gregory waggishly, 'I wot not how it was departed; I trow the purse stole the money.'

When Margaret heard for certain that Edward and Warwick had met and joined forces and that they were advancing on London, she turned round and started on the long journey back to York, hardly realizing what she had lost. She had no particular respect either for the City or for Westminster. The King of France had muddled along for years without Paris. She had captured Henry and she could rule in his name from anywhere.

Edward and Warwick met in the Cotswolds, either at Burford or Chipping Norton. Since their last encounter, each had lost his father and had gained the extra self-confidence which comes from being the head of an important family, but both men knew that if they were to survive they must exercise the utmost forbearance and co-operate with each other against the common enemy. It was certainly not the moment to allude to the fact that the young playboy had won a brilliant victory while his experienced cousin had been caught napping and had lost the puppet king; it was only too painfully obvious, and Warwick must have been cursing his stupidity every moment of the day.

They were in the same predicament; if Margaret ever regained power she would execute them, and so it was essential that Margaret never should regain power. The puppet king must be abolished, and a new king set up in his stead. There was not a moment to lose and, very fortunately, the man with the best title to the throne was Edward, ready on the spot and with an army at his back. Warwick must have resigned himself to the inevitable long before he reached Chipping Norton, but he would have been hardly human if the thought had not crossed his mind that he himself, experienced, wise, a man of the world, would make a far better king than his boyish cousin. However, once Warwick had determined on a course he did not waver, and now he used all his ingenuity to present Edward to the people as a *deus ex machina* who would set everything to rights.

Warwick and Edward entered London on 27 February 1461, ten days after the débâcle at St Albans. The relief was tremendous. Even

Pseudo-Gregory, little given to enthusiasm, remembered the rejoicings with sentimental nostalgia. There was a wave of anger against Henry because he had left them and joined himself to the ravening northmen, and a wave of romantic optimism about the young Prince. People were saying: 'Let us walk in a new vineyard and let us make us a gay garden in the month of March with this fair white rose and herb, the Earl of March.'

Edward was elected king by procedure which roughly followed what had been the custom before the Conquest. In those days it had been essential to fill the throne immediately a king died. There would have been no time to summon a representative council, and to meet in a provincial city was out of the question, and so in effect kings had been elected by whichever peers happened to be in London, backed by moral and financial support from the mayor and aldermen and city merchants, and acclaimed by a cheering crowd; in other words, when English kings were elected, it was London which chose them.

Bishop George Neville, the Chancellor, had returned from Canterbury whither he had fled after the Battle of St Albans and, on 1 March, he addressed a large open-air meeting explaining that Henry had forfeited their allegiance and putting forward Edward's rights to the throne —which were strong enough to need no lying or exaggeration. The crowd, doubtless thickened by a claque of Neville adherents, shouted assent. Then there was a gathering of those peers who were in London, and they also acquiesced. The possibility of rushing through a coronation was discussed, but it was decided to postpone it until after the Queen's army had been defeated, and instead, on 4 March, Edward attended a large meeting outside St Paul's, followed by ceremonies in Westminster Hall and Westminster Abbey, after which he went back to the City by way of the river.

This was the day—4 March 1461—on which Edward's reign officially began, he being eighteen years, ten months and a few days old. He seldom made mistakes which could be attributed to youth and inexperience, but he had one built-in disadvantage which was that the men who had put him on the throne were neither his natural subordinates nor his natural companions; there would be difficulty in establishing a personal ascendancy over them, and a tendency for them to be jealous of his younger associates.

On 6 March the new régime issued a long proclamation of the usual bombastic kind, written in officialese and lawyer's jargon, and touching on various subjects from the misery of England to the loss of France, from the wickedness of Edward's enemies to his own good intentions. All men between the ages of sixteen and sixty were summoned to join the army, and they were commanded upon pain of death to refrain from robbery, sacrilege and rape.[6] Pardons were offered to those who wished to change sides—with certain exceptions—and a hundred pounds was promised to whoever killed Andrew Trollope and some other named men.

There was much to be done before Edward went north; in particular, he had to raise the cash to finance the expedition. As Pseudo-Gregory put it: 'He was sorry that he was so poor, for he had no money but the substance of his meinie[7] came at their own cost.' Fortunately Edward had a flair for finance, and he was quickly able to borrow enough money to tide him over the next few weeks. Usury was forbidden by the church, and so accounts had to be fiddled and interest concealed[8] and hard business deals appear in the records as generous gifts and loans, but it is unlikely that the merchants concerned did not hope to make on the transactions and, as Edward's future was very uncertain, that they did not insist on a high rate of interest.

Edward, Warwick, Fauconberg and the Duke of Norfolk travelled to Yorkshire by different routes, Edward taking the road through Cambridge. They recruited as they went along and about 27 March they converged at Pontefract, having collected between them what is generally agreed to have been a gigantic army.

Queen Margaret, recruiting in Yorkshire, had had equal success. She could truly boast that she and her army had gone south to the wars

---

[6] Richard Beauchamp, Bishop of Salisbury (1430?–1481), writing to Coppini on 7 April 1461, said that the army going north had actually bought provisions, which was 'almost incredible to some'. It is true that Bishop Beauchamp had been taken into favour by Edward, but Warwick—unlike Queen Margaret's friends—had always been careful not to annoy the public.

[7] 'Meinie' is derived from the same root as *maison* and originally meant household retainers, but it had come to signify, like 'affinity' or 'fellowship', any band of armed followers.

[8] One very simple way to do this was to enter the loan as being for a larger sum than had actually been lent.

and had returned loaded with booty, having defeated the Earl of Warwick and captured the King. The great Earl of Northumberland supported her, and so did the disinherited branch of the Neville family. The
semi-royal Dukes of Somerset and Exeter and the Earl of Devon, as well
as a dozen or more other peers were in the city of York, and among her
knights was the famous soldier from France, Sir Andrew Trollope. The
gentlemen of Yorkshire could see for themselves that the Queen was
mighty and invincible and they came in crowds to share in her good
ortune. Her army, also, is said to have been gigantic and, if the figures
given at the time could be accepted, the battle which followed would
be the largest ever fought on English soil; certainly it was much the
largest fought in England during the fifteenth century. [9]

On the Continent, letters from England were eagerly awaited and
wild rumours flew around. It was said that King René (most impro-
bably), was going to the assistance of his daughter; not since Caesar had
the island suffered so many calamities; the whole country was convul-
sed. [1] For want of reliable news the Milanese ambassador, writing from
Brussels on 15 March, passed on what he knew to be mis-information.
'They say here that the Queen of England, after the King had abdicated
in favour of his son, gave the King poison. At least he has known how
to die even if he did not know what else to do. It is said that the Queen
will marry the Duke of Somerset. However, these are rumours in which
I do not repose much confidence. The sea between here and England
has been stormy and un-navigable ever since the 10th.'

The great royal castle of Pontefract [2] stood on a rocky bluff over-
looking the rolling plain of York but separated from it by the River
Aire which, together with the marshes on both sides of the river, formed
a considerable barrier. Observers on the castle towers could see a
good deal of what went on in the surrounding country and on a clear

[9] Otherwise the largest would be the Battle of Marston Moor, fought on 2 July 1644,
when 27,000 Roundheads defeated a rather smaller number of Cavaliers. Lt.-Col. A. H.
Burne is prepared to believe that at Towton Edward had 36,000 soldiers and 12,000 camp
followers, and that Margaret's army was even larger.

[1] *Cal. Milanese Papers.*

[2] Pontefract Castle was besieged three times during the Civil Wars and demolished
in 1649. A public garden has been made among the ruins. It was formerly pronounced
'Pumphrey' but is now pronounced as spelt.

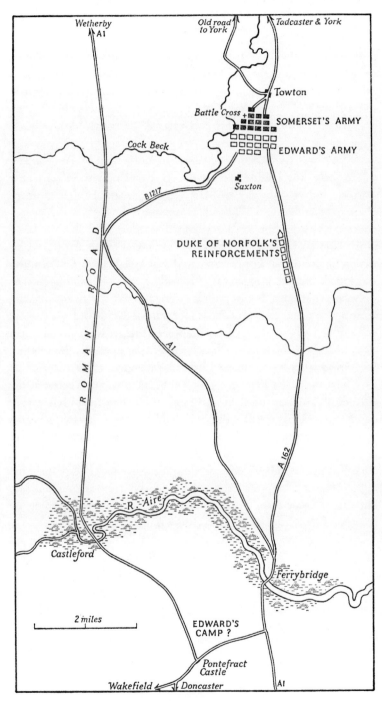

Battle of Towton

day it was possible to distinguish the city of York, twenty-two miles away; closer at hand their view was blocked by small slopes and undulations but they could make out that an enormous army was encamped about halfway between York and Pontefract, and there could be no doubt that if Edward and his host crossed the river a deadly battle would ensue.

The direct route from Pontefract to York went by Ferrybridge, where there was a bridge across the river and causeways across the marshes, and on Saturday 28 March Somerset sent Lord Clifford to destroy the bridge, and Warwick commanded the force which endeavoured to prevent him from doing so. There was some sharp fighting in the course of which Warwick was wounded by an arrow and his second in command, Lord Fitzwalter,[3] was killed, Lord Clifford also was killed, but the bridge was effectually put out of action. Repairs were begun at once, but in the meantime to cross the river Edward's army had to go upstream for about four miles to Castleford where there was a stone bridge and a ford. On the other side there was a good Roman road, but it bore too much to the left and by the time Edward was facing Somerset's army he had marched round three sides of a rectangle.

Somerset had taken up a position in open country between the villages of Towton and Saxton. On his right the ground fell steeply down to a small river called the Cock, and on the left he was protected by boggy ground. This did not leave him a very wide front, and it has been suggested that both armies were drawn up in divisions one behind the other instead of being spread out in the usual lines.[4] They spent the night in the open opposite each other. The next day was Palm Sunday, but that did not deter Edward, and some time in the morning he launched a straightforward frontal attack on Somerset.

The two things that are certain about the Battle of Towton are that it lasted for a phenomenal time and that there was a snow-storm which blew the arrows of Edward's archers into the faces of the enemy. The front line does not seem to have shifted at all until the afternoon, when Edward was reinforced on his right wing. The bridge at Ferry-

[3] John Radcliffe married Elizabeth daughter of Lord Fitzwalter and became Lord Fitzwalter. His widow married John Dynham.
[4] Burne, *The Battlefields of England*.

bridge had at last been mended and the Duke of Norfolk's soldiers,[5] who had been waiting to cross it, arrived fresh and terrible. This was too much for Somerset's weary men and they broke and ran, and the battle ended in a massacre. Penned in by the little Cock river, the fugitives were slaughtered in heaps or drowned when they tried to wade across it.

Among Edward's friends no one of note was killed, but on the opposing side the Earl of Northumberland, Lord Dacre, three other peers and many well-known knights lost their lives, among them that colourful character Sir Andrew Trollope. Queen Margaret, King Henry and Prince Edward, who had been awaiting the result of the battle either at York or some other place to the north, received news of the disaster in time to escape and reached Scotland safely, where they were joined by the Dukes of Somerset and Exeter who had both managed to survive.

The heralds' official estimate was that the dead numbered twenty-eight thousand; this was unprecedented but was soon exaggerated, so that the Croyland Prior wrote that he was told by the grave-diggers that there were thirty-eight thousand dead. Certainly digging the burial pits was unusually heavy work and several large grave-mounds remained until the present century. The duration of the battle was also exaggerated and on 7 April Archbishop Neville (who had not been present) was writing to tell Coppini that the battle had begun at sunrise and lasted till ten o'clock at night, and that the dead covered an area six miles long by three miles four furlongs wide, while on 17 April an Italian doctor in Bruges told Coppini that the battle lasted from Palm Sunday at prime to Tuesday noon.

Entering York the day after the battle, Edward and Warwick found the heads of their respective fathers and brothers still on the gate; these were sent to be interred with their bodies at Pontefract, and the heads of the Earl of Devon[6] and other opponents were put up in their place. They also discovered in York three of their relations who had been taken prisoner at St Albans and who had played their cards so adroitly that their lives had been spared: John Neville Lord Montagu, John

---

[5] According to a later account the Duke of Norfolk was ill in Pontefract, and his men were brought up by other officers.

[6] According to Pseudo-Gregory, he was ill in York and could not flee.

Bourchier Lord Berners, and William Bourchier Lord Fitzwarin. Montagu spent the next few years rounding up supporters of the Queen and they must often have regretted that they did not execute him when they had had the chance.

Having won his sanguinary victory, Edward was most anxious to conciliate the people of Yorkshire and he stayed for three weeks in the city of York trying, by charm and favours, to win over its important citizens; then he went on to Durham where the Bishop was quite willing to make friends with the new King; then on to Newcastle. Here the Earl of Wiltshire was brought in and executed, and his head was sent south to be set on London Bridge. Wiltshire had been captured at Cockermouth in Cumberland and with him was Dr Morton (the future Cardinal Morton), and one or two other men. They were mildly treated, and after a period of eclipse they were free again and Morton rejoined Margaret.

Seldom can civil war have been accompanied by so little ill-feeling, so little deliberate cruelty and so much readiness to forgive and forget. The ordinary citizen, though recognizing the royal family collectively as a superior race, was less than starry-eyed about the individual members of the clan. One was not much different from another. No abstract ideas about a cause were attached to the tug-of-war for the crown. The belligerents were not Cavaliers and Roundheads, French and English, Catholics and Protestants, Whigs and Tories, they were simply individuals, and their frequent realignments were accepted as natural, and the struggle for power, though ruthless, was hardly ever bitter.

Newcastle was as far north as Edward dared go, and it was certainly very necessary that he should return to the capital. Leaving Warwick, Fauconberg and Montagu to beat off attacks from the Scots, he came south by a westerly route, pursuing a zig-zag course through the Duchy of Lancaster where the people were traditionally attached to the descendants of Blanche of Lancaster; they might have a change of heart if they received attentions from their new monarch.

Edward made one-night stops at Preston, Warrington, Manchester, Chester, Stafford, Eccleshall, Lichfield, Coventry, Warwick and Daventry: at Stony Stratford, a popular halting-place on Watling Street, he stayed two nights. Here he was contacted by Lord Rivers who lived

half-a-dozen miles away at his manor of Grafton. He and his son Anthony had fought for Queen Margaret at Towton—in fact Anthony had
been reported dead—but they now considered that Edward had won
and decided to accept the new régime. Edward received him gladly; the
Woodvilles were friends who could be trusted, and he wrote from Stony
Stratford commanding that Lord Rivers should receive a pardon.[7] He
then, in one day, rode the fifty miles or so to his Palace at Shene (Richmond), arriving on 12 June 1461.

On Sunday, 28 June, Edward was crowned in Westminster Abbey
by Bourchier, Archbishop of Canterbury. Sunday was the unlucky day
of the year[8] but Edward cared no more for unlucky days than he did
for holy days, and he insisted on being crowned on the date which
suited him. The Exchequer was bankrupt and his pockets were empty,
but festivity and display were necessary to produce a good impression
and to establish confidence, and he did his best to make the greatest
possible show at the least possible expense. Followers were rewarded by
being made peers or by receiving some licence or office. His uncle[9]
Viscount Bourchier became Earl of Essex, and Lord Fauconberg became Earl of Kent. Hastings, Wenlock and Herbert became Lords and
so did five other supporters.[1] Thirty-two knights of the Bath were
created, including his two younger brothers; moreover, his brother
George was made Duke of Clarence.[2]

One year and two days had passed since the Three Earls landed in
Kent and during that period Edward had fought in three battles[3] and

---

[7] Lord Rivers' pardon was sealed on 12 July and Anthony's on 23 July.

[8] The unlucky day of the year was the day of the week on which the preceding Holy
Innocents' Day had fallen. Louis XI would not even discuss business on it.

[9] Henry Viscount Bourchier, Earl of Essex (1404?–1483), had married Edward's
father's sister, Isabel.

[1] Lord Ogle, Lord Lumley, Lord Stafford of Southwick, Lord Ferrers of Chartley
(Sir Walter Devereux) and Lord Cromwell (Humphrey Bourchier, third son of the new
Earl of Essex). These five were friends of Edward who were rich enough to support a title
but had no particular abilities. Titles were not given lightly—Hastings never became an
Earl, nor Warwick a Duke.

[2] Edward's right to the throne depended on Lionel Duke of Clarence, son of Edward
III. The title was very old and derived from the honour of Clare in Suffolk. The badge of
Clarence was a black bull.

[3] In this, the culminating twelve months of Henry VI's reign, five battles had been
fought in England; Northampton, Wakefield (Yorkshire), Mortimer's Cross (Herefordshire), St Albans (Hertfordshire) and Towton (Yorkshire).

ridden into London triumphantly four times. A great many of his relations and acquaintances had been killed, and he had mounted high above the heads of his cousin Warwick and the other Nevilles. It was a precarious eminence and failure meant death, but he was a young man with good nerves, good spirits and a good head for figures and, whatever the future had in store for him, he was prepared to meet it with dash and courage.

IV

England's Neighbours

WHEN EDWARD CAME TO THE THRONE THE PICTS, SCOTS, Welsh-British, Norseman and Anglo-Saxons who had settled in the territories now called Scotland had not yet fused together. The Lowland landowners had more in common with the Northumbrians than with the Gaelic-speaking clans in the Highlands and some of them owned property in the English Midlands. The great Douglas family toyed with the idea of repudiating the Stuarts and setting up a kingdom of their own, but the various branches feuded between themselves and the head of the family, James, 9th Earl of Douglas, had been living in England since 1455. The Highland clans fought each other and the Western Isles were practically independent, though loosely tied to Norway. The frontier between England and Scotland fluctuated and local cattle-raiders obeyed nobody. The French were always hoping that the energies of the English would be channelled into a Scottish war. Queen Margaret was in Scotland preparing a fresh invasion, and Somerset was said to be the lover of the Queen mother, Mary of Gueldres.

Intelligent men could see that both countries stood to gain if friendly relations were preserved and, over the years, every kind of marriage alliance between members of the English and Scottish royal families was suggested,[1] and Edward, who—in spite of his victories—always preferred peace to war, was in favour of some such alliance, but he had never been to Scotland or seen an accurate map of it and all he knew about the country was what people told him. In 1462 he agreed to a plan which may have originated in the lively brain of Warwick; the exiled Douglas and the Lord of the Isles should, with English help, possess themselves of the whole of Scotland which they would then hold with Edward as their overlord, and a secret treaty, later known as the Treaty of Ardtornish, was actually signed with the Lord of the Isles. When this became known it naturally made the Scots very suspicious of the good faith of the English king. The English on their side found their honest efforts to preserve peace frustrated by the instability of the Scots government and by the fact that none of the nobles stayed in power for very long. Some of them, including the Regent, Bishop Kennedy, were sent annual presents,[2] but when these individuals died or were displaced, the money was lost and other associations had to be cultivated.

A foreigner's impression of the rough and primitive conditions prevailing in Scotland can be found in the autobiography of Pope Pius II.[3] In 1435, before he had taken orders and when he was a career diplomat working for Cardinal Albergata, he was sent on a mission to James I and in middle age he recalled with horror the discomforts of Scotland and the barrenness of the devastated Border country.

He attempted to make the journey overland through England but he was not permitted to travel north of London and was forced to return to the Continent and take ship from Sluys. On this voyage he met with terrible gales and he was blown so far north that the sailors 'who could no longer recognize the stars' abandoned hope. After

---

[1] At last, in 1503, Margaret, daughter of Henry VII, married James IV of Scotland. This did not prevent the Battle of Flodden in 1513, but it paid amazing dividends exactly a hundred years later when, in 1603, James VI of Scotland succeeded to the crown of England and the two countries were united.

[2] It would not be correct to call these presents bribes; they were just the palm oil which is still customary in many countries and in many walks of life.

[3] Pius II. Aeneas Silvius Piccolomini (1405–64). Pope, 1458. His memoirs were written in Latin and continued to the last months of his life. *Memoirs of a Renaissance Pope. The Commentaries of Pius II*, trans. F. A. Gragg, ed. L. C. Gabel (1960).

twelve days they reached Scotland. 'It is a cold country where few things grow and for the most part has no trees. Below the ground is a sulphureous rock which they dig for fuel. The cities have no walls. The houses are usually constructed without mortar; their roofs are covered with turf and in the country the doorways are covered with oxhides. The common people, who are poor and rude, stuff themselves with meat and fish and eat bread as a luxury. The men are short and brave; the women fair, charming and easily won. Women there think less of a kiss than they do in Italy of a touch of the hand. . . . The horses are small and natural trotters. . . . There is nothing the Scotch like better than to hear abuse of the English. . . .'

Having discharged his mission—its nature he does not disclose, but it was probably to incite James I to attack England—and fearing to venture again on the sea, he came south by road, disguised as a merchant. He crossed the Tweed into Northumberland and spent a terrifying night in a very savage village where the women seemed to have even looser morals than the Scots but, as he was expecting raiders at any moment, he was too frightened to take advantage of his opportunities. However, no raiders appeared and he felt that his continence had been rewarded. At daybreak he left with relief and at last reached Newcastle. 'There for the first time he[4] seemed to see a familiar world and a habitable country; for Scotland and the part of England nearest to it are utterly unlike the country we inhabit, being rude, uncultivated and unvisited by the winter sun.'

Still in disguise, he travelled down England, sightseeing as he went. He visited the tomb of the Venerable Bede in Durham, and in York saw the cathedral 'famous throughout the world for its size and architecture and for a very brilliant chapel the glass walls of which are held together by very slender columns'. Foreigners were not permitted to leave the kingdom without a passport and as he dared not ask for one he bribed the port authority at Dover, 'a thing which is easy to do as this class of man loves nothing more than gold'. And so via Calais and Basle to Milan.

---

[4] The *Commentaries* of Pius II were written in the third person, in whimsical imitation of Caesar's *Commentaries*.

THE TWO CONTINENTAL POWERS which really mattered to England were France and Burgundy, and their respective strength was so nearly equal that it was a matter of opinion which of the two was the more valuable ally. Edward, thinking in terms of trade, was inclined towards the rich and peaceful Burgundy; Warwick favoured an alliance with France. The rulers of all three countries unceasingly engaged in negotiations with each other. Embassies came and went. Very important messages were delivered verbally and particularly compromising papers may have been destroyed, but there remains much diplomatic correspondence in the French archives. Occasionally a score was made by one side or the other, but most of the time the ball was cautiously patted to and fro. The rulers had no illusions about each other; a king naturally thought of the welfare of his own country and his own dynasty; all professions of friendship were provisional; if circumstances altered, then alliances altered also.

THE FRENCH KING, CHARLES VII, died on 22 July 1461, and was succeeded by his middle-aged son, Louis XI.[5] Edward and Louis thus began their reigns in the same year.

A great deal is known about the personality of Louis XI, partly because he was more literate than most kings and could dash off fluent and colloquial letters—the printed collection of his letters runs to eleven volumes—and partly because he was attended during the last half of his reign by the intelligent and articulate Philip de Comines who, in retirement, wrote a history of his own times.[6] Comines did not tell all, sometimes his memory played him false, he did not know much about what went on in England, but he had lived at the very centre of French and Burgundian politics and he endeavoured to give posterity a true account of what he thought had happened.

Louis spent his whole life working and worrying; he never relaxed, never rested, never enjoyed. Even hunting, to which he was passionately devoted, gave him more annoyance than pleasure; he set out

[5] Louis XI (1423–83). He died less than five months after Edward IV.
[6] Comines left the service of the Duke of Burgundy and attached himself to Louis in 1472. His memoirs were written between 1488 and 1501.

very early in the morning and came back late at night, tired out and in a foul temper. Louis was grotesque in appearance and eccentric in his habits and dress. In boyhood he had been married to Margaret of Scotland, daughter of James I and Joan Beaufort, who combined the aggressiveness of the Beauforts with the ineptitude of the Stuarts. In spite of her youth and unimportance she managed to become an object of persecution, and she was accused of sitting up all night to write poetry, and of failing to conceive because she drank vinegar and ate green apples and laced herself alternately too tightly and too loosely. Louis detested her and she died aged twenty-one exclaiming in despair: 'Fy de la vie de ce monde! Ne m'en parlez plus!'[7] In 1451 Louis married Charlotte of Savoy. In his younger days he had kept mistresses and acknowledged bastards, but (according to Comines) after a baby son died he took a vow to abstain from all women except his wife, and so great was his self-control that he kept his vow although the Queen 'was not one of those from whom one can get much pleasure, though a very good sort of woman'.

Before his accession, Louis had lived in Burgundy, having quarrelled with his father, but his friendship with Duke Philip did not survive his coronation. The Duke's avuncular attitude was resented by the new monarch and the ostentatious riches of the Burgundians were a source of irritation to the impoverished French. (Comines was of the opinion that the meeting of princes was always unwise as it invariably led to jealousies.)

Much of France was cut up into states and provinces governed by hereditary rulers whose allegiance was only nominal and who would be quite likely to side with the enemy in the event of a foreign invasion, and Normandy and Picardy had not yet recovered from the effect of the Hundred Years War, but Louis fortunately inherited the standing army which his father had instituted and which was accepted as an expensive necessity, and he was able to act independently without much regard for the opinion of the nobles or the rest of his people. His ultimate aim was to produce a strong and united France, an aim which now seems refreshingly sensible.

---

[7] 'I am tired of the life of this world! Don't mention it to me again!'

THE HISTORY OF THE DUKES OF BURGUNDY was short and remarkable. In 1363 King John of France bestowed the small duchy of Burgundy on his fourth and favourite son and, in the space of a hundred years, by dint of adroit deals and clever marriages, the Dukes of Burgundy had extended their domains to include Flanders and Holland, and had obtained possession of what has always been—in spite of frequent wars —one of the richest parts of Europe. They had mines, vineyards, good farmland, water-ways, manufacturing towns and ports, and after Duke Philip the Good[8] pulled out of the Anglo-French war he was able to avoid almost any further fighting and his court became the undisputed centre north of the Alps of art, fashion, luxury, culture, pageantry, tournaments, and what was considered refinement and good manners. His income was supposed to equal that of Venice and to be twice that of the Pope and, supported by the industry of merchants and artisans, the Court played games of chivalry in which the conquerors of Greek and Roman history mingled with the Knights of the Round Table and the Patriarchs of the Old Testament. In his youth Duke Philip had seen real war and he still cherished an aspiration to lead some great crusade, though latent common-sense prevented him from actually embarking on one.

Philip was technically only a duke and not a king; he held part of his Duchy from the King of France and most of his other territory from the Emperor. Nor was Burgundy a nation. It was a collection of different peoples united by chance and held together by the Duke personally. It had no centre. Dijon was the capital of the original French Duchy, but Duke Philip lived much at Bruges and other Flemish towns. His celebrated Castle of Hesdin with its joke rooms where visitors were showered with water, soot, flour and feathers was near Boulogne.

In 1461 Philip was an elderly man with deteriorating health, and he had long allowed the government to be carried on by excellent chancellors while he devoted himself to pleasure; but shadows were

[8] Philip the Good, 3rd Duke of Burgundy (1396–1467). Married (1) Michelle of France; (2) Bonne d'Artois; (3) Isabella of Portugal, mother of his only legitimate son, Duke Charles the Bold. He is said to have acknowledged thirty mistresses and seventeen bastards.

creeping up. He had never been able to get on with his only legitimate son, Charles,[9] a headstrong young man who it was guessed would, when his hour arrived, immediately reverse the peaceful policies of his elders.

THE DUCHY OF BRITTANY, owing to its proximity to the English coast, was also of importance to England. Like Burgundy, it was in fact an independent state whose Duke theoretically owed allegiance to the King of France. The Bretons were in possession of the mouth of the Loire; their coastline stretched from Nantes to St Malo; they had traded across the Channel from time immemorial and they persisted in remaining on good terms with the English in spite of frequent local quarrels caused by acts of piracy.[1]

In 1461 Brittany was enjoying prosperity in a rustic, peaceful, unsophisticated way. Weak, comparatively backward and uncultured, this hilly, poorish province did not attract invading armies and it had escaped the worst ravages of the late wars. Industrious artisans from devastated areas had taken refuge there, and it afforded convenient asylum for noble exiles from other countries. Its ruler, Duke Francis II,[2] who had succeeded in 1458, was neither clever nor ambitious, and his main wish was to be left alone and allowed to hunt in peace.

ENGLAND'S RELATIONS WITH DENMARK and the towns of the Hanseatic League were frequently strained. Merchant ships often turned pirate and attacked those of other countries, and Londoners were jealous of the merchants from the Baltic ports who unloaded at their trading-post in the City. The countries of central Europe hardly affected England one way or the other; they were loosely united under an elected

[9] Charles the Bold, Fourth and last Duke of Burgundy (1433–77). Before he succeeded he was the Count of Charolais. He was known as Charles le Hardi until the beginning of the last century when it became the fashion to call him Charles le Téméraire.

[1] St Malo and Fowey were notorious haunts of pirates.

[2] Francis II, last Duke of Brittany (1435–88). He married twice, but his mistresses were more conspicuous than his wives, and he acknowledged several children by Antoinette de Villequier, formerly a mistress of Charles VII of France.

Emperor and the eastern states were already beginning to suffer from the great Turkish advance across Europe.

On the other hand the English were extremely conscious of the Iberian Peninsula, which was squarely in the way of ships sailing to the Mediterranean. The boundaries of Portugal were much as they are today and over the years the Kings of England had managed to avoid war with the Kings of Portugal, though their trading interests sometimes clashed.

Spain had not yet been united into a single kingdom. The Moors occupied a coastal strip in the south, while Castile, Aragon and Catalonia were independent states. Of these Castile was the largest. In 1461 the king of Castile was a notorious debauchee who, ever since his first marriage had been annulled, was known to his subjects by the crude nickname of Henry the Impotent.[3] Henry possessed a young half-brother and half-sister, and it was the latter, Isabella, who eventually inherited Castile and married Ferdinand, the heir of Aragon.[4]

THE FIFTEENTH-CENTURY ENGLISHMAN who travelled to one of the north Italian towns plunged into a milieu where learning, art and literature were far ahead of what was to be found in England. Dante had died as long ago as 1321, and Boccaccio had died in 1375. In 1461, artists working in Italy included Giovanni Bellini, Filippo Lippo, Andrea Mantegna and Piero della Francesca, but the English traveller may have failed to notice their paintings, his attention being distracted by the savage riots and outbreaks of mob violence, the assassinations and bloody reprisals, the tortures and sinister disappearances, compared to which the occasional affrays and disturbances, imprisonments and hangings to which he was accustomed at home were tame indeed.

The Italian nobles had feuds with their own relations and with other great families and, apart from this, most states were endeavouring to expand at the expense of their neighbours by means of wars con-

---

[3] Henry IV, King of Castile (1425–74). His second wife gave birth to a daughter whom the nobles would not accept, although he persisted in asserting that he was her father.
[4] Isabella the Catholic (1451–1504), married 1469 Ferdinand of Aragon (1452–1516).

ducted by mercenaries led by highly paid condottieri who inconvenienced themselves as little as possible, refraining, by a gentleman's agreement, from fighting on foot or in winter.

The great Duke of Milan, Francesco Sforza, had himself been a condottiere and was the illegitimate son of another famous condottiere. 'He appeared the only man of our time whom fortune loved,' wrote Pope Pius II, adding that he did have some misfortunes as his mistress, whom he passionately loved, was murdered by his wife, two old friends deserted him for the enemy and he was forced to hang a third; he also had to bear the treachery of his brother and to imprison his son who was plotting against him.

Venice was the richest state and was governed by a ruthless oligarchy. Florence, nominally a republic, was controlled by the Medici family, bankers with branches in France, Burgundy and London. Naples, having failed to produce a royal family of its own, was the centre of disputes which reverberated until well into the next century and affected countries as far away as Scotland; it was claimed by both the King of Aragon and by René of Anjou and occupied by Ferrante, the illegitimate son of the last king, Alfonso of Aragon, who had left it to him by will.

Towards Rome, English feelings were ambivalent. The Pope was very powerful; he could interfere in English private affairs in a way that was open to no other foreigner and he could extract money from the English by all sorts of means. Three-quarters of the contents of the pilgrims' offertory box at Eton was supposed to go to Rome, and if an Englishman wanted to marry his third cousin or build a school or endow an almshouse the licence had to be bought in Rome. The Pope, also, was able to lengthen or shorten a man's stay in Purgatory, although there were paintings over the chancel arch in many a village church showing the Holy Father himself being thrown into a fiery Hell. Pseudo-Gregory was a little nervous of the Pope's magical powers, but he enjoyed repeating the jeers of bolder spirits. When the Pope sent a Bull cursing all shoemakers who made shoes with pointed toes or who traded on Sunday, the shoemakers flouted his orders, and the men who were trying to destroy the 'long pykys' were beaten up. 'And some men said that they would wear long pykys whether Pope willy or nilly, for they said the Pope's curse would not kill a fly. God amend this.'

Pius II describes in his autobiography how he was elected to the papal chair in 1458, and how there were villainous cardinals who wished to elect other candidates and how he foiled their plots.

'Many Cardinals met in the latrines as being a secluded and retired place' and decided to elect one Guillaume. 'A fit place for such a pope to be elected! For where could one more appropriately enter into a foul agreement than in latrines?' While the votes were being counted the excitement was terrific but, in the end, the best man won.

Pius was a romantic as well as a poet, a scholar and an egotist, and his grand obsession was that he must organize a crusade against the Turks who, ever since the fall of Constantinople, had been pushing westwards. He knew that even Rome could be sacked by barbarians, and one of his first actions was to summon an international congress at Mantua for the purpose of forcing all the kings of Christendom to make a great concerted effort. In his memoirs he frankly admits that the congress was a failure.

The delegates were supposed to meet in June 1459, and from the first there were complaints and gloomy prognostications. 'They said that Pius had been foolish to come to Mantua, that very few representatives of Princes had assembled, and still fewer were likely to come; the place was marshy and unhealthy; the heat intense; they did not like the flat wine . . . most of them were sickening; very many were catching fever; nothing was heard except the frogs.'

Finally the envoys did arrive, some of them with fine retinues like the Polish ambassador whose men were dressed alike in their national costume, wearing plumed hats, carrying quivers and slings and mounted on well-groomed horses. There was, of course, quarrelling over the seating, but the greatest disappointment was the non-appearance of the Duke of Burgundy; old-fashioned in outlook, his ambition was to go to Jerusalem to challenge the captain of the Infidels to single combat, but he sent the excuse that he dared not leave his duchy for fear of an attack by France. The French said that they could not come on the crusade for fear of being attacked by the English, and though the Pope pointed out that if the French and English each sent the same number of soldiers it would make things equal the French were not to be persuaded. The English were almost insulting; the legate Coppini had failed to secure an interview with Henry and Margaret had been too busy to attend to him, and so they only sent two paltry friars. As for the Venetians, they said straight out that they traded with the Turks and that if they embarked on a war they would probably be left in the lurch by their allies and the Milanese would certainly stab them in the back.

In spite of these depressing rebuffs the Pope did not abandon his great enterprise; he clung hopefully to the vague promises which he had received and made charitable excuses for the countries which had offered nothing. 'England, now racked by civil war, holds out no hope, nor does Scotland, remote as it is on Ocean's furthest bound. Denmark, Sweden and Norway also are too far away to be able to send soldiers and they have no money to contribute as they produce nothing but fish.'

V

The New King July 1461–February 1462

THE MAIN PROBLEMS WHICH CONFRONTED THE YOUTHFUL KING Edward were how to retain his throne, how to drag the nation out of bankruptcy, how to restore order in the provinces and how to protect his frontiers against the French and the Scots.

We do not know to whom he went for advice, nor which of the men who served him were influential and which merely carried out his orders. We do not know how far he planned ahead, how much he was guided by theories, which decisions were instantaneous, which were arrived at after long discussions, and which he regretted later. He was like an energetic young man who has taken over a run-down family business which he means to restore to its former efficiency. At first he must have felt his way tentatively but, seen in retrospect, his policies throughout his reign appear remarkably consistent, and his objectives might be summarized as peace and prosperity, trade with all and to hell with glory—a programme which would have been considered most un-kinglike if he had announced it to his subjects.[1]

Much depended on selecting the right officials. The easiest posts to fill were the secretaries and working deputies who could be drawn from any class on the strength of their abilities; it was essential that they

---

[1] It was despised by the historians of the last century who, from the safety of their libraries, wallowed in the gore of battles long ago.

should be honest and some must have been extremely sagacious, but their various characters and achievements have evaporated and they are just names among other names. The most important of these shadowy men was undoubtedly William Hatteclyffe or Atclif. He was by profession a physician and had attended Henry VI; Edward, at his accession, appointed him his personal doctor and by 1466 Hatteclyffe was called private secretary; eventually he proved capable of undertaking anything from negotiating abroad with foreign powers to arranging a family marriage. Hatteclyffe must have been a very remarkable man, not the least of his achievements being that he seems to have aroused no jealousy.

Besides these middle-class employees, there were the knights of the body, gentlemen of small fortune who were willing to spend a strenuous life travelling round with the King, and who were occasionally sent abroad on responsible missions. Some of them were Edward's personal friends, so far as difference in rank permitted friendship, but again we do not know which were influential and which were no more than agreeable and obedient aides-de-camp.

The really important and lucrative posts could only be bestowed on peers and here the choice was very limited; their numbers were few and of these only a fraction had the brains and the social weight to conduct business of the first importance. In addition there were half a dozen bishops who were prepared to devote their time to affairs of state, and able government officials who were in holy orders could be given the wealth and status of a bishopric as and when a vacancy occurred. There was a tradition that all the members of the royal family should be admitted to state councils, but here Edward was unlucky; his family was large, but it was mainly useless. His brother Rutland was dead and Clarence and Gloucester were still children. His eldest sister was married to the Duke of Exeter who, besides being futile was attached to the Queen's party; his other brother-in-law, the Duke of Suffolk, never took an active part in public affairs;[2] and his youngest

[2] John de la Pole, 2nd Duke of Suffolk (1442–91). Married (*c.* 1460) Elizabeth Plantagenet (1444–1503). The downfall of his father may have made him determined not to meddle in politics, or he may have been a feeble character. He and Elizabeth lived mainly at Wingfield, deep in rural Suffolk. Their castle is now a farm, but it retains a battlemented façade and a moat, and their effigies can be discovered in a large and lonely church.

sister, Margaret, had not yet been found a husband. With the exception of his uncle, Henry Bourchier Earl of Essex, who was reliable rather than brilliant, the only relations who were qualified to occupy the highest positions were his Neville cousins: Bishop Neville was Chancellor; John Neville Lord Montagu was permanently in command of military operations in the North; and Warwick was Captain of Calais, Constable of Dover Castle, Lord Warden of the Cinque Ports, and Warden of the East and West Marches towards Scotland as well as holding many other posts and titles. While Edward wrestled with the internal problems of the nation, Warwick would guard it from attack by foreign countries.

It is not surprising that Warwick was dissatisfied. Under no circumstances today would an ambitious millionaire spend his life playing second fiddle to two cousins, one of whom was mad and the other fourteen years younger than himself. Continental grandees were virtually kings in their own domains but, as a Venetian envoy observed, in England even the greatest peers were nothing more than very rich gentlemen.[3] The blood of John of Gaunt and Catherine Roët surged in Warwick's veins, and yet, unless there was some extraordinary cataclysm and he was elected king by vote of Parliament, he could never be more than he was now, Edward's subordinate, to be ordered about or dismissed at the royal pleasure.

THE PASTONS BELONGED TO AN EAST ANGLIAN FAMILY of minor importance which has intruded into the pages of history through the chance that an enormous accumulation of their correspondence has been preserved, so that while practically nothing is known about the private lives of the personages who swayed the destinies of the nation the insignificant Pastons exhibit themselves to the gaze of posterity with unselfconscious abandon.[4] Several other hoards of fifteenth-century

---

[3] Written in 1497. *A Relation or Rather a True Account, of the Island of England* (Camden Society, 1847).

[4] *The Paston Letters 1422–1503*, ed. James Gairdner, 6 vols (1904), and *Paston Letters and Papers of the Fifteenth Century*, ed. Norman Davis, pt 1 (O.U.P., 1971).

family papers have been discovered and published, but for human and political interest, as well as for quantity, the Paston letters are in a class by themselves, and the Pastons have become the spokesman for the average Englishman of the period.

The thousand-odd Paston letters taken in the lump are a trackless morass. They are badly spelt and clumsily expressed, and if they had been written at a later date they would be considered of no interest whatever. The majority are business letters and, as we are accustomed to read collections of letters from which private business-matters have either been entirely excluded or else are much outweighed by other topics, the first impression is that the writers are money-grubbing monsters; on closer acquaintance, however, they turn out to be ordinary human beings—so ordinary, indeed, that the whole family might be characters in a Victorian novel.

They had only recently come up in the world. A farmer who lived at Paston in Norfolk had had a brilliant son who studied law, became a judge, married an heiress and invested his money in land. Judge Paston had several sons and the eldest, John Paston, became a lawyer and married another heiress. The law was practically the only money-making occupation that could be pursued by gentlemen;[5] owning many manors was the hall-mark of the upper classes, and Lawyer Paston's children were accepted as country gentry. The Pastons had arrived.

John Paston the lawyer (d. 1466) was undeniably crooked. The great coup of his life was to attach himself to an old soldier, Sir John Fastolf,[6] who had made a fortune in the French wars and was a man of considerable taste, perhaps even a dandy, and had built himself a delectable little castle, or fortified manor-house, in the latest foreign style at Caister in Norfolk, a mile or two inland from Yarmouth. Fastolf disliked his relations and, having a bad conscience, intended to

---

[5] Court pleadings were in French; French was not taught at the universities and law was studied at the Inns of Court in London. Sir John Fortescue expressed the opinion that it was a good thing that law was expensive to study as this kept it a profession for gentlemen.

[6] Sir John Fastolf appears in *Henry VI, Part I*. He was nothing to do with the better known Sir John Falstaff.

leave all his wealth to found a 'college'[7] at Caister so that the prayers of the bedesmen would assist his soul through the fires of the next world; but in 1459, when he died, his lawyer John Paston, who had attended his death-bed, produced a dictated will leaving much of Fastolf's property to himself. He occupied Caister Castle, but several local peers also coveted it and the rest of Paston's life was poisoned by the struggle to remain in possession. He was much in London on business while his wife Margaret remained in Norfolk, wrestling with the management and protection of their scattered estates and doing her utmost for her misguided husband and their brood of awkward children. When she had first married, her letters had been loving and skittish, but she led a trying life beset by worries and burdened by cares and responsibilities, and she ceased to be cheerful and was sometimes harsh, though always conscientious.

Of their five sons and two daughters the main letter-writers were the two eldest sons who were both called John. To repeat a Christian name was quite usual and caused so little inconvenience that a diminutive or nickname was not found necessary, but for the sake of clarity the young John Pastons will be referred to as *major* and *minor*.

John Paston *major* was extravagant, selfish and flighty, exhibiting the stock features of an eldest son who is not turning out very well; while John Paston *minor* was an ordinary, responsible, matter-of-fact English youth; however, the two brothers got on very well together and only bickered in a friendly, chaffing way. Had they lived in Victorian times, the elder would have been an officer in a smart cavalry regiment while the younger would have been put into some less expensive branch of the service or perhaps sent out to India; but there was no standing army, so the best they could do was to attach themselves to great men and hope either that fighting would break out, or that by influence they might obtain some salaried post. Naturally they expected to increase their capital by marrying a girl with property, which was practically the only way that any man could get rich *quickly*. By dint of living in the highest society and moving to and fro with their

[7] 'Colleges' were like mission stations and could include, besides a chapel, a school, almshouses, hospital, library and soup kitchen. They filled a need, and many were founded during the fifteenth century.

patrons they were quite well informed as to what was going on at Court, but they were careful not to write anything indiscreet. Neither of the Paston brothers attempted to be clever or literary; they merely aimed to pass on news that was important to themselves, and when they were not sure of the truth of a rumour they used some such formula as 'men say'; and as a result what they wrote is exceptionally reliable.

In the summer of 1461 Lawyer Paston, as one of the late Fastolf's executors, handed back to Edward two brooches which the Duke of York had pawned and which were now needed to create an effect of opulence and inspire confidence. They were showy pieces; one was 'an owch of gold in the fashion of a ragged staff with two images of a man and a woman garnished with a ruby, a diamond and a great pearl' and the other, also an owch of gold, had 'a great pointed diamond set upon a rose enamelled white'. The sum owing was 700 marks,[8] including an 'obligation' of 100 marks (an euphemism for interest), and Edward promised to pay it off at the rate of 200 marks every All Saints' Day.

When August came, Edward set off on a progress through the southern counties, beginning at Canterbury and Sandwich. A wise king was always on the move, keeping in touch with local leaders and inquiring into local grievances; and courtiers, officials and hangers-on travelled along with him as best they could. John Paston *major* had got his toe in the door and was vaguely attached to the Earl of Essex, now Treasurer of England, and his father expected to hear that he had secured the King's interest in some of the squabbles over property in which the Pastons were engaged. Patronage was one of the highly prized perquisites of the great, and all the way up the social ladder there were petitioners buying the intervention of men above them; suppliants, far from being resented, were regarded as a useful source of income, and it was quite in order for Paston *major* daily to badger Essex, and the servant of Essex, about the manor of Dedham and an extract copied from the Court Roll.

By 23 August 1461, they had reached Lewes in Sussex and Paston *major* wrote apologetically to tell his father that he was doing his best;

[8] A mark was worth thirteen shillings and fourpence (two-thirds of a pound).

he had almost given up hope and Essex had kept on putting him off and saying that the moment was not propitious, but at last Essex had broached the subject to Edward, pointing out how much Lawyer Paston had done for him, and Edward (who had many ways of knowing all about the skulduggery that went on in Norfolk and was also a shrewd judge of character) had replied that 'he would be your good lord therein as he would be to the poorest man in England. He would hold with you in your right; and as for favour, he will not be [thought to] . . . show favour more to one man than to another, not to one in England.' When asked about the Court Roll 'he smiled and said that such a bill there was, saying that you would have oppressed sundry of your countrymen . . . and therefore he kept it still. Nevertheless he said he should look it up' at once, and give it them. Paston *major* had not yet actually obtained it, but he would send it as soon as possible. The servant of Essex had pointed out that Lawyer Paston now had to 'do somewhat' for the Earl of Essex, and that there was a little money owing between a gentleman called Durward and Paston, and that there was the same sum between Essex and Durward, and so Paston could pay off his obligation that way. This had the advantage that the transaction did not appear in recognizable form in anyone's account book and to a large part of the human race this would still seem the natural and friendly way of doing business.

All England was quarrelling over the ownership of land. Leaving aside the cases of deliberate swindling and stealing and forging of deeds, the laws of land tenure were out of date. Written records often did not exist or were impossible to find, and Edward was determined that disputes should be settled in the law-courts and not by royal award or by violence; even if the richest man won, that might have happened anyway. But Edward's offer of justice did not satisfy the Pastons, who expected their 'good lord' to support them right or wrong, in the same way that they would support him right or wrong. By giving the Pastons what they demanded he could have bought their swords for ever, but they were not worth buying at the price of sacrificing the principle of impartial law as well as annoying the other parties in the dispute. Edward was a disappointment to the Pastons and ten years later they even fought against him in a battle, but for the most part they accepted the fact that he was king and, though they did not like him, they made the best of him; and Edward, in his realistic way, made the best of them.

Paston *major* stayed on at the court although he needed more money and there were some doubts at home whether the expense was justified. A very youthful uncle of his in London, Clement Paston, discussed the point in a letter to his father;[9] on the one hand, his nephew did not seem to have the push required to get on—he had not even managed to get himself included among those who were fed from the King's kitchen, and he knew no one but one usher—on the other hand, it would look bad if he left, and the King might take it amiss, so, on the whole, the money must be found to keep him where he was and Uncle Clement would make an advance.

EDWARD'S SOUTHERN TOUR PASSED OFF PEACEABLY. It was a voyage of discovery through a part of England which was mainly new to him. In Hampshire the people of East Meon complained that their landlord, Wayneflete Bishop of Winchester, exacted rent in money, service and kind; but Edward, not to be lured into giving snap judgements about matters of which he knew nothing, ordered them to put their case before Parliament.[1] He then went through Salisbury and Devizes and on 4 September 1461, reached Bristol where he was greeted with a pageant of the traditional kind with gorgeous dresses and expensive scenery, mechanical devices, orations, music, singing and dancing, and the hearts of all were exhilarated by a glimpse of William the Conqueror, St George and the Dragon, angels and other glorious apparitions from another world.

Bristol was the second city in England; York, Coventry and Plymouth may have had larger populations (though as there was never

---

[9] Clement Paston to John Paston, senior, 25 August 1461. Clement Paston was born in 1442, the same year as his nephew John Paston *major*.

[1] The case was examined on 15 December 1461 by four lawyers before the House of Lords. The Bishop was able to produce a pile of ancient documents in support of his claim and, inevitably, judgement was given in his favour. This verdict did not satisfy the people of East Meon and they continued to bicker with the Bishop, the incident providing a striking example of an intelligent man bringing the Church into contempt by persisting in legal, but out-of-date, practices.

a census this is surmise) but Bristol was undoubtedly the richest. Here he stayed for nearly a week, lodging with the mayor and negotiating loans in exchange for privileges, and to a young man with Edward's interest in trade and shipping it must have been an enthralling visit. After Bristol he went through Gloucester and Hereford to Ludlow, which he reached on 18 September.

He was back at home again, and he stayed in Ludlow for eight days, rewarding the town with a new charter dated 7 December 1461, which put on record his gratitude for 'the laudable and gratuitous services which our beloved and faithful subjects the burgesses of the town of Ludlow have rendered unto us' and also referred to the 'rapines, depradations, oppressions, losses of goods and other grievances for us and our sake in diverse ways brought upon them by certain of our competitors'. Granting new charters was a well-known way for kings to make money, but Edward was fond of Ludlow and the new charter gave the town exceptional liberties and privileges. His holiday done, Edward returned, by way of the inevitable Stony Stratford, to London and the royal palace at Greenwich.

While Edward was making his southern tour, Lord Herbert was taking over the castles in Wales. There was no hope of relief for them and they all surrendered reasonably with the exception of Harlech which, tucked away in its corner between the mountains and the sea, was hardly worth troubling about.[2] Pembroke Castle, Jasper Tudor's great stronghold, was handed over on 30 September 1461, and was bestowed on Lord Herbert. In it was discovered a most interesting infant, the four-year-old Henry Tudor, son of Margaret Beaufort and the late Edmund Tudor, and potentially a danger to Edward and his heirs.

Margaret Tudor was the daughter of John, 1st Duke of Somerset, who died when she was a baby leaving her heiress to the Beaufort wealth and the Beaufort claim to the throne. The Duke of Suffolk, then all-powerful, secured her as his ward and married her to his only son, but after Suffolk's fall she was extricated from this alliance and in 1455 she married Jasper Tudor's elder brother, Edmund Tudor, Earl of Richmond, who was then in high favour at Court. He died next year,

[2] Harlech Castle held out for seven years, till August 1468.

and in the following January his widow gave birth in Pembroke Castle to a posthumous son, Henry Tudor, the future Henry VII. She was thirteen at the time, an unusually young mother even for the days when the need to acquire an heir was often urgent.[3]

All the portraits of Margaret Beaufort represent her as an old widow and she has gone down to posterity in the likeness of a pious and charitable dowager, as described in the funeral sermon preached by her confessor, Bishop John Fisher, and published with the title 'A Mourning Remembrance'. Fisher did not meet her until she was over fifty and his sketch, written in the reign of Henry VIII, does not do justice to the adventures of the little heiress at the courts of Henry VI and Edward IV. Fisher gravely assured the congregation that when Edmund Tudor asked for her hand there were several other suitors and she did not know which to choose. It is most unlikely that she was consulted in any way, and Horace Walpole may be excused for poking fun at Fisher. 'On so nice a point, the good young lady advised with an elderly gentlewoman, who thinking it too great a decision to take upon herself, recommended her to St Nicholas, who, whipping on some episcopal robes, appeared to her, and declared in favour of Edmund. The old gentlewoman, I suppose, was dead, and St Nicholas out of the way; for we hear nothing of the Lady Margaret consulting either of them on the choice of two other husbands after the death of Earl Edmund.'[4]

By 1464 Margaret Countess of Richmond was married to Henry Stafford, a younger son of the Duke of Buckingham; he had fought against Edward at Towton but had since changed sides, and there is no reason to think that Margaret's life at Edward's court was not a merry one. Her mother, who had married three times altogether,[5] was still

---

[3] Margaret Beaufort was born on 31 May 1443. As a small child she married and was separated from the son of the Duke of Suffolk; she married Edmund Tudor in 1455. He died 3 November 1456. Henry VII was born 28 January 1457. She married Henry Stafford by 1464; he died 1471. She married Thomas Lord Stanley, Earl of Derby (1435?–1504) by 1473. Margaret Beaufort, Countess of Richmond and Countess of Derby, died 29 June 1509.

[4] Horace Walpole, *A Catalogue of the Royal and Noble Authors* (1758).

[5] Marraret, daughter of John, 3rd Lord Beauchamp of Bletsoe, married (1) Sir Oliver St John, (2) John Duke of Somerset, (3) Lionel, Lord Welles, who was killed at Towton fighting for Queen Margaret. She died in 1482.

alive and she was protected by a network of relations. She had kept her Beaufort wealth and her widow's portion and she was extremely rich. She was also of very high rank, she was young, she was clever, she was prudent and—like a true Roët—she knew how to look after herself. Her only son lived with the Herberts and she can have seen him but seldom, but at least he was safe. The estates he had inherited from his father had been confiscated, but he was her heir and Lord Herbert had bought his wardship and marriage for £1000. Lord Herbert had many daughters, and it was far better for everyone that Henry should be down-graded by marrying Maud Herbert than that he should pair off with semi-royalty.

PARLIAMENT HAD BEEN SUMMONED to meet in November 1461 and in the course of the election Lawyer Paston (who managed to get himself elected as one of the members for Norwich) fell foul of a rival candidate, Sir John Howard,[6] and there was an affray; one of Howard's retainers struck Paston twice with a dagger and he was only saved by his thick doublet. Howard happened to hold an appointment in the royal household and he complained about Paston to the King.

An unusual amount is known about Howard because a quantity of his 'household books' have survived.[7] These consist mostly of rudimentary accounts kept by his secretaries and agents and, as they were intended only for the eye of Howard who was obviously capable of doing all really important calculations in his head, the emphasis is on detail. There is little attempt to add up or to indicate money received, or to include everything or to be precise about dates. The secretaries jotted down their disbursements and Howard checked them over and

[6] Sir John Howard (c. 1421–85). Lord Howard, 1469/70. Duke of Norfolk, 1483. His mother was Margaret Mowbray, daughter of the first Duke of Norfolk. He lived at Tendring Hall near Stoke-by-Nayland in Suffolk and when, in 1455, his cousin the 3rd Duke of Norfolk nominated him as one of the members for Norfolk it was objected that he had no property in the county. 'Howard was as wode as a wild bullock' wrote a correspondent of the Pastons. (Paston Letters (1904 ed.) no. 295.) Needless to say, both the Duke's nominees were elected. Howard married (1) Catherine Moleyns and (2) in 1467 Margaret Chedworth.

[7] Manners and Household Expenses of the 13th and 15th Centuries (Roxburghe Club, 1841). Howard's accounts and notes from November 1462 to July 1469, and also from 1463 to 1471. Household Books of John Howard, Duke of Norfolk (Roxburghe Club, 1844). 23 February 1481–20 October 1483.

occasionally added memoranda of his own—his large primitive hand-writing stands out from the curlicues of his secretaries and his spelling is appreciably worse than theirs. The picture is rather lopsided, as it is the unusual expenses which occupy the largest space. Howard's journeys can be traced by payments at inns, laundry, tips to servants at houses he visited, pennies to beggars, purchases. Among foodstuffs, wine and barrels of fish are conspicuous. There are many entries for articles of clothing; shoes for himself, his family and his employees; best clothes for himself from London tailors; lengths of cloth for his retainers—the quantity varied, but the average was two yards for a man and three for a woman. Wages are frequently noted, and there are also payments for fitting out and victualling ships—Harwich was near and he was accustomed to go to sea.[8]

The lists include the names of the men he had recruited for an expedition to north Wales, and the items of armour which he had lent to individuals. Some of the horses are listed, and who was to ride them. Howard always had money in his pockets and he was able to act as a money-lender, and in 1465 his secretary made out a long list of his debtors which included his very rich cousin, the Duke of Norfolk, and the King (for unpaid tallies, for the plate used by the Queen on the day of her coronation, and for the lists at her coronation tournament).[9] Three shillings and fourpence had been lent to Paston *minor* when they had been soldiering together, and eight shillings and fourpence to 'my Lady Scales to play at cards'. There is also the entry, 'Item. Foster the gaoler of Ipswich owes my master £40. And he is condemned therefore and lies in the same gaol.'

Now and again there are notes on such things as the terms on which a new employee is engaged, or how to measure timber or work out the area of an irregular field; and there are a few drafts of letters.

Paston had known Howard for years and he failed to appreciate that he had become a dangerous man and that the new king was a very different proposition from the last one, and he twice ignored a summons to appear in London to answer Howard's accusations. But Edward

---

[8] In the next century the Howard family produced several distinguished admirals.

[9] Until mid-Victorian times it was quite usual for country gentlemen to borrow from each other at four per cent, when today they would borrow from the bank.

was determined to be obeyed, and on 11 October Paston's brother Clement wrote to him in agitation to warn him that he was taking foolish risks. Clement had been told on the best authority that Edward was very angry and he even knew exactly what Edward had said. Few people except born mimics are capable of transmitting another person's turn of phrase and this tirade, having filtered through the imagination of two messengers, probably owes something to the way kings talked in popular romances, but it bears a strong likeness to Edward's other reported sayings in that it is very much to the point. '"We have sent two privy seals to Paston by two yeomen of our chamber and he disobeys them; but we will send him another tomorrow, and by God's mercy, an if he come not then he shall die for it. We will make all other men beware by him how they shall disobey our writing. A servant of ours has made a complaint of him. I cannot think that he has informed us all truly, yet not for that we will not suffer him to disobey our writing; but since he disobeys our writing, we may believe the better his gydinge [behaviour] is as we be informed." And therewith he made a great vow that if you come not at the third commandment you should die there for.'

Clement Paston's informant had urged him to beg Lawyer Paston to come immediately as the King meant what he said and Clement added, 'Come right strong, for Howard's wife made her boast that if any of her husband's men might come to you, there should go no penny for your life; and Howard has with the King a great fellowship. This letter was written the same day that the King said these words'.

At this Lawyer Paston hastened to London where he was put in the Fleet prison for about a fortnight, after which his enemy Howard took his place in gaol. The persecution of Paston at once tipped public opinion in his favour, and his wife wrote on 20 November: 'The people was never better disposed to you than they be at this hour. The bill that Howard has made against you and other, has set the people in this country a-roar. God give grace it be no worse than it is yet.'

Edward did his best to restore order. He appointed Sir Thomas Montgomery,[1] a trusted friend, to be sheriff of Norfolk, and announced

---

[1] Sir Thomas Montgomery (1433–95). Son of Edward's godmother, Lady Say. He was a most useful man.

that he would have his laws kept and that he considered that most of
the shire was well disposed and that only a few ill-disposed people were
stirring up trouble, and that if anyone, poor or rich, had a complaint
they were to bring the matter before the Sheriff and Justice Yelverton;
and if they were not satisfied with the verdict they could make a complaint to the king—though Yelverton hinted that they might be sorry
if they did so.[2] This was a step in the right direction but it was only a
beginning and the nobility and gentry of East Anglia continued to
attack each other's property and assault each other's employees for a
long time to come.

EDWARD'S FIRST PARLIAMENT met at Westminster on 4 November 1461,
and sat intermittently until 6 May 1462. The printed volumes known
as the *Rolls of Parliament*[3] contain a good deal of miscellaneous information about the business transacted, some of it important, some very
trivial. The entries are mostly in English, occasionally in Latin, and now
and then in French. Much space is occupied by the allocation of property. There are transcripts of speeches, pronouncements in the form
of memoranda, and petitions followed by some such formula as 'Le
Roy le voet' or 'Hit is Agreed'. Whatever was written in the parlia-
mentary records was as permanent as any writing could be, though
facilities for consulting them were not good and a considerable number
of the edicts must have been impossible to enforce. Noticeably lacking
from the Rolls are the petitions which were turned down and any hint
of discussion or disagreement. The constantly recurring themes in all
Edward's Parliaments were the repression of dishonest traders, the
maintenance of the quality of merchandise, especially wool, and the
control of foreign imports.

There were always about 300 members of the House of Commons
and the number in the House of Lords varied; according to the 1461
Lords' Journal, it was attended by 2 archbishops, 16 bishops, 21 abbots,
the Prior of St John's, no dukes, 6 earls and 34 barons, making a total of

---

[2] *Paston Letters* (1904 ed.) no. 500. Thomas Playter to John Paston senior.
[3] *Rotuli Parliamentorum ut et Petitiones et Placita in Parliamento* (1761–83). *See* vols 5
and 6.

80.[4] Some peers were too old or too ill to attend and some were too young, and the peers who were with Queen Margaret were not summoned. The largest attendance on any one day was 67 and the smallest 47.

The Speaker of this Parliament was Sir James Strangways, a connection of the Nevilles—it would have been quixotic in the extreme to have selected an impartial Speaker, even if such a man could have been found. In his address he complimented the King on 'the beauty of personage that it has pleased Almighty God to send you', and indeed Edward, tall and elegant, must have presented a striking contrast to the shabby, dotty figure which they were accustomed to see in the monarch's chair. He recapitulated Edward's right to the throne and repeated what had been said in the previous March, that the woes of the times, the 'unrest, inward war and trouble, un-righteousness, shedding and effusion of innocent blood, abusion of the laws, partiality, riot, extortion, murder, rape and vicious living', were due to the murder of Richard II sixty-one years before. The point was easy to understand. The murder of Richard was one of the highlights of modern history. God punished sinners. It *ought* to be very unlucky to murder a king and usurp his throne. In fact the moral was so obvious that in the next century Shakespeare's very mixed audiences accepted it as the natural link between his historical plays.

Most of the peers had sworn allegiance to Henry VI and, to make them feel comfortable, it was announced that their oaths were void because he had technically broken his side of the bargain. Henry could then be attainted of High Treason and the Duchy of Lancaster annexed by Edward, 'and to his heirs Kings of England perpetually'.[5] Enriched by this giant windfall and by the crown lands which Henry had given away and which were now taken back, Edward could manage for the moment without asking the Commons for more money. Many prominent members of the opposition were attainted and the attainders of Edward's friends were reversed, including the attainder of Edward's father's father who had been caught plotting by Henry V just as he was

---

[4] W. J. Dunham Jr, *The Fane Fragment of the 1461 Lords' Journal* (Yale, 1935). Other books give slightly different figures; medieval lists seldom tally unless they are actually copied from each other.

[5] The present Queen is Duke of Lancaster.

setting out for France. This constant shuttling of lands between different owners must have been extremely confusing, but it was one of the inconveniences to which they were accustomed; even in the ordinary way of things property was often shared between people who had a short-term or life interest in it, or it was temporarily held by trustees or guardians of children.

A start was made towards deciding which of the grants, patents, charters and other arrangements made during the reigns of the three 'usurping' Henrys were valid, and complaints and petitions were laid before the King. A feeble gesture was made against the barons' armies by an edict forbidding the giving of liveries—the psychological effect of wearing a uniform was entirely appreciated. Actually, kings were glad of barons' armies as long as the barons were favourable to themselves and did not turn into brigands, and exceptions were made for the King's men in times of crisis and the soldiers of the Wardens of the Scottish Marches when they were north of the Trent. There was also an equally futile edict against playing cards and dicing (except during the Twelve Days of Christmas).

Parliament was prorogued on 21 December 1461 in a very amiable spirit.[6] Edward made a short jaunty speech to the Commons ending with a touch of that personal affection which his great-granddaughter, Queen Elizabeth, could convey so deftly on occasion. 'James Strangways and you that be come for the Commons of this my land', he began, and finished: 'And for the faithful and loving hearts, and also the great labours that you have borne and sustained towards me in the recovering of my said right and title which I now possess, I thank you with all my heart; and if I had any better good to reward you withal than my body, you should have it; the which shall alway be ready for your defence, never sparing nor letting for no jeopardy; praying you all of your hearty assistance and good continuance, as I shall be unto you your very righteous and loving liegelord.'

DURING THE AUTUMN OF 1461 Edward's party had been augmented by an important peer, John Tiptoft, Earl of Worcester, who returned from

---

[6] When it reassembled on 6 May 1462 it was at once dissolved.

abroad in September 1461.[7] He had been educated at University College, Oxford, and he was probably the only peer who could be described as learned. His abilities had early been recognized and he had held various official positions in the reign of Henry VI, but in 1458 he had retired to Italy where he sought the company of scholars. Upright and uncompromising, his reason for leaving England may have been contempt for the Queen's friends coupled with an unwillingness to rebel against the King, but to some people it might seem that he had avoided risking his neck and had come back after the fighting was over to reap rewards which he had not earned, and it is possible that his undoubted unpopularity with the crowd may have originated at the Court where his fellow peers resented his superior education. It is also possible that he had a supercilious manner and had forgotten the nuances of English etiquette. Pseudo-Gregory relates that on one occasion there was a City dinner and that the Earl of Worcester sat himself down in the middle of the high table, oblivious of the fact that within the City of London the Mayor ranks higher than anyone except the King, whereupon the Mayor and some of the aldermen swept out and the Mayor put on a banquet in his own home, and thus preserved his dignity and the honour of the City.[8]

Tiptoft had seen how Italian and oriental despots controlled their states and he may have deliberately cultivated the reputation of being an ogre; he seems, at any rate, to have had no objection to undertaking unpleasant tasks, and in February 1462 he accepted the title of Constable of England with summary powers to try without jury and condemn to death any man whom he considered to be a traitor. This was a new office, created to cope with a particular emergency. It had been dis-

[7] John Tiptoft (1437?–70). Earl of Worcester, 1449. Son of John, 1st Baron Tiptoft, a court official who made a fortune. Married (1) 1449, Cecily Neville, widow of Henry Beauchamp Duke of Warwick. She d. 1450. (2) 1451, Elizabeth Baynham *née* Greyndour. She d. 1452 (3) 1467, Elizabeth Corbet *née* Hopton; by her he had one son.

In 1458 Tiptoft and a suite of twenty-seven persons had visited Jerusalem on the package-tour pilgrim-ship which sailed every year from Venice. They started on 15 May and were back in Venice on 6 September.

[8] Tiptoft's biographer, R. J. Mitchell, protests that Tiptoft cannot have been the man concerned but Pseudo-Gregory, who was apparently personally involved, is unlikely to have mistaken the identity of such a well-known Earl. The blunder was just the kind of unintentional insult which rankles for ever.

covered that the Earl of Oxford was about to launch a rebellion and, without waiting for this to break out, Oxford, his eldest son and three other men were arrested, tried by Tiptoft and executed. Much bloodshed was doubtless prevented, but justice was not seen to be done.

The 12th Earl of Oxford[9] belonged to a family which had come over with the Conqueror and he could look down on practically all other peers as parvenus. In the past he had not played much part in public affairs, and why he could not bring himself to accept Edward's régime is obscure. Edward and his advisers may have panicked, but they would not have taken such a drastic step unless they had believed it to be necessary and a great deal must have been going on which they knew about and we do not.

The mob, who were used to seeing common men hanged, drawn and quartered according to the splendid laws of old England, spotted at once that Tiptoft's powers were something new and they complained that he was judging by the Law of Padua, which was possibly the case. Oxford and his son were executed publicly in London and the event attracted a good deal of notice, the crowd—like posterity—tending to sympathize with victims in exact proportion to their rank.

Unfortunately for Edward, he could not exterminate all the de Veres. There were at least three more sons, the eldest of whom, John de Vere, 13th Earl of Oxford, was only eighteen or nineteen.[1] He obtained the reversal of his father's attainder and he married Margaret Neville, the youngest sister of the Earl of Warwick, but nothing would appease him; in fact, he seems to have been the only peer whose politics were motivated not by practical considerations but by the spirit of revenge.

---

[9] John de Vere, 12th Earl of Oxford (1408–62).
[1] John de Vere, 13th Earl of Oxford (1443–1513). He lived in Essex, at Hedingham Castle.

VI

Queen Margaret and King Henry
April 1462–July 1465

WHILE OXFORD WAS PLOTTING, MARGARET WAS IN SCOTLAND; after his execution it was obvious that she could do nothing more without help from her relations on the Continent, and in April 1462 she set sail from Kirkcudbright, taking her son with her but leaving Henry behind, and for the next six months she travelled from court to court endeavouring to find a backer who would risk men and money on an invasion of England. Her arrival caused much perplexity; continental rulers were completely in the dark as to her chances of successfully staging a return and travellers and spies sent in conflicting reports.

On 16 April Margaret landed in Brittany where Duke Francis, who had nothing to gain by interfering but wished to keep in with all parties, received her politely, gave her some money and sent her on to her father in Anjou, where her reception was cool. King René could not manage his own affairs and was bored by the troubles of his daughter; he had fixed her up with a splendid marriage and no more could be expected of him. Her cousin King Louis, on the other hand, was deeply interested in her proposition; England was ever the enemy at the gate, and it was worth investing a little money in a scheme which would embroil her in civil war and might re-establish a Frenchwoman at the head of the English government. Margaret and Louis struck a secret bargain at Chinon on 23 June 1462, Margaret agreeing to hand over Calais to France—a promise that would have infuriated the English, had they known about it, even more than the gift of Berwick to the Scots. On 28 June a public (and different) treaty was signed at Tours, Margaret's signature being backed by half-a-dozen of her friends, including Jasper and Dr Morton, and the invasion became a certainty.

To lead the French troops Louis loaned Margaret the cultivated and charming Pierre de Brézé[1] who came originally from Anjou and with whom she had long had some special understanding—when he sacked Sandwich in 1457 it was commonly believed that she had encouraged him to do so, and she had presented him with the islands of Jersey and Guernsey. During the reign of Charles VII and especially during the ascendancy of his mistress Agnes Sorel, de Brézé had flourished, but at the accession of Louis he had shared in the general disgrace of the late king's entourage[2] and had been imprisoned. Now, with characteristic abruptness, Louis restored him to favour, but little money was forthcoming and most of the expense of equipping the expedition fell on de Brézé himself. Much else was discouraging. Fauconberg and Sir John Howard had put to sea and were raiding ports in France and Brittany. The Duke of Burgundy was firmly pro-Edward. Louis began to waver and Duke Francis sheered off. But nothing deflected Margaret, and in the autumn she and her son, de Brézé, Jasper Tudor, a few hundred mercenaries and a handful of friends, set out for Scotland and, having successfully arrived there and collected King Henry and Somerset, they landed on 25 October 1462 on the wild Northumbrian coast. Bamburgh Castle became their headquarters and for the next eighteen months Northumberland was the scene of courageous but hopeless efforts to re-establish Henry VI.[3] The struggle centred round the three castles of Bamburgh, Dunstanburgh and

[1] Pierre de Brézé (1410?–65). Grand Seneschal of Normandy.
[2] On his accession Louis dismissed all his father's advisers and supporters—a step he afterwards admitted was an error.
[3] Bamburgh Castle is twenty miles from Berwick-on-Tweed and 324 miles from London. It was on a rocky promontory and considered impregnable. Restored at the end of the last century, it still presents a magnificent appearance.

Alnwick which were close together, and there was also Warkworth Castle, south of Alnwick, and Newcastle, south again on the road to Durham, and Norham Castle right up on the Border. Owing to the remoteness of the region the rest of England was hardly affected, but to maintain a large army in Northumberland was for Edward expensive and inconvenient.

Once in possession of Bamburgh, Margaret took the castles of Dunstanburgh and Alnwick without difficulty, but news came that Warwick was bringing an army against them and she, Prince Edward and de Brézé re-embarked with some of their French mercenaries and set out for Scotland with the intention of recruiting more soldiers while Jasper and Somerset held the three castles. The journey was short, but the coast of Northumberland is notoriously dangerous; it was November; there was a storm and they were all wrecked, and though Margaret and her party obtained a fishing-boat and were able to reach Berwick alive, the mercenaries had to take refuge in Lindisfarne Abbey. This is on a peninsula which is cut off from the mainland at high tide, and here they were in a trap; they were all either killed or taken prisoner.[4]

Edward was in the south when he heard that Queen Margaret had occupied Bamburgh and as soon as he could he set out to go to the assistance of Warwick, but he never reached the scene of action. At Durham he succumbed to a severe attack of measles and he was incapacitated for several weeks, dangerously pegged down in a remote district while the rest of his country was open to attack. From his sickbed he sent orders to the armies; he, not Warwick, was Commander-in-Chief.

Among the more insignificant officers in the royal forces was John Paston *minor* who had taken service with his rich young neighbour, the new Duke of Norfolk.[5] They were stationed well in the rear at Newcastle and, on 11 December 1462, he wrote a long, newsy, slightly homesick letter to his eldest brother, John Paston *major*, and among other things he told him that Bamburgh was being besieged by

---

[4] The two officers were distinguished French knights; they were sent to London and lodged in a model prison built by a female philanthropist called Dame Alice Foster.

[5] John Mowbray, 4th Duke of Norfolk (1444–76). Last of the Mowbray Dukes of Norfolk. In spite of his wealth and his father's prestige he never made any mark in public life. At this time he was only eighteen.

Montagu and Lord Ogle; Dunstanburgh by Tiptoft and Sir Ralph Grey, and Alnwick by Fauconberg and Anthony Woodville (who, it will be noticed, was already in a position of trust and co-operating with a Neville). Warwick was at Warkworth, and rode daily to all the castles to oversee the sieges and to ascertain whether they needed fresh supplies. The King had ordered the Duke of Norfolk to send food and ordnance from Newcastle to Warkworth and so, the preceding day, Paston *minor* had helped to escort a convoy which was commanded by Sir John Howard. Paston *minor* wanted money sent to him by Christmas Eve at furthest, as he had to pay the wages of the men he had brought with him and he was not permitted to dismiss them. No one was allowed to go home, and anyone trying to desert would be sharply punished. There was a rumour that the Scots would send an army within the next week, but 'the Scots keep no promise'. He was in no danger at the moment, and when he was he would let them know. Four Norfolk neighbours who had failed to respond to the King's summons were likely to find themselves in trouble, and they should either bring their excuses or send them to him in writing and he will forward them to the King. 'For I am well acquainted with my Lord Hastings and my Lord Dacre[6] which be now greatest about the King's person and also I am well acquainted with the younger Mortimer, and Ferrers, Haute,[7] Harpor, Crowmer and Bosewell of the King's house.'

He would like his mother to know that he and his fellowship and servants are all well at the moment of writing; he had not been able to write to his father as he could not find a messenger who was going to London, but he asked his brother to pass on his news to him and also to his grandmother, and to show his letter to their agent. He sent his remembrances to his sister Margery, a couple of female friends 'and to all good masters and fellows within Caister'. 'I pray you that you will send me some letter how you do, and of your tidings with you, for I think long that I hear no word from my mother and you.' The letter is signed 'Your John Paston the Youngest'.

[6] Sir Richard Fiennes, Lord Dacre (d. 1484) had married the niece of the Lord Dacre who fell at Towton fighting for Queen Margaret. He was never of more than minor importance though one of the inner circle of Edward's friends.

[7] The Haute family lived at Calais and in Kent, and were cousins of the Woodvilles.

By Christmas both sides were tired of a Northumbrian winter, and the castles of Bamburgh and Dunstanburgh surrendered by amicable agreement. Some of the defenders, including Jasper Tudor, went to Scotland with safe conducts, but Henry Duke of Somerset remained and swore an oath of allegiance to Edward. To trust Somerset was to take a risk, but had the gamble succeeded the gain would have been immense; he had two younger brothers as energetic as himself and if the Beaufort clan had, in reality, changed sides Margaret's party would have been deprived of its most effective leaders. Edward may genuinely have liked his young and gay cousin; at any rate he treated him with ostentatious friendliness which caused much head-shaking, particularly afterwards when Somerset had gone back on his oath and rejoined Margaret's party. The Constable of Bamburgh Castle, Sir Ralph Percy, also swore allegiance to Edward and was left in charge of the two castles. This was another gamble which did not come off, but the pros and cons must have been carefully debated; perhaps the lack of a suitable volunteer to fill his place may have helped Edward to decide to trust him.

Perversely, the defenders of Alnwick Castle would not join in the deal and as a Scottish army under de Brézé and George Douglas, 4th Earl of Angus, was reported to be on its way south Edward (still at Durham) ordered the Archbishop of York to call out all the clergy of his diocese in defensible array and muster them at Newcastle. However, this danger evaporated; the Scots army was too small and too late and, at the beginning of 1463, it retired across the Border and most of the garrison of Alnwick went with them. The remainder surrendered to Warwick, and Edward could return to London.

But by the beginning of June 1463 the trouble in Northumberland had flared up again. Sir Ralph Percy repudiated his oath of allegiance; Margaret, Henry VI and Prince Edward were once more in Bamburgh; Dunstanburgh and Alnwick castles were also in the hands of her supporters; and a Scottish army was over the Border.

Montagu, who had been appointed Warden of the East March, set off at once, quickly followed by his brother, Warwick, and between them they collected an army. The Archbishop of York was told to arm his clergy and send them to Durham. Parliament happened to be

sitting and voted Edward £37,000 for defence against the Scots—
Margaret's march on London two years before was still fresh in
memory. Tiptoft, Earl of Worcester, sailed up the coast with a fleet.
Henry Somerset, too dangerous to be kept any longer at the Court, was
sent into Wales.

But 1463 was not 1461. The invasion crumbled at a touch. The
Scots army came a few miles over the Border and besieged Norham
Castle, and it was easily routed by the combined forces of Warwick
and Montagu, who pursued the enemy back into their own country;
and that was the end of the danger for the time being.

Margaret did not accept defeat. The Scots having failed her, she
decided to go back to the Continent and try to raise men and money
from the Duke of Burgundy. She could hold the three castles, but she
could not march south without foreign mercenaries, and there was no
time to waste. A triangular conference between England, France and
Burgundy was about to be held at St Omar, and if a triple alliance were
formed neither Louis nor Duke Philip would be interested in backing
her. Accordingly, about the end of July 1463, she took ship with her
son and de Brézé and a small number of followers and arrived safely in
Flanders, to the great embarrassment of the Duke of Burgundy. Her
husband she left behind in Bamburgh, and here he lived with a handful
of peers who put up the pretence that he was a ruling monarch and
issued fiats in his name.

Since there was now no need for Edward to go north, he remained
in the Midlands, residing comfortably in his own castle at Fotheringhay
in the company of his friend Lord Hastings. Hastings, by birth an
ordinary landowner, was now a peer, Lord Chamberlain, Master of
the Mint, Receiver-General of the Duchy of Cornwall, Constable of
Rockingham Castle and Master Forester of Rockingham Forest, and
he had married a rich and well-born widow, Catherine, sister of the
Earl of Warwick and widow of William Bonville, Lord Harington.
Edward granted him many forfeited estates, mainly in Leicestershire.
However, in spite of securing so much favour and wealth he appears to
have been universally popular and this is partly explained by two letters
from him which are included in the Paston collection and which are
extraordinarily easy, friendly, considerate and, at the same time, authori-

tative. Men certainly liked serving under him and he built up an army which he could call out when needed,[8] though as he never had to fight a battle on his own it is not possible to tell how he would have shaped as an independent commander.

On 7 August 1463 at Fotheringhay, Hastings composed a letter in French to Jean de Lannoy, a Burgundian who had recently headed an embassy to England. After a few lines of polite salutation, he dictated one colossal sentence which conveyed well enough the picture he intended—Edward nonchalantly amuses himself while his servants utterly crush the fools who dare to rebel. This sentence begins by regretting that previous letters had gone astray and that the English ambassadors have not yet reached the place appointed for the proposed conference, and goes on to relate how 'le noble et vaillant Sr. Mr. le Comte de Warvich' with a few soldiers from the Border has rescued Norham Castle which had been besieged by the King of Scotland[9] with the whole of his resources, and how Queen Margaret and de Brézé had fled overseas while his sovereign majesty, not in the least disturbed, had continued to pass the time hunting 'sans aucun doubte ou effraiment de sa tres honorable personne'; and how the Sire de Montagu had pursued the King of Scotland into his own land, ravaged the countryside, destroyed several fortresses, killed many Scotsmen, and taken a great number of prisoners, so that the Scots would repent and go on repenting till the day of Judgement that they gave assistance to 'Hery et Marguerite'.[1]

In December 1463 the knot of followers who clustered round Henry VI where he held imaginary sway in Bamburgh were augmented by the arrival of Henry Somerset who had escaped from Wales and who, after an adventurous journey, had managed to get through to Northumberland. He became once more the acknowledged leader, and Henry's miniature court flourished unmolested till the Spring, his

[8] In the Huntington Library are 67 indentures between Hastings and men who agreed to be ready to fight for him with their retainers, on terms that were evidently well understood by all parties. Lord Mountjoy and Lord Grey of Codnor are among those who allied themselves to him in this way. The total should be at least 90 and perhaps more. W. H. Dunham, Jr, *Lord Hastings' Indentured Retainers. 1461–1483* (Yale, 1955).

[9] James III of Scotland, then aged twelve.

[1] Bibliothèque Nationale: printed in C. L. Scofield's *Edward IV*, vol. 2, p. 461.

followers (who must have been extremely short of money) living like robber-barons, raiding the surrounding countryside and roving as far as Yorkshire.

Montagu was still in the north with a small band of soldiers, but he did not meet with Somerset until 25 April 1464. Edward, more sure than ever that peace with Scotland was essential, had persuaded the Scots to send envoys to a conference at York, and Montagu was on his way to the Border to act as their escort when he came upon Somerset and his men at Hedgeley Moor in Northumberland. The numbers engaged were probably very few and they may have fought on horseback like cowboys and Indians; the battle, such as it was, ended with Montagu in possession of the field and the treacherous Sir Ralph Percy dead.

After escorting the Scottish ambassadors to York, Montagu gave chase to Somerset and on 15 May 1464 cornered him near Hexham, and here was fought a battle that was final and decisive. Somerset was taken prisoner, and in the next few days all the other leaders were captured. Somerset, who by the standards of the time had behaved very badly, was executed at once by order of Montagu, and Lord Hungerford and Lord Roos were killed shortly afterwards.[2] Others lost their heads as and when they were caught. Fourteen prisoners were executed at York after trial by Tiptoft, which did not tend to diminish the legend of his ferocity.

Montagu followed up his success by calling on Bamburgh to surrender. It was defended by a renegade knight, Sir Ralph Grey, who imagined that it was impregnable, and defied the besiegers. Then heavy guns were brought up, the walls were breached, Sir Ralph was knocked unconscious by a piece of falling masonry and before he came round his men surrendered, and Bamburgh had won the doubtful distinction of being the first English castle to succumb to cannon-fire. Sir Ralph Grey was taken before the implacable Tiptoft and condemned to death, and Queen Margaret's Northumbrian venture was at an end.

[2] Henry Duke of Somerset was unmarried, but he left a bastard, Charles Somerset, b. 1460, by a girl called Joan Hill. When he grew up Charles joined Henry Tudor and was knighted at Milford Haven, and later was created Earl of Worcester. The Dukes of Beaufort are descended from him.

Montagu had undoubtedly been uncommonly useful, and some great reward was due to him. He was already Warden of the East March, and he was now given the Earldom of Northumberland which included the Percy lands as well as the Percy title. The Percy family were the traditional guardians of the Border, but the last Earl had been killed at Towton, fighting on the wrong side, and his young heir was a prisoner; a good soldier was needed to police the Marches and Montagu was the obvious man for the job. The objection to this arrangement was that the north of England was now divided between the two Neville brothers, but there was no feasible alternative, and Montagu was far from being Warwick's obedient servant.

WHEN BAMBURGH CASTLE FELL, Henry VI had already been removed from it. He had mysteriously vanished about the time of the Battle of Hexham, and he was not rediscovered until fourteen months later when, apparently in perfect health, he was handed over to Edward's agents. Many places in the North claim to have sheltered him, and accounts differ as to whether he was captured in Yorkshire or Lancashire and who it was who betrayed him, and this suggests that what really happened was kept completely secret and that myths grew up to fill the vacuum. It is quite possible that Henry was hidden in a secluded manor by people who at first imagined that he would be restored to the throne, and who later decided to sell him to Edward. Seeing him at close quarters must have been disillusioning, and the prospect of having such an embarrassing guest on their hands for ever would appal the most loyal hearts. Several men received annuities and rewards in connection with his capture, but beyond that nothing is certain.

When Henry reappeared his attendants consisted of two chaplains and a groom. One of the chaplains was an ex-Dean of Windsor, 'aged and infected with a white leper': he was soon released. The other was a truculent character who was so unco-operative that he was imprisoned; fortunately he had friends who eventually made him see reason and ransomed him.

By this time Edward was married, and he was at Canterbury with his Queen when word arrived that Henry had been recaptured and—

always quick to make the correct gesture—he at once proceeded to the Cathedral for a service of thanksgiving. It was necessary to give ocular proof that Henry was a prisoner and, on 24 July 1465, Warwick met him outside London at Islington and escorted him to the Tower with his feet bound to his stirrups so that even the most obtuse would understand the truth. Henry had signally failed to carry out any of the functions expected of a king and although the crowd bore him no ill will they were indifferent to him, and it did not occur to them to think him particularly holy. He was lodged comfortably in the Tower with a chaplain and servants and an ample allowance for food, and as there was no longer any need to conceal the fact that he was mad visitors were permitted to see him by arrangement with his keeper, and access to him was easier than it had ever been.

QUEEN MARGARET WAS TEMPORARILY QUIESCENT. In Burgundy she had met with a high degree of formal politeness, but financial backing was not forthcoming. Duke Philip, had always regarded her as a Frenchwoman and an enemy, and at the time of her arrival he had been hoping to arrange a triangular pact with Louis and Edward; while his son Charles, although accustomed to oppose his father, could not on his own finance and precipitate another invasion.

One small piece of luck did fall in Margaret's way, and that was that she met and charmed the Burgundian chronicler Chastellain,[3] and he recorded her story in the flowery and fanciful manner that was then fashionable. It would have been more interesting for posterity if he had written a truthful description of this remarkable woman, who had led three major invasions of Britain as well as several smaller forays, but unfortunately Chastellain preferred art to nature and his ideal woman was the conventional heroine of the period, a featureless victim for the villain to ill-treat and the hero to rescue.

Margaret, says Chastellain, arrived at the port of Escluse in direst poverty, with seven women at the most in attendance. Philip Duke of Burgundy happened to be away on a pilgrimage at Boulogne, so leaving her son at Bruges she set off to find him, in a village cart with a

---

[3] Georges Chastellain (1405–75). Courtier and writer. *Œuvres* (1863), vol. 4.

canvas roof pulled by four mares, taking with her not more than three ladies, Pierre de Brézé and a few other followers, like a poor lady who travels quietly incognito.

She met the Duke at the town of St Pol, and she explained to him that it was a mistake to imagine that her husband had been an enemy of Burgundy. Philip, who was in the middle of negotiations with Warwick, only stayed one night; he gave her money and then 'le Duc monta à cheval at s'en alla'. But the Duke's sister, the Duchess of Bourbon, remained, and listened sympathetically to the recital of her adventures. Margaret related how the King, her son and herself had had nothing to eat for five days but one herring; and how she had been without a coin to put in the church offertory and had to borrow from a rather unwilling Scots archer; and how, escaping after a battle, she and her treasure were captured by robbers and she was taken to the robber chief who wanted to cut her throat and threatened her with tortures and cruelties, so she knelt and begged and prayed and said that she was a king's daughter and had been their queen, and that if they sullied their hands with her blood their cruelty would remain imprinted on the memory of man throughout the ages; and how her prayers were answered for they fell to fighting among themselves over their prey, and a squire with a horse appeared and they escaped. She was then captured by a brigand, hideous and horrible of aspect, to whom she made a three-page speech after which he promised to reform—and so on.

When Margaret returned to Bruges, Charles, the son of Duke Philip, gave a dinner for her. He attempted to make her wash before he did as though she were a reigning queen, which she and her son (young though he was) refused to do. Charles persisted, and they gave way. Chastellain admits that he did not actually witness this edifying scene, but he heard about it at the Duke's court at Hesdin, where it was much discussed. The courtiers disagreed, but the majority were of Chastellain's opinion in thinking that a queen and the son of a king, even in exile, rank above the son of a duke.

Chastellain also mentions that some people considered that her misfortunes were a judgement for the murder of Richard II—royal murders stuck in people's memories and, even on the Continent, Richard had not been forgotten. He later wrote for Margaret a book called

Le Temple de Bocace. Remonstrances, par manière de consolation à une desolée Reyne d'Angleterre, a variation on the ever-popular theme of the dreadful tragedies which have happened to exalted personages in the past, in this case including Richard II, the Duke of Suffolk and Duke Humphrey of Gloucester (who was popularly supposed to have been murdered by Margaret's faction); finally Boccaccio himself gives Margaret a bracing lecture and reminds her of the far worse misfortunes of Job.

Margaret settled down to wait for better times in the Château of Koeur in the Duchy of Bar, between Nancy and Verdun. It was lent her by her father, who also made her an allowance; and a small party of émigrés collected round her. Some of them afterwards drifted away and resided in Burgundy where, according to Comines, Charles gave them pensions because his own mother was descended from John of Gaunt and he preferred not to acknowledge the rival line. As usual the Duke of Exeter got himself into difficulties. 'I saw one of them,' wrote Comines, 'the Duke of Exeter, go on foot without shoes, following the Duke of Burgundy's train, begging his bread from house to house, without giving his name. He was the next in the line of Lancaster and he had married the sister of King Edward. Afterwards he was recognized and had a little pension to support him.'

Among the respected elders living with Margaret was the distinguished judge, Sir John Fortescue,[4] and on 13 December 1464, when Margaret had not been established at Koeur for very long, he wrote a letter which is practically the only surviving private letter written by one of Margaret's party.

Fortescue was writing to the Earl of Ormonde,[5] who was in Portugal and was contemplating joining them at Koeur, and he advised him to bring money as there was no one to lend and many to borrow, though the Queen did as much for them as she could. 'We beeth all in great poverty but yet the Queen sustaineth us in meat and drink, so

---

[4] Sir John Fortescue (1394?–1476?). Chief Justice of the King's Bench (1442). Called Chancellor of England, having been appointed by the fugitive Henry VI. According to G. R. Elton: 'The alleged prominence of Sir John Fortescue in the fifteenth century is that of a mole-hill on a very flat plain.'

[5] John Butler, 6th Earl of Ormonde (d. 1478), younger brother of the Earl of Wiltshire executed after Towton. He is said to have been extremely cultivated, and later he returned to Edward's court.

we beeth not in extreme necessity.' The new Duke of Somerset and his brother[6] had arrived, having travelled through Brittany and Paris without any difficulty; also at Koeur were the Duke of Exeter, Sir John Courtenay[7] and a dozen or so well-known gentlemen, as well as many squires and clerks.

Between them all they had conceived the plan that the King of Portugal should come to their assistance, and Fortescue sent lengthy instructions as to how this was to be arranged. Ormonde was to tell the King that the people of England would rise in their favour if he sent them 'a notable and manly prince or other captain' and three thousand soldiers. Afterwards they would help the King of Portugal in his own wars. And it would be useful if the King of Portugal wrote round to other rulers recommending Henry's cause to them.

The Prince of Wales himself enclosed two polite notes, one to the King of Portugal and one to Ormonde, signed with his own hand 'that you may see how good writer I am', and Queen Margaret also sent him a letter. Unfortunately none of the royalty, nobility and politicians assembled in the Château of Koeur knew the name of the King of Portugal, so Fortescue enclosed a tag, written by the secretary who had penned the Prince's letter, for Ormonde to fill up and stick on.

Alfonso V (who, incidentally, had been king since 1438) was capable of launching out into hare-brained schemes, but even he would hardly have been tempted by Queen Margaret's proposition, and so it did not really matter that Fortescue's engaging and unpractical letter was stopped by a French spy and never reached its destination.[8]

[6] Edmund Beaufort, 4th Duke of Somerset (1438–71) and John Beaufort (d. 1471). They were brothers of Henry Duke of Somerset, executed after Hexham.

[7] John Courtenay, afterwards 8th Earl of Devon (d. 1471). His brother, the 6th Earl, had been beheaded after Towton, but his other brother, the 7th Earl, had been pardoned.

The two Beauforts, the Courtenays and Exeter were all descended from John of Gaunt and heirs to the throne after Margaret's son; which of them had priority was never put to the test.

[8] The original is in the Bibliothèque Nationale. Printed in the *Archaeological Journal*, vol. VII.

VII

Edward's Marriage 1464

'MEN MARVELLED THAT OUR SOVEREIGN LORD WAS SO LONG without any wife and were ever feared that he had been not chaste of his living,' wrote Pseudo-Gregory with facetious under-statement in 1469, looking back to the events of 1465. Soon after Edward's death the Croyland Continuator described him as a man 'fond of boon-companionship, vanities, debaucheries, extravagance and sensual enjoyments'. Sir Thomas More, voicing the gossip of elderly men who could well remember Edward's reign, wrote (about 1515): 'He was of youth greatly given to fleshly wantonness. . . . This fault not greatly grieved the people.' There can be, in fact, no dispute that during his lifetime it was widely believed both in England and on the Continent that he was an ardent womanizer, and it is with this label round his neck that he appeared in the histories of the last century, and it is his 'reputation for lechery which has, more than anything else, in modern times diverted attention from his political successes'.[1]

The reader who hopes for salacious stories will be disappointed. Far from his Court being the scene of orgies, foreigners thought it

[1] J. R. Lander, 'Marriage and Politics in the 15th Century' in *Institute of Historical Research*, vol. 36 (1963).

magnificent but formal. He acknowledged one bastard, Arthur,[2] and at the end of his life it was no secret that the wife of William Shore, a wealthy mercer, was his mistress. Beyond this nothing is certain, and the allegations do not add up to much. After Edward was in his grave his brother Gloucester, for his own purposes, announced that Edward had once been married to a long-dead Eleanor Butler, *née* Talbot, the widow of Lord Sudeley's heir. Sir Thomas More thought that this woman was called Elizabeth Lucy. A gossip at Windsor was told that 'Mistress Grace, a bastard of King Edward's, was on the funeral barge of Edward's widow when it came down the river from London. An Elizabethan Lord Lumley claimed that one of his ancestresses was called Catherine Plantagenet and was Edward's daughter, but the *Complete Peerage* considers this to have been an invention. Even if Edward did have love affairs with Eleanor Butler and Elizabeth Lucy, and if Mistress Grace and Catherine Plantagenet are added to Arthur, the total is small by the standard of other rulers whether of the fifteenth or other centuries.

So little stigma attached to acknowledging bastards that they were to be found at every court and in most families, and the names of illegitimate children frequently occur in wills and law-suits, although their mothers have hardly left a trace. There were two bastard brothers of the Duke of Exeter and two bastard Fauconbergs; Cardinal Beaufort, John Duke of Bedford, Lord Herbert, Jasper Tudor, Anthony Woodville, Lord Dynham and Richard III all acknowledged bastards; there were bastards in the Paston and Plumpton families and Sir Thomas Stonor married the bastard daughter of his great neighbour, the first Duke of Suffolk. According to Malory, Sir Galahad was the bastard son of Sir Lancelot.

It would be interesting to know how Edward acquired his reputation. One possibility is that in his early days he became involved in a public scandal which he never lived down, although the details were

---

[2] Arthur Plantagenet (d. 1542). His mother was probably called Elizabeth Wayte. In 1511 he married the daughter of Viscount Lisle and in 1523 he was created Viscount Lisle. General Monk (1608–70) was descended from Arthur, and for this reason took the royal title of Duke of Albemarle. (*See Complete Peerage* and, for details of Arthur's life, the *Dictionary of National Biography*).

forgotten; another is that he liked to be thought irresistible and enjoyed shocking the bourgeoisie by peacocking about in the midst of a bevy of ladies. A curious point is that, although he had all England to choose from, the victims of his supposed gallantries are said to have been the wives of the merchants of London, and Comines even went to the length of writing that he was popular with the City merchants *because* he seduced their wives, a theory that is so improbable that it begins to look as if Edward's insatiable lust was merely a treasured London myth which, like the legendary excesses of Prince Hal, grew up because he was seen much more often and at closer range than was usual with royalty. It is one thing to hear that a king leads a merry life and another to recognise his horse outside a house from which issues the hubbub of a party. When the King went to dine with a business acquaintance the passers-by would stop and watch the door with fascinated interest and when he finally emerged, rather unsteadily, and gave his hostess a farewell salutation in the manner of the Court they would cheer because they knew that—God bless him—he had been doing just what they would like to do themselves—eating, drinking and cuckolding the aldermen. Eventually the wife of the merchant Shore became his mistress and it confirmed what they had been saying all along.

There were many other sides to Edward. The Paston brothers, who moved in the highest society, never insinuated that he was either soft or debauched, and though it is unlikely that he was more continent or more abstemious than other rich young men of the period, or any period, and though he may have conducted some of his *affaires* with blatant effrontery, when he wished to carry on a secret intrigue he was perfectly capable of doing so.

As soon as Edward was securely established it became desirable that a suitable wife should be found for him—a princess who would bring tangible advantages. When commoners married, any heiress was an acquisition however remote her lands, but royal marriages, from which so much was expected, often worked out badly and led to decades or centuries of rebellion and war. If Warwick's daughters had been older he probably would have forced one of them on Edward but they were too young,[3] and in the early summer of 1462 tentative offers were made for the hand of Mary of Gueldres, the widowed Queen of Scotland, but these came to nothing probably because the envoys spotted that the Flemish woman's brief spell of power was nearly over[4] and that marriage with her would hinder rather than help the much desired peace with Scotland.

Warwick then turned his attention to trying to arrange a marriage that would be pleasing to Louis of France. He could see that ultimately England would be too small for himself and Edward, and he reckoned that if he installed a French queen in England and helped Louis to dismember Burgundy he ought to be rewarded with a Duchy in Holland where he would be virtually an absolute ruler. Louis, ever alert to the possibility of exploiting human frailty, suggested that the Queen of France's sister, Bona of Savoy, should be planted on Edward. He never understood England's internal politics because his informants were mainly Warwick's agents who were at pains to explain that Edward was just a spoilt boy who amused himself while Warwick governed the kingdom; this was sufficiently near to Edward's pose of a king who hunted while his servants did the work to seem very plausible. Neither did Louis understand the mysterious force of English public opinion, because public opinion was something that he himself hardly had to reckon with. Meanwhile Edward pig-headedly kept to his own opinion that trade with Flanders had priority over all other European projects—wine was the only product of France that was imported in quantity. The foreign policy of the English king was thus the direct opposite of that of his principal ambassador, to the considerable mystification of other nations.

Louis was not alone in his miscalculations. Many English observers also misjudged the situation and reckoned that Warwick was a stronger man than Edward, and this was partly because he was able to spend more money. Edward was still saddled with his father's debts and the

---

[3] In spite of Warwick's early marriage, he had only two daughters; Isobel, born in 1451, and Anne, born in 1456. They were very great heiresses, and about the right ages for Clarence and Gloucester.

[4] There was a palace revolution in July 1462 and the young king was taken from her. She died in the late autumn of 1463.

nation's debts, and anything he could do Warwick could do more expensively. For instance, on 30 January 1463 Edward staged at Fotheringhay a showy memorial service for the souls of his father and his brother Rutland, killed at Wakefield, but this was entirely eclipsed and outshone a fortnight later when Warwick transported the bodies of his father and brother from Pontefract to the Neville burial place on the Thames at Bisham near Marlow.[5]

Warwick's negotiations to marry Edward to Bona of Savoy proceeded slowly and nothing had been settled when, in the beginning of 1464, ambassadors from Spain arrived to offer Edward the hand of the twelve-year-old Isabella of Castile. The unhappy girl was in a pitiable plight. The Court of Castile was squalid, violent and dangerous; repulsive husbands had been suggested for her and to marry the King of England would have been a blessed escape. Isabella could not foresee that her brother would die and that she would inherit Castile, and she was deeply disappointed when she was rejected.[6] It is possible that Edward might have accepted Isabella if he had been free, but he had lost his heart and was contemplating marriage to a lady of the English Court, none other than Elizabeth, eldest daughter of the despised Lord Rivers and Duchess Jacquetta, and widow of the Sir John Grey who had been killed at St Albans. She had already two sons Thomas and Richard Grey.[7]

Sir John Grey had not been very rich but he had been extremely well born. His mother was the granddaughter and heiress of the 5th Lord Ferrers of Groby Castle near Leicester and his father, Sir Edward

[5] Edward did not feel rich enough to move his father's body to the family vault at Fotheringhay till 1476, by which time he was able to afford a stupendous feast.

[6] Or so the Spanish ambassador told Richard III in 1483. Isabella had been able to return the snub by refusing, in 1468, to marry one of Edward's brothers—which, is not clear. In 1469 she married Ferdinand of Aragon. Isabella and Edward were distant cousins; she was descended from John of Gaunt, and Edward's great-grandfather, Edmund Langley Duke of York, had been married to a former Isabella of Castile, sister to John of Gaunt's wife.

[7] Thomas Grey (1455–1501), Marquis of Dorset, 1475. He married in 1466 Anne, daughter of the Duke of Exeter. She died in 1473. In 1474 he married Cecily Bonvile, daughter of Lord Harington and step-daughter of Hastings. Their son Thomas, 2nd Marquis of Dorset, was the grandfather of Lady Jane Grey.

Richard Grey, born between 1456 and 1461. Executed at Pontefract by Richard III on 25 June 1483. He never married.

Grey, was a younger son of the 3rd Lord Grey of Ruthin. Sir Edward had been called Lord Ferrers of Groby, but when he died the title was not handed on to his son but was retained by his widow. She did not die till January 1483 when it descended to her grandson, Thomas Grey, Marquis of Dorset. Elizabeth Woodville was generally known as Dame Elizabeth Grey although occasionally incorrectly called Lady Ferrers.

Like most families the Greys bickered over property, and there exist papers relating to a dispute over Elizabeth's dowry and her mother-in-law's claims, a dispute which was probably carried on by the men of the family without any particular ill-feeling. Lady Ferrers had re-married and her husband was Sir John Bourchier, one of the sons of the Earl of Essex and in future times Elizabeth was on the best of terms with the Bourchiers.

The Ferrers family were very friendly with their Leicestershire neighbours, the Hastings family, and on 13 April 1464 Elizabeth and Lord Hastings signed an agreement[8] by which her elder son, Thomas Grey (or, failing him, her younger son, Richard Grey) should marry the eldest daughter of Lord Hastings to be born in the next five years (or, failing that, a daughter of his brother Ralph, or, failing that, a daughter of his sister Anne, who had married a Ferrers cousin). If certain lands claimed by the Greys were recovered, Elizabeth and Hastings were to go half-shares in the rents until Thomas Grey reached the age of twelve. Lord Hastings was to pay 500 marks for the marriage, and if it failed to take place Elizabeth was to pay him 250 marks. Times were dangerous, life was uncertain, and the agreement must have seemed admirable to the parties concerned, particularly as a year or two before Hastings had bought the manor of Kirby Muxloe which was very near to Groby Castle;[9] the contract was only provisional after all, and it could be cancelled if circumstances altered.

The date of Elizabeth's birth is presumed to have been some time between 1436 and 1440, and so she was several years older than Edward. It is probable that she had known him literally ever since he was born,

---

[8] Historical Manuscripts Commission. Hastings, vol. I (1928).

[9] Groby Castle is now a mound. It is separated by the M1 from Kirby Muxloe, where the foundations of Hastings' manor-house can be seen next to the ruins of a castle which he began to build in 1480.

as her father was attached to the Duke of York's staff in Normandy and Duchess Jacquetta's children must surely have played with Duchess Cecily's children in the Castle of Rouen. The acquaintance could have continued in England; Fotheringhay and Grafton are both in Northamptonshire, separated by some thirty-five miles of forest—Rockingham Forest merged into Whittlebury Forest—and hunting was of interest to all. County business would also bring their respective fathers together.

The story goes that Edward and Elizabeth first met in Whittlebury Forest under an oak-tree, when she knelt with her two little orphan sons to beg that the lands of her attainted husband should be restored to them, but it must be a myth because her husband never was attainted, nor were his lands confiscated, and if they ever met under the very big oak-tree at Yardley Gobion which is known as the Queen's Oak it was not for this purpose. For all we know Elizabeth may have been fond of hunting and the oak may have been the rendezvous for hunting-picnics. No descriptions of Elizabeth exist. The paintings of her are only copies of a lost original which would appear to have been rather stylized, but there is nothing to contradict the obvious guess that large, fair, flamboyant Edward fell in love with a woman who was small, dark, neat, quiet and foreign-looking—her mother was half-French and half-Italian. The Woodville family—men, women and children—clung together devotedly, and Edward evidently found the whole group charming; their French accents, which some people found so irritating, reminded him of happy days in the nursery.[1]

Edward was well aware that there would be an uproar if he announced that he wished to marry Elizabeth; he was expected to make a marriage that would be an asset to the country, and she had no powerful relations, very little money, and her parents had been jeered at for twenty-eight years. It was also important not to annoy Warwick while Somerset and Henry were still at large in Northumberland; Warwick had been forced by circumstances to put Edward on the throne, but he

---

[1] None of the chroniclers point out that the Woodvilles were only half English, yet that must have been the main reason why they had not been assimilated by the other courtiers. The eldest members of the family, who had spent some of their childhood in France, could well have had many French mannerisms, and even Thomas and Richard Grey may have looked very foreign.

was quite capable of changing sides if he could get hold of his puppet king again. On the other hand (Edward may well have argued) what is the point of being a king, and a very handsome king too, if you cannot marry the woman of your choice?

ALL THROUGH THE WINTER OF 1463–4, Henry VI had been in Bamburgh Castle, and the peers who supported him had been ranging over the North, waiting for reinforcements from abroad. Edward decided to strike first and, as soon as the spring came, to take a large army up to Northumberland, capture Henry and the castles and destroy the rebels once and for all, and he and Warwick made deliberate preparations. Money was borrowed and the shires were ordered to send soldiers. On occasions like these the Neville brothers were invaluable; Montagu was already in the North, Warwick joined him, and Bishop Neville, the Chancellor, left the Great Seal in London and travelled up to York to meet the delegates who were coming from Scotland to discuss plans for a permanent peace or at least a prolonged truce. It was feared that Margaret was about to launch a great new attack, but it was impossible to know from which direction she would strike. Jasper was somewhere in Wales, and there were rumours of risings in Yorkshire, in Cheshire and in Lancashire.

On St George's Day, 23 April 1464, Edward attended the annual ceremony of the Knights of the Garter in the Chapel of Windsor Castle. Then he started for the North, unaware that on 25 April Montagu had had a brush with Somerset's men on Hedgeley Moor and had come off best. He did not know what was ahead of him; he might have to fight another battle as big and as bloody as Towton, and this time the luck might go the other way. Determined not to attack until his army was large enough to make victory certain, he moved slowly, and reached Stony Stratford on the last day of April.

On the first day of May, early in the morning, he rode over to the Woodvilles' manor of Grafton. He had determined to follow the dictates of his heart and, forestalling opposition, to marry Elizabeth first and break the news afterwards. Perhaps it was one of those perfect May mornings beloved by medieval poets, and everything was green and beautiful. Later in the day he pushed on to Northampton and rejoined his army; in the interval he had made Elizabeth his wife. He was just twenty-two, and king of England. She was several years older, a widow with two sons.

Very few people were in the secret, and no whisper of it leaked out. Doubtless his servants and friends knew that he was in love with Elizabeth, but the idea that he would actually marry her can never have entered their heads. The ceremony may have taken place in a small building known as the Hermitage, which was only a short walk away from Grafton manor house and which, at that time, was hidden in the forest. Recent excavations have uncovered a tiled floor, and some of the tiles bear the Woodville arms and some the white rose, as though Edward was connected with the place in a special way. Edward and Elizabeth could have reached the Hermitage from different directions and without attracting attention, and afterwards they could have arrived separately at Grafton manor house. One chronicler[2] asserts that Elizabeth's mother was at the wedding; she herself had made a clandestine love-match in her youth, marrying beneath her, and she may have felt that her daughter was now putting things right and that a girl who was descended from the noble house of Luxemburg, and whose mother had married the Regent Bedford, was quite good enough for anyone.

From Northampton Edward went on to Leicester. He had ordered the mayor of Salisbury to send soldiers to Leicester by 10 May and this fitted in very well with his private life, for Groby Castle and Kirby Muxloe were just outside the town and a secret honeymoon would have been easy to contrive. Possibly Hastings was an accomplice; anyway, it was only the *marriage* which had to be kept secret. His journey up the Midlands was perfectly sensible from a military point of view, and no one would suspect that he had an ulterior motive.

By the time Edward reached York on 23 May the crisis had passed. Montagu had annihilated Somerset's little army at Hexham, the leaders

---

[2] Robert Fabyan (d. 1513). He was a London tradesman and in no position to know about the private life of the royal family. His chronicle, a synthesis of other London chronicles, was first printed in 1516. It is very unreliable but it was one of the earliest and it was much read.

were captured and risings and rebellions which had broken out in other places had died down. To crown all, the conference at York was being an entire success, and on 1 June 1464 an Anglo-Scots truce was signed that was supposed to last for fifteen years, and actually was effective for a year or two longer.

Edward spent some weeks in the north while Warwick and Montagu stamped out the last vestiges of rebellion and tried in vain to discover where Henry was hiding, and when the King turned south in the middle of July Warwick and the world at large had not the faintest idea that he was not still an eligible bachelor.

THE NAMES OF EDWARD's financial advisors are lost to history; whoever they were, he went to the right people for advice and the results justified the measures they suggested. The country was suffering from a scarcity of bullion and Edward, having accepted the proposition that completely new coins should be minted, prepared to push the scheme through ignoring the grumbles which the change naturally occasioned.[3] Lord Hastings was Master of the Mint, though doubtless everything was deputed to a professional. The scheme was a success, and gold and silver flowed into the London Mint, the mints at Canterbury and York were reopened and new mints were set up at Bristol, Coventry and Norwich.[4]

Edward's coins of 1465 consisted of a ryal or rose noble, worth ten shillings; a half ryal and a quarter ryal; an angel, worth six shillings and eightpence (half a mark) and a half angel or angelet. These were all gold coins. Silver coins were: a groat worth fourpence, a half groat, a penny and a halfpenny. Farthings and copper coins were discontinued.[5]

At the beginning of August 1464 Edward presided over a preliminary meeting at Stamford to explain the proposed new currency, and a

[3] According to Pseudo-Gregory: 'At the beginning of this money, men grogyd passing sore, for they could not reckon that gold not so quickly as they did the old gold. And men might go throughout a street or through a whole parish before that he might change it. And some men said that the new gold was not so good as the old gold was, for it was alloyed.'

[4] They all soon closed down again, except the mint at Canterbury.

[5] Gold sovereigns worth twenty shillings were introduced by Henry VII.

large assembly of the Great Council was summoned to meet at Reading on 14 September for further discussions; it was generally understood that at the same time Edward would announce that he had chosen a Queen.

The Great Council duly assembled at Reading feeling fairly confident that it knew exactly what to expect. After Somerset's forces in Northumberland were smashed, Louis had resigned himself to the fact that Edward was likely to remain king, and the plans to marry him to Bona of Savoy had gone ahead with a rush. The Duke of Burgundy had given a half-hearted assent and Warwick's friend, Lord Wenlock, had been permitted to cross the French frontier and attend a banquet where Bona and her sister, gorgeously dressed, were presented to him. This was the first time for years that an English ambassador had set foot in France and, what was more, in October Warwick himself was to visit the French Court to conclude the bargain. Warwick and Louis had never met previously, and the proposed encounter was felt to be extremely significant.

The Great Council at Reading, therefore, was taken by surprise when Edward informed its members that since last May he had been married to the eldest daughter of Lord Rivers. His choice astounded them. When the greybeards of Troy looked at Helen they said that it was small wonder if men suffered hardships for such a woman, but no one could imagine why Edward should want to marry Elizabeth, who had been around the Court for years without being considered remarkable in any way. She was not said to be beautiful or clever or amusing; she was never even accused of having lovers. How had she done it? The stories which grew up to explain it were not very original—she had aroused his lust and then held out for marriage; she had threatened to kill herself with a dagger when he tried to rape her; Duchess Jacquetta had caught him by witchcraft. Romances and ballads in which true love conquers all were popular enough, but fiction is one thing and real life another, and for a young king to marry for love was so unusual and eccentric that for the rest of Edward's reign when anything happened which seemed sinister, even in Ireland, failing another explanation it was apt to be put down to the malign influence of the Queen and the 'Queen's kin'.

The chroniclers are unanimous in asserting that Edward's marriage gave offence to the nobles, but they are very vague about it and appear to have had no personal opinions on the subject. Among the Howard archives there is the draft of a letter written by Sir John Howard to (apparently) Elizabeth's father, on 22 September 1464, a week after the announcement had been made, saying that he had been going round in Norfolk, Suffolk and Essex spreading the news of the marriage, 'to feel how the people of the country were disposed; and in good faith they are disposed in the best wise and glad thereof; also I have been with many divers estates to feel their hearts and I found them all right well disposed, save one, the which I shall inform your good lordship at my next coming.'[6] Howard was not entirely disinterested as he hoped his wife would be given a place about the Queen, but Lord Rivers wanted a truthful report and it seems quite likely that most people tolerated Edward's choice, and that here and there powerful men were very angry.

Once Edward had got through the ordeal of confessing to Warwick he may have thoroughly enjoyed dropping his bombshell. Sir Thomas More retails the story that when Duchess Cecily voiced her disapproval Edward said 'that she is a widow and has already children, by God's blessed Lady, I am a bachelor and have some too; and so each of us has proof that neither of us is like to be barren', which is probably apocryphal but suggests an unrepentant attitude. It is not at all unlikely that Duchess Cecily was wounded by her son's duplicity and that the whole Court was annoyed because they had been taken in, but there is no reason to think that Edward ever regretted his unconventional step. Even though he was an unfaithful husband, he was an affectionate family man; he certainly trusted Elizabeth implicitly and, in spite of his frequent journeys, they were often together. Whomever he had married, it would have caused annoyance in some quarters; Bona of Savoy would have been extremely unpopular with his ordinary subjects who feared and disliked all foreigners, and loathed the French; any Englishman's daughter would have caused jealousy among the families who were not connected with her, and nothing could have averted the

---

[6] *Manners and Household Expenses* (Roxburghe Club, 1841), p. 197.

eventual show-down with Warwick. It was the Woodvilles themselves who were the real sufferers from Edward's marriage; instead of living out their lives in happy mediocrity they were involved in power politics at the highest level and four of them were executed.

Disappointed and exasperated though Warwick had cause to be, he behaved admirably at Reading; he kept his temper and scrapped his plans. Edward was a silly boy who was besotted by love and had made a terrible blunder, and Warwick had been made to look a fool in the eyes of France and Burgundy; but he did not show that he minded and when, on Michaelmas Day 29 September 1464, there was a ceremony in Reading Abbey at which Elizabeth was formally recognized as Edward's wife and Queen she was escorted by Warwick and Clarence and welcomed graciously into the family. A week of festivities followed, but it was late in the year and her coronation ceremonies were postponed till the following summer. Edward and Elizabeth remained for some weeks at Reading Abbey enjoying a second honeymoon, and then moved to Windsor and afterwards to Eltham for Christmas.

They returned to Westminster for the opening of the final session of Edward's second Parliament. The first elections had been so flagrantly irregular that they were cancelled and held again. Opening on 29 April 1463, it was not dissolved till early in 1465 but it only sat for about three months. The records are largely filled with matters concerning property and the ownership of land. Certain ladies had their rights protected: Margaret Beaufort, now Stafford, was confirmed in her inheritance, and Anne (Edward's eldest sister) was to be treated as a 'woman sole' as though her husband the Duke of Exeter did not exist. There were several acts regulating the export and standard of wool and cloth—the dishonesty of a few could ruin trade for everyone. There was an act to protect work-people who were paid in pins, girdles and other unprofitable merchandise; an act to protect piece-workers who were given over-weight bundles of wool; and an act to protect the silk-women of the City of London—some of them were gentle-women, and it was an old occupation, and trade was now being ruined by silk goods imported by Lombards and other foreigners. There was a long list of objects which should not be imported from abroad, which included galoshes, playing-cards, dice, tennis-balls, and curtain-rings, and to this the King agreed with the stipulations that goods from Ireland and Wales should be exempt, that certain warehouses should not be searched and that the merchants of Almayne having the house called commonly Yeldehalla Teutonicorum should be free to trade as before. He also exempted Robert Stillington, Dean of the King's Free Chapel of St Martin's le Grand, or any successive Dean, or anyone dwelling in St Martin's Lane, which suggests that that was the channel through which Edward carried on his extensive, successful and well-hidden trading activities.

There was a complaint from the Horn-makers (and London horn-makers claimed to be the best in the world) that foreigners bought up horns from butchers and tanners, leaving no good horns 'for the king nor for no Lord, such as they were wont to have, for no money'; and the patten-makers complained that Henry V had made a law that pattens and clogs were not to be made of ash, because ash was needed for arrows; and they pointed out that wood suitable for clogs was not suitable for arrows, and that carpenters used much more ash than they did; and the people of Dover complained that the old law that all ordinary travellers must come to England through Dover was being ignored.

It was agreed that the River Severn should be kept clear for navigation, and that corn should not be imported except in times of scarcity when prices rose above a certain level, and that the Merchants of Calais should be paid £32,856 which they had advanced for the wages of the garrison.

There were also laws regulating dress. Only peers were to wear cloth of gold, or velvet, or purple or scarlet silk. No one under the rank of a lord, squire or gentleman was to wear any gown, jacket or cloak which did not cover his privy members and buttocks when he was standing upright. The fine was twenty shillings, and the tailor responsible was also to be fined. No one under the rank of a lord, squire or gentleman was to wear shoes or boots with pikes longer than eleven inches; the fine was forty pence, and the shoe-maker would also be fined. (Many people were exempt from this rule, including minstrels and the players in interludes.)

ABOUT THE TIME OF THE Council of Reading the Archbishop of York[7] died and Edward hastened to confer the office on Bishop Neville. The new archbishop celebrated his promotion in true Neville fashion during the following September, when he gave (at York) the largest feast that had ever been seen in England. Six thousand guests are supposed to have been fed, and among the more exotic items on the menu were a dozen porpoises and seals, four hundred swans and a hundred and four peacocks.

LOUIS WAS REPUTED TO HAVE spies everywhere, but his agents in England had great difficulty in getting letters back to him.[8] Messengers ran the risk of being robbed, killed or tortured and merchants heard English news by means of their grapevine much more quickly than did Louis; and long after Edward's marriage to Elizabeth Woodville had been made public Louis continued to expect that Warwick would arrive with a formal offer for the hand of Bona of Savoy.[9] On 5 October he heard disquieting rumours, but he refused to believe them, and it was not until 10 October—nearly a month after the announcement at Reading—that he received letters which convinced him of the truth. Louis consoled himself by thinking that Warwick would be so enraged by the affront that he would immediately rise in rebellion and seize the throne, but in this also he was disappointed.

[7] William Booth (1390?–12 September 1464). Half-brother of Lawrence Booth (d. 1480) who was Archbishop of York after George Neville's death in 1476.

[8] In 1442, Bishop Bekynton, in Bordeaux on government business, sent home a letter sewn into the hem of a pilgrim's gown; and in the summer of 1464 ambassadors from the Duke of Brittany came to England disguised as friars.

[9] Bona of Savoy ultimately married Galeazzo Maria Sforza, Duke of Milan. He was later assassinated in church, and she wrote to the Pope to procure absolution for his sins. He was, she said, 'versed in warfare, both lawful and unlawful; in pillage, robbery and devastation of the country; in extortion of subjects; in negligence of justice; in injustice knowingly committed; in imposition of new taxes which even included the clergy; in carnal vices; in notorious and scandalous simony and innumerable other crimes'. The widowed Bona tried to govern for her young son but she was imprisoned by her husband's brother, Ludovico Sforza. 'With luck and good judgement, aided by the silliness of the Duke's mother and the misguided cunning of her lover, Ludovico became regent of Milan.' J. H. Plumb, *The Penguin Book of the Renaissance.*

WHILE ENGLAND, FRANCE AND BURGUNDY were busy with their private concerns, the Pope, Pius II, had died making one last desperate effort to launch an international attack on the Turks. He had admired Joan of Arc and he longed, before he died, to do some great heroic deed. Crippled by gout, a dying man, he resolved to lead a Crusade himself and to shame the rest of Christendom into following him; in particular he hoped to arouse the aged Philip of Burgundy who had vowed in the year that Constantinople fell to take the cross *if* any other great prince would do likewise. The last pages of the Pope's autobiography reveal his brave, mad dreams of an eleventh-hour victory.

'If this method does not rouse Christians to war we know of no other. This path we are resolved to tread. We know that it will be a crushing burden for our old age and that we shall in a sense be going to certain death. We do not refuse. We trust all to God. His Will be done. We must die some time and it matters not where, so long as we die nobly . . . a noble death redeems an evil life.' He went on to say that the Duke of Burgundy would rise from his sick-bed and follow; that a Venetian fleet would meet them; help would come from Hungarians, Sarmanthians, Greeks, Albanians, Servians and Epirotes. In Asia, Karamanians and Iansea would rebel.

'We do not go to fight in person since we are physically weak and a priest, whom it does not befit to wield the sword. We shall imitate the holy patriarch Moses who, when Israel was warring against the Amalekites, stood praying on the mountain, We shall stand on a high stern or some high mountain brow and, holding before our eyes the Holy Eucharist . . . we shall pray Heaven for the safety and victory of our fighting soldiers.'

Philip of Burgundy was still attracted by the idea of a Crusade, but he was getting old and woolly-headed and there was no real possibility of his taking any action. Edward and Louis never had the slightest intention of sending help, and they temporized and made excuses. In the middle of July 1464, when Edward was rejoicing over the collapse of rebellion in the north, discussing the minting of new coins and wondering when it would be safe to break the news of his marriage, Pius II set out on the Last Crusade. Suffering great pain, he was carried over the mountains to Ancona on the Adriatic where he hoped to find that a throng of allies had assembled.

No throng had assembled, and the few soldiers who were there had already lost heart and were beginning to desert. Days went by before the Doge of Venice sailed into the harbour with a mere dozen ships. Courageous to the last, Pius exhorted those around him to continue the Crusade. He died on 15 August 1464, and immediately the Venetian fleet returned to Venice and the papal escort hurried back to Rome to be in time for the election of his successor.

The new Pope was Paul II, a worldly Venetian who did not share in the heroic dreams of his predecessor; and, although in years to come there were many expeditions against the Turks, there were no more Crusades.

VIII

Dangerous Years 1465 — 1468

L IKE THE QUEEN CONSORTS WHO HAD PRECEDED HER, ELIZABETH
had little opportunity to ingratiate herself with the crowd. On
state occasions she was overshadowed by her ebullient husband,
and the Woodville name was still tarred by the scandal caused by her
mother's marriage nearly thirty years before; as late as 1483 a foreigner
collecting information in London was told that the trouble with the
Woodvilles was that they were low born.[1]

Lord Rivers had been a peer since 1448, which was a good deal
longer than many of the other members of the House of Lords;[2] he
had been a Knight of the Garter since 1450, and he was also a Privy
Councillor; as for Duchess Jacquetta, she had once been the highest-
ranking lady in England. The assertion that the Woodvilles were resented because they had fought for Henry VI is also pure nonsense;
everyone—including Edward himself—had started as a loyal subject

---

[1] Dominic Mancini, *The Usurpation of Richard III.*

[2] On an average peerages died out after three generations and between 1439 and 1504
sixty-eight new peerages were created; of these twenty-one were bestowed on the husbands or sons of heiresses and forty-seven were totally new. J. R. Lander, *The Wars of the
Roses.* For a reappraisal of the Woodvilles, *see* J. R. Lander, 'Marriage and Politics in the
15th Century. The Nevilles and the Wydevilles', in *Institute of Historical Research*, vol. 36
(1963).

of Henry VI and no stigma whatever attached to changing sides provided it was done in an open manner and not too often. Allegations that they were grasping and pushing seem to be totally without foundation; they did not meddle in affairs of state. Lord Rivers, a professional soldier, conscientiously carried out the duties entrusted to him to the best of his ability, and Anthony Woodville, Lord Scales, was positively admired for his elegance and his prowess at jousting; the rest were ciphers. The Paston brothers heard all the gossip of the Court, and the only thing they held against the Woodvilles was that they were not useful patrons and had no influence.

Taken singly, none of the honours or rewards received by the Woodvilles was unreasonable; in 1466, Edward promoted his father-in-law to the rank of Earl and made him Lord Treasurer, and Earl Rivers carried out his duties as honestly and efficiently as any other peer would have done and better than some. Anthony was already Lord Scales; he was given the Isle of Wight, which might have been bestowed on him anyway. The other members of the family received only minor prizes.[3] Edward was always acutely aware of the dangers of arousing jealousy, and he was also able to recognize which of his friends lacked talent; nothing was to be gained by building up the Woodvilles as he had built up Hastings and Herbert, and, in terms of power, they were negligible compared to the Neville bloc.

There was a silly story, considered amusing at the time, which appears in *The Great Chronicle of London*,[4] to the effect that a man arrived at the Court with bare legs and explained that to get there he had had to wade through *rivers*, and this joke spotlights one of the reasons that other people beside the Nevilles found the Woodvilles annoying. Outsiders are apt to be irritated by any large family, especially if it is united and devoted. There were too many Woodvilles, and anyone approaching the King might have to walk past the Queen's father and mother,

[3] When Edward married Elizabeth many of her family were still children. Warwick was dead before 1475, when Thomas Grey (who, in any case, was heir to the Barony of Ferrers of Groby) was made Marquis of Dorset; Lionel Woodville was not made Bishop of Salisbury until 1482.

[4] *The Great Chronicle of London* is based on other City chronicles, and was not compiled by anyone very knowledgeable.

her five brothers, her seven sisters, her two sons by her first marriage and any number of Haute cousins.[5]

Looking more closely, something else can be discerned. Edward used Elizabeth's sisters and her elder son to block the dynastic marriages which the nobles might otherwise have arranged between themselves. 'The over-mighty subject' was a phrase which had not yet been coined[6] but the danger of allowing a rich man to become even richer was one which any intelligent king could figure out for himself, and the rise of Warwick—not to mention his own rise by the union of York and Mortimer—was a constant reminder of what could happen when wealth married wealth. Six of Elizabeth's sisters were married to peers, which must have infuriated the parents of other eligible girls as well as the families of the bridegrooms who had been looking forward to doubling their capital by capturing an heiress. Anne, the only child of the Duke of Exeter and thus a potential pretender to the throne, was bought back from Montagu's son (to whom she had been promised) and married instead to Elizabeth's elder son, Thomas Grey, and the motive for this manœuvre must have been quite obvious to the Nevilles. Another child who might become dangerous was the immensely rich Henry, Duke of Buckingham,[7] whose mother was the eldest sister of the Dukes of Somerset: he and his brother were brought up in the Queen's household and he was immunized as far as possible by being married to Catherine Woodville, though this did not prevent him from playing a very equivocal role when he grew up. John Woodville was married to Edward's aunt, the sixty-six-year-old Dowager Duchess of Norfolk,[8] who had got through three husbands and was involved in lawsuits over

---

[5] Joan Woodville, one of the sisters of Lord Rivers, married Sir William Haute of Calais and Kent, and they had at least four sons and one or two daughters. He also had a daughter by a previous marriage and, in due course, some grandchildren. Most of them had comparatively minor posts about the Court but Alice Haute married Sir John Fogge of Ashford, Kent, who was Treasurer of the Household, 1461–67, and prominent enough to arouse the jealousy of Warwick.

[6] It first appeared in *The Governance of England*, written by Sir John Fortescue some time after 1471.

[7] Henry Stafford, 2nd Duke of Buckingham (1455?–83). His father died in 1458, and his grandfather, the 1st Duke of Buckingham, was killed in 1460 at Northampton.

[8] Catherine Neville, an elder sister of Duchess Cecily. She married (1) John Mowbray, 2nd Duke of Norfolk; (2) Sir Thomas Strangeways; (3) John, Viscount Beaumont, killed at Northampton; (4) Sir John Woodville.

Mowbray and Beaumont property, but Elizabeth's other brothers and Richard Grey were not found partners.

Edward was determined that his wife should be treated with as much respect as if she had been a princess, but he could not afford to be lavish and her settlement was less than that of Margaret of Anjou. Lands which brought in a moderate income were made over to her, she was given the royal palaces of Shene (Richmond) and Greenwich so that she had pleasant homes where she could live in security and dignity while her husband was away on his incessant journeys and, in addition, she was given a town house at Smithfield, just outside the wall of the City.[9] The Bourchiers and her own family were the mainstay of her household. Her two highest-paid officers were John Bourchier, Lord Berners, and her brother Sir John Woodville, the next two were Sir Humphrey Bourchier and one of her Haute cousins. Her ladies were headed by Anne, Lady Bourchier and Elizabeth, Lady Scales (now married to the Queen's brother Anthony, and formerly married to Henry Bourchier). Such accounts as exist suggest that she spent less than the Queens who preceded and succeeded her.

Elizabeth was crowned by Archbishop Bourchier in Westminster Abbey on Whit Sunday, 26 May 1465. There were the usual processions and feastings and a tournament, and Edward created nearly fifty Knights of the Bath, including the Mayor of London and other City merchants, and the young Earl of Oxford whose father and brother had been beheaded by Edmund in 1462. Duchess Jacquetta's younger brother, Jacques of Luxembourg, had come over for the occasion, to show that the Queen had at least one aristocratic relation, and there were also representatives sent by the Duke of Burgundy—under cover of the festivities there could be informal diplomatic discussions. Warwick, Wenlock and Hastings were absent in Calais where they had hoped to meet envoys from Burgundy, France and Brittany, but a rebellion had flared up in France and the conference petered out.

Everyone knew that great changes were inevitable in Burgundy. Philip the Good was growing old; his son Charles was beginning to gain control of the government and the years of peace were drawing

---

[9] Ormonds Inn in Knightrider Street, now Giltspur Street.

to a close. Philip's dreams of knight-errantry had been harmlessly dissipated in pageants and tournaments, and his chancellors—even if they had not what the Milanese ambassador referred to as 'the supernatural instinct which God has granted to princes'—had managed so well that they had brought the Duchy to its high watermark of prosperity. With Charles it would be otherwise. Tournaments would be replaced by real battles and he would attempt to emulate the deeds of the heroes of antiquity; stories of warriors and conquerors had been dinned into his ears from his earliest youth and in particular he held in veneration Alexander the Great whose father, like his own, bore the name of Philip.

In this summer, 1465, the French nobles whom Louis had antagonized were temporarily united under the pious name of the *Ligue du Bien Public*. The nominal leader of the rebels was his own brother, Charles Duke of Berry. Charles, son of Philip Duke of Burgundy, had joined in and extorted from his unwilling father some soldiers, although Burgundy had been at peace for so long that the art of war had been almost forgotton. The *Ligue* also included the Duke of Brittany; the Count of St Pol;[1] Dunois, Bastard of Orleans, the friend of Joan of Arc, who was sixty-three and so crippled by gout that he travelled in a carriage; Edmund Beaufort, Duke of Somerset; and John of Calabria, son of King René, dressed up like an Italian condottiere.

Louis, most unwillingly, found himself fighting a pitched battle at Montlhéry near Paris on 16 July 1465. The gallant de Brézé was among his officers and according to Comines (who was with the Burgundians) he was suspected of being in correspondence with the rebels, and Louis asked him straight out whether he had some written agreement with the enemy. 'The Grand Seneschal replied yes, and that the writing should remain with them and that his body should belong to Louis; and he said it jokingly for that was the way he was accustomed to talk.' Louis was not particularly appreciative of other people's jokes and he put de Brézé in charge of the advance guard; de Brézé told his friends that he would bring the armies so close to each other that they would

[1] Louis of Luxembourg, Count of St Pol (1418–75). Duchess Jacquetta's eldest brother, Constable of France. Owing to their geographic position the Counts of St Pol sat on the fence, leaning now one way and now the other, and their friendship was anxiously courted.

be very clever if they could disentangle themselves. 'And this he did. And the first man who died, it was him and his people'. Comines was told all this by Louis himself.

The Battle of Montlhéry was a bungled draw, but it gave Charles of Burgundy a taste for blood and confirmed him in his belief that he was indeed a second Alexander. The terms of the Treaty which followed were dictated by the *Ligue*, but the rebels were soon quarrelling among themselves, and in a very short time they had muddled away all the advantages which they appeared to have gained, and Louis once more had the upper hand.

IN THE LONG RUN ELIZABETH proved to be extremely fertile, but she did not present Edward with a child until 11 February 1466, a year and three-quarters after their marriage. Disappointingly the baby was a girl, but any heir was better than none and she was christened with every appearance of rejoicing. Other things being equal, Edward preferred to behave correctly, and his daughter was christened Elizabeth by George Neville, Archbishop of York; her godfather was the Earl of Warwick, and her godmothers were Duchess Jacquetta and Duchess Cecily.

An account of the ceremonies when Elizabeth was churched was written by a German traveller, Gabriel Tetzel of Nuremburg, who came through London in the suite of a Bohemian nobleman, Lev Lord of Rozmital.[2] Starting from Nuremburg in November 1465, they visited Burgundy, England, Brittany, Anjou, France, Spain, Portugal, Milan, Venice and many minor states, and reached home in the early months of 1467. Bohemia had long been disturbed by fanatical religious sects and was at loggerheads with the Pope, and the tour, ostensibly a pilgrimage, was undertaken for the purpose of enlisting allies, and they met with receptions varying from extreme courtesy to downright hostility. Edward knew little about Bohemia and had no intention of becoming involved in the wars of central Europe, but he was polite to

[2] Mrs Henry Cust, *Gentleman Errant* (1909). The Lord of Rozmital was brother of oanna, wife of George of Podebrad who, in 1458, was elected King of Bohemia.

foreigners on principle and showed the Lord of Rozmital and his suite the hospitality which etiquette demanded; he paid out £100,[3] hung orders round their necks, knighted anyone who wanted to be knighted, gave a banquet in their honour and invited them to the Queen's churching.

Gabriel Tetzel wrote up his travels from memory after he got home, and his account does not agree with that of another member of the party who kept a kind of diary; it is only a general impression, which is coloured both by the desire to boast of the marvels he has seen and the admiration which his party excited, and an underlying resentment that their journey was completely fruitless.

The Lord of Rozmital had started with an escort of forty men, fifty-two horses and one baggage-wagon, but he reduced this by half when he reached Calais. They crossed to Sandwich and 'the sea suited my Lord and his comrades so ill that they lay in the ship as though they were dead'. They did not like England, but they were impressed by its air of prosperity and the frequent towns, castles, churches and holy relics. London was full of busy goldsmiths' shops. The women were beautiful, and kissed strangers instead of shaking hands. The crowd stared at them and asked if their long hair was fastened on with glue. The Court was very grand, but appallingly stiff.

After the churching ceremony in Westminster Abbey there was a banquet held in several halls and, their hunger satisfied, the Bohemians were permitted to stand in a corner of the inner room where the Queen dined, seated in a golden chair alone on a dais. Everyone was very silent, and there was a great deal of kneeling—the chief sufferers, apparently, being Elizabeth's mother, Duchess Jacquetta, and the King's sisters. Afterwards there was dancing by the Court ladies who curtsied to the Queen with superlative elegance;[4] and then there was some very beautiful singing by the King's choristers.

[3] It was the custom to give both presents and money to distinguished foreigners. The Patriarch of Antioch who arrived in December 1466, bringing 4 dromedaries and 2 camels, received £404 16s 4d, while an envoy from Ferrara in 1467 was given 100 marks, a piece of scarlet cloth and a grey horse. In 1482 Andrew Palaeologus, nephew of the last Emperor of Constantinople, received £20 a month for about six months.

[4] Fashionable ladies dressed like fairy-tale princesses and wore tight jackets and full skirts and either heart-shaped head-dresses or steeple-shaped 'hennins'.

Subsequently the Bohemians were entertained by two Earls, and it is significant that one of these banquets was more lavish than that given by the King—sixty courses, Tetzel reckoned, against fifty courses. 'After this my Lord invited many earls and lords to his house and provided a banquet in the Bohemian fashion. They thought this very strange.'

Wherever they went the travellers attempted to exhibit their prowess at jousting (this also they did after the Bohemian fashion) but Edward obstinately refused to hold a tournament for their gratification, and Tetzel says they gave away their tilting horses and jousting armour—which sounds extremely unlikely. From London they went to Windsor, where they were entertained by the 'poor knights' of St George's who ran down the street after them in a final attempt to unravel their names. At Salisbury they were received by the Duke of Clarence; at Poole they once more embarked on the stormy sea. The horses were hoisted on board by ropes and dropped through a hole in the deck, where they were wedged together in misery. Bad weather drove them to Guernsey where they were marooned, short of food, for eleven days, and nearly three weeks had gone by before they reached St Malo.

IN THE AUTUMN OF 1465 THE WIFE OF CHARLES OF BURGUNDY DIED;[5] the question of whom he would choose for his third wife became a matter of great interest and, early in 1466, an envoy arrived in England with a tentative offer for the hand of Edward's sister Margaret. Edward was in favour of any plan that would bind England to Burgundy and he suggested a further alliance—that his brother Clarence should marry Charles' daughter Mary, who, unless Charles fathered a son, was the heiress of Burgundy. From Edward's point of view this would have been a perfect arrangement. Margaret was devoted to her brother, and Clarence—who was already showing signs of becoming a liability—would be safely occupied abroad. But Mary was too valuable to be lightly pledged and the embassy which went over to the Continent to

[5] Charles of Burgundy, in 1439, married Catherine (aged ten), daughter of Charles VII of France. She died in 1446, and in 1454 he married Isabella of Bourbon, the mother of Mary of Burgundy (1457–82). Isabella died on 26 September 1465 and, on 2 July 1468, Charles married Edward's sister Margaret (1446–1503).

discuss the matter was headed by Warwick, who was against a Burgundian alliance and had other schemes for Clarence. Not surprisingly, the negotiations fell through but the dream of marrying the heiress of Burgundy was one which Clarence did not forget.

The Anglo-Burgundian conference at Boulogne was followed by an Anglo-French conference at Calais, and Warwick returned with the names of four suitors for Margaret who were protégés of the King of France. Cautious messages were carried backwards and forwards between the three rulers, and Louis hoped much from Warwick's pro-French leanings.

ON 14 FEBRUARY 1467, the Milanese ambassador at the French court wrote home to warn the Duke and Duchess of Milan (Galeazzo Maria Sforza and Bona of Savoy) that Louis was in communication with the Earl of Warwick, and he reported a conversation which he had overheard at a dinner-party when Louis had entertained John of Calabria, who was still hoping to obtain a kingdom, he did not mind where. After falcons and hunting had been discussed the talk turned to politics, and John of Calabria abused Warwick for driving Queen Margaret out of England, and Louis replied that Warwick was the friend of France. John of Calabria then said that Louis ought to help Queen Margaret to regain her kingdom and Louis had enquired what security would she give—would she offer her son as a hostage?

The Ambassador here explained primly that the Prince already showed undesirable tendencies. 'This boy aged about thirteen already talks about nothing but cutting off heads or making war, as if he had everything in his own hands or was the god of battle or was seated on the throne.'[6]

Then Louis again asked about a guarantee and 'John of Calabria, frowning, said that if his nephew promised and did not keep his word,

[6] This is second-hand gossip, which sounds suspiciously like the stories about Prince Edward which circulated in London after Margaret's triumph at St Albans. On the other hand, it is quite on the cards that his extraordinary childhood did have a bad effect on him and that his boastful and autocratic way of talking shocked Sir John Fortescue, and caused him to write *De Laudibus Legum Anglia*, a book addressed to the Prince in which he explains the laws of England.

he would have to reckon with himself and others, and they would fly at him and tear out his eyes'. John of Calabria added that Louis had never liked the family of Anjou to which Louis retorted that they had never given him cause to do so. 'Thus, half joking, they said very sharp things to each other after dinner.'

JUNE 1467 SAW THE MOST CELEBRATED TOURNAMENT of Edward's reign, in which the star performers were Anthony Woodville Lord Scales and Antoine, Bastard of Burgundy,[7] the eldest of Duke Philip's illegitimate children who, although a middle-aged man of forty-six, was still considered to be practically unbeatable. The idea that the two Anthonys should meet for a trial of skill had originated as far back as 1465, and all the preliminaries which the game of chivalry demanded—tokens and challenges, the provocations of fair ladies and the flourishes of heralds—had been punctiliously carried out, but two years elapsed before the great event actually took place.

At the English Court knights practised energetically, and among them was Paston *major*. He had been knighted in 1463, his father had died in 1466, and he was now the head of his family and an established courtier. On one glorious April day at Eltham—the most glorious of his life—he even found himself taking part in a match with the King himself. Naturally he wanted the people at home to share in his exaltation and, as casually as he could, he wrote to his brother:

'My hand was hurt at the tourney at Eltham upon Wednesday last. I would that you had been there and seen it, for it was the goodliest sight that was seen in England this forty years. . . . There was upon the one side, within, the King, my Lord Scales, myself and Sellenger;[8] and

---

[7] Antoine, The Bastard of Burgundy (1421–1504). Besides being a noted jouster, he had recently taken part in a kind of crusade and assisted the King of Portugal to rescue Ceuta from the Moors. In 1477 he was taken prisoner at Nancy, and he spent the last years of his life in the service of the King of France.

[8] Sellenger, Seintleger, Selyngere, Salinger or Chalanger was Sir Thomas St Leger. In 1465 Tiptoft, Steward of the Household, had ordered that his right hand should be struck off for brawling in the Palace of Westminster but Edward pardoned him. In 1472 he married Anne, Duchess of Exeter. In 1483 he rebelled against Richard III and was executed. Like Sir Thomas Montgomery and Sir John Parre, he was one of the King's inner circle of friends.

without, my Lord Chamberlain [Hastings], Sir John Woodville, Sir Thomas Montgomery and John Aparre.'

John Paston *minor*, desperately worried by estate troubles in Norfolk, replied coldly: 'and whereas it pleases you for to wish me at Eltham at the tournay, for the good sight that was there, by trowth, I had liefer see you once in Caister Hall than to see as many king's tournay as might be betwixt Eltham and London.'[9]

The lists for the great tournament were set up in a large open space at Smithfield near the town house of the Queen (who, incidentally, was again pregnant). The arrangements were made by Tiptoft assisted by Sir John Howard. Howard's cousin, the young Duke of Norfolk, was hereditary Earl Marshal and by rights should have been in charge of the entertainment, but he was too ill to attend. 'God has visited me with great infirmity and disease,' he wrote to Howard, and implored him to officiate in his place; Howard could keep any emoluments and Norfolk would repay him the remainder of his expenses next time they met.[1] Howard, a masterly organizer, was far more efficient than his feeble cousin would have been, and grand-stands were built, decorations put up and elaborate arrangements made for a whole week of entertainment. At the end of May the Bastard duly arrived, accompanied by a large suite which included Louis de Bruges, Seigneur de la Gruthuyse, a favourite envoy of Duke Philip, who had already been on a mission to England and to Scotland. They were lodged in the Fleet Street house of Richard Beauchamp, Bishop of Salisbury, and they also were given the use of his Chelsea residence where they could practise jousting in secrecy.

Edward had now been king for six years and, though he had a long way to go before he could feel that his financial situation was satisfactory, it had improved remarkably. He was slowly reorganizing government offices, the crown estates were managed more efficiently and he quietly continued to trade like a private merchant—a specially privileged private merchant. On the other hand, Warwick was as determined as ever to be the real ruler of England and continued to pursue

[9] *Paston Letters* (1971 ed.), nos. 236, 327.
[1] *Paston Letters* (1904 ed.), no. 668, 18 May 1467.

a foreign policy which was opposed to that of the King, and while Edward's secretary Hatteclyffe and his good friends Beauchamp, Bishop of Salisbury, and Thomas Vaughan[2] were in Flanders trying to push through the marriage of Edward's sister Margaret to Charles of Burgundy Warwick and his colleague, Wenlock, were in Rouen negotiating with Louis. Both embassies met with a measure of success. Hatteclyffe made five journeys to Burgundy in the course of arranging Margaret's marriage, and Bishop Beauchamp—singularly untrammelled by episcopal duties—stayed in Flanders until after it had taken place in the following year. Charles was a very unwilling bridegroom, and only the fear that Margaret would marry a Frenchman, and Edward's refusal to be put off by obstacles and readiness to pay a very large dowry and to give way on the long-disputed point of exporting English cloth to Flanders, ultimately secured his acquiescence. In 1467 the outcome was still very doubtful and on 1 May Paston *major*, when buying an ambling horse from a friend, agreed to pay six marks (eighty shillings) if Margaret's marriage took place within two years, otherwise only forty shillings.[3]

About 7 June 1467 Warwick met Louis for the first time. When he chose, Louis could be very fascinating, and he showered Warwick with presents and treated him with every mark of respect, and Warwick quickly agreed to plans for dismembering Burgundy. Besides persisting in his own foreign policy, Warwick cherished the disloyal plan of marrying his daughter Isobel to the Duke of Clarence with the intention that, when opportunity offered, he would kill Edward and replace him with his daughter and son-in-law.

Clarence, who was nearly eighteen, had taken readily to the scheme. He was tall, good-looking and a glib talker, but he seems never to have attracted a circle of friends, or even of parasites, perhaps because his selfishness and irresponsibility were so glaring that other young men fought shy of him. Edward could block the marriage for a time by making it worth the Pope's while to refuse to send the neces-

---

[2] Thomas Vaughan, knighted in 1475, held numerous positions of trust. He was keeper of the jewel-house from 1465 to 1483 and Chamberlain to the Prince of Wales, afterwards Edward V. He was executed by Richard III in 1483.

[3] *Paston Letters*, no. 667. An ambling horse, trained to move its two feet on the same side in unison, was very comfortable to ride.

sary dispensation, but Warwick and Archbishop Neville also had agents in Rome who might out-bid him. It was a dangerous situation, and the whisper that the Nevilles were turning against the king they had set up undermined Edward's authority and weakened the hands of his officers who were trying to impose law and order in the provinces.

Edward's third Parliament assembled on 3 June 1467, and he took the opportunity to make the welcome announcement that he purposed henceforth to 'live upon his own' and not to ask for further taxes or grants; he added, however, that he was confident that if there was a war the nation would come to his assistance.

By rights, the opening speech should have been made by the Chancellor, Archbishop Neville, but he was absent, pleading illness. Something treacherous that he had done had been discovered, though it is not clear what it was, and on 8 June Edward took the drastic and insulting step of going round to the Archbishop's house[4] accompanied by Lord Herbert, and dismissing him from the post of Chancellor and removing the Great Seal.

The emergency had arisen so suddenly that no new Chancellor was immediately forthcoming and Robert Kirkham, the Keeper of the Rolls, held the Seal temporarily until a Cabinet shuffle could be arranged; then Stillington, the enigmatic Bishop of Bath and Wells, was promoted to Chancellor and the Privy Seal went to Thomas Rotherham.[5] Stillington turned out to be one of Edward's few really bad appointments, while Rotherham was a capable and useful man who served Edward well to the end of his reign.

Meanwhile London was busy with preparations for the great Smithfield tournament. All the elegant preliminaries went swimmingly and on Thursday, 11 June, Anthony Lord Scales and Antoine Bastard of Burgundy entered the lists. Parliament had been adjourned for a long weekend and crowds turned out to watch the glorious spectacle of a contest between two of the most famous jousters in Western

---

[4] The London residence of the Archbishop of York was altered and improved by Cardinal Wolsey. Henry VIII confiscated it and renamed it Whitehall Palace.

[5] Thomas Rotherham (1423–1500). Afterwards Bishop of Rochester, Bishop of Lincoln and Archbishop of York. Chancellor, 1474–83.

Europe. Tournaments had originally been miniature battles fought over several square miles of country, the object being to take prisoners for ransom, and they had been as dangerous as any sport ever invented by a military caste, but over the years there had been many modifications and they were now fought in an arena, the rules were strict, and serious injuries were rare. Combatants were separated by a barrier, and they wore thick 'frog' helmets which protected their faces and eyes.[6]

A Burgundian court official, Olivier de la Marche, described the tournament in his memoirs. On one side of the lists was a high grandstand for the King, and on the other a slightly lower one for the Mayor and Aldermen. Oddly enough he does not mention the presence of any ladies. 'The King was dressed in purple and wore the Garter on his leg and carried a great staff; and certes he seemed a person who was worthy to be a king, for he was a handsome prince and tall and had style.'

For the first charge Anthony and the Bastard carried lances and they missed each other altogether. For the next they carried swords, and the Bastard's horse contrived to crash his head into Anthony's saddle and drop dead with his rider under him, and Anthony, the flower of chivalry, the hope of England, was accused of fighting in an unknightly manner and of having a saddle that was against the rules. He was quickly exonerated and both sides agreed that it was an accident, but the incident created an unpleasant atmosphere. Next day the Anthonys fought on foot with axes and daggers, and the duel was declared a draw, and then the tournaments and feasting continued happily until, towards the end of the next week, the festivities were brought to an abrupt close by the news that Duke Philip had died. He had been nearly senile, but while he lived he had been a restraining influence and now the headstrong Charles was untrammelled ruler. Too late for the funeral, the Bastard and most of his followers hurried home, but Louis de la Gruthuyse remained behind for some weeks and if Edward and he were not already close friends they had become so by the end of his visit.

As an extra complication it was plague year; two members of the

---

[6] There was a slit like a frog's mouth through which they could see when they charged with their heads down but at the moment of impact they put their heads back and were blind.

House of Commons had died, and Parliament adjourned on 1 July, the same day that Warwick arrived back in London, elated by his confabulations with Louis and accompanied by a posse of French envoys whom he had invited to England on his own initiative and who mistakenly imagined that their sponsor Warwick was the power behind the throne. Edward welcomed them with cold politeness and then retreated to Windsor, where he saw a great deal of de la Gruthuyse who was given to understand that Edward was willing to make almost any concession for the privilege of becoming the brother-in-law of Duke Charles.

In July, Edward made a trade alliance with Castile. His father's grandmother had been a princess of Castile and English ballad-makers liked to boast that their king was also king of Spain, but it was not a claim that was taken very seriously and there was no outcry when he announced that he had renounced his rights to the throne of Castile in exchange for a trade treaty.

The French envoys ultimately were given an audience at Windsor, and found to their surprise that their propositions aroused little interest and they returned to France disconsolately with nothing more to show for their visit than some presents of hounds, hunting horns, leather leashes and leather bottles. All these were English specialities, but Louis did not consider that they were offerings of sufficient value and interpreted them as an insult.

The Court was still at Windsor when, on 11 August, Elizabeth gave birth to another child. The Woodvilles, of course, clung together, and her mother had been at Windsor since the middle of July. A male heir was badly needed to diminish the pretensions of Clarence, but unfortunately the baby was a girl. She was christened Mary.[7]

MEANWHILE THERE WAS TROUBLE IN IRELAND WHICH, since the death of the Duke of York, had been left to its own devices with the Duke of Clarence as nominal Lieutenant and the Norman-Irish Earl of Desmond[8]

[7] Mary (1467–82) died at Greenwich on 23 May 1482, and was buried in St George's Chapel, Windsor.
[8] Thomas Fitzgerald, 8th Earl of Desmond (1426?–68).

acting as his deputy. Desmond was experienced and active, but in 1467 the situation became chaotic and Edward appointed Tiptoft, an impartial outsider, to take over the post of Deputy Lieutenant. This appointment was not relished by either the Earl of Desmond or his equally powerful brother-in-law, the Earl of Kildare.[9]

Tiptoft relinquished his office of Constable to Earl Rivers and arrived in Ireland in September 1467, having married for the third time on his way through Ludlow.[1] As usual he took a strong line and had no scruple in trying to kill the leaders whom he considered were stirring up trouble; he was used to passing the death sentence on noblemen, and he executed the Earl of Desmond. In the long run this was possibly of benefit to the country, but Desmond became a martyr and by the next century the story had been improved and it was believed that Tiptoft had added to his crimes by killing the two smallest of Desmond's many sons. The Earl of Kildare was also condemned, but he managed to escape.

In 1470 Edward was in great difficulties in England, and he recalled Tiptoft; but with a flash of insight he reinstated the Earl of Kildare, making him deputy in Tiptoft's place. Kildare restored order and eventually was succeeded by his son, Gerald Fitzgerald, 8th Earl of Kildare, the famous Garret More who ruled Ireland from 1477 to 1513.

IN THE SPRING OF 1468 THE TROUBLES of Duke Francis of Brittany demanded attention; Louis was encroaching on his Duchy, and he implored Edward to send him a large force of archers. To Edward it was of the utmost importance that Brittany should remain independent and, little though he wanted to engage in a war, he promised the archers on condition that any parts of Normandy that were captured should be handed over to England. For a short time a victorious campaign did not seem impossible; Duke Charles (who had agreed to marry Margaret) was longing to take the field against somebody and,

---

[9] Thomas Fitzgerald, 7th Earl of Kildare (?–1477).
[1] He married a local heiress, Elizabeth Hopton, widow of Roger Corbet and afterwards wife of Sir William Stanley. They had one son, Edward, 2nd Earl of Worcester (1469–85).

with Burgundy as an ally, there was just a chance that they might pulverize Louis so that he would never be a danger to them again.

Parliament reassembled on 5 May 1468, and on 17 May the Chancellor, Bishop Stillington, made an eloquent speech, enumerating the wonderful trade treaties which Edward had made with different countries and explaining that now was the time to make an expedition against France and regain Normandy, Gascony and Guienne. Parliament was delighted at the idea of a war with France, and money was voted willingly, and although Edward knew in his heart that to hold land in France was impossible and pointless he gratefully accepted the subsidies offered and the contributions voted by various other bodies, all of which came in very useful as security on which he could borrow the first instalment of Margaret's dowry. Raising the annual sums which he had promised to Duke Charles would always be tiresome, but there was no difficulty about the method of payment; the London agent of the Medici Bank was Gerard Canizini[2] who had long had financial dealings with Edward, and the Medici Bank in Bruges was managed by Thomas Portinari[3] who was in very close touch with Duke Charles.

Edward's third Parliament was dissolved on 7 June 1468. It had been in existence for about a year and had met very intermittently, sitting for seven or eight weeks altogether. The business transacted had been of the usual kind. It was agreed that the people of Norwich must be prevented from making shoddy worsteds, and it was petitioned that robbers who stole from churches should be burnt—a request which received the cautious assent, *Le Roy s'advisera*. One of the governors of the Mint defended himself against accusations of dishonesty arising out of the new coinage and the rate of exchange. There was also a new regulation against the giving of liveries (but the Barons' armies flourished as before).

On 18 June 1468 Edward's sister Margaret set out on her marriage

[2] Gerard Caniziani was operating in England at least by 1459. He married an Englishwoman and was naturalized in 1473. Later he severed his connection with the Medici and continued in business on his own. He died in 1484.

[3] Several portraits of Thomas Portinari exist. The best-known is the Portinari altarpiece by Hugo van der Goes in the Uffizi. He and his wife, sons and daughter are depicted on the wings.

journey. She was now a strong-minded young woman of twenty-two, quite old for a royal bride, and she went into marriage with her eyes open. She knew that Duke Charles was a difficult man, and she knew that she would have to live the rest of her life in a foreign country; the previous autumn she had appeared before the Royal Council (which happened to be meeting at Kingston-on-Thames) and had affirmed that she was willing to accept the husband which her eldest brother had chosen for her. Warwick had opposed her marriage at every point, but he could be counted on to help keep up appearances, and Margaret rode through the City pillion behind him, which was a beautifully simple way of concealing from the citizens the dissensions which were tearing the royal family to pieces. After this demonstration of solidarity, Margaret stayed for several days with the King and Queen at the abbey of Stratford Langthorne, just east of the City. She then proceeded to Margate where she embarked for Flanders. Her very large suite of important ladies and gentlemen was headed by Anthony Woodville and the Duchess of Norfolk. Sir John Woodville, Lord Wenlock, Sir John Howard and the Paston brothers were among her followers, and somewhere in the crowd was Pseudo-Gregory.

Duke Charles of Burgundy and Margaret were distant cousins, and Louis had done his utmost to prevent the Pope from sending a dispensation: when his efforts were unavailing, he spread the rumour that Margaret was no better than she should be and had actually given birth to a son; according to the Milanese ambassador, Duke Charles dealt with this by announcing that anyone mentioning the subject would be thrown into the river. It is quite possible that Margaret left her heart behind her in England, but during her bleak marriage and long widowhood she led a life of utter propriety and much as some people disliked her they did not accuse her of having lovers. She was a woman who would have been an excellent helpmate to a sensible man, and she was unlucky in that, despite her great position, her sterling qualities were of so little use. As far as he was able, Charles avoided living under the same roof with her, but they always remained on speaking terms and he recognized her intelligence. Greatly to Margaret's credit, she managed to get on with her mother-in-law, Isabella of Portugal, who was descended from John of Gaunt and maintained that she was the rightful Queen of England,[4] and she became devoted to her thirteen-year-old step-daughter, Mary of Burgundy.

On Saturday, 2 July 1468, Margaret was married to Duke Charles at Damme, a small town outside Bruges; Beauchamp, Bishop of Salisbury, officiated. The time was five o'clock in the morning and the moment the essential part of the ceremony was over Duke Charles rode home to Bruges and went to bed because—according to de la Marche—he was conserving his energies for the ardours of the forthcoming night. Provision for children was made in the marriage settlement, but Charles seems to have been uninterested in sex of any kind; perhaps the excesses of his father had nauseated him. If it could be proved that he had become impotent it would explain both his evasiveness towards Margaret and his almost insane aggressiveness.

After the rest of the ceremonies had been completed at Damme, the whole company proceeded in pouring rain to Bruges where ten days of festivities followed. Duke Charles, spartan though he was in some ways, had a passion for grandeur and pomp, and the pageants were as magnificent as any in the history of Burgundy. Flemish art was at its peak and the best artists had been gathered from all over the Duchy, so it is probable that the tableaux were very beautiful, grotesque though they sound. There were tableaux of famous married couples including (according to Olivier de la Marche) Adam and Eve, and Alexander and Cleopatra (sic); there were tableaux of all the Labours of Hercules, there were dwarfs, giants, mermaids and, above all, people dressed up as animals.

The jousting was led by the Bastard of Burgundy, and it was woven into a drama in which the Bastard represented the Knight of the Golden Tree who had received a letter from the Princess of the Unknown Isle about a chained giant guarded by a dwarf—all of which was completely in tune with the taste of the audience.

Paston *minor* enjoyed himself enormously and on Friday 8 July he wrote an ecstatic letter to his mother, who would perhaps have preferred to hear rather less about the jousting and more about the ladies.

---

[4] Isabella of Portugal had several brothers, but perhaps her mother, who was a daughter of John of Gaunt and Blanche of Lancaster, had bequeathed her the crown by will.

He and his brother and their fellowship were all well. Everything was perfect. Never had Englishmen been so well treated abroad. The Bastard had jousted with twenty-four knights over eight days, and next Monday he and the twenty-four knights were to tourney against twenty-five other knights.[5] They were all wonderfully arrayed in cloth-of-gold and silk and silver and jewels. Anthony Lord Scales fought against a Burgundian lord; he could not fight against the Bastard because they had sworn eternal friendship at Smithfield, but the Bastard had escorted him onto the field and while he was doing so a horse kicked the Bastard on the leg and hurt him so badly that he might not be able to fight again, 'and that is great pity for by my truth I trow God made never a more worshipful knight'.

As for the Duke's court, 'I heard never of none like to it, save King Arthur's court'.[6] He will tell them more about it when he gets back. They are all starting for home next Tuesday, except for the few who are staying on with the new Duchess of Burgundy. The gathering is breaking up sooner than expected because the Duke has heard that the French king intends to make war on him and is within four or five days' journey of Bruges, and so the Duke is setting out on Tuesday to meet him. 'God give him good speed and all his, for by my troth they are the goodliest fellowship that ever I came among, and best can behave them, and most like gentlemen.' The Duke of Somerset and his following left Bruges the day before Duchess Margaret arrived, and the Duke of Burgundy will not again give them shelter or assistance. Will his mother look after his small servant, 'little Jack', and send him to school; and give his remembrances to his two sisters and all other friends at Caister?

Those lower down the social scale were less charmed with Bruges, and Pseudo-Gregory complained that after the first day or two the English attendants were not allowed into the ducal court and the Burgundians 'showed no more favour unto Englishmen than they would do unto a Jew'. Food and drink was as dear as if it had been wartime and a shoulder of mutton cost twelve pence. And, as for

[5] Jousts were single combats, tourneys fights between teams, but the terms were often used loosely.
[6] This expression is also used by Comines and was evidently a popular cliché.

lodging, 'Lyard[7] my horse had more ease than had some good yeomen', for the horse was under shelter while yeomen lay in the street; not a bed was to be had for less than fourpence. 'Lo! How soon they could play the niggards!'

A minor aftermath of the Anglo-Burgundian rapprochement was that in the late summer of 1468 a number of London craftsmen worked themselves up into a frenzy of jealousy against the Flemish artisans in Southwark, and a plan was made to attack them at night and to put an end to foreign competition by cutting off their thumbs. Fortunately somebody sneaked to the authorities and the conspirators were intercepted and imprisoned.

AFTER SEEING OFF HIS SISTER MARGARET on her wedding journey, Edward went back to London and turned his attention to the dangers which were threatening him on all sides. Warwick was now as great a menace as Queen Margaret of Anjou, and there were risings in the provinces. Edward could not tell which outbreaks were serious, nor who was behind them and how they would turn out. On 24 June Jasper Tudor, financed by Louis and with a small force of French soldiers, landed near Harlech and attempted to relieve the castle which had now been besieged for seven years. Foiled in this endeavour, he collected some Welsh chieftains and marched to Denbigh which he took and burnt, and after this brave but foolish venture he returned to France. In retaliation Lord Herbert's brother led a savage punitive expedition through North Wales, while Harlech abandoned hope and surrendered on 14 August. The defenders, some fifty men, were sent to London where two were beheaded and the rest pardoned—treatment which compares very favourably with the way that Duke Charles or Louis massacred the garrisons of captured towns.

Earlier in the year a messenger had been arrested carrying compromising letters and, under torture, he had implicated many people;[8] in

---

[7] 'Lyard' means grey.

[8] The great period of torture, witch-burning and religious persecution which disgraced western Europe for two centuries was just beginning. In England, torture was supposed to be used only for cases of high treason but sometimes it was used illegally. The rack had been introduced into the Tower about 1440 by the Governor, John Duke of

particular, a prominent alderman, Sir Thomas Cook, fell under suspicion. Cook had been made a Knight of the Bath at the time of the Queen's coronation; he had been Mayor of London in 1462–3; he had lent money to Edward; and he was possessed of wealth that appears to have been almost bottomless and which he was now using for some nefarious purpose. His case emphasizes the dilemma of the frustrated and ambitious merchant who had risen to the top of his own world and yet could not break into the other world which governed England. Edward hob-nobbed socially with merchants, but there was not one who gained political eminence.[9] Cook's activities are extremely obscure, but a likely explanation is that he was making a daring bid to gain entry into the closed circle of power and privilege by helping to finance Queen Margaret.

For some months there were arrests, fines, pardons; two insignificant men were hanged without exciting much attention, but the trial of Sir Thomas Cook caused a buzz of excitement. Very powerful interests were involved on both sides, and there was a tug-of-war between the King's influence and Cook's money. The crowd, completely in the dark over the real issues, found solutions of their own and some people believed that the Woodvilles were at the bottom of it—particularly as Duchess Jacquetta had disagreed with Cook over the price of some tapestries—although they must have known perfectly well that no Woodville was powerful enough to pervert justice in the City of London, and that Edward would not have prosecuted such a prominent man unless he had had the backing of many of the other merchants. The case first came before a commission which included Warwick, Earl Rivers, Clarence and the Mayor of London. The latter was 'a replete and lumpish man' and Clarence caused great amusement

---

Exeter, and it was known as the Duke of Exeter's daughter. The inaccurate statement that it was Edward IV who first made torture legal in England is due to Stubbs, and it is often repeated as a way of blackening Edward's name; even if true, it would only have been a manifestation of the spirit of the age. No one would hold Henry VI responsible for the rack in the Tower.

[9] The children of landowners and merchants seldom intermarried, perhaps because their respective families found it difficult to handle each other's kind of property. Sir William Stonor's first wife was a City madam, but she was considered extravagant and unsatisfactory.

by saying, 'Sirs, speak softly, for the Mayor is asleep.'[1] Afterwards Cook was tried before a judge and jury and escaped with his life, but he was fined the enormous sum of £8000 plus 'Queen's gold', a recognized percentage amounting to eight hundred marks. Edward was probably trying to break Cook financially, but he did not succeed in doing this and Cook continued to take an active part in City intrigues.

It is impossible now to tell what Edward suspected, what he knew, what he was actually able to prove, what it was inexpedient to state in court and what did, in fact, come out at the trial—let alone what other courses were open to him, and what would have happened if he had acted differently. His secret service must have been extensive, but it has left practically no traces. During the autumn there were other alarms and arrests. The Earl of Oxford was imprisoned and released, and three unimportant men were executed on Tower Hill. Hugh Courtenay, Earl of Devon, and Thomas, Lord Hungerford,[2] both men whose fathers had been prominent members of Queen Margaret's party but who themselves had agreed to accept Edward, were arrested in Wiltshire, their trial being postponed to the New Year when Edward was able to come to Salisbury. There must have been something unusual about their case as they were not even allowed an honourable execution, and on 16 January 1469 they were hanged, drawn and quartered at Bemerton outside Salisbury. Courtenay's lands and the title of Earl of Devon were given to Lord Stafford of Southwick, a lightweight who had been Edward's friend and supporter ever since Calais days.

IN THE MEANTIME the war to save Brittany had petered out. Edward had planned to send six thousand archers under Anthony and Lord Mountjoy, but he did not intend to sacrifice them rashly, and by the

---

[1] *The Great Chronicle of London.*

[2] Hugh Courtenay, 7th Earl of Devon. His elder brother was killed at Towton and his younger brother was among the émigrés on the Continent.

Thomas, 4th Lord Hungerford. His father had been executed after Hexham. The Hungerford property was around Heytesbury, and the family were buried in Salisbury Cathedral.

Both Courtenay and Hungerford had been pardoned, but they had not been reinstated and their titles were in abeyance.

time they had been equipped Duke Francis had caved in. Duke Charles, unable to co-operate with anyone for very long, failed to send the support which he had promised and, on 10 September 1468, Duke Francis signed a treaty with Louis and English hopes of reconquering France receded into the background for the time being, no doubt to the great relief of King Edward.

IX

Open Rebellion 1469

FOR EIGHT YEARS EDWARD AND WARWICK HAD MANAGED TO WORK together but in 1469 there was a showdown and blood was shed. Then for two years Edward and Warwick were openly at war, and no one could tell what would be the outcome, or which side it would be wise to back. To use a phrase of the Pastons, the times were right queasy.

With rebellion imminent, the King suffered acutely from the lack of a standing army. Although perfectly aware of the intentions of Warwick and Clarence, he could not afford to hire soldiers until after his opponents had taken the field. Nor did he know where to concentrate his strength. Disturbances at one place might be a blind, and a day's march in the wrong direction might make the whole difference between victory and defeat; the best he could do was to hover round a central depot, and he began amassing arms in Fotheringhay Castle.

The first ominous signs appeared in the spring of 1469, when two separate bands of rebels, one under 'Robin of Holderness' and the other under 'Robin of Redesdale', were reported from Yorkshire. The name 'Robin' was emotive, and hinted that the leader was the people's champion and the redresser of the wrongs of the poor as well as having magical powers like Robin Goodfellow and that, on top of all, he was of noble birth like Robin Hood who was really the Earl of Huntingdon. At first it was not clear whether either of these risings were serious: with luck they might fade away naturally when money ran out.

Montagu, now Earl of Northumberland, was in the North. He had had great experience of rounding up rebels, and soon he was able to suppress the rebellion of Robin of Holderness which turned out to be a small spontaneous protest against local grievances. One of the demands made was that the Earldom of Northumberland, which included much land in Yorkshire, should be restored to its hereditary ruler, the heir of the Percies. This suggestion did not appeal to Montagu; he beheaded Robin of Holderness and the rebellion was over.

The Robin of Redesdale outbreak, on the other hand, had been engineered by Warwick, who had provided it with a manifesto which accused Edward of excluding the royal family from his councils and listening to unworthy favourites such as Earl Rivers, Duchess Jacquetta and their sons, Lord Herbert, Lord Stafford of Southwick (now Earl of Devon), Lord Audley and Sir John Fogge—a list which seems to have been dictated by Warwick's personal dislikes. Lord Hastings was not included, either because he was too popular or because he had married Warwick's sister and had managed to keep Warwick guessing. Denunciation of a king's unworthy favourites was always a success with the mob, and the Nevilles exploited the possibilities to the full.

When June came, Robin of Redesdale and his followers were still at large in the North and, methodically, Edward set about mobilizing a large army. The Herbert brothers were sent to gather a force from Wales, and Lord Stafford of Southwick raised soldiers on his new estates in Devonshire, while Edward himself went to East Anglia on a recruiting tour thinly disguised as a pilgrimage to Walsingham, taking with him Anthony, John Woodville and his youngest brother, Richard Duke of Gloucester.

The Duke of Gloucester was now sixteen and Warwick had already tried to coax him into the Neville party, but Gloucester had nothing to gain by deposing Edward and substituting Clarence and he elected to remain with his eldest brother, who was very thankful to have the assistance of a new and energetic supporter—one, moreover, who could not possibly be called lowborn.

It appears that Richard suffered from some slight deformity; Polydore Vergil and Sir Thomas More, both of whom must have spoken to many people who had seen Gloucester at close range, assert that one shoulder was higher than the other.[1] More was sceptical about a rumour that he was born with teeth, but was fairly confident that his birth had been a difficult one, that he was born feet first and 'that the Duchess his mother had so much ado in her travail that she could not be delivered of him uncut'. These obstetrical details, however obtained, make sense, and although More retails them merely as a sign of Gloucester's ingrained fiendishness they could easily account for a dislocated shoulder. Something very similar happened at the birth of Kaiser William II, who was permanently injured in the course of a bungled delivery and who went through life with a 'withered arm' which was certainly never depicted in portraits, barely shows in photographs, even in the bitterness of war was not caricatured or jeered at, and did not prevent him from spending his old age chopping down trees—but which was, to him, a very grievous affliction. Gloucester was the eleventh of Duchess Cecily's twelve children and it is relevant that he and Clarence were the only two of the last six to survive infancy.

More and Polydore Vergil also say that Gloucester was very small, and this is corroborated in a Latin speech addressed to him by Scottish envoys in 1484; never, they said courteously, had nature enclosed so great a mind or such remarkable powers within a smaller frame.[2] In childhood he must have felt inferior to attractive Clarence and clever Margaret who, besides being respectively three and six years older than himself, were a devoted pair, and it would not be surprising if he resented the casual way in which he was treated.

Nor was Gloucester's childhood of a kind to produce a well-balanced adult: there were too many changes of fortune. He was just

---

[1] The first evidence of Gloucester being called a hunchback dates from 1491, when one William Burton of York was accused by one John Paynter of having called Richard III a hypocrite and crouchback'.

[2] A German traveller, Nicolas von Poppelau, who wrote an account of a visit which he made to England in 1484, states that Richard III was very tall, but as he also states that he was entertained by Richard for a week at Pontefract at a date when Richard is known to have been at York and Middleham his testimony is not worth very much. Dominic Mancini, *The Usurpation of Richard III*, Appendix.

seven when his father and his older brothers fled from Ludlow and his home was looted by Queen Margaret's troops. The following year his father and his brother Rutland were killed and then, after desperate alarms, he and Clarence sailed to Flanders where they were fêted by the famous Philip, Duke of Burgundy. In no time at all he was back in England for the coronation of his tall and domineering brother Edward who—the applauded victor of two pitched battles—had unexpectedly become King of England. Richard, having been made a Duke and a Knight of the Garter, was then sent up to Yorkshire to be educated in Warwick's castle at Middleham. In the absence of upper-class boarding-schools, it was quite usual for the nobility to take in each other's young people, and Middleham was a pleasant place of residence on the edge of a small town, beside a river, and among green fields and fine trees, but it was a long way from the palaces where the rest of his family were enjoying themselves. Edward may have hinted to him that it would be convenient if he learned to like living in the north, and Gloucester may have taken the point and, turning the matter over in his mind, have decided that supposing he did choose to reside in Yorkshire when he was a man it would be to please himself, and not to pull Edward's chestnuts out of the fire.

IN EAST ANGLIA THE SHAKINESS of the throne was perceived, and the landowners seized the opportunity to attack each other. By 1469 the Pastons had added to their list of enemies the Duke of Norfolk, the young man in whose troop Paston *minor* had assisted at the sieges of the Northumberland castles; the Duke had become obsessed by the idea that he must obtain Caister Castle, and Paston *major* was equally determined to keep it. Since the beginning of the year Paston *major* had been courting Anne Haute, the Queen's first cousin, and all Anne's relations endeavoured to forward the match and were so far successful that the pair became entangled in a contract which was not actually a marriage but which was so binding that they could only be released from it by squaring officials in Rome.[3]

[3] By April 1473 he was determined to break his engagement, but he was not able to do so till 1477.

The Pastons were full of woes. On 9 January 1469 a well-wisher had written to tell the Paston's bailiff that this day in the grey morning three men of my Lord of Norfolk with long spears carried off three good horses from John Poleyn, one of their farmers, and 18 January the King sent from Salisbury to command Paston to stop bickering with the Duke of Norfolk and to appear immediately before the Council of Westminster, as he had already been told to do. Edward was writing on the very day on which he had hanged Lord Hungerford and the Earl of Devon, and he was in no mood to put up with turbulent country gentlemen. On 12 March Paston's mother informed him that Norfolk's men had again been giving trouble; they had felled the wood of Paston's tenants, drained ponds and taken fish. 'And they ride with spears and lances like men of war so that the said tenants are afraid to keep their own houses. Therefore purvey a ready remedy or else you lose the tenants hearts and you [are] greatly hurt; for it is greaty pity to hear the sorrowful and piteous complaints of the poor tenants that come to us for comfort and succour sometimes by six or seven together. Therefore for God's love see that they be helped. . . .' She also reminded him to get a kerchief for his sister Anne and to settle up his father's will as quickly as possible, because the present Archbishop would not require a very large gratuity and he might not last long. 'For he is an old man and he is now friendly to you and if he happened to die who should come after him you wot never;[4] and if he were a needy man, inasmuch as your father was noised of so great value, he will be the more strange to entreat.' She also pointed out that it might be awkward if a new archbishop asked them for their accounts, and that if Paston had not been so dilatory he could have got everything settled up while his patron, Archbishop Neville, was Chancellor.

Inevitably the other large landowners in East Anglia were drawn into the quarrel over Caister. Anthony, Lord Scales, had become pro-Paston because of his cousin, Anne Haute, and another neighbour, Sir Thomas Wingfield, was also an ally, but the King remained firmly neutral. After the royal tour of Norfolk in June, Paston *minor* told his

---

[4] Archbishop Bourchier survived for another seventeen years; he died in 1486.

brother that Wingfield had told him that Edward Brandon[5] (who had established an ascendancy over the Duke of Norfolk) had tried to persuade the King to favour the Duke, and that Edward had said, 'Brandon, though thou can beguile the Duke of Norfolk and bring him about the thumb as thou list, I let thee weet thou shalt not do me so; for I understand thy false dealing well enough.' The King added that if the Duke of Norfolk acted contrary to the law 'Brandon should repent it every vein in his heart', for he knew perfectly well that the Duke was completely ruled by Brandon.

Wingfield had also arranged that when the King rode through Hellesdon Warren towards Walsingham he would point out the ruins of the Pastons' house which the Duke of Norfolk had destroyed. The young Duke of Gloucester, rashly plunging into the troubled waters of landowners' quarrels, promised to put in a word for the Pastons, but when they passed the ruined house the King, who had more important things to think about, merely remarked to the Pastons' uncle William that he supposed that it might have fallen down by itself, for if it had been pulled down they could have brought the matter up before the judges in Norwich. None of the Woodvilles did anything to help, and Paston came to the gloomy conclusion that promises from courtiers were not of much value.

All the lords were recruiting followers, and some Norfolk neighbours had joined the Duke of Gloucester. Lord Scales had tried to persuade Paston *minor* to enrol with the King, but he had replied that he was not worth a groat without his elder brother and that he must first ascertain his brother's intentions.

AFTER VISITING THE SHRINE OF WALSINGHAM, Edward pushed on into south Lincolnshire and at the end of June he stopped a night at Croyland. The causeways across the Fens were cleared of obstacles and the King and two hundred retainers rode along the embankment to the

[5] Edward Brandon, later Sir Edward Brampton, was a Portuguese Jew who had settled in England and been baptized. He traded successfully, married an heiress and sometimes commanded naval expeditions. Later he attached himself to Sir John Howard (Lord Howard, Duke of Norfolk) and he continued to flourish in the reign of Richard III. Finally he returned to Portugal, and died in 1508. E. F. Jacob, *The Fifteenth Century*.

Abbey. The Prior was the same mild creature who had recorded the visit of Henry VI and, charmed by Edward's easy good manners and quite unaware of his desperate plight, described him as 'a well-pleased guest. On the morrow, being greatly delighted with the quietude of the place and the courtesy shown to him, he walked on foot through the streets to the western water-gate and after greatly admiring the plan of the stone bridge[6] and the houses, there embarked with his attendants; and setting sail, made a prosperous voyage to the Castle of Fotheringhay where the Queen was awaiting his arrival.'

While Edward was building up his forces in the east Midlands, Warwick was in Kent. He was still Warden of the Cinque Ports and Captain of Calais; his brother the Archbishop was with him and so was Clarence, and they were joined by an important new ally, the young Earl of Oxford, who was ready to back Clarence, or Warwick, or Queen Margaret or any other rebel, and to dash into any plot that was against Edward and would enable him to avenge the execution of his father and brother.

Warwick's agents at the Vatican had outwitted Edward's; the vital dispensation had arrived and Isobel could now marry Clarence. Duchess Cecily appeared at Sandwich, but nothing she could say had any effect; Clarence and the Nevilles went over to Calais where Isobel was awaiting them and, on 11 July, Archbishop Neville performed the wedding ceremony. It was a great score for the Nevilles, but not one that was likely to endear them to other members of the peerage.

Back in England they issued a proclamation to the effect that they had been appealed to by the people of England to rescue them from the unworthy favourites of the King, and they called on the men of Kent to rise in their support. Oxford had recently become 'good lord' to the Pastons and on 18 July he sent Paston *major* a breathless note asking him to procure three sets of horse harness of the best quality; Lord Hastings had obtained some for six or seven pounds, though 'I would not mine were like his'. Lady Oxford will give Paston the money, though she will have to borrow it. 'And I trust to God we shall do right well.'

[6] The remarkable three-armed bridge is still one of the sights of Croyland, though the channels which it spans are now dry.

Warwick, the Archbishop, Clarence and Oxford moved swiftly to London and with barely a pause to raise a loan they were out on the road to the North.

Edward was in the Midlands, waiting for Lord Herbert with his army from Wales and Lord Stafford of Southwick with his army from Devonshire and hoping that they would arrive before Robin of Redesdale from the North and Warwick from the South converged on him. Herbert and Stafford met according to plan and combined forces, but somewhere in North Oxfordshire the two armies drew a little apart and Stafford went on ahead. One story is that the soldiers quarrelled over billets in the small town of Banbury, which is quite believable, though it is also possible that there was a shortage of food and congestion on the roads, so that the leaders agreed that progress would be quicker if they split up; whatever the reason, Edward would never have divided his forces without first ascertaining whether the enemy were in the neighbourhood, and it turned out that they had made an error of the first magnitude.

On 26 July 1469, Herbert's army, after leaving Banbury, was surprised by the army of Robin of Redesdale at a place called Edgecott. Stafford cannot have been far off, because before the battle was over he had returned and joined in the fighting; but it was too late and by the time he arrived the Welshmen had been cut to pieces. Stafford's men, coming fresh to the battle, achieved an initial success, but then an army sent by Warwick appeared and the final result was that the two armies on which Edward had been relying were annihilated. So many Welsh chieftains were killed that in Welsh history Edgecott is almost what Flodden is to the Scots. Lord Herbert was taken prisoner and brought before Warwick in Northampton. There was no chance for him and he was executed, but he was permitted to write a farewell letter to his wife.

After directions about his burial and some charitable bequests he asked her to take the order of widowhood, 'as I love and trust you', by which means she could escape a second marriage and would be left free to manage his estates and look after his children. 'Wife, pray for me, and take the said order that you promised me, as you had in my life my heart and love. God have mercy upon me, and save you and our children, and Our Lady and all the saints in heaven help me to salvation. Amen.'[7]

Not only was Lord Herbert killed but his brother[8] and Lord Stafford were hunted down and executed, and furthermore Warwick's agents discovered Earl Rivers and Sir John Woodville in Monmouthshire and they also were despatched. Thus, by the victory of Edgecott, Warwick was able to liquidate five of his particular bêtes noires.

'Robin of Redesdale' is believed to have been either Sir William Conyers of Marske (d. 1495) or his brother, Sir John Conyers of Hornby, whose son was killed at Edgecott, but neither of them seem to have received rewards for their services or credit for winning this overwhelming victory, and perhaps no real Robin existed. Warwick, with his extraordinary talent for intrigue, may have organized every detail of the rebellion, and the victory itself may have been the purest fluke, the result of Herbert's and Stafford's blunder and the quick thinking and prompt action of some quite insignificant captains.

The news of the defeat of his armies and the executions of his friends was an appalling blow to Edward and it would have suited Warwick and Clarence if, driven to desperation, he had now collected such forces as were left to him, and with foolish gallantry engaged in a hopeless battle and fallen in the thickest of the fray. But this was not Edward's way. Instead of attempting to fight against impossible odds he dismissed his soldiers and, about 29 July, surrendered at Olney in Buckinghamshire to Archbishop Neville who—taking advantage of the general chaos to indulge his natural tastes—was at the head of some troops.

Edward was a prisoner but he was still king, and king he remained while he was moved to Coventry, to Warwick Castle, and then to Yorkshire to Warwick's castle at Middleham. In London, government officials carried on as if nothing had happened, the mob indulged in a little violence on its own account, and the mayor and alderman showed their sympathy to the Queen by making her a present of wine. Two

[7] Nicolas, *Testamenta Vetusta* (1826). Lord Herbert also had an illegitimate family by Maud, daughter of Adam Ap Howell Graunt, from whom the present Earl of Pembroke is descended.

[8] Sir Richard Herbert, ancestor of Lord Herbert of Cherbury the philosopher, and George Herbert the poet.

men were incited to say that Duchess Jacquetta was a witch and had made wax figures. An accusation of witchcraft was practically the only way by which a great lady could be brought low and by this means the widow of Henry IV and the wife of Duke Humphrey of Gloucester had been imprisoned, but after the unprovoked murder of Duchess Jacquetta's husband and son public opinion was in her favour and the case against her collapsed.

Owing to Edward's popularity, Warwick did not dare kill him and there was a period of deadlock which was ended by an unexpected rising on the Scottish Border in favour of Henry VI. This was led, ironically, by two members of the disinherited branch of the Neville family and it completely upset Warwick's plans. He could not raise soldiers to suppress it while the King was a prisoner and so Edward was set at liberty and, early in October, he re-entered London at the head of a great cavalcade, while Warwick was left to capture his cousins and cut off their heads at leisure.

Paston *major* saw Edward ride into London and he sent a thoroughly puzzled letter to his mother. She, also, had her troubles. While Edward was a prisoner the Duke of Norfolk had seized the opportunity to send men to attack Caister Castle. The siege had lasted several weeks and Paston *minor* held out bravely, but on 26 September 1469, after one of the Pastons' men and two of the Duke of Norfolk's had been killed, he was forced to surrender. Paston *major* did not accept this as final, but he needed a 'good lord' who would assist him to regain Caister and it was very unfortunate that his new protector, the Earl of Oxford, appeared to be out of favour.

The King, wrote Paston *major*, had ridden into London with Gloucester, Suffolk, Montagu, Essex, Hastings, Arundel, Dacre, Mountjoy, the Duke of Buckingham and his brother, a thousand horsemen (some in armour and some not), the Mayor of London and twenty-two aldermen in scarlet, and two hundred craftsmen in blue. The Earl of Oxford was absent; he was staying with the Archbishop of York at The Moor[9]

---

[9] Archbishop Neville had built himself a country mansion in Hertfordshire near Rickmansworth. It was called The Moor and it afterwards belonged to Cardinal Wolsey and to the Duke of Monmouth. The name was changed to Moor Park and it was rebuilt in the early eighteenth century.

and some said that they went three miles along the road to meet the King and he stopped them with the message that they could come when he sent for them. Edward pretended that nothing was amiss. 'I wot not what to suppose therein. The King himself has good language of the Lords of Clarence, of Warwick, and of my Lords of York, of Oxford, saying they be his best friends, but his household men have other language; so what shall hastily fall I cannot say.'

An unexpected peer in Paston's list is Montagu, Earl of Northumberland, but probably the whole Court was aware that Edward had managed to detach him from Warwick in the same way that Warwick had captured Clarence. Montagu was now rising forty, and he had spent most of his life soldiering, policing the Border and rounding up rebels. He had won the Battles of Hedgeley Moor and Hexham single-handed, and there was no reason why he should forward his brother's career at the expense of his own, particularly as he had a son and heir which his brother had not; there was no reason why he should wish to dethrone Edward and crown Clarence.

Edward and Montagu had agreed on a deal: they were to go into partnership and Montagu's son George was to marry Edward's eldest daughter, Elizabeth, the heir to the throne, so that if Edward were killed —which did not seem at all unlikely—Montagu could step into the breach, rally the country and ensure that Elizabeth and George were crowned and not Clarence and Isobel. To check Warwick's power in the north, young Percy was to be released from prison and given back the title and estates of the Earls of Northumberland (as Robin of Holderness had demanded) and, in compensation, Montagu would be raised to the rank of marquis and endowed with other estates as opportunity offered, while his son should bear the venerated title of Duke of Bedford.[1]

Henry Percy had been imprisoned as a youth when his father was killed at Towton eight years before;[2] now, totally inexperienced, he found himself a great clan chieftain with the task of defending the

---

[1] George Neville (c. 1461–83). This was the boy whom Edward had prevented from marrying the daughter of the Duke of Exeter. He was created Duke of Bedford on 5 January 1470.

[2] Henry Percy, 4th Earl of Northumberland (1446–89). He was finally killed by a mob which was demonstrating against a tax imposed by Henry VII.

Northumbrian Border against the Scots and assisting in maintaining law and order in the north of England generally. Every magnate had a 'Council' which performed the functions of an estate office, and in ordinary matters could carry a lazy or stupid employer, but the new Duke would have to make great decisions and perhaps lead an army into battle. A boyhood spent in confinement could sometimes be turned to advantage, as the careers of James I of Scotland and Henry VII prove; while other young men were hawking and hunting, Henry Percy had had time to think, and the chief conclusion he had reached was that, once free, he would proceed with the utmost caution. As a consequence, he never showed his hand until he was quite sure who had won.

The execution of five of Edward's trusted helpers had left many posts vacant; Lord Herbert and Lord Rivers in particular had been key men whom it was not easy to replace. To fill the gaps Sir John Howard, ruthless and clever, was made a peer[3] and Tiptoft was sent for from Ireland. Edward also began to build up Gloucester; he was given commissions in Wales and also the opprobrious office of Constable of England, which had fallen vacant when Earl Rivers was executed. It was not a suitable post for a very young man, but he was eager for responsibility.

By December 1469 Warwick and Clarence were back at Westminster attending a Council of Peers, and a pardon was granted to all those who had taken part in the rebellion of the previous July. After Warwick's murder of Edward's friends it must have been difficult for them to associate as though nothing had happened, but they could not avoid each other's company. England was small, public life narrow, and Edward's hands were tied. Warwick was still the richest peer in England; only the Pope could take the archbishopric of York away from George Neville; and no power on earth could prevent Clarence from being Edward's brother.

IT WAS IN THIS TROUBLED YEAR, somewhere between 4 March 1469 and 3 March 1470, that a man completed the most famous English literary

---

[3] Sir John Howard became Lord Howard either in 1469 or early in 1470.

work of the fifteenth century. He was a one-book author, and he was writing in captivity. These are his final words:

'I pray you all, gentlemen and gentlewomen that read this book of Arthur and his knights, from the beginning to the ending, pray for me while I am alive, that God send me good deliverance. And when I am dead, I pray you all pray for my soul. For this book was ended the ninth year of the reign of King Edward the Fourth, by Sir Thomas Malory, knight, as Jesu help him for his great might, as he is the servant of Jesu both day and night.'

Le Morte Darthur by Sir Thomas Malory is a prose synthesis of a number of French manuscripts and English stories and poems dealing with the adventures of King Arthur and his knights. The romantic legends had been growing for nearly a thousand years and they were mixed with primitive folk-tales, but to Malory the knights and ladies were dressed like his contemporaries and the tournaments took place in fifteenth-century lists. It is not known when his book first began to be read; Caxton printed it in 1485, and there survives one very early manuscript version which was discovered in 1934 in a safe in the bedroom of the Warden of Winchester College, but both these are supposed to have been copied from texts which were already corrupt.

As for Sir Thomas Malory himself, five men of that name have been discovered, and for a long time the laurels were worn by a War-wickshire knight who would have been over seventy in 1469 and who was the leader of a band of ruffians, but he has now been displaced in favour of a Yorkshire Thomas Malory whose family lived at Hutton and Studley, and it has been pointed out that the vocabulary of the *Morte Darthur* has a northern tinge.[4] The problem of how Malory came to have access while in prison to so many French romances is tentatively answered by the suggestion that he had been taken prisoner by Jacques d'Armagnac, Duke of Nemours (1433–77), who owned the castle of Carlat south of the Auvergne mountains, and who was one of the very few men who possessed the sort of library that would contain the necessary manuscripts and who, at about the same date, did employ a French scholar to make a synthesis of his Arthurian romances. This

---

[4] William Matthews, *The Ill-framed Knight* (University of California, 1966).

theory does at least provide a possible explanation. Adventurous Englishmen have found themselves in many strange prisons, and genius is so unaccountable that it might be possessed by an obscure Yorkshire knight as well as by anyone else.

For the most part Malory kept to the realms of fantasy, but there is one paragraph which might refer to the deplorable behaviour of Clarence, news of which could have reached him in France. It comes towards the end of the book, when King Arthur's bastard son, Sir Mordred, is attempting to dethrone his father.

'And many there were that King Arthur had made up of nought, and given them lands, might not then say him a good word. Lo! ye all Englishmen, see ye not what a mischief here was! For he that was the most king and knight of the world, and most loved the fellowship of noble knights, and by him they were all upholden, now might not these Englishmen hold them content with him. Lo! thus was the old custom and usage of this land; and also men say that we of this land have not yet lost or forgotten that custom and usage. Alas, this is a great default of us Englishmen, for there may no thing please us no term. . . . And the most part of all England held with Sir Mordred, the people were so new fangle.'

X

Fluctuating Fortunes 1470

WARWICK AND CLARENCE PUT UP A SHOW OF FRIENDLINESS
which lasted until March 1470, when Warwick was able to
turn a local quarrel among the landowners of Lincolnshire
into a rebellion against the King. The events of the preceding year had
made Edward seem less formidable and during the winter of 1469–70
Lord Welles, his son Sir Robert Welles, and his brother-in-law Sir
Thomas Dymoke took to arms and destroyed property belonging to
Sir Thomas Burgh, an officer of Edward's household. Confused,
Edward tried to quell from afar the disturbances which followed, and
Warwick won over Lord Welles and his faction while putting it about
that there was a Lincolnshire rising in favour of Henry VI, and Clarence
was assuring Edward that he and Warwick were bringing soldiers to
subdue the rebels.

There exists a memorandum of the rebellion[1] which appears to
have been written by one of Edward's secretaries as a kind of apologia,
and which gives a day-to-day account of the King's movements, and
the fact which most clearly emerges is that Edward was unable to make
out what was happening; he had had, however, the prescience to
summon Lord Welles and Sir Thomas Dymoke to London and to keep

---

[1] *Chronicle of the Rebellion in Lincolnshire, 1470* (Camden Society, 1847).

them under partial arrest. On 7 March Edward was at Waltham Abbey in Essex when he learnt that a large army was collecting in Lincolnshire, and on 9 March was at Huntingdon and informing Lord Welles and Dymoke that unless they immediately called off the rebellion they would be executed. He still could not be certain whether Clarence and Warwick intended to help him or the rebels. On 11 March he was at Fotheringhay, and Sir Robert Welles—who had intended to join Clarence and Warwick at Leicester—changed his course and went south in the hope of rescuing his father. He camped at Empingham near Stamford and Edward, informed of his proximity, made a dash through the night to Stamford[2] where he arrived 'early in the morning before day'. Lord Welles and Dymoke were now executed by general consent, and then Edward and his army pushed on to Empingham with such celerity that the rebels were taken by surprise and put to rout; the fleeing soldiers threw off their heavy padded coats as they ran and the Battle of Empingham was mockingly called Loosecoat Field. In the evening the King returned to Stamford. By this time he knew that the rebellion had been organized by Warwick and Clarence, and he sent one of his equerries, John Donne,[3] with letters summoning them to his presence, but they returned evasive and untruthful answers and moved away. Edward followed them and captured Sir Robert Welles who was executed at Doncaster on 19 March. On 21 March Edward was at Rotherham, but he could not follow Warwick further west because the country had been stripped of food and so he turned north reaching York on 22 March. Here he stayed for some days to collect provisions for his army, and to discover Warwick's intentions. Warwick, meanwhile, had doubled back and when Edward again picked up the trail he had been left far behind.

Warwick had already instructed the ladies of his family to await him at Exeter, and Isabel had arrived there on 18 March. She was in the last stages of pregnancy, and she was escorted by Lord Dynham who

---

[2] Fotheringhay to Stamford is about ten miles, and Empingham is about another five miles further on.

[3] The portraits of Sir John Donne, his wife and daughter, can be seen in the Memlinc triptych in the National Gallery. His arms were the same as those of the poet, though no connection between the two men has so far been traced. His wife was Elizabeth, sister of Lord Hastings.

arranged for her to lodge in the Bishop's Palace.[4] Her mother and her sister Anne soon joined her, and Warwick and Clarence appeared on 3 April and, as soon as they could, they all took ship for Calais, Lord Dynham remaining behind. The part he played in this affair is very obscure and, in the absence of evidence to the contrary, can be called chivalrous; not much more than ten years had passed since he and Edward and Warwick had escaped together to Calais and, a rational and honourable man, he must have regretted that their adventurous partnership was ending in this deplorable strife.

On the day that Warwick arrive at Exeter, Edward had only got as far as Coventry, whence he sent out letters appealing to friends to bring soldiers to assist him against 'our traitors and rebels the Duke of Clarence and the Earl of Warwick'. He reached Exeter on 14 April, and just stayed one night, and whether or not he noticed that the rafters of the Guildhall were decorated with bears and ragged staffs—the badge of the Earls of Warwick—he left his sword behind him as a reminder that it was he who was king.[5]

The whole of the south coast was now in danger of attack by Warwick, and some of his partisans were captured at sea and brought to Southampton for trial. They were tried by Tiptoft, who had not been mellowed by his experiences in Ireland and who decided to make an example of them. One or two gentlemen were executed and twenty seamen were hanged, drawn and quartered, and then he scandalized public opinion by putting the bodies together again and impaling them on spikes. To modern minds this would appear harmless after the barbarities which had gone before, and Tiptoft had doubtless seen much worse sights in the Levant, but it was a novelty and it added to his reputation for cruelty.

Warwick had been Captain of Calais for years and the deputy who held if for him was his friend Wenlock, and so he expected to be welcomed with enthusiasm; instead, when his ship reached the mouth of the harbour, he received a warning that feeling was running high against him and that it would be very unwise to attempt to land. Isobel

---

[4] John Dynham of Hartland had been created Lord Dynham in 1467.
[5] The bears and the sword are still in Exeter Guildhall.

was now in the throes of childbirth and Wenlock sent her wine, but that was all he could do for them. The baby was born dead, or else died shortly after birth, and Warwick and his family had no option but to throw themselves on the mercy of Louis; they headed for the mouth of the Seine and, at the beginning of May, they landed at Honfleur after a long and distressing voyage.

By the time Warwick landed in France he had readjusted his plans and had made up his mind to jettison Clarence, marry his younger daughter Anne to Queen Margaret's son, Prince Edward, and restore Henry VI to the throne. The possibility of this combination had of course occurred to other people, and Louis was far from averse to it; he would have to put up most of the money but, win or lose, it would cause disturbance in England.

These promising schemes were nearly wrecked at the very beginning by a small international incident caused by Warwick's nephew, Thomas Bastard of Fauconberg. The Bastard was a daring leader, and he and Lord Howard had been entrusted by Edward with a fleet with which to guard the coast. Changing suddenly to Warwick's side, the Bastard recklessly seized some Burgundian merchant ships and Warwick, who badly needed the money and who in his youth had taken part in pirate raids, accepted the plunder thankfully and sold it in Normandy. The Duke of Burgundy retorted by arresting the French merchants who were attending Antwerp fair, and Louis was put in such an awkward position that he might have repudiated Warwick had he not been too deeply involved to retreat.

The greatest difficulty of all was to get Queen Margaret to agree. She loathed Warwick, the man who had driven her into exile and cast aspersions on her morals, and the noble émigrés at her court did not relish the prospect of returning to England in Warwick's train; on the other hand, they had been away from their homes for nine years and Sir John Fortescue was greatly in favour of a reconciliation. Louis used all his powers of persuasion, and Warwick apologized abjectly for his past conduct, and finally Margaret consented. Money was borrowed from a merchant in Tours to pay for a dispensation, but it took some weeks to push the marriage through, and it was not till 25 July that Anne Neville and Prince Edward were formally betrothed at Tours. Clarence dissembled his chagrin; but as soon as he was able he secretly got in touch with Edward.

Philip de Comines was, at that time, still in the employment of the Duke of Burgundy; Wenlock had the reputation of being untrustworthy, and Comines was sent to Calais to keep him true to the Anglo-Burgundian alliance; and while he was in Calais he was much amused to meet a lady-in-waiting of Isobel's who was acting as an intermediary between Edward and Clarence, without Wenlock being aware of it. Comines did not think it right to name ladies, and gives no clue to her identity. 'This woman was not foolish nor over-talkative; she obtained permission to rejoin her mistress and she managed better than a man could have done. And although M. de Wenloc was a very clever man, this woman deceived him.' Comines then remarks that one ought to suspect everyone who comes and goes, but that suspicions should be reasonable, and it is foolish to be too suspicious.

An invasion of England seemed imminent, and English and Burgundian ships blocked the mouth of the Seine until the middle of September when they were scattered by a storm and Warwick's ships were able to slip out. Warwick, Clarence, Jasper, Oxford and a small force of mercenaries landed at Dartmouth and Plymouth on 13 September 1470. Edmund, Duke of Somerset, and John Courteney, Earl of Devon, had already reached England, but Queen Margaret and her son and Warwick's wife and daughters remained in France.

Warwick's plans worked to perfection. Edward had been decoyed into the north by a diversion created by Lord Fitzhugh[6] who staged a pretended rebellion at the end of July. Montagu and Northumberland between them should have been able to deal with it, but neither of them could be trusted and, loth though he was to leave London unprotected, Edward himself went to Yorkshire. Elizabeth was expecting another baby, and first he installed her in the Tower, providing it with extra weapons and ammunition, and ordering big guns to be sent from Bristol. Lord Fitzhugh had disappeared over the Scottish border by the time Edward reached Ripon, but he and his staff were convinced that Warwick was about to make a landing on the coast, and they stayed in

[6] Henry, 6th Lord Fitzhugh (c. 1429–72). Married Alice Neville, Warwick's sister.

Yorkshire for the next few weeks. They were still there when word reached them that they had been fooled and that, on 13 September, Warwick had landed in Devonshire. At once Edward started south with a small escort and a party of close friends, leaving Montagu to follow more slowly with the army he had mustered at Pontefract. Edward was at Doncaster, fifteen miles south of Pontefract, when he was woken up in the middle of the night to be told that his agents in Montagu's army had sent word that Montagu had switched over to Warwick's side. It was an appalling predicament; he was pinned between Montagu and Warwick and there was no time to rally his supporters; as at Ludlow, flight overseas was the only possible course.

Edward, Gloucester, Anthony, Hastings, Lord Say and a few attendants took horse and rode the hundred miles or so to King's Lynn, a port on the Wash near Middleton, Anthony's castle; local contacts enabled them to charter a ship and by 29 September 1470 they had set sail. Eventually they reached Holland and landed near Alkmaar, having been chased by ships of the Hanseatic league and stuck on a sandbank from which they were lifted by the tide before their pursuers could come alongside. Short of money, Edward rewarded the captain of his ship with a fur coat, and then got in touch with his friend de la Gruthuyse, Governor of Holland, and by 11 October the English fugitives were safely at the Hague. Afterwards, Edward stayed with de la Gruthuyse at Bruges, where among the amenities possessed by his host was a magnificent library, and later Edward commissioned a number of books illustrated by Burgundian artists—some of then volumes of indescribable splendour—which formed the beginning of a Royal Library and became the nucleus of the British Museum Library.

MEANWHILE, IN LONDON THE STREETS were in an uproar and the Men of Kent were running wild. As soon as it was known that Edward had fled, the Queen and her children and her mother left the Tower for the greater security of Westminster Sanctuary, which was a hostel on the island of Westminster and considered inviolable. Other people took refuge in the sanctuary of St Martin le Grand near St Paul's. The Tower was handed over to the insurgents; Archbishop Neville, whose attachment to Warwick was never in doubt, arrived hot-foot, and on 6 October 1470 Warwick and Clarence entered the City.

Warwick had returned with the avowed purpose of restoring the rightful king to his throne, and Henry VI was immediately brought out of the Tower. The extremely unreliable chronicler Warkworth recalls that he was 'not worshipfully arrayed as a prince and not so cleanly kept as should beseem such a prince', and for once he may be accurate; at the best of times Henry had persisted in dressing poorly, dirt was considered holy and lunatics are notoriously difficult to keep clean. On 13 October Henry VI was re-crowned[7] in St Paul's with Warwick holding his train and Oxford the sword of state, but the cherished assertion that the King of England was also the King of France had to be omitted from the service out of respect for the feelings of Louis who had financed Warwick's enterprise.

The cynical Croyland Continuator was amused by the way people quickly changed over to the winning side. 'You might then have heard persons innumerable ascribing this restoration of the most pious King Henry to a miracle and this change to the working of the right hand of the Most High; and yet, behold! how incomprehensible are the judgements of God and how inscrutable are his ways! for within six months after this, it is a fact well known, there was not a person who dared own himself to have been his partisan.' Comines also was tickled to find that after Edward's flight from England everyone in Calais seemed to be wearing Warwick's badge; Wenlock wore in his cap a ragged staff of gold, and those who could not afford gold wore a badge of cloth. 'This was the first time that I appreciated that the things of this world are very unstable.'

THE EARL OF WARWICK had at last achieved his ambition. He was the ruler of England, in possession of a completely passive king, but there was little pleasure in it. For one thing, he was not supported either by the approbation of the crowd or by a strong party of peers. No one was impressed by his sudden enthusiasm for Henry VI, whom he

---

[7] Henry VI's restoration was officially known as his re-adeption.

himself had led prisoner through the streets of London, and the way he had treated both Edward and Clarence did not inspire confidence. Edward would undoubtedly return. Clarence had a justifiable grievance and was a dangerous liability. Montagu had deserted him once before, and might desert him again at a pinch. The Neville faction and the Queen's faction had been antagonists for years and could not be expected to pull together all of a sudden, and there was always the possibility that when Margaret was re-established she and the Beauforts would find ways of getting rid of the Nevilles.

Warwick by this time was a man of vast experience, and he acted carefully and correctly. Order was restored. The sanctuaries were not violated. The holders of key posts were changed, but there were no unnecessary upheavals and government offices continued to function smoothly. The rewards to his followers were moderate, and Edward's friends were not persecuted. Bishop Stillington, the Chancellor, was in St Martin's sanctuary, and Archbishop Neville was given back the Great Seal. The Earl of Oxford received nothing very noticeable, apart from the right to try and condemn Tiptoft, who had executed his father and brother. Tiptoft was nearly lynched as he walked through the streets to the Tower, but he was rescued and on 18 October he died in style on the scaffold, requesting that his head should be cut off with three strokes in honour of the Trinity. His behaviour on this occasion was much admired and Caxton, who later printed a translation made by Tiptoft, extolled him as an example to all. Montagu bought a pardon for the year which he had spent in alliance with Edward, and went north to guard the Border. Sir Thomas Cook again became an alderman.

Jasper Tudor recovered Pembroke Castle from the widow of Lord Herbert. Here he found his nephew, Henry Tudor, now aged thirteen, and he brought him to London, which may have been the first occasion on which the future Henry VII set foot in England.[8] Perhaps, also, he had a reunion with his youthful mother, whom he can have seen but rarely since he was a baby, but with whom he was able to establish a very affectionate relationship. However, Henry Tudor was too near

---

[8] Nothing definite is known about his childhood.

the throne to be welcome at any English court; the Beauforts feared him as much as Edward did, and after a fortnight Jasper and his nephew retreated to Wales.

Warwick returned to his old custom of entertaining lavishly, but for the first time he found himself hard-pressed for money; there were other calls on his purse, and his private income was needed to supplement the deficiencies of the Exchequer.

On 2 November 1470 Queen Elizabeth, in Westminster Sanctuary, gave birth to the longed-for son and heir. She evidently had the art of endearing herself to her immediate circle and, unlike Queen Margaret, in all her troubles she was treated kindly. Warwick did not harry her; she was attended by her usual midwife, her friend Lady Scrope and her mother; and a butcher supplied her with half a beef and two sheep every week with such regularity that afterwards he was rewarded by being given permission to load a ship called the *Trinity of London*, 30 tons, at any port, with oxhides, lead, tallow and all other merchandise except staple ware, and to trade with her for a year.

The baby was christened Edward by the sub-Prior of Westminster; the godparents were the Abbot and Prior of Westminster and Lady Scrope, but he could not become Prince of Wales until the title was bestowed upon him. By the end of the month, Edward IV and all his descendants had been officially disinherited by reviving an old story to the effect that Duchess Cecily had had an affair with an archer called Blackburn and that Edward was a bastard. Parliament met on 26 November and it was agreed that Henry VI was once again King and that if his heirs should fail then Clarence, the eldest *legitimate* son of the Duke of York, should succeed him. Duchess Cecily was thus publicly branded as an adulteress by her son Clarence, her nephew Warwick and both Houses of Parliament, but there was nothing that she could do about it.

LOUIS WAS EXPECTING AN IMMEDIATE return from his investment; Prince Edward had signed a paper promising to send English mercenaries to assist in the dismemberment of Burgundy, and Louis imagined that as soon as Warwick was established in London the mercenaries would arrive. In December 1470 French ambassadors came to England, accompanied by a trade mission bringing samples of manufactures which it was hoped would attract English buyers. The London merchants scented unfair foreign competition and the trade mission was a pathetic failure, but the ambassadors were greeted with fair words and false promises and they reported back that Warwick was quite ready to despatch the promised army.

Erroneously confident of Warwick's support, Louis took the plunge and towards the end of December he massed troops on the French Burgundian border and began moving them into the territory of Duke Charles. This at once galvanized Duke Charles into action.

XI

Edward's Return 1471

W HEN EDWARD LANDED IN HOLLAND HIS BROTHER-IN-LAW
had not rushed to greet him; in fact, Duke Charles allowed
three months to elapse without vouchsafing him an interview, and it was only when it became known that Louis was launching
an attack on Burgundy that he hastily arranged a conference. The meeting took place at Aire near St Omer on 2 January 1471. Edward was
accompanied by de la Gruthuyse, while his sister Margaret—somehow
reconciling the interests of her husband, her eldest brother and her
adored Clarence—worked for him behind the scenes.

Whether or not Edward and Duke Charles disliked each other as
much as they expected, they were in such straits that they were able to
suppress their mutual antipathy and come to the agreement that Duke
Charles would announce that he did not intend to assist Edward but
that he would secretly provide him with men and money. Edward had
already arranged loans with adventurous investors and his old friends
the Calais merchants; now, assured that Duke Charles would put no
impediments in his way, he was able to go ahead with his preparations
and by the middle of February his invasion force was ready.

In England Warwick was still awaiting the arrival of Queen
Margaret and Prince Edward. He badly needed an attractive figurehead
round which he could rally his supporters, and the Prior of St John's,

Sir John Langstrother,[1] was sent over to France to fetch them. This produced no results and though Warwick himself went to Dover on 27 February it was a fruitless journey; Queen Margaret was either afraid to trust herself to the odious Warwick, or else she hoped that any battles that were necessary would have been fought before she arrived. When at last she did embark storms drove her back into harbour.

London buzzed with the news that Edward was about to return. The French envoys and the trade mission packed up and hurried back to France.[2] The Mayor of London, uncertain how to proceed, feigned illness, whereupon Sir Thomas Cook sprang forward and became Deputy Mayor. Most people decided to wait and see what happened. As usual, the advantage lay with the invader, who might land at any point; and, following the usual course, Warwick began collecting an army in the Midlands.

The story of Edward's reconquest of England is better documented than any other part of his reign because, after the fighting was over, one of his followers composed an official account of it which was circulated among his friends and backers on the Continent. It is known as *The Arrivall*,[3] and several versions of it exist.

The writer was a non-combatant, probably a chaplain, and he claimed that he was an eye-witness of most of the events he described and 'the residue knew by true relation of them that were present at every time' and, except at the very end, he seems as though he were writing from personal experience. Edward must have vetted the story, but he does not appear to have added anything and it is a war-correspondent's article rather than a general's despatch. Considering that this nameless reporter had never before attempted such a task and had no models to copy, he acquitted himself rather well. Like all beginners, he could not pick out the important from the trivial, but he endeavoured to be truthful, and his testimony is all the more convincing because the

---

[1] Sir John Langstrother (d. 1471) had been appointed Prior of St John's in September 1469 when Edward was Warwick's prisoner. On regaining power, Edward extracted from him an oath of fealty but this had been cancelled during Henry VI's re-adeption. He was now Warwick's Treasurer.

[2] The French trade mission continued to be unlucky, and crossing back to France they lost two ships—one to the Bastard of Brittany and one to the Easterlings.

[3] *Historie of the Arrivall of Edward IV in England* (Camden Society, 1838).

impression left is that of doubt and hesitancy and caution and disappointment. Edward was to him a figure in the distance, conferring with his staff or waiting for his scouts to return and occasionally riding on ahead.[4] Hastings, Gloucester and Anthony were subsidiaries who were taken for granted, but Clarence, Montagu and Northumberland were of great interest because their intentions were doubtful.

Always a bit of an actor, Edward commenced his hazardous enterprise by walking three miles from Bruges to the quay at Damme, thus presenting the populace with a free show and astounding them by the sight of a magnifico at eye-level. This wooing of the crowd, which nowadays every royal personage and politician attempts as a matter of course, was then considered quite extraordinary and one chronicler hints that Edward was a little too aware of his own good looks. He had mustered about 1200 mercenaries and on 2 March they embarked on sea-going vessels at Flushing. Edward, Hastings and 500 soldiers were on the *Anthony*, which belonged to the father-in-law of de la Gruthuyse and came from the Dutch port of Veere;[5] Gloucester was on a ship with 300 men, and Anthony on another with 200. Contrary winds held them back for over a week and they did not get away until 11 March.

On 12 March Edward reached the Norfolk coast and at Cromer sent ashore a reconnaissance party, which reported that the Earl of Oxford[6] was in the neighbourhood and that it would be most unwise to land. They then headed for Yorkshire, and on the way encountered 'storms, winds and tempests'; a shipload of horses was lost, but on 14 March they arrived off the sparsely inhabited coast north of the Humber.

Edward's navigator hailed from Hull[7] and knew the coast intimately, and the *Anthony* put in at Ravenspur,[8] a derelict little port

---

[4] The account of Edward's prowess on the field of Barnet has been lifted wholesale out of some Arthurian romance.

[5] After Edward's restoration, Veere was given special trading rights.

[6] Possibly this was one of Oxford's brothers.

[7] In July 1471 Robert Michelson of Hull, navigator of the *Anthony*, was granted a life annuity of 100 shillings from the customs of Hull. (*Patent Rolls*.)

[8] In 1305 Ravenser and Ravensrod sent two members to Parliament but soon afterwards the sands shifted, high tides made the houses uninhabitable and the ports were abandoned in favour of Hull, further up the Humber. It is believed that 'Ravenspur' is under the sea about two miles east of the present Spurn Head.

which has now totally disappeared and which, even then, had been long abandoned; it was the very place where 'the usurper Henry of Derby, after called King Henry IV' landed in 1399 when he arrived to seize the throne and murder Richard II—a coincidence not lost upon the men who had come to dethrone Henry of Derby's grandson. Rough weather made landing difficult, and at first only Edward and a few followers went ashore and spent the night at 'a poor village'. Gloucester was four miles up the coast and Anthony ten miles beyond him, and 'the remnant of the fellowship where they might best get land'. The next day 'the rage of the tempest somewhat appeased', and the whole force disembarked.

Collecting his little army, Edward set off. The news of his arrival had spread round the district and the local gentry were armed and watchful. People on the north side of the Humber did not greatly care who was king in London, and they had not forgotten the Battle of Towton and how they had joined what had appeared to be a triumphant host and had then been killed in their thousands. What concerned them was to be legally correct whichever side won, and Edward, disappointed by their attitude but appreciating their dilemma, announced that he was not returning to recover the crown—merely to claim his personal estates. This was not only a flat lie, but the very same lie which Henry of Derby had told in similar circumstances; however, it covered his partisans if he lost,[9] and if he won the weight of it on his conscience would not be intolerably heavy. Again it served its purpose; Edward was not assisted and he was not molested, and a point was gained.

The direct route to London was due south through Lincolnshire, but they could not cross the Humber without re-embarking on their ships and this, after the recent tossings they had endured, 'they abhorred for to do'; besides, it might have given the impression that they were retreating abroad. Edward therefore informed his army that they were proceeding to York, and that they must keep up the pretence that he had merely come to claim his estates.

[9] The Aldermen of York did use it as an excuse in 1485, when they were trying to ingratiate themselves with Henry VII.

Hull did not dare to admit them: Beverley risked it. They could not tell how York would react.

Three miles outside York Edward was met by the Recorder, a supporter of Warwick's called Conyers, who assured him that if he attempted to enter the City he was 'lost and undone'. Edward, unable to go back, decided to 'abide what God and good fortune would give him', so, 'notwithstanding the discouraging words of the Recorder', he continued boldly towards York. Then two prominent citizens came to meet him and told him that, as he was only seeking his estates, he could enter the City. Then up came the Recorder again 'and put him in like discomfort as before. And so, sometimes comforted and sometimes discomforted, he came to the gates before the city where his fellowship made a stop.' Edward, with sixteen or seventeen of his followers, went into the town while the army waited outside. Presently the gates were opened again and the little army entered and received food and shelter for the night.

Next morning, refreshed, they started on their journey south, by way of Tadcaster and Sandal Castle, leaving on their left Pontefract Castle which was held by Montagu. Few sympathizers had joined them and they had hardly more soldiers than their original twelve hundred mercenaries, and so they expected that Montagu would march out and bar their way; however, to their surprise and relief, Montagu remained in Pontefract. This was felt afterwards to have been one of the crucial moments of the expedition, and there was much discussion as to why Montagu had not attacked, and the conclusion they reached was the very simple one that he had not been able to raise enough soldiers to make interception feasible. The most powerful local magnate was the Earl of Northumberland,[1] who had played for safety and 'sat still', and the lesser landowners of the neighbourhood had followed his example.

Even around his own castle Edward had difficulty in attracting followers. 'About Wakefield and in those parts, came some folk unto him, but not so many as he supposed would have come; nevertheless,

---

[1] The Earl of Northumberland's castle, Wressell, was less then 20 miles northeast of Pontefract.

his number was increased.' The Earl of Oxford was at Newark with the Duke of Exeter, but they also were meeting with rebuffs and they felt themselves to be so weak that they fled at the approach of Edward's scouts. As Edward came south, partisans did begin to join him; William Dudley[2] brought in 160 men at Doncaster, Sir William Parre and Sir James Harington brought in 600 at Nottingham, and at Leicester, the centre of the Hastings' country, Edward's army was suddenly more than doubled by the addition of two or three thousand men under Sir William Stanley and others.

This completely changed the situation: Edward had now about five thousand soldiers and, taking a bold line, he marched straight towards Coventry, which he reached on 29 March. Warwick was supposed to have assembled six or seven thousand men inside its walls[3] and Edward, with a show of confidence which he can hardly have felt, challenged Warwick to bring out his army and fight a pitched battle. Warwick did not accept, he was waiting for Oxford and Montagu to join him with reinforcements, and there was still a chance that Clarence would come in on his side. Edward repeated his challenge for three days running and then moved off to the town of Warwick, eleven miles distant. From here he sent messengers to his cousin in the manner of a conqueror dictating terms of surrender; Warwick was offered his life, but Warwick was by no means beaten, and he refused to parley.

Clarence was coming up from Somerset and, at first, it was not known on which side he intended to fight. The writer of *The Arrivall* alludes to the 'inconveniences' which he had caused his two brothers, and remarks that his eventual change of heart was only because he had been jettisoned by Warwick and he thought that if Queen Margaret regained power she would probably 'procure the destruction of him and all his blood'. The go-betweens who had arranged the reconciliation were his mother and sisters—especially his sister Margaret—the Archbishop of Canterbury, Bishop Stillington, the Earl of Essex and Lord Hastings.

---

[2] William Dudley (d. 1483) a younger son of John, 6th Lord Dudley. He was in holy orders and in 1476 he became Bishop of Durham.

[3] Coventry had no castle but strong walls, begun in 1355 and finished forty years later.

DURING THIS TIME OF EXCITEMENT AND ALARM, a courtier called Henry Vernon, who was living at Haddon in Derbyshire, received a succession of letters[4] which reflected very clearly the desperation of the leaders. The majority of them came from Clarence, and the first of them was written at Bristol on 15 March. He asked for help and news, and it was followed next day by one written at Wells; Vernon was to send spies to find out what the Earl of Northumberland, Lord Stanley and Lord Shrewsbury were doing. He should have two spies in each place, one to collect information and the other to convey the messages. 'We be ascertained that it is said about London the K.E. is sailed by the coast of Norfolk towards Humber',[5] and so Vernon must be ready to come at an hour's warning.

On 23 March Clarence commanded Vernon to come at once. 'Wherever we be, with as many persons defensibly arrayed as you can make.' He did not mention on whose side he intended to fight; he may not yet have made up his mind. On 25 March it was Warwick who was sending Vernon a circular letter appealing for help and ending with a postscript in his own hand: 'Henry I pray you ffayle not now as ever I may do ffor yow. R. Warrewyk.' On 30 March it was Clarence again: he and his army were moving towards the Midlands, and he wrote from Malmesbury. On 31 March he wrote from Cirencester and, on 2 April, from Burford. But Henry Vernon did not leave home.

THE MEETING OF EDWARD AND CLARENCE was arranged to take place publicly so that the whole army could see that there had been a reconciliation, and it was carried out in the grand style, both brothers acting their parts with gusto. The place selected was a stretch of open country a few miles outside the town of Warwick on the Banbury road. The King, 'upon an afternoon', issued out of Warwick with all his fellowship and drew them up in battle array with their banners displayed. Clarence, less than half a mile away, also spread out his troops. Then

[4] *Historical MSS. Commission, 12th Report*, Appendix Part IV (1888). Also *HMC Rutland* vol. IV (1905).

[5] This was written on 16 March and Edward was off Norfolk on 12 March. Cromer is about 250 miles from Wells.

Edward advanced towards Clarence, taking with him Gloucester, Hastings, Anthony and other friends, and Clarence came towards him with a few supporters and was received effusively. 'The trumps and minstrels blew up', and the King introduced Clarence to his foreign mercenaries, whom Clarence welcomed to England in an eloquent little speech. The King then said a few words of welcome to Clarence's followers and they both returned 'to the King's host, when either party welcomed and jointly received the other, with perfect friendliness'. Short of murdering Clarence on the spot, there was no alternative to a demonstration of brotherly love, and Clarence's effrontery helped to carry off an awkward situation.

Clarence is said to have brought 4000 men with him, but the Earl of Warwick had also been reinforced: Montagu, Oxford, Exeter and their armies had joined him in Coventry so, with one final challenge to come out to fight, Edward turned his back on them and set out for London as fast as he could get his troops to move.

They started from Warwick on Friday, 5 April, and reached Daventry next day. On the morning of Palm Sunday, 7 April, Edward attended Mass in Daventry parish church where there appeared a propitious omen which made a great impression on the writer of *The Arrivall*. Just in front of the King, fixed to a pillar, was a very ordinary alabaster shrine of St Anne which was hidden from sight by four small wooden painted doors which had been closed, as was the custom in Lent. Suddenly there was a loud crack and the doors opened a little, and then closed again, and then they opened violently and remained open in the sight of all; whereupon Edward remembered that he had prayed to St Anne when he had been in danger on the sea. The congregation was awed and the army continued on its way much heartened by such a 'fair miracle'; although Edward, after putting a donation in St Anne's box, seems to have taken no further notice of her.

As Edward rode down the familiar Roman road towards London, the City Fathers were once more thrown into confusion. Messengers coming from the two armies announced that both Edward and Warwick would shortly be arriving. The Deputy Mayor, Sir Thomas Cook, besought his colleagues to shut the gates and Archbishop Neville endeavoured to rally the crowd to Henry VI by parading him round the City.

According to one Chronicler,[6] the procession was small and insignificant with just a few men on foot and one horsemen holding a long pole on which were two fox-tails. Henry wore his usual old long blue velvet gown 'as though he had no more to change with', and Archbishop Neville held his hand the whole way, while Lord Zouche,[7] 'an old and impotent man', carried the royal sword. As Edward and his army drew nearer, fear of assault and sack tipped the scales in his favour; the City Fathers decided to open the gates and Archbishop Neville, making a quick volte-face, sent Edward a secret message of welcome.

On Thursday 11 April Edward re-entered his capital. He had come from Ravenspur without striking a blow, but Warwick and Montagu were close behind him. After a quick ceremony in St Paul's, he went to the Bishop of London's palace where Archbishop Neville 'presented himself to the King's good grace' and handed over Henry VI: then he hurried on to Westminster and, after another quick ceremony in the Abbey during which the crown was placed for a moment on his head, he at last arrived at the Sanctuary, where he 'went to the Queen and comforted her', and made the acquaintance of his son who was now five months old. The Queen and her children came back with Edward into the City and spent the night at Baynard's Castle,[8] palace of Duchess Cecily, and next day they moved for safety into the Tower, which was also accommodating Archbishop Neville, several Bishops and old Lord Sudeley.

'The King took advice of the great lords of his blood and others of his council for the adventures that were likely for to come', and they agreed to go back up the road down which they had ridden the day before and to meet Warwick's army head on. It was important that they should annihilate it before Margaret arrived and as this day was Good Friday there was some discussion as to whether it would be permissible to fight a battle on Easter Day. The writer of *The Arrivall* thought that Warwick intended to take Edward by surprise while he

---

[6] *The Great Chronicle of London.*

[7] As a matter of fact Lord Zouche was only a boy, and the sword-bearer was Ralph Butler, 7th Lord Sudeley, who was called 'aged and infirm' in 1462 and died in 1473. This error is an example of the unreliability of the City Chronicles even when the writers had been eye-witnesses.

[8] Baynard's Castle was on the river, just inside the west wall of the City.

was occupied with his devotions, 'but the King was well advertised of this evil and malicious purpose'. As the Croyland Continuator sarcastically put it, 'This prudent prince, paying more attention to urgent necessity than absurd notions of propriety', decided to forestall Warwick by himself launching an attack on Easter Sunday.

On Saturday 13 April, Easter Even, Edward set off up Watling Street carrying with him Henry VI who, for a man of peace, had now been present at a remarkable number of battles. Edward had been reinforced by some of the Bourchiers and Lord Howard and his son, but Warwick's army was still supposed to be the larger.

This same day, Saturday, Queen Margaret and Prince Edward landed in England.[9] They put in at Weymouth, which is about a hundred and thirty miles from London, and neither Edward nor Warwick knew that she had arrived.

Edward's army reached Barnet late on Saturday evening after a twelve-mile march. His advance guard found the enemy advance guard already in the streets and drove it back, and Warwick's army stopped short on the ridge above the town and camped in a line across the road. Edward's men had hoped that they would spend the night comfortably under cover in Barnet, but the King would not 'suffer one man to abide in the same town but had them all to the field with him'. It was a pitch-black night[1] and he made them creep forward and camp close in front of the enemy—much closer then he intended or Warwick realized. Throughout the night guns were fired at them, but the shot went over their heads. Edward also had some guns, but he was able to restrain his men from sending answering shots, 'or else right few', and also from talking or making noises which might have given away their position.

The ensuing battle was fought in thick fog, and nobody can have had a very clear idea of what happened. The writer of *The Arrivall* did not know who was commanding in which sections, but it is fairly safe to guess that Edward was in the centre of his line, with Gloucester, Hastings and Anthony on the wings and Clarence wedged in some

[9] *The Arrivall* states that she landed on Sunday, but this must be a mistake. A letter signed by Prince Edward, summoning one John Daunt to join him, is written from Weymouth and dated Saturday.

[1] As it was Easter and there should have been a moon, they must already have been wrapped in thick fog.

place where he could not desert. On the opposing side, Warwick must have been in the centre; Oxford is known to have been on his right, which leaves Montagu to command the left wing. It is true that Exeter was a Duke and should have had precedence, but the battle was crucial and it was no time for the niceties of etiquette.

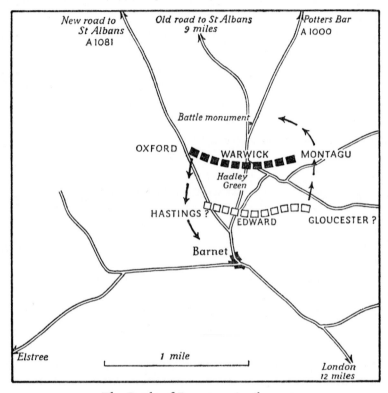

The Battle of Barnet 14 April 1471

On Easter morning, 14 April 1471, between four and five, just as it was getting light, Edward 'committed his cause and his quarrel to Almighty God, advanced banners, did blow up trumpets and set upon them'. Shooting was quickly superseded by hand-to-hand fighting, but so thick was the mist that they did not realize that the two armies were not exactly opposite each other and that Warwick's right wing, under

Oxford, and Edward's right wing had little in front of them. Oxford, a Prince Rupert on foot, led his men with tremendous dash and, breaking through such opposition as there was, ran down the hill to Barnet, and the news that the battle was lost and the King killed was carried to London and beyond. In Barnet, Oxford's soldiers began looting, but he succeeded in collecting them and forced them to return up the hill to where the combatants continued to struggle in the fog. All was confusion, and the return of Oxford's men facing the wrong way caused sudden panic in Warwick's army. Montagu went down fighting, Warwick was killed 'fleeing somewhat', and the battle was over.

Though the action had lasted for over three hours it was still only eight o'clock in the morning. Edward refreshed himself briefly in Barnet, ordered that the wounded should be attended to and then rode to London, where Cardinal Bourchier[2] was in St Paul's ready to combine a thanksgiving for victory with the Easter celebration. It must have been a macabre occasion. When Edward and his knights stalked up the aisle, fresh from the battlefield, everyone knew that there would inevitably be another battle which might end in a different way. And casualties had been heavy. The fog had produced freakish results, and Edward had lost some loyal friends. Lord Say (who had fled with him to Flanders) and Lord Cromwell[3] were dead, and so was Sir Humphrey Bourchier[4] who, according to Paston *major*, was 'a sore mourned man'. Sir William Blount[5] was wounded and died later, and Lord Howard's son was badly wounded but recovered.[6] Gloucester and Anthony were slightly wounded. Two Gascon gentlemen who had commanded the mercenaries were also killed, 'and many other good knights and squires, good yeoman and many other menial servants of the King'.

Warwick's supporters had not fared too badly, and Oxford and his brothers had managed to escape into the fog. The Duke of Exeter was wounded, stripped, and left for dead. 'He was little known' and his

---

[2] Archbishop Bourchier became a cardinal in 1467. Archbishop Neville had hoped to be the recipient of this honour but Edward persuaded the Pope to give it to Bourchier.

[3] Humphrey Bourchier, Lord Cromwell. Third son of the Earl of Essex.

[4] Sir Humphrey Bourchier, son and heir of Lord Berners.

[5] Sir William Blount, son and heir of Lord Mountjoy.

[6] Thomas Howard (1443–1524), Earl of Surrey 1483, and afterwards 2nd Duke of Norfolk. Educated at Thetford Grammar School.

body was unrecognized; he was rescued by his servants and smuggled into St Martin's sanctuary, a refuge which he afterwards exchanged for the greater comfort of an apartment in the Tower where he lived with a chaplain, a cook and a number of servants.[7]

The day after the battle, the corpses of Warwick and Montagu were brought to St Paul's where they lay in state, so that all could see that they were truly dead, and then they were decently interred in the family burial place at Bisham Abbey.[8] The name of 'Kingmaker' has stuck to Warwick and given him a certain posthumous fame, but the story of the two noble brothers slain together as they battled in the fog failed to catch the popular fancy. The Nevilles' prestige had depended entirely on their success, and when they failed their glamour vanished leaving nothing behind.

DURING THE PREVIOUS AUTUMN when Edward was in exile, Paston *minor* had been very cock-a-hoop; his 'good lord' was now the Earl of Oxford who, impetuous in everything, was ready to assist the Pastons in their quarrels. On 12 October 1470, Paston told his mother that his late patrons, the Duke and Duchess of Norfolk, sued to Oxford 'as humbly as ever I did to them. . . . My master the Earl of Oxford bids me ask and have. I trow my brother Sir John shall have the constable-ship of Norwich Castle with £20 of fee; all the lords be agreed to it.'

Unfortunately Oxford's patronage caused the Pastons to fight at Barnet on the losing side, and four days after the battle, on 18 April, Paston *major*, a semi-prisoner, was writing to their mother to let her know that his brother was alive although he had been wounded by an arrow in his right arm below the elbow. The surgeon reported that the wound was not serious. One of his brother's men, John Mylsent, was dead, God have mercy on his soul! but William Mylsent was alive and probably his other servants had all escaped. 'As for me, I am in good

[7] The Duke of Exeter had been born in the Tower when his father was the Governor.
[8] Bisham Abbey was destroyed at the Reformation and a dwelling-house built on the site. The Neville tombs were swept away, but an antiquarian must have discovered some remains, for two battered alabaster effigies believed to represent Warwick's parents are now in the parish church of Burghfield, Berkshire.

case, blessed be God, and in no jeopardy of my life.' His patron Archbishop Neville was in the Tower, but would probably 'do well enough'.
He gave a list of prominent people on both sides who were killed at
Barnet, estimated that there had been more than a thousand dead, and
passed on the news that Queen Margaret and her son had landed in the
west country and that King Edward would shortly set forth to 'drive
her out again'. He was still quite hopeful that Oxford's side would emerge
victorious, and he sent a warning to a cousin to be very careful as to
what he said, '. . . for the world I assure you is right queasy, as you shall
know within this month; the people here fear it sore. God has showed
Himself marvellously like Him that made all and can undo again when
him list; and I can think that, by all likelihood, shall show Himself as
marvellous again and that in short time. And, as I suppose, oftener than
once, in cases like.' He said he had lent his brother money and was now
short himself, and he reflected that, whoever won, the Pastons would
come through all right, concluding 'Be you not adoghted of the world,
for I trust all shall be well. If it thus continue I am not all undone, nor
none of us; and if otherwise, then etc.'

Paston *minor*'s wound healed quickly, and on 30 April he wrote to
his mother about money, clothes, horses and so on, adding, 'And if it
please you to have knowledge of our royal person, I thank God I am
whole of my sickness and trust to be clean whole of all my hurts within
a seven-night at the furthest.'

Unlike the Pastons, the Earl of Oxford had no thought of compromise; he was determined to battle on until he had dislodged Edward
from the throne. Escaping from Barnet, he eventually made his way up
to Scotland, but while he was still on the run in the south he sent his
wife an urgent letter which somehow found its way into the Pastons'
archives.

Right reverent and worshipful Lady, I recommend me to you, letting you weet that
I am in great heaviness at the making of this letter; but thanked be God, I am escaped myself; and suddenly departed from my men for I understand my chaplain would have
betrayed me—and if he come into the country let him be made sure etc. Also you shall
give credance to the bringer of this letter, and I beseech you to reward him to his costs, for
I was not in power at the making of this letter to give him [anything] but as I was put in
trust by favour of strange people etc.

Also you shall send me in all haste all the ready money that you can make, and as many
of my men as can come well horsed; and that they come in divers parcels. Also that my

horse be sent, with my steel saddles; and bid the yeoman of the horse cover them with leather.

Also you shall send to my mother and let her weet of this letter, and pray her of her blessing, and bid her send me my casket, by this token: that she hath the key thereof but it is broken.

Also you shall send to the Prior of Thetford and bid him send me the sum of gold that he said that I should have. Also say to him by this token: that I showed him the first privy seal etc.

Also let Paston, Fellbrigg, Brews, come to me. Also you shall deliver the bringer of this letter an horse, saddle and bridle.

Also you shall be of good cheer, and take no thought, for I shall bring my purpose about now by the grace of God, whom have you in keeping.

[Signed with a squiggle.]

MARGARET HAD EMBARKED AT HONFLEUR on 24 March 1471, but she was held up by bad weather and did not arrive at Weymouth until 13 April. She was now a woman of forty-two, she had been absent from England for eight years and she was as determined as ever to regain the crown. Her oddly assorted and (one might suppose) rather draggled party included her son Edward, Prince of Wales, who was seventeen: his fourteen-year-old wife, Anne Neville; Lord Wenlock, who was over seventy and had first seen war under Henry V; Sir John Langstrother, Prior of the military order of the Knights of St John; Doctor Morton, who was about fifty and had the most interesting part of his life still to come; and the famous judge, Sir John Fortescue, who was getting on for eighty. The soldiers they had brought with them were mainly French mercenaries.

The Countess of Warwick (aged forty-four) had come over on another ship which had put in at Portsmouth, and she had reached Southampton when she heard that her husband had been killed in battle. Whether she had loved him is unknown now, and was immaterial then; what mattered was that she was without a protector and that her vast estates had reverted to her and that she was once more a marriageable heiress. This she understood extremely well, and she quickly slipped into the inviolable sanctuary at Beaulieu Abbey which was conveniently near.

On Monday, 15 April, Margaret and her party moved inland to Cerne Abbas, the abbey where Doctor Morton had been educated, and here they were met by the semi-royal cousins, Edmund Duke of

174

Somerset and his brother John Beaufort, and John Courtenay, Earl of Devon. These three had just come from Salisbury, a town which had promised them forty soldiers (soldiers which were afterwards sent to Edward), and they brought the news of the Battle of Barnet. To Wenlock the death of Warwick was a disaster, but the others may have been able to persuade themselves that it was a blessing in disguise. Edmund Duke of Somerset had fought with the Burgundian army, and he appears to have been the ablest general of his family; the faithful Jasper was collecting an army in Wales; Courtenay's dependants in Devonshire were ready to rise at his call; and so, not unduly depressed, they set out for Exeter on a recruiting tour. After Exeter, they visited Wells where the soldiers looted the Bishop's palace and broke open his gaol—yet one more mysterious incident in the life of Bishop Stillington.

IMMEDIATELY AFTER THE BATTLE OF BARNET, Edward disbanded his English soldiers; letters summoning fresh men were sent out on Tuesday, and by the following Friday, 19 April, he was at Windsor assembling a new army. Somerset did not intend to risk an engagement until he had joined up with Jasper, but he ingeniously kept Edward guessing by sending small detachments here and there as though he meant to go through the southern counties to Kent or through Reading to London. Edward, determined not to leave open the road to London, celebrated St George's Day in the Garter Chapel at Windsor, and then moved cautiously first to Abingdon and then to Cirencester. His scouts were busy, but it is quite possible that he had not yet discovered that Jasper was in Wales, and he evidently expected Somerset to attack immediately—as he himself would have done in his place. On the night of Tuesday, 30 April, he made his army sleep out in the fields in readiness for a battle in the morning, but when day broke there was no sign of his opponents.

Somerset and the Queen had dodged back through Bath to Bristol, where they obtained both men and guns—the Recorder of Bristol was an enthusiastic supporter and joined their army himself. On Thursday, 2 May, they started on a dash north to join up with Jasper, who was separated from them by the wide River Severn. Edward erroneously suspected that Somerset intended to fight him near Sodbury, and his suspicion became almost a certainty when the King's quartermasters, who had gone on ahead to secure billets in Sodbury, were set on by some of Somerset's men who had laid an ambush in the town while the main body of the army hurried on to Berkeley. Edward, completely nonplussed, encamped on Sodbury Hill, while his scouts attempted to locate the enemy. This was the night of Thursday, 2 May.

'Early in the morning, soon after three of the clock, the King had certain tidings that they had taken their way to Berkeley towards Gloucester.' At once a council of war was called. Edward had been deceived, and he now understood that Somerset was racing to Gloucester where there was a bridge across the Severn.[9] It was too late to overtake them, but a messenger was sent to the Governor of Gloucester with the command that he was on no account to permit them to enter the town or cross the river and when Somerset and his army arrived at Gloucester in the middle of the morning—having come the fourteen miles from Berkeley since daybreak—they found the gates shut against them. Edward was close behind them and, hot and weary, they had no alternative but to hurry on.

The next town upstream was Tewkesbury; here there was only a ferry, but they were too tired to go further. The majority of the men were foot-soldiers, but even 'them that were horsemen were right weary of that journey and so were their horses', particularly as they had had to struggle through 'a foul country, all in lanes and strong ways, betwixt woods, without any good refreshing'.

Edward's army followed a track that was on high ground, and which ran parallel to the road taken by Somerset in the valley, and the writer of *The Arrivall* vividly remembered the exhausting day he spent trailing along in the rear.

The King, the same morning, the Friday early, advanced his banners and divided his whole host in three battles, and sent before him his fore-riders and scourers, on every side of him, and so, in fair array and order, he took his way through the champaign country called Cotswold, travelling all his people, whereof were more than three thousand footmen that Friday, which was right-an-hot day, thirty mile and more; which his people might not find, in all the way, horse-meat nor man's meat, nor so much as drink for their horses,

---

[9] Gloucester remained the first point at which the Severn could be crossed by road until 1967, when the great bridge was opened near Chepstow.

save in one little brook,[1] where was full little relief, it was so soon troubled with the carriages that had passed it. And all that day was evermore the King's host within five or six miles of his enemies; he in plain [open] country and they among woods; having always good espials upon them. So continuing that journey till he came with all his host to a village called Chiltenham,[2] but five miles from Tewkesbury.

Here they learnt that Somerset had halted at Tewkesbury, and had taken up a position on the edge of the town where he intended to give battle; and so, after a brief pause during which such provisions as they had brought with them were doled out, they marched on again and camped at Tredington, a village three miles from Tewkesbury. By this time they had marched thirty-five miles.[3]

The next morning, Saturday 4 May, Edward 'advanced directly upon his enemies'. His aim was to win a victory which would be absolutely final, and doubtless word was passed down the line that prisoners were not required and that anyone who looked like an officer should be knocked down and killed.

Somerset had chosen a strong defensive position and had drawn up his army 'in a close, even at the town's end, the town and the Abbey at their backs; before them and upon every hand of them foul lanes and deep dykes and many hedges with hills and valleys; a right evil place to approach as could well have been devised'. Edward Prince of Wales was in the centre; he had been brought up to believe that one day he would win England by his sword, and now the day had arrived. Wenlock supported him. Courtenay commanded the left wing and Somerset the right.

On the King's side, Edward took the centre, Gloucester the left wing and Hastings the right. (Anthony had been left behind to defend London.) Psychologically they had the advantage. They had recently defeated the famous Earl of Warwick; Edward had never lost a battle; Hastings was well known and much liked, and the young Duke of Gloucester was a promising prince: while the leaders on the other side had no reputation except Wenlock who, rightly or wrongly, was neither liked nor trusted. The Queen's army had fewer guns than their

[1] The River Frome.

[2] Cheltenham is nine miles from Tewkesbury.

[3] See Burne, *The Battlefields of England*. He reckons that in three days both armies had covered precisely the same distance, fifty-nine miles.

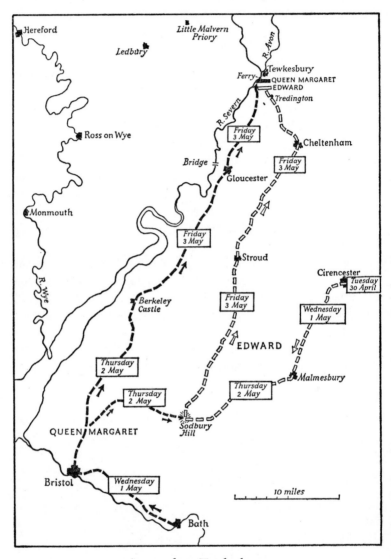

Approach to Tewkesbury

opponents and, on top of all, they had been trying to escape for days and now were only standing at bay because they were too tired to go further.

Somerset did his best. He placed his men among the trees and scrub, and he discovered a hidden path by which he could lead a party

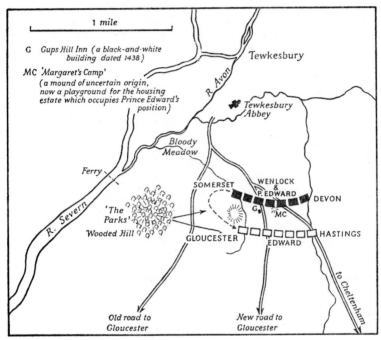

Battle of Tewkesbury

of his men round the end of Gloucester's wing, and this manœuvre— had it succeeded—might have caused such confusion that it could have tipped the battle in his favour. Unfortunately for Somerset, Edward (who was said to be a lucky commander) had noticed some way off on the same side a wooded knoll which he thought might conceal an ambush, and he detailed two hundred mounted spearmen to explore this wood and, if they found no ambush, to act on their own initiative.

The battle began with the usual exchange of fire and then Edward's soldiers tried to close with the enemy, but they were impeded by the hedges and scrub. Somerset's party crept round the by-lanes according to plan and they were about to fall on Gloucester's flank when the mounted spearmen, who had found nothing in the wood, caught sight of them and charged down. Taken by surprise, sandwiched between the spearmen and Gloucester's wing, Somerset and his men panicked and rushed back towards the town. With Somerset in flight morale collapsed, and the whole army turned and ran. The rout became a massacre. Many were drowned in the Avon, others killed in a field which is still known as Bloody Meadow. There were no prisoners.

The Arrivall states that 'Edward called Prince was taken fleeing to the townwards and slain in the field' and baldly adds that Courtenay, John Beaufort and Wenlock were also slain.[4]

Somerset managed to get back to the town alive and, with a crowd of fugitives, took refuge in the Abbey. As Prince Edward was dead, he could have put himself forward as the heir to the throne and it was out of the question to leave him alive. Hundreds of men had been killed that morning, and hundreds more would be killed if he was set free to raise fresh armies. Technically the Abbey had no particular rights of sanctuary and, though they felt uneasy, Edward's soldiers swarmed into the building and dragged out everyone they found hiding inside, to the fury of the Abbey authorities who considered the building polluted and unfit for divine service until it had been purified.

It was no time for squeamishness. There was a rising in the north and, though they did not yet know it, London was about to be attacked by the Bastard of Fauconberg. The common soldiers were released; they belonged to no faction and would do no further harm. Somerset was the man who mattered, and on Monday he and seventeen others— including Sir John Longstrother, the Recorder of Bristol and a mason of Westminster—were tried before the Constable of England and the Earl Marshal, found guilty and executed in the market square of Tewkesbury. The Constable who undertook the task was the eighteen-year-old Richard Duke of Gloucester, and the hereditary Earl Marshal was the feeble Duke of Norfolk, who is only now remembered because he sent his men to besiege the Pastons in Caister Castle. The whole

---

[4] The stories told about the deaths of Prince Edward and Wenlock appear to be later inventions.

business was an unpleasant necessity, and the heads were not stuck up on spikes. Prince Edward and the others who were of note were buried in or around the Abbey, except for Sir John Longstrother whose body was put in a lead coffin and sent to the church of the Knights of St John in London. Shame, however, was tempered by elation: at one swoop four men claiming to be heirs to Henry VI had been removed from the world.

There was no respite for the conquerors and on Monday 6 May, the same day that Somerset was executed, Clarence was again writing to Henry Vernon. Fresh armies had to be raised to march against the rebels in the north, and Clarence tried to entice his friend to join him by mentioning that Prince Edward and Courtenay had been killed and Somerset executed. On Tuesday the King himself wrote, asking Vernon to bring twenty men to Coventry, and on Wednesday he wrote from Worcester pointing out that though Margaret had been captured and Prince Edward, Somerset and Courtenay were dead there was still a rising in the north. On Friday Clarence wrote, half pleading and half bullying, and reiterating that though Margaret was captured and Prince Edward, Somerset, John Beaufort and Courtenay were dead it was essential that he should join them. His excuses for not coming before would be accepted 'and you shall find us your good lord'. Even this had no effect on Henry Vernon.[5]

Queen Margaret had probably slipped across the Severn by Tewkesbury ferry before the battle began, and she was not discovered till Tuesday 7 May when she was found in 'a poor religious place' which may have been Little Malvern Priory.[6] With her was a sad little party; her French lady-in-waiting Catherine (who had married an English knight, Sir William Vaux), Anne Neville and the Countess of Devon, each of whom had lost her husband in the battle. Margaret was taken

[5] Henry Vernon's career was not damaged by his caution. He became a squire of the body to Edward IV, got into trouble for brawling, took no notice of a summons from Richard III to fight at Bosworth, was a rather slack Controller of the Household to Arthur Prince of Wales, was knighted, and lent money to Henry VII. The upper class was very small and it is no surprise to find that Henry Vernon and Paston *minor* shared an annual ten marks raised on a Derbyshire manor and granted to them in 1468 by John Mowbray Duke of Norfolk.

[6] Little Malvern Priory church has a rather battered stained-glass window representing Edward IV and his family which was put up by Bishop Alcock about 1482.

to Edward at Coventry; if they had ever met before it must have been years earlier when he was a boy, and there is no record of what the two found to say to each other on this occasion.

As soon as the result of the Battle of Tewkesbury was known, the Earl of Northumberland announced that he was on the side of King Edward and the rising in the North collapsed; he then excited surprise by arriving in Coventry with only a small escort and without his armour, as though the troubles were over. It turned out afterwards that Edward had fought his last battle, but at the time nothing was certain and news came in that London was being attacked by the Bastard of Fauconberg and an army said to number 17,000 men. Edward at once sent on an advance guard of 1500 men and followed after them as soon as he could.

The Bastard of Fauconberg's rebellion was the last fling of the Nevilles. Since the previous May, when he left Lord Howard's fleet, he had been a kind of pirate, sometimes allying himself with his cousin Warwick and sometimes acting on his own, and he had even been so irresponsible as to attack ships belonging to England's old allies, the Portuguese. While Edward was occupied on the other side of England, he came up the Thames with his fleet and anchored at St Katherine's, just below the Tower, while at the same time the Mayor of Canterbury, Nicholas Faunt, brought to the south bank a large and bellicose contingent of the Men of Kent. He also had the assistance of numbers of foreign adventurers and a few peasants from Essex who (according to the *Great Chronicle*) were dissatisfied with the prices which they received in London for their farm produce. The Bastard's nominal purpose was to reinstate Henry VI, but it may not be over-cynical to suspect that he and Archbishop Neville planned to become joint dictators.

Fauconberg's attack was extremely frightening for the people of London. Anthony and the Earl of Essex had been left in charge of the defences, and old Lord Dudley[7] was Constable of the Tower, but their soldiers were few. Fauconberg's ships fired their guns at the Tower (which sheltered the Queen and her children, and a variety of prisoners)

[7] John Sutton, Lord Dudley (1400–87).

and the Tower guns replied. On 12 May the Men of Kent tried to rush London Bridge but were repulsed; then the Bridge was set on fire and all the houses on the south side of the drawbridge were burnt. Lives were lost, property destroyed, prisoners taken. There were also traitors within the City walls, some of them genuine partisans of Henry VI and the Nevilles, and some of them poor people 'who would have been right glad of a common robbery'.

The writer of *The Arrivall* must have got this part of his story second-hand and, from a certain similarity in the narratives, it would seem that his chief informant was the Croyland Continuator, a man who was more inclined to deflate than exaggerate, and whose account of London's week of terror is likely to be fairly near the truth.

Unable to get across the Thames at London Bridge, Fauconberg led his men upstream to Kingston where there was an unguarded bridge, but Anthony sent boat-loads of soldiers up the river and Fauconberg dared not cross it for fear of being cut off from his line of retreat. Returning to his ships, he ferried his soldiers across to the north side of the Thames and then he attacked the City walls on the east at Aldgate and Bishopsgate.

The inhabitants of London were now united by anger, and the peers and gentry organized a force of volunteers to defend the gates. Anthony led a dashing sortie from the north postern of the Tower and fell on the rear of the rebels attacking Aldgate, 'and so killed and took many of them, driving them from the same gate to the waterside. Yet nevertheless [in] three places fires were burning all at once.'

The rebels then recrossed the Thames and camped at Blackheath for three days, from 16 to 18 May when, having no further plans and hearing that Edward was approaching with 30,000 men, Fauconberg abandoned his ambitious enterprise. The rebels dispersed; 'they of Calais, to Calais the soonest they could; such as were of other countries into theirs; many of Kent to their houses; the mariners, and mischievous robbers, rebels and rioters with them, to their ships, and drew down to the sea coast.'

On 21 May Edward re-entered London at the head of a large army which proved to be no longer needed. It was a kind of victory parade, and somewhere in the procession was the unhappy Margaret who had played high and lost all. This was Edward's third triumphant entry in six weeks, but too much blood had flowed too recently for it to be a merry occasion, and there had been so many convulsions in recent memory that no one could feel much confidence about the future. Edward knighted the Mayor, the aldermen and the Recorder, and once more resumed his reign.

Fauconberg's attack on London had sealed the death warrant of Henry VI; had any doubt existed, it had proved only too clearly that while he lived unscrupulous men would make insurrections in his name and, soon after Edward arrived in London, Henry died in the Tower. He was forty-nine and, from the accident of having been born a little sub-normal, he had caused much fighting, murder and general anarchy in the country which had had the misfortune to accept him as its baby king nearly half a century before. According to *The Arrivall*, he died of shock when he was told of the reverses which his party had suffered, 'not having before that knowledge of the said matters, he took it to so great despite, ire and indignation that of pure displeasure and melancholy he died the twenty-third day of the month of May'.

There is a rule known to novelists that only unfortunate coincidences can be introduced into a story because readers will not believe in lucky ones, and Henry's demise was so convenient for Edward that everyone assumed that he had not died a natural death. If we too make this assumption, we can hardly doubt that the decision to liquidate Henry was taken with the tacit approval of Edward's Council of War. Its members were used to hangings and executions, they had just seen the corpses of hundreds of strong young men, their hearts were sore for the death of friends, and one more death did not count for much; there would be no peace in England till Henry was dead. Edward could have vetoed the sentence, but he had been through a long period of danger and acute anxiety and he entirely agreed with it. The killing of prisoners excited public disapproval only if the victims were of very high rank, and to kill a king was bound to be unfavourably criticized, but the men responsible for his death are unlikely to have regretted it afterwards, although they would not wish to appear to be connected with it.

Gloucester was Constable of England, and it was probably his duty to make the arrangements, but there is no reason for saying that he witnessed the deed although in later years when he had acquired a sinister reputation by ordering the execution of Hastings, Anthony, Richard Grey and the Duke of Buckingham and contriving the disappearance of his young nephews, it was commonly said that he stabbed Henry with his own hand—a violent action which would not seem to be at all in character.

Once Henry was safely dead the people of London, who had taken no interest in him during his lifetime, could afford to be sentimental; a murdered king appeals to the crudest and most facile emotions, and in a short time he was being venerated as a saint. The body was exposed to public scrutiny in St Paul's, and then taken up river to be buried in Chertsey Abbey. Inevitably the story became current that the corpse had displayed the authentic signs of murder by bleeding, first at St Paul's and afterwards at Blackfriars, while Chertsey, a pleasant outing from London, drew a stream of pilgrims till 1484 when Richard III had the remains moved to St George's, Windsor, where the elegant almsbox can still be seen. In later times Henry VII contemplated transferring the coffin to Westminster Abbey, a suggestion hotly resented both by the authorities at Windsor and the monks at Chertsey who made a bid to regain their former money-spinner. Henry VII also requested the Pope to canonize his step-uncle[8] but he died before he was able to push the matter through.

In 1910 George V gave permission for Henry's remains to be examined, and some writers now make the assertion that it was proved that Henry was clubbed on the head. This might seem to be an odd way to kill a man when it is desirable that he should seem to have died from natural causes, and whose corpse will be put on view, and those who take the trouble to read the original report of the exhumation will find that nothing of the sort came to light.[9]

Henry VI had no visible tomb, but there was a traditional burial-place in St George's Chapel, and this was opened up on 4 November 1910 by workmen in the presence of the antiquarian W. H. St John

[8] Similar requests in the twentieth century were equally unsuccessful.
[9] W. H. St John Hope, 'The Discovery of the Remains of King Henry VI', in *Archaeologia*, vol. LXII.

Hope, the Dean of Windsor, the Provost of Eton College (Dr Warre), the Provost of King's College, Cambridge (Dr M. R. James), the Cambridge Professor of Anatomy (Dr Macalister), three canons, a verger, and the architect and surveyor of St George's Chapel.

The vault had been filled in with rubble, but they were able to recognize the metal corners of what had once been a six-foot coffin, now rotted away. In the centre of these was a somewhat dilapidated plain lead box. Inside the lead box was a very decayed wooden one, with a sliding lid; it was three foot, three-and-a-half inches long, ten inches wide and nine inches deep, and crammed into this was a quantity of old bones mixed with fragments of cloth and rubble. Dr Macalister put the bones together and wrote a short account of them.

The skeleton, he reported, had clearly been dismembered before it was put in the box. Not all the bones were there, and the right arm was completely missing. On the other hand, there was the unexpected addition of the left humerus of a small pig. The three teeth found were much worn and the only bit of jaw had lost its teeth some time before death. The bones of the head were much damaged, but seemed thin and light and the skull, though well shaped, was small in proportion to the body. He thought the bones were those of a fairly strong man between forty-five and fifty-five, and five foot nine or ten inches tall. 'I am sorry I can add nothing more. The state of the bones was so unsatisfactory that I could not make any trustworthy measurements.'

The antiquarian, W. H. St John Hope, added that the bones were moist and mixed with rubbish and adipocere[1] and that he discovered a piece of skull to which was attached some brown hair stained with what he decided (quite arbitrarily) was blood, and from this has grown the legend that Henry was hit on the head.

The body was then reburied, and nothing had been proved except that the monks of Chertsey had been in the habit of selling bones as relics.

QUEEN MARGARET, HAVING LOST HER HUSBAND and her son, was no longer dangerous; nobody wanted her, least of all her father who had married

---

[1] A fatty substance resulting from the decomposition of animal bodies in damp conditions.

a young wife for love and, having abandoned Anjou and imperial ambitions, now lived in Provence where he devoted himself to a life of Watteauesque gaiety; he was very fond of his illegitimate daughters, and the Jews gladly financed his extravagances in exchange for favours and privileges. Margaret was moved from the Tower to Windsor and then to Wallingford Castle,[2] one of the largest and finest of the King's castles and wonderfully suitable in every way. Political prisoners had often been confined in it, and it had also been inhabited by royal ladies; Isabella, wife of Edward II, had lived at Wallingford; it had been done up for the widow of the Black Prince, and again for Catherine of France, and when Henry VI was a boy he had used it as a summer palace. Furthermore, the post of Constable of Wallingford was generally held by a member of the family of her old friend, Alice, Duchess of Suffolk,[3] whose manor of Ewelme was only two or three miles away. Margaret still had her lady-in-waiting, Catherine Vaux, as well as attendants called 'Petronilla and Mary', and her physical surroundings were made as comfortable as possible, but her son was gone, her hopes were gone, her power and prestige were gone. She who had been a queen and had bargained with kings, had raised armies and won battles, was now a person of no account, and it is unlikely that even with sweet Thames flowing softly past her windows and the Dowager Duchess of Suffolk coming to call she was anything but bored and miserable.

EDWARD COULD ONLY SPEND A DAY OR TWO IN LONDON before pushing on into Kent. On 26 May he was at Canterbury, where the City Council hurriedly spent ninepence on three-quarters of a yard of white kersey from which to make white rose badges, a belated attempt to show their devotion to Edward which did not, however, prevent them from having to pay for the stupidity of attacking London by the loss of their Charter and the expense of buying a new one. There were probably some hangings—though, as usual, this point is very obscure.

[2] Little now remains of Wallingford Castle but a very large enclosure, some mounds and some stones.
[3] Alice herself had been Constable of Wallingford, and so had her father, husband and son.

Gloucester had gone straight to Sandwich where Fauconberg coolly awaited him and, unfair as it may seem, when Edward arrived Fauconberg was able to drive a good bargain; he surrendered his ships, his life was spared, and in the middle of June he and Gloucester went north together. It is not clear why his preposterous behaviour should have been so easily overlooked: perhaps Edward was ready to give another chance to an old friend, or perhaps his talent for leadership was too valuable to throw away; Montagu, who had guarded the Border for so long, was dead; the new Earl of Northumberland was no soldier, and Gloucester, though keen, was very young and inexperienced. But the attempt to turn poacher into game-keeper did not come off; Gloucester and he soon fell out, and by 15 September Paston *major* in London was writing to his brother: 'I understand that Bastard Fauconberg is either headed or like to be, and his brother also; some men say he would have deserved it and some say nay.' On 28 September Paston wrote: 'Item; Thomas Fauconberg's head was yesterday set upon London Bridge, looking into Kent-ward; and men say that his brother was sore hurt and escaped to sanctuary to Beverley.' There were still local disturbances and Paston added some third-hand gossip for what it was worth. 'Sir Thomas Fulford escaped out of Westminster [Sanctuary] with a hundred spears, as men say, and is into Devonshire, and there he has struck off Sir John Crocker's head, and killed another knight of the Courtenays, as men say'; after which he drifted into esoteric jesting about Mistress Elizabeth Higgens of the Black Swan and her daughter.

Edward returned to the capital as soon as he could, and a commission headed by Lord Dynham, Sir Thomas Bourchier and Sir John Fogge was entrusted with the task of levying fines on the rebels and convincing the Men of Kent that the power of the Nevilles was no more and that, in future, they would have to obey King Edward. Two captains who had led the attack on Aldgate were executed, and their heads sent to decorate the very gate they had tried to capture, and the Mayor of Canterbury, Nicholas Faunt, was hanged, drawn and quartered at the end of July; but for most people it was a question of buying pardons, and ruefully readjusting their political allegiances.

Calais and Guisnes also had to be brought into line. Warwick had been in command of Calais, on and off, for some fifteen years, but fortunately there was Hastings, loyal and capable, to take it over.

Several months passed before control of south Wales was regained. There was no good substitute for Lord Herbert, and Jasper was able to defend himself in Chepstow Castle, and then to retreat to Pembroke Castle. Here he held out until he saw that it was useless and then, taking his nephew Henry Tudor with him, he embarked at Tenby, meaning to sail to France but, through some contretemps, landing in Brittany. Duke Francis bore them no ill-will, but they were valuable prisoners who might come in useful one day, so he kept them in semi-captivity and refused to give them up to anyone. Jasper, who had in the past dedicated all his courage, energy and ingenuity to the cause of Henry VI, Queen Margaret and Prince Edward, now transferred his devotion to his nephew, and from then onwards he worked ceaselessly, secretly and eventually successfully, to place him on the English throne. Meanwhile Henry Tudor continued to lead the same constricted life that he had always done; he was in a castle in Brittany instead of in a castle in Wales, but he was at least safe.

CONTINENTAL RULERS WERE COMPLETELY BEWILDERED by the twists and turns of events in England, particularly as they had persistently over-rated Warwick and underrated Edward. In the January of 1471 the Duke of Milan had tried to send a spy to England under cover of buying horses, but the man had been stopped on his way through Burgundy and his presents to Henry and Margaret impounded. A second spy fared even worse; he had started on 16 April with a letter congratulating Henry VI on the recovery of his kingdom and apologizing for the absence of presents, but by 23 June he had got no further than Paris. He had instructions to buy horses and dogs, English stirrups and horn, and was quite ready to go on to Ireland 'where all the best hackneys come from', but the Milanese ambassador to France advised him not to set out as it might possibly be suspected 'that he is going for something besides dogs and harness'. This ambassador confessed that English politics defeated him. 'I wish the country and the people were plunged deep in the sea because of their lack of stability, for I feel like one going to the torture when I write about them, and no one ever hears twice alike about English affairs.'

For a long time Louis refused to believe that Warwick had been defeated. As usual, merchants received news before court officials. Warwick had been killed on 14 April, and on 26 April an Italian merchant in Bruges was writing to tell his father that he had met three men who had actually seen the bodies of Warwick and Montagu lying in state in St Paul's, and in his next letter he remarked that the death of Warwick might help Queen Margaret as so many people had disliked him. But long after that, on 18 May, the Milanese ambassador at the French court was seriously reporting that Louis had just had a letter from Queen Margaret saying that Warwick was wounded and recuperating in hiding, and that the Prince of Wales was in London with a large following. On 26 May another envoy reported news was difficult to get, as the Burgundians, Bretons and Easterlings controlled the sea, and that two friars asserted that the Prince of Wales was flourishing and that Warwick was not dead—but no one believed them.

It was a whole month after the Battle of Tewkesbury, on 2 June, that the Milanese ambassador wrote to say that on the previous day Louis had heard that the Prince of Wales had been killed in a battle near Wales, that the Queen had been sent to join Henry, and that Edward was without a rival. The Duke of Burgundy's joy could be imagined. He had shown it by public demonstrations, constant processions, ringing of bells, and bonfires so that one would think the whole country was on fire. On 17 June the report was that both Henry and Margaret had been assassinated in the Tower, but on 19 June an Italian agent at Grenoble wrote: 'Today they say that the Earl of Warwick is alive and victorious. We have such different reports that I cannot possibly find out the truth.'

By 16 July Louis had at last accepted the unpleasant fact that Edward was once more King of England, and he fell back on his old tactics of trying to incite the Scots to invade England. The Duke of Milan had had much the same idea and his ambassador wrote back to him, 'His Majesty thoroughly approves of the suggestion of your Highness about it being desirable to keep up some disturbances in England. He says he is doing so with all his might.'

Edward IV. (Windsor Castle)
It is possible that this portrait was drawn from life.

Margaret of Anjou (Victoria and Albert Museum)
Gilt bronze medal, made 1462/3 by Pietro di Milano

Louis XI (British Museum)
Bronze medal by F. Laurana (Enlarged)

James III of Scotland and his son, afterwards James IV. (National Gallery of Scotland). Detail from the wing of an altarpiece commissioned in Flanders from Hugo van der Goes? in 1478. The faces were probably painted in Scotland.

AROLVS · DVX · BVRGV

Charles the Bold, Duke of Burgundy. (Musée de Dijon)

Elizabeth Woodville. An early Tudor copy of a lost original.
(Queens' College, Cambridge)

Ludlow, from an early Georgian painting.
To the left is the bridge over which Edward and his
friends escaped unseen.

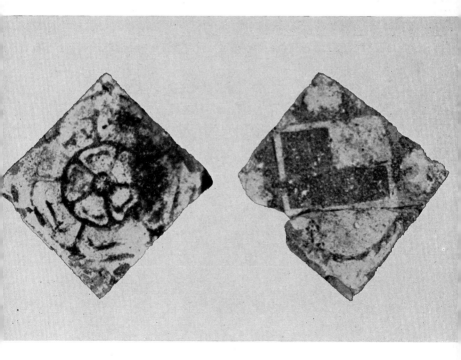

Tiles excavated near Grafton Regis.
On one is a white rose and on the other is a shield with the Woodville arms. They
were part of the floor of a small chapel and perhaps marked the site of the
marriage of Edward IV and Elizabeth Woodville.

Pontefract Castle, Yorkshire, *c.* 1630.
(Pontefract Public Library)

Bamburgh Castle, Northumberland.
(A recent photograph by Alexander Knox)

The Treaty of Picquigny, 1475. (St George's Chapel Windsor)

Misericord under the seat of the Sovereign's Garter stall. On the right Edward stands in front of his tent. On the left Louis emerges from his castle. In the centre the two kings meet on the bridge. The head of Louis has been knocked off but otherwise the carving is in excellent condition.

St George's Chapel, Windsor, looking west.
Begun by Edward IV in 1473 and finished by Henry VIII
in 1528.

XII

Edward Resumes His Reign 1471-1474

TEN YEARS HAD NOW PASSED SINCE EDWARD HAD FIRST BEEN crowned, and they had been years of dangers, rebellions, battles, sudden changes of fortune, flights and returns: he was to reign for nearly twelve years more and, although holding many anxious moments, they were to be, by comparison, almost placid. Once Warwick was dead there was no question as to who was the ruler of England, and the possible pretenders to the throne—Clarence, Henry Tudor, Duke Charles of Burgundy, the Duke of Buckingham, the Duke of Exeter—were never given a chance of putting an army in the field, and the raids of the Earl of Oxford were small and abortive.

In the reorganized Court many faces were missing, and several rising men were able to consolidate their position. Hastings continued to be Edward's most intimate friend, and for the rest of the reign he was the best-known and best-liked member of the peerage. Among the new peers, the most conspicuous was Lord Howard. Ageless, tireless, versatile and immensely capable, he could lead a naval foray, negotiate at a foreign court, or turn his mind to accounts: he was also honest in the sense that he was not a double-crosser, and the reason that he had had to struggle so long before getting his head out of the crowd may well have been that Edward recognized that his ambitions were so great that he was potentially dangerous. Howard was already growing rich, and Edward was unwilling that he should become any richer. On the other hand Lord Stanley,[1] another rising man, was considered so harmless he was allowed to become the fourth husband of Margaret, Countess of Richmond, who had again become a widow. It was certainly not a marriage of passion and Margaret's confessor, Bishop Fisher, when he preached her funeral sermon, thought fit to proclaim to the congregation that soon after her last wedding she had taken a vow of chastity.

Judge Fortescue and Doctor Morton, finding that their party had ceased to exist, offered their services to King Edward. Fortescue was too old to take any further part in public affairs, but he still possessed his intellectual faculties and, besides sending in the usual formula to the effect that he was truly contrite, he dashed off a treatise[2] confessing that he had made a mistake when he wrote that Edward's ancestress Philippa was illegitimate. This recantation bought him a pardon and he retired to Ebrington, his manor high up in the Cotswolds (by a happy chance it had been given to Wenlock and so could now be returned to him), and he spent the last years of his life in pastoral surroundings, composing or up-dating his famous work, *The Governance of England*, the first book on the constitution to be written in the English language.

Doctor Morton was only middle-aged and still extremely active; his cleverness was valuable and his political career, interrupted by ten years in the wilderness, was smoothly resumed; by 1473 he was Master of the Rolls and by 1479 he was Bishop of Ely.

There were also some falls, and among the men who overreached themselves was Bishop Stillington. At Edward's restoration he again became Chancellor, and on 8 April 1473 he acted in his official capacity and prorogued Parliament. Two months later he was disgraced and removed from office, and in 1475 he was summoned to Rome to face accusations the nature of which are so far undiscovered, although there may be relevant papers in the Vatican archives.

---

[1] Thomas, Lord Stanley (1435–1504). Earl of Derby, 1485. Married (1) Eleanor Neville, sister of the Earl of Warwick; (2) Margaret, Countess of Richmond. He was very rich indeed and owned much land in Cheshire and south Lancashire. From 1471 he was Steward of the Household.

[2] Sir John Fortescue, *Declaration upon Certain Writings sent out of Scotland*.

Archbishop Neville was another man whose intrigues led to his downfall. He was as guilty as any of the rebels who had fought and died, and Edward would have been insane to trust him, but he was granted a pardon and, secure in the knowledge that he could not be executed without shocking the public, and that he could not be deprived of his Archbishopric except with the consent of the Pope, he went back to his former way of life, entertaining magnificently at The Moor. In January 1472 Paston *major*, who had spent the beginning of Christmas with his uncle and aunt in Surrey, finished the 'twelve days' at the Archbishop's palace, 'where I have had as great cheer and been as welcome as I could devise'. Paston was still obsessed by the determination to get back Caister Castle from the Duke of Norfolk and, having lost the Earl of Oxford, he was looking for another patron who would support his claim. Archbishop Neville was probably in correspondence with Oxford, who was financed by Louis and who was known to be planning an invasion, but Paston was not in the secret and he was astonished when, at the end of April, the Archbishop was suddenly arrested and hurried across the Channel to the Castle of Hammes.

In Warkworth's unreliable chronicle there is a story that Edward entertained the Archbishop at Windsor and invited himself to dinner at The Moor. The Archbishop brought out his valuables from their hiding-places and borrowed plate from his neighbours, whereupon Edward arrested the Archbishop and confiscated all the plate. Warkworth disliked nearly everyone, and though he thought this trick reflected no great credit on Edward he also felt that it served the Archbishop right.

The equally unreliable chronicle known as *Hearne's Fragment* has quite a different version of the incident. According to this writer, Edward went to dinner at The Moor and before supper he was warned that there were a hundred men-at-arms ready to kidnap him, 'whereupon the King, faining himself to make his water, caused a good horse to be saddled and so with a small company rode to Windsor'.

Paston's account has no embroidery. 'My Lord Archbishop was brought to the Tower on Saturday at night,' he wrote on 30 April 1472, 'and on Monday at midnight he was conveyed to a ship and so into the sea, and as yet I cannot understand whither he is sent nor what is befallen of him; men say that he has offended . . . some men say nay.' In

spite of the disruption of his own plans[3] Paston could not help enjoying
the discomfiture of the stuck-up scholars who frequented The Moor.
'But all his meinie are dispersed, every man his way; and some that are
great clerks and famous doctors of his, go now again to Cambridge to
school. . . .'[4] The Countess of Oxford is still in St Martin's. I hear no
word of her.'[5] Perplexed, Paston resolved to take the safe course and to
attach himself to Hastings. 'And as for my Lord Chamberlain he is not
yet come to town; when he comes then shall I wot what to do.'

Paston *major* accordingly took service with Hastings, and went
happily backwards and forwards from London to Calais. He liked
working for Hastings and he looked on the warlike activities of his late
patron Oxford with a critical eye. On 16 April 1473 he wrote to his
brother from Canterbury, on the way to Calais: 'Item, the Earl of
Oxford was on Saturday at Dieppe and is purposed into Scotland with
a dozen ships. I mistrust that work.' Paston feared that he had been too
indulgent with his servants, who were now taking advantage of his
good nature. Four of them had let him down. The road was crowded
with soldiers coming home from Calais, and his baggage had arrived
two hours behind time but fortunately intact. 'Calais is a merry town.'
Some rich young people were going there and he was in high spirits.
On 3 June of the same year he was back in London and ready to start
for Calais again, except that he was held up for lack of men. 'Wherefore
if you know any likely men and fair conditioned and good archers, send
them to me, though it be four, and I will have them, and they shall have
four mark by year and my livery.'

The Earl of Oxford was incorrigible. He made raids on Calais,
toyed with the idea of launching an invasion from Scotland, landed in
Norfolk, moved off to Thanet, raided shipping. On 30 September 1473
his daring reached its height, and with his two brothers and Lord

---

[3] Archbishop Neville owed Paston *major* a thousand marks, not all of which he recovered. Paston *minor* blamed his uncle William for his brother's unwise investment and
in 1484 was trying to extract the last hundred pounds from his uncle.

[4] Among the scholars whom Archbishop Neville supported was a Greek scribe called
Emmanuel of Constantinople.

[5] The Countess of Oxford probably stayed in sanctuary until after her husband's
arrest in 1474. If she had been at liberty she would obviously have communicated with him.
Oxford's lands were mostly given to Gloucester, but eventually a small annuity was
settled on his wife.

Beaumont (an old friend)[6] he seized St Michael's Mount at the tip of Cornwall.

The occupation of St Michael's Mount was an act of folly. The castle had no strategic value, although its remoteness meant that some time elapsed before an effective siege was organized, and it was not till December that an energetic member of the Fortescue family was put in charge of the land operations and four ships were sent under the command of Edward Brampton (the Portuguese Jew) and one William Fetherston. Pardons were offered to the rank and file, and as it was disagreeable to pass the winter on a rocky island with no particular prospect of better times, Oxford presently found himself without a garrison and, on 17 February 1474, he was forced to surrender. He had bargained that his life should be spared, but he could not be left at large and, like Archbishop Neville, he was immured in the Castle of Hammes, and for the next decade the Earl of Oxford was hors de combat though events were to prove that ten years in prison did nothing to quench his fire.[7]

THE WOODVILLES STILL CLUTTERED THE ROYAL PALACES and, though there were no Nevilles to be jealous of them, the legend that the Woodvilles were low did not die. Now that the dangers which had united Edward's friends were relaxed, there was leisure for personal dislikes to grow into quarrels. The devotion of the Woodvilles to each other continued to be an annoyance and, a fresh irritation, Edward was very indulgent towards his elder stepson, Thomas Grey, afterwards Marquis of Dorset. Dorset had only just grown up, and had fought in no battles: he appears to have been an innocuous youth without any particular talents and perhaps Edward, who had taken on the burdens of kingship when he was eighteen, vicariously enjoyed the boyish pleasures of this callow

---

[6] William, 2nd Viscount Beaumont (1438–1507). Son of a prominent supporter of Henry VI. Taken prisoner at Towton and pardoned. Fought at Barnet and escaped. In 1487 he was mad and being looked after by Oxford. He died in Oxford's house at Wivenhoe, Essex, and Oxford married his widow.

[7] Fifty pounds a year was allowed for his keep. On 25 August 1478 Paston *major* reported that Oxford had jumped into the moat, either to escape or to drown himself. Archbishop Neville was released from Hammes in November 1474 and died in June 1476.

representative of a new era. We now know that the period which is called the Middle Ages,[8] and which had lasted for five hundred years, was coming to an end, and that another chapter of history was about to begin, but the people at the time must merely have thought that the younger generation was peculiarly decadent.

Anthony[9] continued to be a conspicuous figure at the Court. He was a perpetual knight-errant, exotic in England and a puzzle to foreigners who could not make out why Edward treated him as if he were of the blood royal when he was merely a member of the Queen's family which, they had been given to understand, was extremely low. Energetic in a crisis, he had no taste for court intrigues or for humdrum administration. In the summer of 1471, when Paston *minor* was still in prison after the Battle of Barnet, Margaret Paston approached Anthony and arranged a pardon without realizing that Anthony was trying to collect an escort to accompany him on a pilgrimage to St James of Compostela.[1] Her son wrote to her in some annoyance that he had been told 'that the Lord Scales had granted you to be my good lord, whereof I am nothing proud, for he may do least with the Great Master; but he would depart over the sea as hastily as he may. And because he weens that I would go with him, as I had promised him of yore an he had kept forth his journey at that time, this is the cause that he will be my good lord and help to get my pardon. The King is not best pleased with him for that he desires to depart, insomuch that the King has said of him that whensoever he has most to do, then the Lord Scales will soonest ask leave to depart and weens that it is most because of cowardice.' Paston added that to get a pardon he needed money, and that he had not been sent enough.

In 1473 Ludlow Castle was given to the Prince of Wales to be his permanent home, and Anthony was put in over-all charge, and this

[8] The term 'Middle Ages' dates from 1722, 'Medieval' from 1827, and 'Renaissance' from 1840. *O.E.D.*

[9] Anthony was now Earl Rivers, but was generally still called Lord Scales.

[1] The pilgrimage to Compostela ranked next after Jerusalem and Rome. Like Canterbury, it owed its popularity to its position, which was difficult of access but not too difficult. Margery Kempe, a religious fanatic, visited it about 1417. The journey there took her seven days from Bristol; she had fourteen days in Spain and came back in five days. Anthony did not make the pilgrimage till July 1473 and, as Paston *minor* was said by his brother to be going there that summer, they may have travelled together.

worked out so well that the Prince and Anthony were both at Ludlow when Edward died ten years later. The setting up of an establishment for the Prince of Wales was combined with a commission, made out in the name of the Queen and Prince, to restore order on the Welsh Marches. They represented the King, and nominally presided over a temporary court of law at Hereford where notorious gangsters were tried, and this gave the professionals who deputized for them the authority to take a strong line. At the same time Edward set up a permanent Council to govern the Welsh Marches, an institution which continued to function at Ludlow till 1689. The nominal head of the Council of the Welsh Marches was the infant Prince of Wales and orders were issued in his name and phrased as though he were dictating them, but the actual head was the President of the Council, Bishop Alcock, an able official who was also responsible for the Prince's education. Book-learning was becoming fashionable, and Edward was determined that his son should have every advantage, and some zealous official composed rules for his upbringing which, at first sight, appear quite unsuited to a small child and curiously Victorian, though in reality they are fairly elastic and capable of being interpreted in a rational way.

The Prince was to get up 'at a convenient hour according to his age' and to spend the morning 'in such virtuous learning as his age shall suffer to receive'; he was to be read aloud to during dinner and in the afternoon to take exercise. After supper he was to play, and his attendants were to 'enforce themselves to make him merry and joyous towards his bed', and he was to be in bed with the curtains drawn by eight o'clock. Like the grown-ups, his day was to be sprinkled with moments of prayer and praise, and the people round him were to have good characters and were not to use bad language.[2]

Perhaps it was partly Edward's own fault that neither of his brothers could be persuaded to co-operate with him for very long. Gloucester had risen to the occasion splendidly in the hectic days of 1471—commanding one of the ships, leading a wing at Barnet and at Tewkesbury, going ahead to Sandwich in pursuit of Fauconberg, toil-

[2] J. Halliwell, *Letters of the Kings of England* (1846). When Prince Edward was eleven, lights-out was changed to nine o'clock.

ing up to the Scottish Border—and Edward was prepared to build him up as a great landowner in the North, who would replace Montagu, balance the Percies and be a buffer against the Scots. Gloucester was given many of the confiscated lands of rebels, but that was not enough for him and he determined to marry Anne Neville, the widow of Queen Margaret's son, and acquire with her half of the Countess of Warwick's inheritance. Clarence, married to Isobel, was determined to have the whole of the vast property, while the Countess of Warwick herself, still in Beaulieu sanctuary under guard so that she could not escape, wrote to the royal family pointing out that her estates were still legally her own. The quarrel between Clarence and Gloucester raged for the next three years, and Edward was so afraid of the consequences if either of them were thwarted that he tried to appease them both, giving them alternatively large grants of lands, titles, honours and sinecures. Gloucester received Middleham Castle and Sheriff Hutton, the Neville strongholds in Yorkshire, while Clarence was again Lieutenant of Ireland and acquired estates mainly in the south and west.

The Croyland Continuator tells a story which sounds absurd but, as he lived in close proximity to the Court, may have some foundation of truth. According to him, Clarence disguised Anne as a kitchen-maid but Gloucester discovered her and placed her in St Martin's sanctuary. Unfortunately he does not give the least indication as to what was the attitude of Anne herself. She must have had some views about the matter but *nothing* is known about her character or personality, her tastes or preferences, and there is not the smallest clue to show whether her gruelling experiences had left her cowed or made her tough. It is possible that, as a child, she had known Gloucester when he had lived in Middleham Castle; on the other hand she may have been brought up at Warwick Castle and never have seen him before.

Another story related by the Croyland Continuator is that Clarence and Gloucester debated in public their respective rights to divide the Countess of Warwick's fortune. The confrontation took place in the royal Council Chamber with Edward as umpire, and 'all those present, and the lawyers even, were quite surprised that these princes should find arguments in such abundance by means of which to support their respective causes. In fact these three brothers, the King and the two dukes, were possessed of such exceptional talents that if they had been able to live without dissension, such a threefold cord could never have been broken.'

A similar thought must often have occurred to Edward. How strong they would be if only his two younger brothers were not so greedy, and would accept him as their leader and obey his orders!

On 17 February 1472 Paston *major* in London wrote to his brother: 'Yesterday the King, the Queen, my lords of Clarence and Gloucester, went to Sheen to pardon; men say, not all in charity. What will befall men cannot say. The King entreats my Lord of Clarence for my Lord of Gloucester and (as it is said), he answers that he may well have my Lady his sister-in-law, but they shall part no livelihood, as he says; so what will befall can I not say.'

Later in the spring of 1472 Gloucester married Anne, he being nineteen and she nearly sixteen. He had not obtained a dispensation from the Pope and so the marriage was not, strictly speaking, legal; nor did he ever seek to legalize it.

The dispute over the Countess of Warwick's property then raged more fiercely than before. In June 1473 the Countess left Beaulieu sanctuary and was conducted north to live on estates which were now Gloucester's, but which had once belonged to the Neville family. Perhaps she was lucky that things were no worse;[3] her late husband had behaved despicably and betrayed every ally in turn, but at least her two daughters had married princes and her confiscated wealth would, in the natural course of things, descend to her grandchildren.

In the autumn of 1473 the quarrels between Clarence and Gloucester had become so acute that it seemed that a civil war was inevitable, and on 6 November Paston *major* in London wrote to his brother: 'The world seems queasy here. For the most part [those] that be about the King have sent hither for their harness, and it [is] said for certain that the Duke of Clarence makes him big in that he can, showing as he would but deal with the Duke of Gloucester, but the King intends . . . to be as big as them both and to be a stifler between them.' There

---

[3] The Countess of Warwick outlived Clarence, Gloucester and her two daughters. She made various financial arrangements with Henry VII who allowed her enough to live on in modest independence. She died in 1492 aged sixty-six.

might be more in this quarrel than met the eye and Paston, now comfortably settled in the service of Hastings, had not the slightest intention
of being drawn into it and decided to go to Calais. 'It were better for
me to be out of sight.'

The question of who was to get the Countess of Warwick's estate
was finally settled by an Act of Parliament dated 1474. The King, 'by
the advice and assent of the Lords and Commons', decreed that Clarence
and Isobel, and Gloucester and Anne, should share the property of the
Countess of Warwick 'in like manner and form as if the said Countess
was now naturally dead'. If either Isobel or Anne should die, her husband should have her estates for his life. Neither Clarence nor Gloucester
should try to obtain each other's share. Because of the peculiar circumstances of Gloucester's marriage there was a clause to say that the
arrangements held good even if he and Anne divorced and then
remarried each other, or if they divorced and Anne refused to remarry
him, provided he did not marry any other woman. Tied up like this,
Anne could not escape from Gloucester without forfeiting all her
property.

The long-drawn-out struggle for the Countess of Warwick's fortune was at best tiresome, and at worst very dangerous, and it showed
that in his own way Gloucester was as irresponsible as Clarence and that
when it came to pursuing his own interests he would not hesitate to
endanger the peace of the nation. Edward, however, had had much
practice in the art of getting on with relations who were less than
perfect; he believed that family solidarity was of prime importance and
he continued to treat his brothers as though they were honourable and
reliable. They were both young, and as they grew older their greed
might be appeased and they might steady down.

Meanwhile the out-of-date machinery of English government was
being reorganized, and it is now generally acknowledged that the successful methods of Henry VII were based on foundations laid by
Edward IV. He selected officials carefully, seldom changed them, consulted the appropriate councillors and conducted home affairs with a
high hand but remarkably little friction. His system had no long-term
future as it depended on there being a king who was both intelligent
and hard-working, and the time would come when the public would

prefer the appearance of self-government to the rule of even the most enlightened despot, but it satisfied the demands of the moment and was a great improvement on the way in which the country had been run in the previous reign.

Edward has often been accused of both extravagance and avarice. The first charge is obviously untrue as his household expenses were less than those of previous kings, and also than those of Henry VII, while the latter charge may be traced to his determination to become solvent. His domestic reforms aroused indignation. Any concern which employs a large staff has to fight a ceaseless war against carelessness and waste, pilfering and embezzlement, and the larger the staff the greater can be the losses and the pettier seem the precautions that must be taken to block the leaks. The royal household had been run with prodigal carelessness as long as anyone could remember, and Edward instituted unpopular economies while occasionally putting on a magnificent entertainment to impress and amuse his subjects. Eventually he did succeed in straightening out the financial tangles left by his father and previous governments, though accounts are too sketchy to reveal exactly how this was achieved, and how much was due to good management of existing resources, and how much to the success of his trading ventures.

A relic of his determination to economize in his expenditure is a composition known as *The Black Book*[4] which is part of a draft of rules for the Royal Household. It was written in the year 1471 or 1472 and it was apparently the work of a member of the staff, perhaps Sir John Elrington[5] who was Cofferer till 1474 and then Treasurer of the Household till his death in 1483. Similar books of directions for royal households are known from the twelfth to the seventeenth centuries, and noble families also drew up rules with the emphasis on the duties of

---

[4] A. R. Myers, *The Household of Edward IV. The Black Book and the Ordinance of 1478* (1959). The original is lost, but there are several old copies extant. Besides a very interesting introduction, Myers provides lists of Household officials during Edward's reign.

[5] Sir John Elrington had a quietly successful career. He was Treasurer of the Army during the invasion of France in 1475, and one of the eleven members of Edward's staff who, in 1483, were allowed to wear a short tunic like a peer. He married the widow of the heir of Lord Mountjoy.

servants and the maintenance of orderly behaviour, but *The Black Book* is the most elaborate known work of its kind. One of the most striking things about it is that the writer is completely unaware that the world is changing rapidly; he does not boast that his ordinances are novel or modern, or a sign of progress, but offers them with the recommendation that they are a return to the good old days; he is like a man who imagines he is rowing about on a pond when in reality he is drifting down a river and about to be swept over a weir.

The preamble describes some of the excellent domestic arrangements at the courts of Solomon, Lud, Cassivellaunus, Harthacnut, Henry I and Edward III, after which the writer gets down to the problems of his own day and the allocations of food, wine, ale, fuel and lighting. There are torches and candles of different sorts to be distributed, straw for stuffing mattresses and rushes for the floors. Quantity and quality varies with the rank of the guest. A ducal visitor can bring with him one knight, a chaplain, three squires and four yeomen, all of whom may eat in the hall where they will receive befitting rations; fuel and light for them will vary with the season. A Duke can also have twelve servants waiting on him, and the rest of his meinie are to be lodged within seven miles. If the Duke goes away for a short time, a yeoman may keep his room for him. A Baron is only permitted to bring one gentleman and one yeoman to eat in the hall, and four servants to wait on him. And so on down. It is all worked out with precautions against quarrelling, insubordination, thieving, abuse of hospitality, bogus claims and frauds, battening and scrounging, food taken away to give to friends, and horses stabled among the royal horses. Candle-ends are to be given back in the morning. Everything is to be checked by the counting-house.

The King has more food, fuel, light and servants than anyone else, and it is laid down what each of his servants is to do, who is to stuff the King's mattress every night and who is to clear up the 'faults of hounds'. The Queen and her attendants are only mentioned in passing and apart from that there is no reference to females at all, which makes the picture of palace life a trifle unrealistic; in fact, *The Black Book* describes an ideal at which to aim rather than putting on record what actually happened.

In 1478 another 'ordinance' was made, readjusting the expenses, cutting staff, tightening up the rules and blocking loopholes, and disgusted servants doubtless spread around the town the distressing news that the King had become even meaner than before.

EDWARD SPENT THE FIRST CHRISTMAS AFTER HE WAS REINSTATED at the Palace of Westminster. On Christmas Day both he and Elizabeth wore their crowns, and the festivities ended in a 'disguising'—the time-honoured way by which a limited society achieves an illusion of novelty and mystery. On Twelfth Night the King again wore his crown though the Queen, being pregnant,[6] was excused from wearing hers, and the season of carnival ended with a great banquet for the Mayor and aldermen and merchants from the City; it was assumed that Edward was ingratiating himself with them for ulterior motives, but there is every reason to suppose that he really liked their company and was interested by their conversation.

This Christmas merry-making followed conventional lines, but a tremendous effort was made in the autumn of 1472 to provide superlative entertainment for Edward's friend and helper, de la Gruthuyse, who paid a state visit and could hardly have been received with more honour if he had been a visiting king, and an official account was written by a herald, Bluemantle Pursuivant.[7]

Beginning at Calais, where Lord Howard, the Deputy Captain, did the honours, de la Gruthuyse was feasted practically without stopping for about a fortnight. At Windsor he was ceremoniously welcomed and, after supper on the first night, the King took de la Gruthuyse to the Queen's apartments where she and her ladies were playing at morteaulx and closheys of ivory[8] and dancing. 'Also the King danced with my Lady Elizabeth,[9] his eldest daughter.'

[6] The Queen bore a daughter, Margaret, at Windsor on 10 April 1472. She died in the following December and was buried in Westminster Abbey.

[7] *Archaeologia* (1835), vol. XXVI.

[8] Marbles and ninepins.

[9] Princess Elizabeth was six. The daughters of Kings were not called 'princess' until the next century.

Next morning after Mass the King gave de la Gruthuyse 'a cup of gold garnished with pearls and in the midst of the cup is a great piece of an unicorn's horn[1] to my estimation seven inches compass. And on the cover was a great sapphire. Then he went to his chamber where he had his breakfast.'

Later de la Gruthuyse was shown the Prince of Wales, who was carried in by his chamberlain, old Thomas Vaughan, and afterwards he hunted in Windsor Park and Edward presented him with a horse, and a cross-bow with silk strings and a velvet cover embroidered with the royal arms and badges, and showed his garden and his 'vineyard of pleasure'. At night there was a banquet in the Queen's apartments, and among those present were little Princess Elizabeth, Edward's sister Anne, the wife of Anthony, the Duke and Duchess of Buckingham, Hastings and other ladies and gentlemen. The Queen's ladies sat on one side of a long table and the Burgundian followers of de la Gruthuyse on the other. After supper there was dancing, and the Duke of Buckingham danced with Princess Elizabeth.

At nine o'clock everyone escorted de la Gruthuyse to three 'chambers of pleasance, all hanged and beseen with white silk and linen cloth and all the floors covered with carpets. There was ordained for him a bed for himself of as good down as could be thought, the sheets of rennes, also fine fustian, the counterpane cloth of gold furred with ermine, the tester and the seler also shining cloth of gold; curtains of white sarsenet; as for his bedsheet and pillows [they] were of the Queen's own ordinance. In the second chamber was another [bed] of estate the which was all white. Also in the same chamber was made a couch with feather beds, hanged with a tent knit like a net; and there was the cupboard. Item, in the third chamber was ordered a bath or two, which were covered with tents of white cloth.' The company then withdrew leaving only Hastings, who helped de la Gruthuyse to undress. They 'went both together in the bath . . . and when they had been in their baths as long as was their pleasure, they had green ginger, diverse syrups, comfits and hippocras; and then they went to bed.'

The King returned to London for the opening of Parliament on

[1] Unicorn's horn guarded against poison.

6 October, and on 13 October 1472 de la Gruthuyse was created Earl of Winchester with a grant of £200 annually to be paid out of the customs of Southampton. The ceremonies on this occasion began in the Parliament chamber at ten o'clock in the morning; the King and Queen wore their crowns, Clarence carried the train of de la Gruthuyse, there were speeches, processions, and a banquet, and the festivities went on till six o'clock.[2]

SCEPTICAL AND MATTER-OF-FACT as were people like Pseudo-Gregory and the Paston brothers, from time to time the country was swept by superstitious panics, and these seem to have occurred in years which were otherwise uneventful. The addiction of the English to omens and prophecies was a byword on the Continent and in 1473 a prophet called Hogan caused alarm by announcing that great disasters were impending. The authorities took prompt steps to silence him, and in March he was under arrest in the Norwich Guildhall and in April he was in the Tower. 'He would fain speak with the King,' wrote Paston *major* on 12 April 1473, 'but the King says he shall not vaunt that ever he spoke with him.' On 3 June Paston reported that the raids of the Earl of Oxford had 'saved Hogan his head', because he was able to claim that his prophecies had come true.

Among the chroniclers it is Warkworth (who was Master of Peterhouse) and the Prior of Croyland—both educated men—who are so gullible that they take the trouble to write down fantastic rumours. Warkworth saw more and brighter comets than are otherwise recorded, and he relates that in 1473 a sinister water called Womere or woewater ran at Markayte, seven miles from St Albans; this was a very bad sign and there were other similar waters at Lewisham, Canterbury, Croydon, and Hungervale near Dudley. Moreover, a headless man had been seen, and also a voice heard crying 'Bowes! Bowes!' in the air between Banbury and Leicester.

[2] De la Gruthuyse did not come to England again. In 1481 he complained that his annuity was in arrears. He died in 1492, and Henry VII cancelled the peerage of Winchester in 1500.

The Prior of Croyland, on the other hand, remembered 1467 as being a specially ominous year. It had begun badly with terrible floods round Croyland in January, and later there were seen in the heavens three suns and a shower of blood, 'as the grass and the linen clothes stained therewith abundantly testified. . . . Besides this, horsemen and men in armour were seen rushing through the air; so much so that Saint George himself, conspicuous with the red cross, his usual ensign, and attended by a vast body of armed men, appeared visibly to great numbers. . . . A certain woman too, in the County of Huntingdon, who was with child and near the time of her delivery, to her extreme horror, felt the embryo in her womb weeping and uttering a kind of sobbing noise. The same was also heard by some other women who were surprised at no slight degree thereat.'

XIII

The Invasion of France 1475

LTHOUGH HIS MILITARY SUCCESSES HAD BEEN SO DRAMATIC, Edward had not developed a taste for war; he was still the trader-king who wanted world peace and a patriarchal home life, but his subjects were extremely jingoistic and his neighbours interpreted peaceful overtures as a sign of weakness.

It took him some years to restore good relations with the merchants of the Hanseatic League who, ejected from their English trading posts, had become a menace to shipping. He persistently sent envoys whose efforts were frustrated by the quarrels among the different German towns, by the fact that England traded with Cologne which had left the League, and also by the repeated failure of delegates to turn up at the place and time appointed. Much patience was needed; devoted envoys made countless journeys to and from the Continent, and at last a treaty was concluded at Utrecht on 28 February 1474. The English signatories were Edward's secretary and ex-physician, William Hatteclyffe, who had acted as chief ambassador throughout, John Russell (a government official who afterwards was given a bishopric), and a merchant called William Rosse. The treaty was confirmed by Parliament early in 1475, after which the Hanseatic merchants returned to their premises known as Steelyards (from *stål*, a sample) in London, King's Lynn and Boston.

In Spain Edward's diplomacy was also successful, and in May 1475 there was a renewal of the treaty between England and Castile. He had the acumen to back Ferdinand and Isabella who eventually emerged as the ruling powers. Isabella's half-brother, Henry the Impotent, died on 11 December 1474 and the Cortes chose Isabella as his successor, but her title was disputed by Alfonso V, King of Portugal.[1] who did not relinquish his claims till 1479, by which time the old king of Aragon had died and Ferdinand and Isabella were able to settle down to their celebrated joint reign.

Edward also persisted in his efforts to establish a permanent peace between England and Scotland and—his mind moving along its usual groove—he suggested a marriage alliance between his third daughter Cecily and the eldest son of the King of Scotland.[2] On 25 October 1474 Cecily was betrothed by proxy to the future James IV, and so determined was Edward that this marriage should take place that he arranged to send annually to Scotland an instalment of her dowry.

Reflections of these intrigues appear in the papers of the Dukes of Milan who continued to receive reports about England; the island of madmen described by their correspondants at least had the fascination of the mysterious and the fantastic. 'God in his mercy grant what is best for Christians!' exclaimed one writer in despair.

On 25 November 1472 Galeazzo Maria Sforza, Duke of Milan, was sent a furious letter by Pietro Aliprando, a Papal envoy who happened to be in the pay of the Duke, and who had just paid a visit to England. Archbishop Neville was at the moment imprisoned in the Castle of Hammes, and Aliprando, suspected of corresponding with him, had been arrested at Calais and was now stuck at Gravelines on the Calais-Burgundian frontier. 'In the morning', wrote Aliprando, '[the English] are as devout as angels but after dinner they are like devils, seeking to throw the Pope's messengers into the sea ... I mean

---

[1] Alfonso V of Portugal (1432–81) proposed to marry his niece Joanna, the daughter of the second wife of Henry the Impotent. Joanna, who was generally called Beltraneja after her alleged father, was born in 1462. She nominally retired into a convent in 1479, but she remained active and a nuisance until her death in 1530.

[2] Cecily was born in 1469, and James in 1473. He eventually married Edward's granddaughter Margaret, daughter of Henry VII and Elizabeth of York. He was killed at Flodden in 1513.

to excommunicate them . . . for the trick they have played upon me. . . .
They do not keep faith, they are evil islanders and are born with tails.
. . .[3] They are now engaged in London upon the Great Parliament of
the three estates of England, to reform the kingdom; but so far they have
done nothing but talk. They devote every moment to gourmandizing.
. . . The King can do no more as he is a tavern bush [*circulo ad tabernam*].'
After giving all the news that he had heard he regained his temper and
changed his mind about Edward. 'The King is indeed a most handsome,
worthy and royal prince, the country good, the people bad and per-
verse. . . . O my Lord, when I speak of the English, your Excellency
must understand those old prelates, abbots or other fat priests who rule
the Council, and who have represented to the King that he must have
all who come from Rome arrested.'

On 12 May 1473 the Milanese Ambassador wrote from the French
Court at Tours to say that the Scottish ambassadors had arrived and
were offering to invade England if the English invaded France, but
that they must have what their predecessors had had in the past, a
subsidy of 60,000 crowns a year. This demand for money was causing
some annoyance, but the Scots said that if they did not get it they would
not invade England.

Among other tit-bits which the Duke of Milan received in 1474
was the information that the Earl of Usumforch (Oxford) had seized
St Michael's Mount; and the quite unfounded rumour that an English
army had landed in Brittany—he was told that Louis hoped to tire them
out without fighting and send them home in pieces, because 'the English are sturdy artisans and do not obey their Lords'. On 17 September
1474 the Milanese ambassador in France passed on a hint from Louis
that the Duke of Milan might care to marry his daughter to the baby
prince of Scotland. 'For instance supposing your Excellency wished to
make war on the Venetians or any others, in a very short time they
would always be able to send across to Normandy 10,000 to 12,000
Scots at a moderate rate, as at a crown per man you can hire as many as

---

[3] Foreigners were told that the people of Strood near Rochester were born with tails
because they cut off the tail of Thomas à Becket's horse. Pius II and Polydore Vergil were
also interested in this phenomenon.

you please. His Majesty added that, as he experiences every day,[4] they are a fierce and war-like people.' Edward was trying to marry his daughter to the heir of Scotland, so even if the Duke did not like the plan (and certainly Scotland was *in finibus orbis*) the negotiations would please Louis.

To this the Duke replied primly that if it would please Louis he would certainly commence negotiations with Scotland; but he would like Louis to know that he did not intend to carry matters through to a conclusion for two reasons, firstly because, as Louis knew, he had already married his daughter and secondly because, even if he had another, he would not want to marry her as far away as Scotland.

EDWARD'S FOURTH PARLIAMENT MET in the Autumn of 1472. This was the Parliament which welcomed de la Gruthuyse and was accused by the papal envoy of doing nothing but talk and eat, and it created a record by lasting for two and a half years, from October 1472 to March 1475: it assembled spasmodically in six sessions, and it gradually voted supplies for the invasion of France.

Among its by-products were resolutions to improve water-ways and drains, and a plea for cheap bow-staves. These were now an 'outrageous price'; a hundred bow-staves cost a hundred shillings, and the buyer had to take the good with the bad. Formerly they were forty shillings a hundred, and bows for boys were ten shillings or, at most, thirteen and fourpence; as a result, instead of practising shooting, young men now played at cards and dice. In future, any ship coming from Venice[5] or any other place which exported bows must bring a quota of them which would be checked by the port authorities to make sure that they were not below standard.

Edward had long ago come to the conclusion that to be King of both England and France was an impossibility, but the bulk of the nation cherished the illusion that just across the Channel there lay a rich empire, temporarily mislaid but easily regained with a small expendi-

---

[4] Louis had a guard of Scottish archers, as readers of *Quentin Durward* will remember.
[5] The best yew-wood for bows came from the north side of mountains, three or four thousand feet up. English yew-wood was not close-grained and had too many knots.

ture of money and some brave English archers. Edward was permanently afraid that Calais would be attacked and, between bluffing Louis and Duke Charles and trying to make his subjects believe that he shared their foolish dreams, he eventually muddled into war against his better judgement and his inclinations.

Paston *major*, now completely on the side of the Establishment, was seized with a desire to sit in the 1472 Parliament[6] and he hoped to be chosen as one of the members for Norfolk, although he did not trouble to leave London. On 21 September 1472 his brother had to break it to him that the Dukes of Norfolk and Suffolk had settled on the two knights of the shire more than a fortnight ago. There had not been time to stop the Pastons' supporters from coming to Norwich to vote in such numbers that it cost nine shillings and a penny, but Paston *minor* met them and told them that his brother was not standing after all, as he would be abroad, thus averting the ignominy of a defeat. Yarmouth had selected its members already, but there was Maldon in Essex, and if Maldon failed there were a dozen towns which did not even pretend to select their members and where, with the right influence, he could get in.

The Duke of Norfolk still occupied Caister Castle, but the Pastons had now become extremely friendly with the Duchess of Norfolk, a woman with a mind of her own, and Paston *minor* suggested that Jane Roden, her lady-in-waiting who had been pushing their cause, should be sent some present, 'some goodly ring, price of twenty shillings or some pretty flower of the same price and not under'.

The agent of the Duchess of Norfolk had already written to the bailiff of the town of Maldon commanding them to elect Sir John Paston, he being both the protégé of the Duchess and one that 'stands greatly in favour with my Lord Chamberlain [Hastings]; and what my said Lord Chamberlain may do with the King and with all the Lords of England, I trow it be not unknown to you'. If they voted for Paston it would give the Duchess as much pleasure as if they gave her a hundred pounds, and he added in a postscript that he was shortly coming round to look at their accounts. However, in spite of these powerful arguments, Paston *major* did not obtain a seat.

[6] He had been M.P. for Norfolk in 1467–8, and was M.P. for Yarmouth in 1478.

The Parliament of 1468 had voted a small sum of money for an invasion of France which had never taken place, and very suspiciously, in November 1472, the new Parliament promised Edward 13,000 archers. They were conscious that Edward was not dedicated heart and soul to a French war, and they suspected that his demands might merely be a ruse to procure money for his own private amusements. Edward, on his side, was quite determined not to be rushed into a reckless foray and he set to work to build up stores and equipment and to pin down Duke Charles with a written treaty of alliance. The archives of France reveal in tedious detail the correspondences which passed between England, France, Burgundy and Brittany; the protestations of friendship, the temporary truces, the bargains, the promises, the suggestions, the demands and the offers—most of which cancelled each other out and, in any case, were much modified by secret messages delivered verbally. Duke Charles was the only one of the four rulers who actually wanted a general war, but all understood the nature of power-politics and when, as frequently happened, one of them found himself overreached, deluded or let down he may have been annoyed but he can hardly have been surprised. Duke Charles vacillated between old schemes of attacking Louis with the help of Edward, and new ones of expanding eastward, and he was obviously so unreliable that Edward did not entirely close the door to the possibility of a pact with France.

By November 1474, Louis was very frightened and he sent an embassy to London. Edward, however, would not receive it. The Duke of Berry (the brother of Louis who had caused him almost as much trouble as Clarence had caused Edward) and John of Calabria had recently died and, rightly or wrongly, Louis was suspected of causing their deaths; Paston *major*, writing from London on 20 November, gave one explanation why Edward had rebuffed the French ambassadors: 'The King came to this town on Wednesday. And as for the French embassy that is here, they come not in the King's presence, by likelyhood, for men say that the chief of them is he that poisoned both the Duke of Berry and the Duke of Calabria'.

PARLIAMENT, BESOTTED WITH DREAMS of ransom and pillage, voted more and more money for the war; collecting it was another matter. By the end of 1474 preparations had gone too far for the expedition to be called off, but there was a shortage of cash and Edward fell back on the old and unpopular expedient of 'benevolences'. This was a rough and ready income tax demanded from those who could afford to pay and the name was extremely annoying—suggesting as it did that the payments were voluntary. The people affected were the articulate classes; echoes of complaints reverberate in the chronicles, and the Pastons' mother (23 May 1475) was plunged into gloom. 'I wot not how we shall live [unless] the world amend!'

Edward was beginning to put on weight, but his personal charm was unimpaired, and he toured the country collecting subscriptions with the aid of blandishments and blarney. In after years the story was told that a rich widow who offered him ten pounds for his handsome face doubled it when he kissed her, and an Italian merchant living in London gave his version of the King's methods in a private letter written on 17 March 1475, in a tone of mingled disapproval, admiration and amazement.

The King, he wrote, had plucked the feathers of his magpies without making them cry out. The previous autumn he had travelled extensively and extracted money from whomever possessed more than £40 sterling. 'Everyone seemed to give willingly. I have frequently seen our neighbours here who were summoned before the King; and when they went they looked as though they were going to the gallows, and when they returned they were joyful, saying they had spoken to the King, and because he had spoken to them so kindly they had not grudged the money they had paid. According to what I have been told by people he went about it this way; as soon as the person arrived he gave him a tremendous welcome as though he had known him always and after some time he asked how much he would subscribe towards this expedition. If the man offered something appropriate he had ready his secretary who made a note of the name and the sum, but if the King thought it insufficient he said, "So-and-so, who is poorer than you has subscribed so much; you who are richer can well give more." And thus with fair words he brought him up to scratch. In this way it is supposed that he extracted a very large sum.' In spite of the great military preparation, some people were still 'kinsmen of St Thomas', but the writer thought that the expenditure on armaments had been so great that an invasion was really intended.

In France the consternation increased, and the Milanese ambassador reported that Louis was in a frenzy. 'His Majesty is more upset than words can describe and he has almost lost his wits. In his desperation and bitterness he uttered exactly the following words among others: 'Ha! Our Lady! Even when I have given thee 1400 crowns thou dost not help me a bit!'[7]

As a matter of fact, Edward was in a dilemma. On the one hand, his subjects were determined that their old enemy should be invaded and for this purpose had subscribed large sums so that his credit would be lost for ever if he disappointed them; on the other, success depended entirely on the co-operation of Duke Charles, and Edward suspected that when it came to the point no Burgundian army would be forthcoming.

The year before, in July 1474, Duke Charles had attempted to enlarge his eastern boundaries and had taken his army to the Rhine near Düsseldorf and had begun to besiege Neuss, a fortified city which turned out to be capable of resisting indefinitely, and in April 1475 Edward sent Anthony to Neuss to try to persuade Duke Charles to cut his losses, abandon the seige and concentrate on his original plan, an Anglo-Burgundian attack on France. But Duke Charles refused to leave Neuss and when, in the middle of June 1475, the English army began crossing the Channel there was no certainty that he intended to carry out any of his promises, and those who were in Edward's confidence must have known how uncertain was the outlook. Duke Charles had recommended the mouth of the Seine as a suitable landing-place, but Edward chose the shortest sea-crossing and a friendly port, and landed his troops at Calais.

Before leaving England Edward appointed a Council consisting of the Archbishop of Canterbury, six bishops, five peers[8] and about seven government officials. The Chancellor, Rotherham Bishop of Lincoln, was due to go to France with the expeditionary force, so

---

[7] A similar story is told of Louis XIV and it may be a court joke of great antiquity.
[8] Most of the active peers went to France with Edward. The peers on the Council were Essex, Arundel, Dacre, Dudley and Dynham.

Bishop Alcock was made deputy Chancellor, and in May the Prince of Wales had been brought up from Ludlow, knighted, named 'Keeper of the Realm', and left in charge of his mother. Until the very last Edward was negotiating loans from Italian bankers and City merchants, and at Sandwich on 20 June 1475 he sealed his will.[9]

Fifteenth-century wills varied enormously; some were much the same as a modern will, while others were more like a paper of 'wishes'; and, as it often was the case that all the testator's property was already tied up in settlements and trusts, a will could merely be a statement of who was next of kin. Other wills consisted of frantic last-minute bequests to churches and charities. Edward, so careful and far-sighted, must have made all his important arrangements before he left London, and the Sandwich will was only a kind of codicil. Such as it was, it gave directions for his body to be buried in St George's Chapel, 'by us begun of new to be builded', in the place he had showed to Beauchamp, Bishop of Salisbury. There was to be an elaborate tomb with a figure of death bearing the King's scutcheon, and an image of himself 'of silver and gilt or at least copper and gilt'. Elizabeth was to have any household goods she wanted and it was left to her discretion to dispose of the rest. Besides his two sons, Edward had three daughters of which only Cecily was provided for; Princess Elizabeth and Princess Mary were allotted suitable marriage portions if they were 'governed and ruled in their marriages' by the Queen and their elder brother (if he had reached a reasonable age). The Queen was pregnant and if she gave birth to a girl baby it should have a similar dowry. Out of the ten executors the only peer was Hastings.

HOW THE INVASION APPEARED FROM the French side is graphically described in the memoirs of Philip de Comines who, in 1472, had transferred his services from the Duke of Burgundy to the King of France. Louis had recognized his exceptional abilities and had induced him to emigrate to the French Court, and though it can be said that Comines had been bought he can hardly be blamed; it must have been very

---

[9] The original does not exist. A copy is printed in *Excerpta Historica*.

disagreeable for anyone of his intelligence to serve such a megalomaniac as Duke Charles. He clearly saw and sincerely deplored the faults of his new master, but he was fascinated by Louis and ended by becoming extremely fond of him.

Comines was much impressed by the great size of the English army: he reckoned that there were fourteen thousand mounted archers and fifteen hundred men-at-arms, as well as foot-soldiers. This could be approximately correct, as the records of the English Exchequer, which are incomplete, get the numbers of the archers up to nearly eleven thousand and the men-at-arms to nearly twelve hundred. There were no unnecessary attendants, and all agree that it was extremely well equipped with artillery and engines of war, tents, tools, and stores of food. The peers brought contingents of different sizes and, as Edward made a point of knowing exactly what every landowner was worth, they had probably all been given quotas; and the numbers listed are more likely to be an indication of their relative wealth than an exact count of the soldiers in their contingents.[1] Clarence and Gloucester were expected to bring much the largest forces—1000 archers and 120 men-at-arms each, but so enthusiastic was Gloucester that he finished up with more than his quota. The young Duke of Buckingham, who had brought 400 archers, returned home, and perhaps Gloucester took over his contingent. The next largest force was brought by the Earl of Northumberland (350 archers and 60 men-at-arms). Norfolk, Suffolk, Hastings and Stanley brought 300 archers and 40 men-at-arms, while Lord Howard and Anthony were in the group which brought 200 archers and 20 men-at-arms. Of the Scottish refugees at the English Court the Earl of Douglas brought 40 archers and 4 men-at-arms, and Lord Boyd 20 archers and 2 men-at-arms. William Hatteclyffe brought 13 archers, one man-at-arms and a gentleman. Dorset did not bring any soldiers, neither did the Duke of Exeter who apparently was let out of the Tower for the occasion. There were fifteen doctors and surgeons of different grades and the professional head of the army was John Stur-

---

[1] Francis Pierrepont Barnard, *Edward IV's French Expedition of 1475. The Leaders and their Badges: From a M.S. at the College of Arms* (1925). The heralds' lists do not quite tally with the Exchequer lists. This book also contains much information about the minor characters at the court of Edward IV.

geon, Master of the Ordnance. The King's Household Treasurer, John Elrington, was Treasurer of the expedition. Some of Edward's merchant friends were present as sightseers and the Croyland Continuator was among the clerical staff. Paston *major* was with Hastings, Paston *minor* was with the Duke of Norfolk and their brother, Edmund Paston, was indentured to the Duke of Gloucester. He was to serve for a year with three archers; he was to have eighteen pence a day for himself and six pence for each archer; and it was very precisely settled how they were to share the 'winnings of war'.[2]

DUKE CHARLES HAD SENT A fleet of flat-bottomed Dutch boats for the transport of horses, and among the agents who collected them was William Caxton[3] formerly a merchant in Bruges and now the financial adviser of Margaret Duchess of Burgundy.

It took three weeks to get the whole army across the sea, and Comines considered that if Louis had known more about naval matters he could have prevented the landing—but here he may have been wrong as the Straits were guarded by Lord Dynham and had there been a sea-battle Dynham would probably have won it.

Before Edward set out from England, he sent a herald to Louis bearing a letter of defiance couched, according to Comines, 'In fine language and a fine style (I cannot believe that any Englishman had had a hand in it)', demanding that he should be given the kingdom of France of which he was the rightful king. Official letters could not be taken at face-value and Louis, having read the missive himself, withdrew into a *garde-robe* with the herald, who there gave him to understand that Edward was quite prepared to make peace, but that he would not name his terms until he was actually in France. Louis intimated to the

---

[2] *Paston Letters* (1971 ed.) no. 396. The original indenture is in the Pierpont Morgan Library. It is a quite lengthy form, with a gap left for the retained person's name and the number of his archers, and it was signed by Gloucester himself.

[3] William Caxton (1422–91). On 23 April 1475 Caxton set out to visit Delft, Rotterdam, Middleburg, Flushing and other Dutch towns; the boats were forthcoming but the sailors gave trouble and insisted on a month's pay in advance. Caxton returned to England and set up his press at Westminster in the autumn of 1476. W. J. B. Crotch, *The Prologues and Epilogues of William Caxton* (Early English Text Society, 1928).

herald that he would gladly meet Edward half-way, and he gave the herald a very handsome present. Publicly, the herald was given a small present and handed a letter of defiance from Louis to Edward.

While the king was talking to the herald there were many people waiting in the hall who were anxious to know what the king was saying and what his expression would be when he emerged, but all Louis told them about was the letter of defiance, which he showed to several people, and his manner was very confident because he was delighted with what the herald had told him. Comines was instructed to keep watch on the herald and to allow no one to speak to him until he had left the Court.

Edward crossed over to Calais on 4 July and on 6 July his sister Duchess Margaret arrived on a short visit, but she left Calais, escorted by her brothers Clarence and Gloucester, before her husband arrived on 14 July. Duke Charles had at last abandoned the siege of Neuss after nearly a year of wasted effort, and to the disappointment of the English he had sent his army to invade Lorraine and was only accompanied by a small escort. It became painfully obvious that the grand strategy of war which he had evolved was that the English and French armies should slaughter each other while he sought fame and fortune elsewhere. According to the Croyland Continuator, he said publicly that the English army was so large and well equipped that it needed no help; if he were at the head of it he would march triumphantly through the midst of France and to the very gates of Rome; and the Continuator adds that in his opinion if the English and Burgundian armies had met the first battle would have been between them, for food and billets.

A puzzle to all three rulers was the attitude of Louis, Count of St Pol, Duchess Jacquetta's eldest brother, who was both Constable of France and in touch with Duke Charles. His lands lay between Burgundy and France and, trying to make something for himself out of the fluid situation, he offered to hand over the town of St Quentin to Edward. On 18 July the English army left Calais and set off towards St Quentin through Burgundian territory, and—extraordinary as it may seem—it was only now that Louis discovered that Edward and his army were on the Continent and that his worst nightmare had come true. The English were back.

Throughout Edward's march Duke Charles behaved in an infuriating manner, leaving him and returning. At Peronne he entered the town himself, but excluded the English army which was forced to camp outside. Some of the soldiers wandered off and, falling in with units of the French army which was mustering at Compiègne, a few were killed. Duke Charles having returned to his own army, Edward pushed on to St Quentin which he reached on 11 August, only to find that the Count of St Pol had changed his mind and, instead of being welcomed with the ringing of bells as they had expected, they were fired on. A few soldiers were killed or taken prisoner, while the rest of the English army retreated precipitately through heavy rain.

The English, forsaken by Duke Charles and rebuffed by St Pol,[4] would appear to have been in a critical situation, but Comines considered that Louis was at Edward's mercy. If the nobles revived the Ligue du Bien Public and allied themselves with Edward, all would be lost. English heralds had been in communication with the French, and now a released prisoner brought word that the time was ripe to discuss terms of peace. At first Louis thought that the prisoner was a spy but then, having sat down to dinner, he had an idea and, with that suddenness which looked so irrational and capricious, he whispered that Comines must go out and find a certain servant of one of the courtiers and have dinner in his own room, so that he could ask the man secretly if he would go to the English camp dressed up as a herald. Comines was amazed when the servant arrived, as he appeared to be quite unsuited to the errand, but it turned out that he had sense and was a good talker as Louis had noticed (although he had only seen him once). This poor man was horrified and fell on his knees before Comines, who did his best to allay his fears, entertaining him to a tête-à-tête dinner and promising rewards. When Louis sent to know how they were getting on, Comines suggested other more suitable messengers, but Louis would not be deflected and came himself to talk to the man 'and re-assured him more with one word than I had been able to do with a hundred'. Then a herald's costume was hastily cobbled together out of odds and ends and

---

[4] The Count of St Pol's attempts to be clever resulted in Edward, Duke Charles and Louis combining against him, and he was arrested by Louis and executed in December 1475.

hidden in a bag, his boots and travelling clothes were secretly fetched, his horse was brought round and he was sent off to the English camp and told to ask for Lord Stanley and Lord Howard.[5]

When he was brought before King Edward, the man delivered his message most persuasively. He said Louis had never fought the English and had never wanted to fight the English: he had only backed Warwick to embarrass Duke Charles—whom Edward would find, incidentally, a very awkward ally. The season was getting late. A conference could be arranged.

It was a case of a willing seller and a willing buyer. On 13 August, at a village near Peronne called Lihons-en-Santerre, the English leaders drew up an agreement among themselves. 'Considering the poverty of his army, the nigh approaching of winter and the small assistance of his allies', the King would send Lord Howard, Thomas St Leger, Dr Morton and William Dudley to discuss terms of peace. (Howard and Morton had hard heads and could speak French, St Leger was Edward's brother-in-law and Dudley was both aristocratic and literate.) This resolution was signed by most of the important people in the camp, including Clarence and Gloucester.[6]

Soon envoys from both sides were discussing the peace terms. The English went through the form of demanding all, or a large part, of France, but they soon abated their demands to 75,000 crowns cash down and 50,000 crowns annually: also a seven-year truce, mutual assistance if either country was attacked, and the marriage of Princess Elizabeth to Charles the Dauphin[7] when they had both reached a suitable age. Louis was also to ransom Queen Margaret of Anjou who was still a prisoner in England, and who would then make him heir to whatever rights she might inherit from her father.

Louis felt that he was escaping very lightly, and though some of his courtiers tried to persuade him that there was some catch or trap he decided to close with the offer immediately, before Edward could change his mind. News of the projected treaty reached Duke Charles

[5] Comines records with slight surprise that the messenger did, in fact, receive the rewards promised to him.

[6] Thomas Rymer, *Foedera* (1707). A collection of miscellaneous documents the originals of many of which have now disappeared.

[7] Charles VIII (1470–98).

who reappeared on 18 August in a towering passion, while the Count of St Pol wrote begging Edward not to make peace. Compared to Edward's nominal allies, Louis seemed positively simple and honest, and the peace talks went with amazing smoothness.

The French army moved to Amiens on 22 August, and the English camped outside the town. Comines was with Louis when he inspected the invaders from the top of the town gate, and he agreed that they looked a very undisciplined crowd, and that the long string of carts carrying a gift of Bordeaux wine to Edward made a much better show. Louis, recovered from panic, became increasingly hospitable and the officers who came into the town were entertained gratis. More and more Englishmen poured in and eventually they became so obstreperous that, although it was the unlucky Holy Innocents' Day on which Louis usually refused to receive bad news or discuss business, Comines plucked up courage to tell him that there were nine thousand English in the town and that he was in danger of attack. Louis at once abandoned his prayers and told Comines to get hold of some responsible English officers and eject the English troops.

It turned out that their fears were groundless. In one tavern there were already a hundred and eleven reckonings, although it was not yet nine o'clock in the morning 'The house was full; some were singing, others were sleeping and were drunk; when I realized this it seemed to me that there was no danger.' Edward was ashamed when he heard how his soldiers were behaving, and somehow they were got under control.

The site chosen for the meeting of the two kings was Picquigny, thirteen kilometres from Amiens on the Somme, a place where the river was narrow but not fordable. A strong wooden bridge was built and in the centre of the bridge and reaching right across it was a lattice, such as might be on a lion's cage, the space between every bar being no bigger than a man could get his arm through. The top was covered to keep off the rain, and there was room for ten or twelve men to stand on each side. In the river there was only a little ferry-boat, rowed by two men. Louis was resolved that there should be no way round or through the partition because when, in 1419, John the Fearless, second Duke of Burgundy, was assassinated on the bridge at Montereau at just such a conference as this he had been lulled into a false sense of security by the pleasant tone of the conversation and had gone through a gate onto the other side of the barrier.[8]

At last, on 29 August 1475, everything was in readiness and the King of England and the King of France came face to face. Louis, who had lodged in a castle close to the bridge, came first; he was backed by six hundred men and cannon placed in strategic positions. Edward appeared supported by his entire army, drawn up in order of battle; they were not all in view, but Comines and Louis could see enough to feel nervous. Each king was accompanied by twelve nobles, four of whom took up stations on the enemy side of the barrier. To confuse assassins, Comines was wearing identical clothes to Louis, a duty which often fell to his lot.

The English had to approach the bridge along a causeway across a marsh which, Comines points out, would have been very dangerous for them if the French had not kept faith. He was amazed how casual they were. 'And without any doubt, as I have said elsewhere, the English are not cunning in treaties and negotiations like French people are; and in spite of what people say they are clumsy in business. But one must have a little patience and not argue angrily with them.'

Edward advanced along the causeway with a regal air. He was wearing cloth of gold and a black velvet cap decorated with a large jewelled fleur-de-lys[9] and he was attended by Clarence, Hastings, Northumberland, Bishop Rotheram (the Chancellor) and others. 'He was a very handsome prince, and tall as well, but he had begun to get fat, and I had seen him when he was better looking, for I do not remember ever to have seen a handsomer man than he was when M. de Warwick forced him to flee from England.'

Edward took off his cap and bowed nearly to the ground as he approached the barrier, and Louis bowed in return, and then the two kings embraced each other through the grille. Louis spoke a few words

---

[8] This was the best-known incident in Burgundian history, though exactly how it happened was never decided. It was believed to have been planned in revenge for the murder of the Duke of Orleans which had taken place twelve years before, but it may have been unpremeditated.

[9] Bad taste or legitimate teasing? He had had a seal cut with fleur-de-lys stops between the words, the only known impression of which is on the Picquigny Treaty in the French archives.

of welcome and Edward replied in quite good French, and then they both solemnly swore to observe the treaty. Formalities over, Louis, who was always ready to chat, suggested jokingly that Edward should visit Paris and amuse himself with the ladies; he could have for his confessor the Cardinal de Bourbon who would certainly absolve him for any sins he committed.

The attendants then withdrew a little, and the two kings talked together in private; different though they were, they got on far better than did Edward and Duke Charles. Then Comines was called forward and introduced, and Edward, who had a royal memory for faces, at once recollected meeting him in Burgundy, and all about him. They discussed Duke Charles, and Edward said that if he would not join the treaty Louis could do as he liked with him, but when Louis delicately worked round to the question of how Edward would react if Brittany were attacked Edward said firmly that Duke Francis had always been a good friend and that he must be left alone. After this, Louis returned to Amiens and Edward to his camp to which Louis had sent provisions, down to torches and candles.

It will have been noticed that, while Clarence backed up his brother, Gloucester had been conspicuously absent from the scene. He had signed the agreement along with other courtiers, but apparently he now wanted war and, with lamentable absence of esprit de corps, he suddenly refused to co-operate. According to Comines, there was a little group who were against the treaty, 'but they changed their minds and very soon afterwards the before-mentioned Duke of Gloucester called on the King at Amiens and the King gave him some very fine presents such as plate, and horses splendidly caparisoned'.

As they came away from the meeting, Louis spoke to Comines about two things which worried him. One was that he feared that Edward had taken his joke seriously and that he really would come to Paris. 'He is a very handsome king; he is fond of women; he might find in Paris a cunning one who would know how to make such pretty speeches that he would want to return.' Louis went on to say that Edward's ancestors had already been too often in Paris and Normandy, and that he would be a good friend on the far side of the sea but not on this side of it. The other trouble was Edward's alliance with Duke Francis; and envoys were sent to try to persuade him to think again, but they only received the answer that if anyone invaded Brittany he would again cross the sea to defend it.

Some of the English lords who dined with Louis the night after the meeting on the bridge took up the subject of the suggested visit to Paris, and Lord Howard whispered to Louis that he thought that it might be arranged. Louis answered evasively, and when, after dinner, they again raised the subject he told them in desperation that he would have to depart immediately to make war on the Duke of Burgundy.

The treaty having been settled in this satisfactory manner, the next day the streets of Amiens were full of Englishmen selling their spare horses. They boasted that peace had been made by the Holy Ghost and gave as proof of it the fact that during the time of the interview on the bridge, a white bird was perched on the top of Edward's tent and had refused to be frightened away; but Louis de Bretaylles, a Gascon in the service of Anthony, told Comines that it was not a miraculous dove but, on the contrary, a very ordinary pigeon which had been wetted by a shower of rain and was drying itself, choosing the King's tent because it was higher than the others.[1]

The treaty was so unexpected and unprecedented that people did not know what to make of two kings who seemed utterly indifferent to glory. Comines had observed that it is much easier to drift into a war than to get out of it again, and he had no doubt at all that France had had a lucky escape. An Italian summed it up in a private letter: 'I feel sure that this agreement will appear very extraordinary and indeed it seems so to everyone, and rather the work of God than human agents, that so valiant a king should come to France with so large an army and with the support of Burgundy, and then return, without striking a blow, the enemy of Burgundy and the friend of France.'[2]

Louis, who now had to wring the money out of his already over-taxed subjects, consoled himself by pretending that he had outwitted Edward and was paying him a 'pension' and that the English were quite wrong to call it 'tribute'. He was a great believer in greasing palms and,

---

[1] Louis de Bretaylles was disappointed because he had hoped to win back his family estates in Gascony. Louis XI tried to buy him over, but he preferred to stay with Anthony.
[2] *Cal. Milanese Papers.* Written on 12 September 1475 by an Italian at Lyons.

besides giving presents to many of Edward's courtiers, he promised annuities to those he took to be really influential. The list of these is incomplete, but payments to Hastings, Howard, Bishop Rotherham, Dr Morton and Sir Thomas Montgomery appear for the next three years in the accounts of a certain Restout, a merchant of Rouen, who also brought Edward's annuity to England. Hastings refused to sign a receipt for his, as he was already receiving an annuity from the Duke of Burgundy, but Louis continued to send it all the same.

Needless to say, the Croyland Continuator detected that money had changed hands and wrote sarcastically: 'Our lord the King returned to England having thus concluded an honourable treaty of peace—for in this light it was regarded by the higher officers of the royal army, although there is nothing so holy or of so high a sanctity that it may not be desecrated by being sneered at.'

The Duke of Burgundy was invited to join the Anglo-French pact, but he was furious, and wrote angrily to Edward. His secretary told the Milanese ambassador that Edward was going about saying that when Duke Charles heard of the treaty, 'he tore up the Garter with his teeth into more than six pieces. But it is not true.' Shortly afterwards the Duke made his own pact with Louis.

Two hostages were left behind as a token of good faith until the English army left France; they were Lord Howard and Sir John Cheyne, Master of the Horse. Men who wished to see some real fighting, two thousand of them it was said, went off to join the Burgundian army in which there were already English mercenaries; but most of the soldiers were glad to be going home before winter. The army had no wish to linger in either France or Burgundy, and they were back in Calais in an incredibly short time. On 11 September Paston *major* wrote to his mother: 'Blessed be God, this voyage of the King's is finished for this time, and all the King's host is come to Calais as on Monday last past, that is to say the fourth day of September; and at this day many of his host be passed the sea into England again; and in especial my Lord of Norfolk and my brethren.' He went on to say that he hoped soon to get Caister back, because the King was beginning to take his part and to question the Duke of Norfolk's title to it; he would rather like to come home to look after his property and the air of Calais did not really suit him.

There was one casualty on the return journey. The Duke of Exeter fell overboard and was drowned, thus ending a ridiculous career in a ridiculous manner.[3] The Duke of Burgundy said that he had been thrown overboard by Edward's orders, however, the Duke of Burgundy was feeling aggrieved. Disbanded soldiers gave a little trouble in the south of England, but ruthless punishment put a stop to their depredations; otherwise the great invasion of France ended without incident.

Edward stayed in Calais till at least 18 September, perhaps enjoying a nostalgic holiday among old friends, perhaps arranging business deals. Many of the guns and munitions he had brought with him were left in Calais and he may have been seeing to the defences of the town. Foreigners hoped that the people of England would be indignant that there had been no battles fought nor towns captured, but they took it very calmly. They had joyously waved their army off to the war and now, a little over two months later, they joyously waved it back again. A deputation from the City of London met Edward at Blackheath and conducted him in triumph to Westminster. Those who were intelligent realized that their money had not been spent in vain, and that in future many of their national expenses would be paid by the French. The unhappy French realized (it is to be hoped) that anything was better then being overrun by an English army.

Edward has been much abused by historians for not reopening the Hundred Years' War. The ethics of levying Danegold may be questioned, and that he was a blackmailer may be laid to his account, but at least he did not repeat the atrocities and follies of the Black Prince and Henry V; in any case, without the help of the Duke of Burgundy success would have been impossible.

Edward himself considered that the expedition on which he had embarked so unwillingly, and which had started so dismally, was an unmitigated triumph, and when he came to select a subject for the misericord[4] on the under side of the royal stall in the new chapel of the Knights of the Garter—that Holy of Holies of chivalry—he did not

[3] He may have merely died on the journey. He was too unimportant to be worth murdering, and the lack of animosity towards him suggests that personally he was rather liked.

[4] The seats in the chancel of St George's Chapel are permanently turned down, and so the crowds who mill through it do not see the misericords.

choose to be represented as the victor of Mortimer's Cross, or Towton or Tewkesbury; instead he was portrayed as a very astute monarch driving a hard bargain with another astute monarch on the bridge at Picquigny. The carving is still there; the figures are tiny, but what Edward is telling posterity is perfectly clear. This, he says to us, was my finest hour.

XIV

Peace and Prosperity 1475–1482

QUEEN MARGARET OF ANJOU RETURNED TO ANJOU. LOUIS HAD bought her at Picquigny for the sum of 50,000 crowns, which was a good bargain on both sides: it saved Edward the trouble and expense of maintaining her and, for the price of her ransom money, Louis would become her heir. Margaret's two brothers had died childless; she had quarrelled with her sister; Louis was her first cousin; it was a very sensible arrangement.

By this time Alice Duchess of Suffolk had died, and Margaret had returned to the Tower where doubtless life was more entertaining than in Wallingford Castle. She set out for France on 13 November 1475, escorted by one of the Hautes, and at Rouen on 29 January 1476 Sir Thomas Montgomery handed her back to the French—nearly thirty-one years after the French had sent her to England. On 7 March she renounced all her hereditary rights in favour of Louis in exchange for an annuity; as Louis pointed out, he had spent a great deal of money on her behalf in the past and furthermore Anjou and Provence belonged to her father, who was still living, while Lorraine, the property of her late mother, was at the moment occupied by the army of Duke Charles.

'The Duke of Burgundy has conquered Lorraine and Queen Margaret shall not now by likelihood have it,' wrote Paston *major* at Calais to his mother on 21 March, 'wherefore the French king cherishes her but easily.' He cannot really have known how Louis was treating Margaret, but he liked stories about haughty ladies who came to bad ends.

Margaret retired to Anjou, the country of her childhood, and lived quietly at the Château of Dampierre. Her father wrote to her from Provence to tell her to trust in God, not man. 'If you wish to feel your troubles less, think of mine. They are great, God knows them.' And he continued to give endless pageants and fêtes, feasts and festivals.

Margaret died in August 1482 at the age of fifty-three, two years after her ebullient father. She had been able to keep a first-class pack of hounds and immediately after her death Louis wrote to one of her ladies commanding that they should be sent to him. She was not to conceal any, '*car vous me feriez terriblement grand déplaisir*', and if she knew of anyone else who had got some of them would she tell his equerry. Among the witnesses to Margaret's will was Catherine Vaux, so at least she had one old friend at her death-bed. Many dethroned queens have fared worse.

DUKE CHARLES SURVIVED THE Treaty of Picquigny by less than a year and a half, during which time his egotism almost reached the point of madness. Having attacked Lorraine and captured its capital, Nancy, he turned his attention to the Swiss; at the same time, he was looking westward, and he told the Milanese ambassador on 9 February 1476 that he had a better claim to the throne of England than Edward IV, and that he would press his claims when things had settled down a little. 'Accordingly he enlists Englishmen into his army in order to win popularity in England, where he says he has a strong party and is much beloved. Once he has that kingdom, he need only lift the other shoulder and forthwith he will be king of France.' Knowing as we now do what in fact happened to Duke Charles, these wild boasts seem unimportant, but his contemporaries had to give them due consideration. They would be reported to Edward, who could not afford to ignore them and who was aware that Duke Charles was almost certainly in communication with Clarence, and that the intrigues of Duchess Margaret were unpredictable.

Comines, who had known Duke Charles well, mentions that he was tireless, fearless, ready to rough it when he was with the army: 'He was the first that rose and last who went to bed in the camp and he slept in his clothes like the poorest soldier,' but that at his court ceremony was carried beyond all bounds; now, when he set out on his expeditions against the Swiss, some romantic aberration inspired him to take with his army a fantastic collection of jewels, tapestries and objets d'art, an eccentricity which was duly noted in other armies. His first exploit, towards the end of February 1476, was to capture the town of Granson on the Lake of Neuchâtel and to hang and drown the defenders; but this, far from frightening the Swiss, infuriated them, and on 2 March they fell on the Burgundian army and, attacking from behind and above, routed it. Duke Charles escaped with his life, but he had to abandon his military stores and his treasures.[1]

Paston *major*, writing to his mother on 21 March, had already heard about the Burgundian defeat, and was able to comment on it far more freely than if it had concerned his own countrymen. 'And so the rich sallets, helmets, garter-ouches gilt and all is gone, with tents, pavilions and all; and so men deem his pride is abated. Men told him that they were froward karls but he would not believe it; and yet men say that he will to them again. God speed them both! . . . I pray you send me some word if you think likely that I may enter Caister when I will. . . . Written at Calais in reasonable health of body and soul, I thank God.'

Paston's information was perfectly correct; Duke Charles was not to be deterred by his defeat at Granson, and immediately he began recruiting a new army which he assembled at Lausanne. By April the Milanese ambassadors to Burgundy and Savoy were both writing home in agitation, describing the scuffles among the soldiers, the street fights, the murders. The English mercenaries were particularly unruly, and fought with the Italians. Antoine, Bastard of Burgundy, calmed them down, and the Duchess of Savoy[2] said that it was nothing, one must

---

[1] Some of his treasures can now be seen in Swiss museums.

[2] Yolande, Duchess of Savoy, was the sister of Louis XI. She was a widow and regent for her son, and she was inclined to ally herself with Burgundy until Duke Charles attempted to kidnap her and her children. The children escaped, and Yolande was rescued by her brother Louis.

expect quarrels and murders among so many troops of so many nationalities.

The two ambassadors continued to describe quarrels and affrays
in the heterogeneous army. English and Lombards killed each other.
'The English are a proud race without any respect, and they claim
superiority over all other nationalities.' On 1 May the news was that
the Duke of Milan's courier had been murdered and his letters stolen.
The English were probably responsible. Some men had been tortured,
but nobody had confessed. On 7 May: 'Last night the Italian infantry
had a broil with the English, Picards and Greeks, and also men from
Gheler, who sacked the quarters of these infantry and men were maim-
ed and wounded on all sides, seven or eight being killed. The Bastard
hastened thither and the uproar ceased. It was about a woman. So
many races cannot always remain of one mind, especially in the
evening.'

At the beginning of June, Duke Charles set out for Berne and
encamped outside the small fortified town of Morat on Lake Morat.
Here, on 7 July, Anthony Lord Scales turned up.

Anthony had been on a pilgrimage, or tour, with some other
gentlemen, and outside Rome, with his usual bad luck, he had been
robbed of his valuables. The Pope, Sixtus IV, offered a reward of 300
ducats and a pardon, and put a curse on whoever concealed them, and
they were discovered on sale in Venice and returned to him, as a compliment to the King of England. His visit to Duke Charles was from
curiosity, and he made it clear that he did not intend to stay—there was
no reason why he should want to fight for the Duke of Burgundy, and
a good many why he should not. Duke Charles, whose allies were
shaky, was very disappointed that he could not induce Anthony to
join him, and he went about saying that Anthony had offered to fight
but had changed his mind when he discovered that a battle was imminent—a slander which the Milanese ambassador duly repeated. 'This
is considered great cowardice in him and lack of spirit and honour.
The Duke laughed about it to me, saying, 'He has gone because he is
afraid.'

Anthony was well out of it. On 22 June 1476 the Swiss attacked
Duke Charles and again won a smashing victory; the Burgundian

casualties were even higher than before, though the booty taken was less. However, Duke Charles continued to believe that he was a second Alexander, the wealth of Burgundy was not yet spent, and he set about raising another army.

His course was nearing its end. In October the Duke of Lorraine recaptured Nancy, and at the end of the year Duke Charles settled down to besiege the town. On 5 January 1477, for the third time, he was surprised by the Swiss, his army routed and his camp looted and, in the thick of the fighting, Duke Charles disappeared. Snow added to the confusion, and some days passed before his Portuguese doctor and his page identified a mutilated corpse as being that of the Duke of Burgundy. It was hard to believe that he was really dead, and a story grew up that he had gone into retirement and become a hermit.[3]

The heir of Duke Charles was his only daughter, Mary of Burgundy. She was unmarried, and as soon as it was realized that the ferocious warrior was no more the vultures gathered. Louis could correctly claim that when the King of France had originally bestowed the Duchy of Burgundy on his youngest son it was with the proviso that if the male line failed it should revert to the crown of France, but he wanted the whole of the late Duke's dominions and for the next six years there was a desultory Franco-Burgundian war. Some of the richer Flemish towns dreamed of becoming independent city-states, and in particular the citizens of Ghent were violent and truculent. Comines wrote: 'I cannot understand why God has preserved for so long this city of Ghent which has caused so much harm and which is little use either to the public or to the country in which it is situated, much less to its prince. It is not like Bruges, which is a market and a great meeting place for people of all nations and in which more merchandize changes hands than in any other town in Europe.'

That Mary should marry immediately was essential and among the suitors suggested was her half-uncle, a bastard of Philip the Good, who might have infused some solidarity into the state. Louis offered the hand of the Dauphin, who was five and nominally engaged to Edward's eldest daughter. Duchess Margaret suggested her brother Clarence,

---

[3] Similar myths attached themselves to Barbarossa, Richard II, Joan of Arc, Kitchener, Lawrence of Arabia and Hitler.

whose wife had just died, but Edward vetoed it; there was a time when he would gladly have set Clarence upon a foreign throne but that had gone by, and Mary had inherited her father's claim to the English crown. Louis pointed out to Edward that Clarence again had become a menace, but Edward was only too well aware of it. He passionately wanted to prevent the union of France and Burgundy, but he had no candidate of his own to put forward except Anthony, who was only an ordinary Earl and did not impress foreigners.

Mary of Burgundy was in the unusual position of being able to choose her own husband, and she selected Maximilian of Hapsburg,[4] the son of the Emperor, a suitor whom her father had tentatively encouraged. He was young, handsome and a bachelor and they married on 19 August 1477. Politically the connection did not turn out so well as had been hoped; in theory Maximilian should have been able to protect Burgundy against France, but his own liabilities distracted his attention and he always remained a foreigner in his wife's duchy, resented by the Burgundians and without much authority. Domestically it was a signal success. Mary and Maximilian were a devoted couple; they hunted, made music and read aloud to each other; they had two children, Philip the Fair and Marguerite d'Autriche; and they stayed on the best of terms with Mary's stepmother.

Duchess Margaret, now a young but formidable dowager, spent her great energy and large income on good works and political intrigue; her morals were irreproachable. She kept great state at Malines, and by sheer force of personality made herself repected and feared. With dogged persistence she tried to induce Edward to join Burgundy in an attack on Louis, and in July 1480 she came over to England to try the effects of sisterly persuasion. Edward fêted her, but refused to be coaxed into a war and when she returned to Flanders she was met by the unwelcome news that in her absence Maximilian had made a pact with Louis.

TO GO BACK TO THE YEAR 1477, and the problems of King Edward: foreign policy was clear—not to commit himself one way or the

[4] Maximilian I (1459–1519). Emperor, 1493.

other; the appalling question was at home—what to do about Clarence?

This year of Clarence's life is very mysterious. Information which was well known to the Royal Council failed to percolate down to the people who wrote chronicles; even matters that were discussed in Parliament did not necessarily become common knowledge. Only the simplest of facts, the crudest of gossip, the shortest of anecdotes, the most childish of explanations, made any impact on the public, and Clarence's murderous schemes and wicked and criminal actions were unknown to them. Clarence, moreover, now lived mainly at Warwick Castle or in Somerset, and the people of London were not affected by his gangster tactics and were mystified by the commotion they caused.

Many pieces of the puzzle are missing, but the following are some of the clues that remain.

According to the chronicle of Tewkesbury Abbey, Clarence's wife Isobel gave birth to a child in the new chamber of the Abbey infirmary on 6 October 1476.[5] She was very ill and on 12 November, still ill, she was taken home to Warwick Castle where she died on 12 December. Her baby died on 1 January 1477; on 4 January her body was brought back to Tewkesbury and, after lying in state for 35 days, she was buried in a vault behind the high altar. Some of this may be inaccurate, as the dates do not tally with those in the story of Ankarette Twynho which is unfolded in the Patent Rolls and in the Rolls of Parliament.

Ankarette Twynho was a widow belonging to a well-known county family, and she had formerly been in attendance on Duchess Isobel; her kinsman and heir, Roger Twynho, put in a petition[6] on 20 February 1478, two days after the death of Clarence. Ankarette, he declared, had been at her home at Cayford near Frome in Somerset when, at two o'clock on the afternoon of Saturday 12 April 1477, eighty of Clarence's men suddenly arrived and carried her off to Bath. On Sunday they took her to Cirencester, and they reached Warwick at eight o'clock on Monday evening. (From Frome to Warwick via

---

[5] Quoted by C. L. Scofield, *Edward IV*, vol. II, p. 184. This was Isobel's fourth child. Besides the baby born dead in the ship outside Calais in April 1470, she had had Margaret, b. 14 August 1473 and Edward, b. 21 February 1475.

[6] *Patent Rolls.*

Bath would be about ninety-five miles.) Her daughter and her daughter's husband had followed in pursuit, but they were forced to go immediately that very night to Stratford-on-Avon, and Ankarette was incarcerated in Warwick prison, having been stripped of all her jewels, money and goods. Next morning she was brought into the Guildhall before the Justices of the Peace and a jury of twenty-four, and the accusation was made that on 10 October of the previous year, at Warwick, she had given the Duchess Isobel 'a venomous drink of ale mixed with poison', after which Isobel sickened until the Sunday before Christmas when she died. The jury, terrorized by Clarence, found her guilty and she was straightway taken to the gallows outside the town at Myton, and hanged; the trial and execution being over in three hours. Some of the jury came to Ankarette and begged her to forgive them. It was flagrantly unlawful to bring a prisoner through three counties, and the King was asked to cancel the verdict so that Roger Twynho could inherit her property; and this was done. According to the Rolls of Parliament, a John Thursby of Warwick was accused of poisoning Isobel's baby and was hanged at the same time as Ankarette, and a Sir Roger Tucotes was also condemned but managed to escape.

The crucial question is: Why did Clarence go to such lengths to murder these three people? As Sir Roger Tucotes escaped, Edward and his confidential council must have known the answer, and it was evidently something which they agreed to hush up.

In May 1477 three men called Burdett, Stacy and Blake were tried on the charge of using magical arts against the king. Their trial was in London and, unlike the Ankarette case which had passed unnoticed except by a small provincial circle, it excited great interest. It was felt, as we feel today, that the accusations were frivolous and a cover for something else, but the true story, whatever it was, did not emerge at the trial. Burdett (who was a member of Clarence's household) and Stacy were hanged; Blake was condemned and reprieved at the last moment. On the day of the hanging the Ankarette case was reopened and Sir Roger Tucotes came out of hiding.

Clarence's riposte to this was to wait till Edward had gone to Windsor and then to appear in the council chamber at Westminster, accompanied by Dr John Goddard (formerly a partisan of Henry VI) who read aloud a declaration of innocence made by Stacy and Burdett. About the same time there was a rising in Cambridgeshire and Huntingdonshire, presumably inspired by Clarence and led by a man who claimed to be the Earl of Oxford. Edward decided—and his decision was probably backed up by his Council—that Clarence was too dangerous to be left at large, and he was summoned to Westminster. The Mayor and aldermen had also been told to attend and, in front of a crowd of witnesses, Edward accused Clarence of 'going above the law' as though he were a king when he arrested and hanged Ankarette Twynho. Edward may have made other accusations as well, and there can have been little sympathy for Clarence among the listeners; he had a black record, and he could no longer be excused on the grounds of youth. Clarence was sent to the Tower, where he remained till his death some six or seven months later.

In the interval between Clarence's arrest and his arraignment by Parliament the two brothers must have communicated with each other, and Duchess Cecily and the other members of the family must have expressed opinions. Edward had forgiven Clarence much, and had helped him to become immensely rich, but it would not be surprising if he now actually hated him: all the same, he did not want to condemn him to death. Fratricide had been execrated ever since the time of Cain and Abel, and Edward had great family feeling and had once been fond of his attractive little brother. On the other hand, he could not incarcerate Clarence in prison for the rest of his life, and experience had shown that nothing would prevent Clarence from plotting. There were always discontented and ambitious men who would join a rebellion. Edward's sons were still very young, life was uncertain, and if he died Clarence would certainly make a bid for the throne. Edward endeavoured to find other solutions, but he finally resolved that Clarence must die and he summoned Parliament to meet in the New Year. It is often said that Edward mishandled this affair, though no feasible way out has ever been suggested.

Parliament met on 15 January 1478. The Speaker was William Alyngton, who had conducted the Long Parliament of 1472–1475, and everyone knew that the main reason that they were there was to share the responsibility of killing the King's brother.

Edward had had a long time in which to think over the case against Clarence, and to discuss with lawyers how to frame the accusations so that Parliament would find Clarence guilty of high treason and pass a Bill of Attainder without asking for proofs or washing more dirty linen in public than was necessary. The indictment as it is printed in the Rolls of Parliament seems rather woolly, but it served its purpose of convincing the Lords and Commons that Clarence had committed the crime of being about to rebel; they knew that he would stop at nothing, and they were quite ready to find him guilty. The murder of Ankarette and the other private crimes which Clarence had committed were not referred to as they would have confused the issue, but most people knew about them. As there was no real trial, justice was not seen to be done, but it can hardly be doubted that Clarence was guilty of high treason, and that the accusations made against him were true.

According to the indictment, Clarence had paid people to say that Burdett was wrongfully put to death, and that he said that the King wrought by necromancy and used craft to poison his subjects, and that he said that the King was a bastard; that he made people swear allegiance to him; that he complained that he had been disinherited; that he had a document with Henry VI's seal naming him heir if Henry's son died; and that he ordered the Abbot of Tewkesbury to send a strange child into Warwick Castle with a view to smuggling his own child to Ireland or Flanders, but the Abbot refused to comply.[7]

Edward pointed out that he had already forgiven Clarence a good deal, but that he was incorrigible, and that as the first duty of a king was to prevent bloodshed and to keep the country and all its people in peace and tranquillity Clarence must be attainted.

There was no reason why anyone, Peers, Bishops or Commons, should want to spare Clarence. He was not *their* brother, he was just a

[7] This is not as crazy as it sounds. Clarence's son was evidently in Tewkesbury Abbey and Clarence intended sending him abroad so that soldiers could be raised in his name. Clarence had no well-known peers on his side and the child would have been a token that his representatives were not impostors—a few years before, Edward had sent the baby Prince of Wales to Hereford to give authority to the judges on the Welsh Border. Parliament would understand that his request to the Abbot of Tewkesbury could only mean that he was planning an invasion with foreign soldiers. At that time Duke Charles was still alive and it is likely that Clarence had been promised the hand of Mary if he could dispose of Isobel.

contemptible prince who was also a rebel, a traitor, a murderer and the leader of a gang of ruffians. Judged by ordinary laws he had earned death several times over. If he were released, there would be disturbances with loss of life or even a foreign invasion.

Clarence was found guilty of high treason and attainted, and the Duke of Buckingham (who had grown up to be a foolish young man with grand ambitions[8]) was given the title of Seneschal of England so that he could pronounce the death sentence, which otherwise would have been the duty of the Duke of Gloucester. The dread words were said on 7 February 1478 and, when no steps were taken to implement them, the Commons sent a deputation to the Lords demanding that Clarence's death should not be further delayed. There is no reason to think that this was play-acting, or that the hesitation on Edward's part was humbug, or that the Commons were not determined that Clarence should receive his just deserts. They knew only too well how often great men were pardoned while small men were hanged. Accordingly, Clarence was put to death in the privacy of the Tower on the night of 18 February 1478. He was buried in Tewkesbury Abbey beside his wife Isobel and not far from 'Edward called Prince of Wales' and other men who had fallen at Tewkesbury.[9] He was twenty-eight.

Almost at once it began to be said that Clarence had been drowned in a butt of malmsey wine and the phrase was, and is, considered so amusing that today it is familiar to people who know of few other incidents in medieval history, and the essentially insignificant Clarence has won immortality by the supposed manner of his death. Whether this messy and extravagant way of killing him was really used can never now be known; had the executioner wished to avoid shedding royal blood, a water-butt would have been more convenient, and the sheer popularity of the story suggests that it is a little too good to be true. Its origins may have been a joke, thrown off on the spur of the moment; Clarence could have been a notorious drunk, and there might

---

[8] His mother, Margaret Beaufort, was the eldest sister of the Duke of Somerset and in 1471, when the last male Beauforts were killed at Tewkesbury, she inherited their pretensions. The Duke of Buckingham's claim to the throne was very similar to Henry Tudor's, and only one degree weaker on paper.

[9] The site of the Clarence vault is marked by a grating in the floor behind the altar.

have been some punning connection between the Frankish Castle of Clarence in Greece and malmsey, a Greek wine.[1]

Once Clarence was safely out of the way and the danger of a rebellion past, opinion swung round in the familiar fashion; his life had been muddled and shapeless, and so it was turned into a neat hard-luck story. Ankarette Twynho, whom nobody in London knew anything about, was completely forgotten[2] and all that was remembered was the handsome young prince. In time it was said that Edward was gnawed with remorse, and that when people begged for pardons he would think of Clarence and exclaim, 'O unhappy brother, for whose deliverance no man asked!' which does not sound like Edward's usual style. Naturally he could never forget what he had done, but it may well be that if someone referred to Clarence with regret he retorted that it was all very well to talk like that afterwards, but that nobody spoke up for him at the time. This last point is not without significance; in spite of his enormous wealth, Clarence does not seem to have had a single friend.

Clarence's son and daughter were treated like other orphans; their wardship and marriages were bought by suitable nobles, and they were brought up by people who had an interest in keeping them alive. In later years it turned out that they were too near the throne for their own happiness, but for the moment they were so young that they were no threat to the reigning king.

On 6 March 1468 Bishop Stillington was sent to the Tower, and on 20 June he was released after paying a fine; some writers have connected this with the death of Clarence, but there does not seem to be any logical reason why the two events should be cause and effect, and

---

[1] The reason for the title of 'Clarence' had become dim. (*See* note 2, p. 51.) Clarencia (now Glarentza) is a long way from Monemvasia which gave its name to malmsey, but close enough to get a laugh.

[2] Polydore Vergil, a disinterested Italian, who some thirty or forty years later attempted to find out why it had been necessary to kill Clarence, heard nothing about Ankarette, but was told that Edward had been warned that he would be succeeded by a man whose name began with a "G"—George or Gloucester—that Clarence was really older than Edward, and that the Woodvilles had killed him for spite. Mancini, in 1483, was informed that Clarence had been killed because of the machinations of Edward Woodville, Dorset and Richard Grey. It would have been better for Edward's posthumous reputation if Clarence had had a proper trial, but there may have been some reason why this was not expedient.

his few months in the Tower must remain as mysterious as the rest of his life.

A week after Clarence's death Parliament was dissolved, and it was not called again for five years, a deprivation which the country bore with great equanimity. It had been a short session, but there had been time to take away all titles from Montagu's son who, in a moment of crisis, had been made Duke of Bedford.[3] There were also new regulations controlling goldsmiths and silversmiths and the Courts of Piepowder (which arbitrated at fairs), and for paving the streets of various towns. There were laws to keep up the quality of cloth and the quality of roof-tiles, to forbid the playing of dice, quoits, football, closshe, kyles, half-ball, hand-in-and-hand-out and quickboard instead of practising archery. There was a law to send people born in Ireland back to Ireland, with a few exceptions which included students at Oxford and Cambridge and the London law-courts. Those who refused to go were to be taxed, and the money thus obtained was to be used to maintain order in Ireland; the King agreed to this measure, but made a special exception for a goldsmith called Hugh Bryce. There was also another sumptuary law, apparently made by the more middle-class members of Parliament, which positively stated what they and their womenfolk could wear and the lower classes could not.

Apart from the refusal of his brothers to march in step, Edward's family life presented a picture of harmonious domesticity. Besides her two sons by her first marriage, Elizabeth gave birth to ten children, three sons and seven daughters, and for most of these Edward arranged state marriages. Large dowries were sometimes demanded, but Edward considered foreign alliances so important that he was prepared to pay a stiff price to get what he wanted. Princess Elizabeth was to be Queen of France; Mary, Queen of Denmark; Cecily, Queen of Scotland; Anne was engaged to the son of Mary of Burgundy and Maximilian,

[3] George Neville (*c.* 1460-4 May 1483). Only son of John, Marquis of Montagu. Created Duke of Bedford in January 1470 and promised the hand of Princess Elizabeth. His father had been loyal to neither Warwick nor Edward, but had not actually been attainted, and though some of George Neville's lands were confiscated it was worth Gloucester's while to buy his wardship and marriage for £1000, and his five sisters made quite good marriages. He died unmarried in Sheriff Hutton Castle.

and Catherine was suggested for the son of Ferdinand and Isabella. None of these marriages took place.

The future of the Prince of Wales was more important still, and the daughter of Bona of Savoy (Duchess of Milan) was considered, and so was the daughter of Ferdinand and Isabella, but in May 1481 the Prince was plighted to Anne, daughter and heir of Duke Francis of Brittany; it was agreed that their eldest son should inherit England and their second son Brittany—a plan so likely to miscarry that it was fortunate that it was never put to the test.

It is not known at what moment Edward made the acquaintance of the woman referred to by contemporaries as Mistress Shore or the wife of Shore, and who is known to posterity as Jane Shore although her real name was Elizabeth.[4] Her husband, William Shore, was a mercer and a well-known figure in the City; he was apprenticed in 1452 and died in 1494. Her father, John Lambert, was another prosperous mercer. In March 1476, Pope Sixtus commissioned three bishops to decide the case of Elizabeth Lambert alias Shore, wife of William Shore, who was petitioning that her marriage should be annulled on the grounds that her husband was 'frigidus et impotens' and that she desired to have children.[5] It can be assumed that the bishops found in her favour. At the end of Edward's reign he was keeping her openly; he had by that time grown immensely fat and his subjects pictured his life as being one happy round of guzzling, swilling and committing adultery.

Sir Thomas More wrote an account of Mistress Shore at a time when he believed that she was still alive. He had never met her, but what he had been told about her had fired his imagination and, unaware that one day he would bear the burden of a reputation for abnormal holiness, he described her with lyrical enthusiasm. He had no doubt in his mind that Edward was genuinely devoted to her. 'For many he had, but her he loved.' She was very small and her greatest charm was her engaging personality. 'Yet delighted not men so much in her beauty as in her pleasant behaviour.' She could read and write and was clever

---

[4] Nicolas Barker, 'The Real Jane Shore' and Sir Robert Bailey, 'Jane Shore in Literature' in *Etoniana* (4 June 1972).
[5] *Calendar of Entries in Papal Registers Relating to England*, XIII 487–8.

and amusing. 'The King would say that he had three concubines which in three divers properties diversely excelled. One the merriest, another the wiliest, the third the holiest harlot in his realm. . . . The merriest was this Shore's wife.'[6] Her influence, says Sir Thomas More, was exerted wholly for good, and she was not mercenary. 'In many weighty suits she stood many men in great stead, either for none or very small rewards, and those rather gay than rich.' More assumed that the Queen detested her rival, but that may not have been so; she may have been grateful for the bright little person who kept her husband amused and away from more grasping women.[7]

THE ROYAL ACCOUNTS DO NOT SHOW HOW EDWARD'S FINANCES really stood at any given time, but fifteenth-century financiers were adept at calculating in their heads and, after 1475 when Edward acquired the annual tribute from France, he knew that he had money to spare, and in July 1476 he went to the expense of transferring the remains of his father and brother Rutland from Pontefract to Fotheringhay. He had waited a long time, but now it was done superbly. The procession stopped for five nights on the way, and everyone who came to gaze received a penny and every pregnant woman twopence. For the ceremonies in Fotheringhay Church Edward wore a mourning robe of blue, and he was supported by Clarence (at that time still persona grata at Court), Gloucester, Anthony, Dorset, Hastings and a great crowd of courtiers. An opportune arrival was Guillaume Restout, a merchant from Rouen, who had been sent by Louis with the first instalments of the French annuities. Afterwards there was a banquet at which it was claimed 20,000 guests were fed which, if true, would be more than three times the number entertained at the great Neville feast when George Neville became Archbishop of York.

There was another notable week of entertaining in January 1478, when Edward's second son, Richard Duke of York, aged four, was

---

[6] This anecdote sounds rather literary; after Edward's death, Elizabeth Shore was the only mistress persecuted by Richard III.

[7] In some ways, Edward IV and his Queen resembled Edward VII and Queen Alexandra, and the latter accepted her husband's mistresses philosophically.

married to Anne Mowbray,[8] aged five, only daughter of the late John Mowbray, 4th Duke of Norfolk, who had died in January 1476. The Duchess was pregnant when her husband died, but her baby did not survive, and as soon as it was ascertained that Anne was sole heiress Edward secured her hand; he entirely agreed with Sir John Fortescue that the King must be the richest man in the kingdom—in other words, the greatest landowner. For Anne it was, of course, the most brilliant match open to her. Usually, very young children were merely betrothed, but Edward was particularly anxious to make sure of her fortune which, if she died unmarried, would be divided among her relations, Lord Berkeley and Lord Howard—the latter, incidentally, had a grandson of about the right age to marry Anne.[9] Prince Richard was created Duke of Norfolk and Earl of Nottingham soon after his wedding, and Parliament passed an act providing that in the event of Anne's death most of her estates would remain with him instead of returning, in the normal way, to her own family. Had Edward appeased the Howards by letting them have the Mowbray inheritance and the Dukedom of Norfolk, the history of England might have been different—though not necessarily better.

The wedding of Richard and Anne took place at St Stephen's, Westminster, on 15 January 1478.[1] The bride was given away by the King and she was escorted first by Anthony and the young Earl of Lincoln,[2] and then by Gloucester and Buckingham. There was one gap in the family circle, a ghastly gap, caused by the absence of the Duke of Clarence who was in the Tower and would shortly be brought to trial; but life was too short and too tragic for people to wish to cultivate the luxury of delicate sensibility; stoicism was a virtue and, whatever happened, the show went on.

The week's festivities ended with a tournament organized by Anthony and Dorset. Anthony came in the costume of a white hermit

---

[8] Anne Mowbray (10 December 1472–19 November 1481).

[9] Thomas Howard, 3rd Duke of Norfolk (1473–1554). Eventually he married Anne fifth daughter of Edward IV. Her children died young and his heir, Henry Earl of Surrey, the poet, was the son of his second wife.

[1] *Illustrations of Ancient State and Chivalry* (Roxburghe Club, 1840).

[2] John Earl of Lincoln (*c.* 1462–87). Eldest of the seven sons of the Duke and Duchess of Suffolk and thus the eldest of Edward's nephews. He flourished under Richard III but took part in Lambert Simnel's rebellion and was killed at the Battle of Stoke.

in a black velvet hermitage with glass windows. His servants wore blue and tawny, embroidered with columbines enrampled with drops and flames, and when they had removed his hermit's costume he rode to the tourney on a horse enrampled with flames, with three decorated horses following him. The entry fees were ten marks for Earls, four pounds for Barons, forty shillings for Knights, twenty-six and eight pence for esquires, and some gentlemen complained that this was too high and that they could not afford to enter. Anthony 'sent of his benevolence to the officers of arms twenty marks like a noble man, and desired them so to be contented for him and his hermitage, to whom God send good life and long. Amen.' Prizes were an 'A' of gold set with a diamond, an 'E' of gold set with a ruby (won by one of the Hautes) and an 'M' of gold set with an emerald. One of the competitors who jousted against Anthony was Sir Thomas de Vere, Lord Oxford's brother, who had helped to seize St Michael's Mount in 1473—yet another example of the readiness to let bygones be bygones.

The child-marriage lasted less than four years, and Anne Mowbray died at Greenwich on 19 November 1481. She was given a costly funeral and buried in Westminster Abbey in a chapel which Queen Elizabeth had endowed and dedicated to St Erasmus, the patron saint of pregnant women.[3] On 11 December 1964 her lead coffin was unexpectedly discovered by a man working an excavator during road-widening operations in Stepney. It was alone in a sealed vault eleven feet underground and weighed over a hundredweight, and after being taken to a police station it was transferred to the London Museum. When Henry VII was adding to Westminster Abbey he demolished the chapel of St Erasmus and temporarily transferred some coffins to a nunnery at Stepney known as the Abbey of the Minoresses, and presumably when the time came to return them Anne's was overlooked. Late in the evening of 31 May 1965, Anne Mowbray was reburied in Westminster Abbey as near as possible to her original resting-place.[4]

[3] St Erasmus was a martyr whose entrails were wound off on a windlass.
[4] The discovery of Anne Mowbray's remains created a mild sensation, particularly as only the very erudite were aware that the younger of the Little Princes was a widower. Crowds came to see part of the coffin, which was exhibited for a short time in the London Museum and an animated correspondence was carried on in *The Times:* should she have a Catholic or Protestant re-burial? should the Dean and Chapter of Westminster and the

OF ALL THE CASTLES AND PALACES which were at the disposal of the medieval English kings, Windsor Castle is the only one which is still a royal residence, and the palaces have so completely disappeared that it is difficult to visualize what any of them looked like. Many were on or near the Thames, and the favourite home of Edward and Elizabeth finally became Eltham Palace which occupied a charming site on a hillside a few miles from Greenwich Palace. About 1479 Edward added to its amenities by building a very large hall which is still standing, though little else remains, and here on 11 November 1480 was celebrated the christening of Princess Bridget[5] who was Edward's tenth child and Elizabeth's twelfth. A hundred knights, esquires and 'other honest persons' bore torches which they lit at the moment of baptism, and the baby was carried by Margaret Countess of Richmond 'assisted' by Dorset. The godparents were Duchess Cecily,[6] Princess Elizabeth, and old Bishop Wayneflete who must have been about eighty-five but was still capable of holding his own in court and college.

During the last, affluent, part of his reign Edward did much building, but for one reason or another his achievements have been forgotten. He made repairs and additions to royal castles, and particularly to the Tower, but his great work was the building of St George's Chapel, Windsor. The Order of the Garter, picturesque and with an underlying idea of friendship and good will, appealed to his imagination, and in spite of the difficulty of finding money for the invasion of France he began to plan, soon after his restoration, a large new Garter Chapel to be built next to the old one. In February 1473 he instructed Richard

---

London Museum be prosecuted by the Home Office? Feelings ran high. The Peers then took up the cry and made indignant speeches in the House of Lords until they were persuaded to continue their maunderings in private. The Press were told that ultimately a scholarly report would appear, but the obstructionists brought pressure to bear and though a report was written it was never published. The whole incident, which would appear farfetched in the pages of a comic novel, demonstrates the peculiar obstacles which are strewn in the way of the simple historian.

[5] Bridget (1480–1517). She became a nun in the Dominican Convent at Dartford, Kent and is assumed to have been subnormal. The account of her christening is printed in *The Gentleman's Magazine* (1831), p. 25.

[6] Besides Baynard's Castle in the City, Duchess Cecily lived at Berkhampstead Castle. In February 1482 she was still of sufficient importance for Lord Howard to think it worth his while to give her three and a half yards of white russet. She died at Berkhampstead in 1495.

Beauchamp, Bishop of Salisbury,[7] to find workmen, and the ground began to be cleared; in June 1475 the walls had started to go up, and by the time Edward died the choir had a temporary roof and services could be held in it although the chapel was not entirely finished until 1528.

Edward also contributed £1000 and a gift of timber to King's College, Cambridge, and there are records of his dining in the hall and attending services in the chapel. Henry VI had laid the foundation-stone in 1446, but money ran out and when it was only half built work on it came to a standstill. By the time funds were again available, architectural fashions had changed and expert eyes can detect where the shape of the pillars was altered to fit a fan roof. The parchment for drawing out the plan of this roof was bought in 1480. Elizabeth Woodville also did not disdain to follow in the footsteps of her predecessor and, in 1465, she became the patroness of Queen's College, Cambridge. The foundation-stone of the chapel had been laid in 1448 by Wenlock, when he was Chamberlain to Margaret of Anjou, but the apostrophe was now placed after the 's' in Queens' to include both Margaret and Elizabeth.

Edward's relations with Eton College, after a see-saw start, also became extremely friendly. Eton was founded by Henry VI when he was eighteen and perhaps owed its origin to the Duke of Suffolk who, besides inheriting a charitable foundation in Hull and a 'college' at Wingfield in Suffolk, had just built another 'college' on his wife's property at Ewelme in Oxfordshire.[8] Henry's interest was concentrated on the chapel, which he twice pulled down and rebuilt on a larger scale, intending that ultimately it should be as long as a cathedral, but Suffolk's death and Henry's mental collapse halted the work. On 27 February 1461, the hectic day on which Edward arrived in London just before he was proclaimed king, the Provost of Eton, William Westbury, who had a house in Westminster, pushed in front of him a

[7] Bishop Beauchamp was made Chancellor of the Order of the Garter; king and bishop are portrayed together on a boss in the centre of the vault at the east end of the south choir aisle.

[8] Like Eton, the almshouses and school at Ewelme are built of red brick. Their endowments have increased in value, and they continue to be used for the purposes for which they were built.

document promising to protect the Provost and Fellows of Eton, and this he hurriedly signed 'E. York'.[9] Subsequently he borrowed money from the Provost, but when he had had time to examine the vast unfinished chapel which greeted his eyes every time he looked across the river from Windsor Castle he decided that it was an absurd extravagance and, in 1463, he endeavoured to amalgamate the endowments of Eton with those of St George's, and he obtained a Papal Bull abolishing Henry's 'college'. But Provost Westbury and Bishop Wayneflete (who was passionately interested in education) fought back, and they persuaded Edward that the chapel could be truncated and finished at Wayneflete's expense. In 1470 the Pope's Bull was reversed, and the bells and vestments which had been taken from Eton and given to St George's, were returned. The hospital which had originally been envisaged had never been built and, during the lean years, the almsmen had faded out, and so by this time Eton had become solely a school with a superb chapel.

Everyone concerned was very matter-of-fact: at the end of May 1471 Provost Westbury went to London to attend the obsequies of the Founder, who had died mysteriously in the Tower, and by the following September Edward and his Queen had paid Eton three state visits. After that, all was fair weather between the Castle and the College. Elizabeth Woodville was so generous that Provost Bost—who succeeded Provost Westbury—boasted on his tomb that *Illius auspiciis elemosyna conjugis uncti Edward Quarti larga pluebat opem*,[1] while Anthony's benefactions earned him a daily mass at 7.15 a.m., preceded by sixty strokes of the bell and a memorial service for the whole Woodville family every year on 30 October—all of which was faithfully carried out until the reign of Edward VI. However, the royal family cannot be given credit for the remarkable wall-paintings in the College Chapel, which were painted between 1479 and 1480 by (apparently) one William Baker, and which were paid for by Bishop Wayneflete.[2]

---

[9] This is now in the library of Eton College.

[1] While He was in office, the bountiful charity of King Edward IV's wife showered wealth.

[2] Wayneflete was Bishop of Winchester, and it can be no coincidence that there are rather similar paintings in the Lady Chapel of Winchester Cathedral.

Edward also embellished the York family 'college' at Fotheringhay, which was next to the parish church and has now almost completely disappeared.[3] He added a cloister and, in its hey-day, it had eighty-four stained-glass windows and seven windows in the library; there was a master, eight clerks and thirteen choristers, and it owned property in Northamptonshire, Worcestershire, Huntingdonshire, Gloucestershire, Wiltshire, Lincolnshire, Southampton and Holborn.

EDWARD'S TRADING ACTIVITIES HAVE LEFT VERY LITTLE TRACE; it is known that he exported wool and cloth to the Mediterranean, that he made use of Italian ships and that, like other merchants, he spread his risks over a variety of enterprises. Among the King's imports, taken from the London customs' accounts for February 1470, are figs, raisins, oil, sugar, oranges, a popinjay, alum, rice, copper, lead, salt fish, wainscots, hops, madder, hats, cards, baskets, wire, pins, pack-thread, fans, soap, brushes and spectacles.[4] This part of their sovereign's activities continued to escape the notice of most of his subjects, and when he entertained his business friends it was considered an extraordinary act of condescension, and the chroniclers were particularly amazed by one hunting party which he gave in Waltham Forest on 10 July 1481 and to which he invited London aldermen and their wives, middle-class people who normally were excluded from aristocratic sports.

Competition in Europe was growing, and there was a constant search for new markets and new sources of supply. These probes were furtive. The Portuguese made a spirited attempt to monopolize the West African trade, but they were not wholly successful and when, in 1480, a ship from Bristol carrying cloth touched at Madeira there were twenty non-Portuguese vessels in the harbour loading sugar. In 1481, Edward asked the Pope to sanction his African trade, and to ante-date the authorization, but it was more important to maintain a friendly trade with Portugal than to compete against them in unknown lands.

[3] The church itself has lost its chancel, but retains an exquisite tower, the bones of Edward's father, mother, and brother Rutland, and an elaborate pulpit given by Edward; this has recently been splendidly repainted in red, blue and gold.
[4] Scofield, *Edward IV*, II, 410.

There were also speculative voyages into the Atlantic to find 'the Islands of Brasile and the Seven Cities' which were believed to exist in the far west. About 1478, English fishing-boats were expelled from the Icelandic fisheries, and it is just possible that in casting about for alternative fishing-grounds the cod-banks off Newfoundland were discovered. On 6 July 1481 the *George* and the *Trinity*, which were owned by a Customs Officer named Croft, sailed out from Bristol, nominally in search of the famous 'Brasile'; they were loaded with salt, and it is surmised that they definitely knew of some base across the Atlantic where they could salt fish. Whatever they found, it was kept secret, though—for what it is worth—Bacon, in his *History of King Henry VII*, casually mentions that Columbus had heard about islands discovered in the north-west.[5]

Craftsmen in England were far behind their continental equivalents, and it was always a surprise to foreigners when they first arrived in England which, judging from its exports of wool, hides and tin,[6] they imagined to be extremely primitive, to find that the houses of the merchants were crammed with expensive luxuries which they had imported, and also that (in spite of the battles and executions of which they had heard so much) there were none of the horrid sights which they associated with civil war—no battered towns, no burnt villages, no devastated fields. The people ate and drank an enormous amount, and the women were so emancipated that it was rather disgusting. According to an Italian visitor, women even went hunting with bows and arrows.[7]

EDWARD'S RELIGIOUS LIFE WAS THAT OF AN ORDINARY JOHN BULL—correct in form and not likely to run to enthusiasm or excess. He got on

---

[5] See David B. Quinn, *The Geographical Journal*, vol. CXXVII, pt 3 (September 1961); and *The Mariner's Mirror*, vol. XXI, no. 3 (July 1935).

[6] Almost the only sophisticated wares exported were small alabaster shrines which were mass-produced for the continental market. Alabaster was quarried in several places, particularly Cellaston in Derbyshire and Tutbury in Staffordshire, and shrines, tombs and altar-pieces were produced by workshops in Nottingham, London, York, Norwich, Lincoln and other towns.

[7] Dominic Mancini, *The Usurpation of Richard III* (1936).

very comfortably with the cultured Sixtus IV[8] who had succeeded Paul II, and in 1479 he was given permission to eat meat on fast days along with eight friends, two doctors and two cooks.[9] In 1481 he obtained a further concession, the Pope having learnt that fish was injurious to Edward's health, and that if he persisted in eating it his life would be in danger. This was not exceptional. Sir Thomas Montgomery and two companions had received much the same permit in 1479, and so had the King of Scotland and three friends in 1476.[1]

In the Venice archives there are several letters from Edward to Sixtus, and though they are polite they are by no means humble. On 25 February 1476, Edward was writing to explain that the Knights of St John in England had always elected their own Prior and that it was out of the question for the Pope's nominee to be accepted, and on 23 May 1477 he was explaining that the monastery at Westminster was a special case: it was now dilapidated because all the money which should have been used for repairs had been sent to Rome during the time that it had been without an abbot, and he would be much obliged if the abbot elected by the monks were recognized by the Pope, and if the money properly belonging to the monastery could be used to repair the buildings.

On 24 February 1476 Edward wrote for permission to prosecute readers of the books of Reginald Pecock,[2] formerly Bishop of Winchester, a request which must surely have been made to please some Bishop. Religious persecutions were not very common in England at that time, and Pseudo-Gregory noted one or two as if they were something out of the ordinary; there were some friars who preached that Christ was a beggar and therefore churchmen should not be rich—a heresy which appealed to the crowd, but not at all to the bishops, and one of the friars found himself in the Castle of St Angelo. Pseudo-Gregory was also amused by the audacity of William Balowe who was

---

[8] Pope Sixtus IV (1471–84). Patron of art and literature. Built the Sistine Chapel.
[9] Scofield, *Edward IV* II 249, 482.
[1] *Calendar of Papal Registers*, vol. XIII, part I, 1471–84.
[2] Reginald Pecock (1395?–1460?) Bishop of Winchester. He denied the authenticity of the Apostles' Creed and suggested converting Lollards by argument instead of by burning them. 'His writings alienated every section of theological opinion,' and he was obliged to resign his bishopric.

burned on Tower Hill in 1467, and who refused to make confession saying that 'no priest had no more power to hear confession than Jack Hare'. While he was being burnt he said to the parson of St Peter's in the Cornhill, who was trying to persuade him to believe in the Holy Sacrament: 'Bawe! Bawe! Bawe! What means this priest? This I wot well, that on Good Friday you make many gods to be put in the sepulchre, but at Easter Day they can not arise themselves, but that you must lift them up and bear them forth or else they will lie still in their graves.'

THE LIFE OF WILLIAM CAXTON (1422?–1491) is a story of well-directed energy, good fortune and success. He was born in the Weald of Kent, received an excellent education and, at the age of sixteen, was apprenticed to a prominent member of the Mercers' Company, the most powerful of the City Guilds. His master dying in 1441, Caxton finished his apprenticeship in Bruges where he resided, on and off, for the next thirty-five years. He was successful in business, and from about 1462 to about 1470 he held the onerous post of Governor of the Flemish branch of the Merchant Adventurers (the association of London guilds trading abroad), during which years he made the acquaintance of most of the important people in England and Burgundy and picked up a smattering of French and Burgundian culture.

In 1471 Caxton, a rich man, retired from the Merchant Adventurers and became the salaried financial adviser of Margaret, Duchess of Burgundy. Encouraged by her, he occupied some of his unaccustomed leisure in translating into English *Le Recueil des Histoires de Troyes*, a popular book of stories based on the Trojan War, 'which work was begun in Bruges and continued in Ghent and finished in Cologne'. This translation met with immediate appreciation; his friends asked for copies and Caxton, after attempting to make copies by hand, turned his practical mind to the possibility of setting it up in type and printing it.

As long ago as 1456 Johann Gutenberg, an inventive man perpetually in financial difficulties, had printed a Bible, probably at Mainz, and struggling presses were in existence in several German towns.

Caxton mastered the art of printing at Cologne and in 1473 set up his own press at Bruges and, in collaboration with a Fleming named Colard Mansion, published in 1475 *The Recuyell of the Historyes of Troye* which thus had the distinction of being the first book in the English language to appear in print. It was dedicated to his employer, the Duchess of Burgundy.

Caxton, who had never even possessed a sheet of carbon-paper, was enchanted with his wonderful machine which could turn out duplicates with such celerity, and he next printed *The Game and Playe of the Chesse*, another translation, in which he fused two French versions of a chatty moral treatise originally written in medieval Latin. This was dedicated to the Duchess of Burgundy's favourite brother, the Duke of Clarence.

Caxton was now an addict. From thenceforward translating, printing, publishing and book-selling were his passion and fortunately he had the money to pursue his hobby without the need to find partners and backers. Always very English at heart, about 1476 he returned to his native land and set up a press in a strategic position in the precincts of Westminster Abbey, as close as he could get to the palace and the government offices. Everyone who was anyone passed by, and here he stayed for the rest of his life in close association with royal and aristocratic patrons, keeping in touch with his City friends and doing his duty as a respected parishioner of St Margaret's. Edward IV, Richard III and Henry VII were all complimented in his prefaces.[3]

In theory, the whole of the known literature of the western world lay at Caxton's disposal, waiting for him to select the hundred best books or whatever he thought his patrons would like to read, but in practice he was limited by the manuscripts of which he could borrow a good copy and he even had difficulty in obtaining a fairly authentic *Canterbury Tales*. One of the first books which he printed at his Westminster press was *The Dictes or Sayengs of the Philosophres* which he dated 1477 and which was a translation made by Anthony Earl Rivers from a popular French original; it was a success and second and third editions followed. Anthony's prose is very halting; nevertheless, in his

[3] In 1479 Caxton was paid £20 'for certain causes and matters performed by him for the said Lord the King', and he may have done some Secret Service work.

preface he does manage to bring to life a perfect day at sea in the far-away summer of 1473 when he and his friends were sailing to St James of Compostela.

'Then I determined me to take that voyage and shipped from Southampton in the month of July the said year; and so sailed from thence till I came into the Spanish sea, there lacking sight of all lands, the wind being good and the weather fair. Then for a recreation and a passing of time I had delight, and asked to read some good history. And among other, there was that season in my company a worshipful gentleman called Louis de Bretaylles, which greatly delighted him in all virtuous and honest things, that said to me he had there a book that he trusted I should like it right well; and brought it to me. Which book I had never seen before, and it is called *The Sayings or Dictes of the Philosophers*.'

There was a great shortage of readable English authors. Caxton printed the two giants, Chaucer and Malory, and also the standard English history known as *The Brut*. He gave his public other histories and romances, doggerel verses—many of them by the prolific Lydgate —*Aesop's Fables*, pamphlets, tracts, prayers, lives of the saints, and indulgences; anything for which there seemed to be a demand. He translated *Reynard The Fox* from the 'Dutch' and, in 1489, he translated a romance called *Blanchardyn and Eglantine* at the request of Margaret, Countess of Richmond, the mother of the King—she had not yet met Bishop Fisher. By the time he died, Caxton had printed nearly a hundred different books, including over twenty translations which he had made himself with light-hearted eclecticism, and he emerges as a middle-brow man of the world—the very opposite of contemporary Italian printers who were scholars, and devoted their lives to preserving the works of Greek and Latin authors.

Unlike the Prior of Croyland, Caxton did not feel that he ought to remain anonymous, and he interpolated his own comments and reminiscences,[4] now lamenting the good old days when everyone was contented and happy, and now discussing the difficulty of choosing a vocabulary when there were so many local dialects and the language

[4] W. J. B. Crotch, *The Prologues and Epilogues of William Caxton* (Early English Text Society, 1928).

was changing so fast—'and certainly our language now used varyeth far from that which was used and spoken when I was born'. Some readers, he said, liked colloquial English and some preferred an elevated style. Spelling did not worry him, and he printed indifferently 'here', 'hyer' and 'ere', but he stressed, not always entirely seriously, that what he was purveying was very moral and improving. Caxton's exact address is known only because in one advertisement for ready reckoners of movable feasts he wrote that if any man wanted them 'let him come to Westminster into the almonry at the Red Pale, and he shall have them good cheap'.

Nothing is known about the financial side of his printing business, and perhaps the fact that he did not become involved in litigation is so extraordinary that it indicates that he ran his press very competently and made a profit. By the time he died other printers were operating in England,[5] and after his death the Westminster press was carried on by his assistant, Wynken de Worde.

Although uninterested in the refinements of typography, Caxton slightly improved his layout and, in the course of time, he straightened his right-hand margins and used eight sets of type, but his letters were always an imitation of the writings in fine manuscripts and remained blotchy and irregular. After 1481 he frequently introduced lively illustrations cut on wood-blocks, which helped to bring home the story even if they had no particular artistic pretensions. It would appear that right to the end Caxton regarded printing as just a splendid way of duplicating manuscripts quickly, and that he had no conception that he was helping to unloose a terrific force and that something had been invented that would change the world for ever. Never was sorcerer's apprentice gayer than he.

---

[5] 'In 1480 John Lettou, a native of Lithuania, set up as a printer in London. . . . He had evidently learnt the art from one of the more advanced European printers of his time and, as a result his work was technically superior to Caxton's in every way.' Crotch, *ibid.*

XV

Edward's Last Years 1480-1482

IN MARCH 1479 LOUIS BEGAN FIGHTING A LOSING BATTLE AGAINST physical break-up. According to Comines, he had a slight stroke while he was sitting at dinner in a village near Chinon and this affected his speech, and for some time afterwards he was forced to use Comines as an interpreter. One of his first actions when he recovered was to degrade and banish those of his courtiers who, when he collapsed, had prevented him from getting fresh air and had shut the windows and carried him to the fire. Determined to conceal his affliction from the world, he insisted that state papers should be read aloud to him. 'He acted as though he were listening', wrote Comines, 'and taking them in his hand he pretended to read them, when really he had no idea what they were about. . . . This illness continued for about a fortnight, after which he recovered his understanding and speech as well as ever, but he remained weak and in fear of a relapse.'

One effect of Louis' illness was to make him much more aggressive, and for the next few years the English were acutely anxious that they would lose Calais. The strip of Burgundy between Calais and French territory was no longer the protection which it had been in the days of Duke Charles, and Hastings, the Captain of Calais, supervised the strengthening of the fortifications. In the summer of 1481 Louis ostentatiously held a grand review of his army in Normandy, and though he wrote to tell Hastings that he had not the slightest intention of attacking Calais and that if anyone attempted to do such a thing he would defend it to the best of his power the fears of Hastings were not allayed. Louis was in no condition to carry through a prolonged enterprise and the advantages of capturing Calais would have been small compared to the cost of a war with England, but Hastings could not be sure that he was bluffing. The outside world did not know that Louis was slowly dying, though in April 1481 Maximilian had passed on to Edward the welcome information that envoys returning from the French Court reported that Louis looked very ill, and in September of that year he had another seizure and for two hours his courtiers thought him dead as he lay on a straw mattress in a gallery. As soon as he recovered, Louis started again on his perpetual journeys; Comines, meeting him, was amazed to find him so thin and weak and wondered how he was able to go on travelling 'but his great spirit carried him through'.

Louis was now living in the misery proper to dying tyrants. Accustomed to have everything his own way, illness made him furious. He was feared and disliked both by his peers and his people and, terrified of assassination, he even became suspicious of men who owed everything to him and who had a selfish interest in preserving his life. Comines was one of the few whom Louis continued to trust; he was sorry to see his master in such a plight and he asked himself the question, Would the miseries endured by Louis in this world lessen the punishments which were due to him in the next?

Louis chiefly resided in the Château of Plessis-les-Tours which he had built on the outskirts of Tours. It was guarded by 400 archers, and fenced with iron grills and four guard-houses in which cross-bowmen were on the alert night and day, with orders to shoot anyone who came near the castle before the gate was opened in the morning. He constantly changed his servants and paid his doctor, a coarse bully, an enormous sum to keep him alive.

Terrified of Hell, Louis gave great gifts to churches, released Cardinal Balue who had been incarcerated in an iron cage for eleven years, and borrowed from the Pope vestments in which St Peter had said Mass.[1] He sent to Calabria for a hermit whose sanctity had become famous. 'Please', wrote Louis to one of his household officers, 'send me some lemons and sweet oranges and muscadel pears and water-melons, and it is for the Holy Man who eats neither meat nor fish.' The hermit arrived at Plessis in April 1482 and rather impressed Comines by his conversation, which admittedly sounded all the better for being in Italian, though some of the courtiers despised him.[2]

Instead of endeavouring to make amends for the sins of his past, Louis clung to the prerogatives of an earthly king. 'To look at,' wrote Comines, 'he was more like a dead than a living man; so thin he was no one would have believed it. He dressed richly, which he had never done before, and only wore gowns of crimson satin trimmed with marten's fur. And he gave money away without being asked for it, for no one dared ask for anything. He inflicted very severe punishments to inspire dread and from fear of losing his authority, as he told me himself. He removed officials, disbanded soldiers, reduced pensions or cancelled them, and he told me a few days before his death that he passed his time in making and ruining men.'

To show that he was still very alert Louis sent abroad for animals, paying exorbitant prices. He bought dogs from all countries, including mastiffs from Spain, greyhounds and spaniels from Brittany and little shaggy dogs from Valentia. He got a special mule from Sicily and horses from Naples, and from Barbary 'a species of little wolf which are hardly bigger than little foxes and are called adits [jackals]'. He paid enormous sums for elk and reindeer from Denmark. 'In fact he did so many things like this that he was more feared by his neighbours and his subjects than he had ever been, for that was his object and the reason he did it.'

---

[1] Cardinal Balue (d. 1491) had been imprisoned since 1469, when a compromising letter he had written to Duke Charles was intercepted. On his release in 1480 he went to Italy. The origin of the 'iron cages' is obscure. Comines believed they were invented by Balue's confederate Guillaume de Haraucourt, Bishop of Verdun, who spent fifteen years in one. Comines himself was shut in a cage for five months during the reign of Charles VIII; he bribed his way out by means of money which he had deposited in the Medici Bank at Lyons. Disagreeable as these cages were, they were evidently not lethal.

[2] The hermit, St François de Paule, died in France in 1507 aged 91 and was canonized by Leo X.

IN THE MIDST OF HIS TRIBULATIONS Louis had one great cause for rejoicing; his persistent intrigues in Scotland had at last produced results and, in spite of Edward's equally persistent determination to stay on good terms with James III (who on his side was most unwarlike and had always wanted peace with England), the truce between the two countries, which had lasted so well, broke down. James had lost control of his nobles, Louis was able to incite an irresponsible faction to make raids and for the rest of Edward's reign there were intermittent expeditions against the Scots.

In 1479 all had been friendly: Princess Cecily was engaged to the heir of the Scottish throne and Edward annually sent north instalments of her dowry, while Anthony was engaged to Margaret, sister of King James.[3] Suddenly Border-raiding began on a large scale, and in the spring of 1480 Edward instructed his envoys to adopt a truculent tone. Soon both sides were arming. At the beginning of September 1480 a Scottish force entered Northumberland and burnt the town of Bamburgh—an act of deliberate aggression for which Louis had probably paid cash down—and reprisals became inevitable.

Perhaps the feebleness of the Earl of Northumberland on the East March, and the pugnacity of the Duke of Gloucester on the West, contributed to the drift towards war. Edward can have had only a vague idea of what was going on inside Scotland, and how the conflicts at the Scottish Court would develop, but he was determined to keep the initiative. Gloucester made a raid into Scotland in return for the attack on Bamburgh, and before the year was out Edward was raising money by direct appeal to towns and counties and public bodies with a view to invading Scotland in 1481. He took the decision to make war without going through the formality of calling Parliament, and it is not clear what he really intended to do. He may have had some wild idea of making a lightning dash into Scotland and frightening James into submission as he had frightened Louis at Picquigny, but the Scots had no money to pay him tribute and it would have been rash to take all

[3] Anthony's first wife had died in 1473, and according to the *Complete Peerage* by October 1480 he had married Mary, daughter of Sir Henry Fitzlewis and granddaughter of Edmund Duke of Somerset; but this does not square with the fact that Margaret of Scotland was awaited in England from early in 1479 to August 1482. King James could not find the money for Margaret's dowry and so it was deducted from Cecily's.

available soldiers to Scotland and to leave the French free to attack Calais and the southern ports.

Records of the period are very sparse; the greater part of England was at peace and good news is no news. Paston *major* had died in the plague of 1479 and Paston *minor*, now married, was living quietly at Caister, and the absence of letters between the two brothers is a great loss. As a slight compensation, there are the *York Civic Records*, which begin in 1476 and illumine a completely different side of English life.[4]

The ancient city of York was going through a black period of its history. It had once been prosperous and had acquired a very large population, but now the river was silting up and it was so poor that from 1464 to 1476 the King had not only waived the annual tax or 'fee farm' but had granted it £40 yearly out of the revenues of Hull, the port which had taken York's trade.[5] Some of the *Records* were preserved on loose sheets, but most of them were written into a book by the secretary or clerk of the City Council who copied them from rough notes without any method and at irregular intervals.[6] In some years there are many entries and in others very few. Hard times brought out the worst in people, and scarcely anybody emerges with credit—except the people who swore that their friends had not said the things that they were accused of saying.

The richest men in York were the merchants who controlled the City Council to the exclusion of the guildsmen, who were known as the Commons or Commonalty and who struggled to make their voices heard. At one time it had been the custom for the retiring mayor to nominate two aldermen, and for the Council to select one of them to be his successor, but Edward had decreed that the two candidates were to be elected by representatives of the guilds and that the Council should choose between them by secret ballot. However, this had not broken the stranglehold of the merchant oligarchy and from time to time the anger of the Commons broke out and there was a riot.

The City Council consisted of a Mayor, twelve aldermen, 'The

---

[4] *York Civic Records*, vol. 1 (1939), ed. Angelo Raine.

[5] Kingston-on-Hull had been founded by Edward I and from the start it had flourished.

[6] The Editor does not reveal if or when the handwriting changes, so it is not apparent whose opinions are being voiced.

Twenty-four', the Recorder, two sheriffs and a clerk, and there were minor officials as well. Meetings were never full, and in February 1477 the mayor was elected by five aldermen and seven of The Twenty-four. Subsequently, fines for non-attendance or lateness were imposed but they made no difference whatever.

Copies of letters to and from the King, the Duke of Gloucester, the Earl of Northumberland and other important personages occupy much space in the *Records*; their help was solicited, but their interference was resented. The two ever-recurring topics are the fee-farm and the fish-garths (salmon-traps placed across the river by such people as the Archbishop of York and the Bishop of Durham); the Council persisted in attempts to get the fish-garths removed, but they were never successful. There are also a good many paragraphs relating to the traditional plays and pageants—collecting money for them, keeping up their quality and so on. The subject which gets most entries in the index is wine.

Many petty incidents are recorded. A man brings twelve witnesses to prove that he is not a Scot, but was christened in the font at Darlington. A butcher swears that he heard the parson of St Peter the Little say that the mayor 'was not able to be mayor of this worshipful city and bad fie upon him for he was but a begger'. (With medieval evasiveness, the result of this case and most others is not given.) An inn-keeper loses his franchise and is fined, for allowing a vestmentmaker from London to work from his inn. York dyers are not to dye cloth from outside the town. Aliens are to be harried in various ways. 'Common women and other mis-governed women shall inhabit them in the suburbs without the walls of the city and not within.' The next mayor is to provide a barge for the Council, and if he refuses he is to be fined £10. This last is almost the only resolution which can be called constructive: otherwise the *Records* are a catalogue of suffocating restrictions and a memorial of a rigid way of life that in the past had been advantageous, but which no longer met the needs of the times. Improvements are not contemplated, enterprise is stifled, criticism punished.

The two outstanding men on the York Council were Miles Metcalf, the Recorder, and Alderman Thomas Wrangwyshe. On

3 July 1471, the Council received a letter from the King informing them that their Recorder would shortly retire and that Miles Metcalf was the man to elect in his place, and so on 1 September Miles Metcalf was unanimously elected by ten aldermen and eleven of The Twenty-four. Miles Metcalf was already—or shortly became—a protégé of the Duke of Gloucester, and subsequently he lent him money and did what he could to assist his schemes.

Alderman Wrangwyshe was a merchant of moderate means who found the walls of the city too narrow for his ambitions, and valiantly endeavoured to get out onto a larger stage. He too attached himself to the Duke of Gloucester, and he jumped at any opportunity to be a member of Parliament or to lead soldiers into the unknown, but the times were against him and he never obtained a permanent foothold in the outside world. Wrangwyshe was mayor in 1476, and deputy in 1481 when the mayor was ill, and he ran again for mayor in 1482 against a determined opponent, Sir Richard York. Deadlock was reached and appeal was made to the King who commanded that the retiring mayor should stay in office until he could look into the matter and Miles Metcalf, the Recorder, having explained to him that Wrangwyshe was the right man, the King commanded that Wrangwyshe should be elected. However, by that time, Sir Richard York had been elected, and nine representatives of the Council and three servants travelled all the way to London to tell the King the true inner story—the Commons, who do not seem to have liked Wrangwyshe, being ready to pay the costs of the journey.

According to the Croyland Continuator, after Warwick's death Edward 'performed the duties of his office with such a high hand that he appeared to be dreaded by all his subjects, while he himself stood in fear of no one, for as he had taken care to distribute the most trust-worthy of his servants throughout all parts of the kingdom as keepers of castles, manors, forests and parks, no conspiracy whatever could be made in any part of the kingdom by any person, however shrewd, without a charge immediately being brought against him'. Edward was not always as successful as the Continuator thought, and the *York Records* show him trying to force his nominees into key positions but sometimes having to back down gracefully. In 1476 the Council's clerk was dismissed for dishonesty, and at first the King was inclined to take the clerk's part, but Gloucester wrote to Hastings and Stanley about it, Edward asked two lawyers to make a report, and finally he allowed the Council to choose a new clerk; and then, in 1482, the King tried to induce the Council to reinstate the official sword-bearer who had been dismissed—owing, it seems, to the machinations of Wrangwyshe—but in this also he was defeated.

Possibly it was due to the vigilance of Miles Metcalf that several citizens of York were arrested at different times for speaking disrespectfully of the Duke of Gloucester. In June 1482 a tailor got one Roger Brere into trouble for reporting that Master William Melrig had said that he had heard Roger Brere say 'that as touching my Lord of Gloucester, What might he do for the City? Nothing but grin of us!' William Melrig stoutly testified that 'he heard never the said Roger say none such words', and Roger escaped. There was a rather similar case in 1483, just about the time of the election of the mayor. On the last day of January, a number of men were sitting in an ale-house and one of them said, 'Sirs, who shall we have to our mayor this year?' Another replied, 'If it please the Commons, I would we had Master Wrangwyshe for he is the man that my Lord of Gloucester will do for.' Then Robert Rede, a girdler, said 'that if my Lord Gloucester would have him mayor, the Commons would not have him mayor'. Robert Rede was arrested and examined, and all his friends testified that what he had really said was either 'that the mayor must be chosen by the Comnalty and not by no lord', or else, 'that my Lord of Gloucester would not be displeased whomsoever it pleased the Commons to choose for their mayor'.

As these extracts show, the people of York—Council, Commons and men in ale-houses—were very conscious of the Duke of Gloucester. His wife, Anne Neville, and their son Edward[7] apparently resided permanently in Middleham Castle, about forty miles to the north-west of the city. His other castle, Sheriff Hutton, was about ten miles to the north-east, and perhaps it was here that he kept his two acknowledged

---

[7] Edward, afterwards Prince of Wales (1473?–1484). He is believed to have been an invalid on the grounds that in 1483 he travelled in a carriage instead of riding a horse, and that he died the following year.

bastards, John of Pontefract and Catherine Plantagenet.[8] Nothing has been discovered about their mother or the dates of their birth, but John at least must have been born after Gloucester's marriage, as before he settled in the north his mistress would not have lain in at Pontefract Castle.

THE EVENTS OF THE YEAR 1481 are almost as obscure as those of 1480. Edward intended—or pretended that he intended—to lead an army into Scotland, and in May he gave this as an excuse to the Pope who was urging him to join a war against the Turks; he would, Edward said, have much preferred to fight the Infidel, but unfortunately he had to fight the Scots. Gloucester and the Earl of Northumberland were sent instructions, and asked to estimate the number of men that could be raised; Edward also wanted to know what was the general reaction to the idea of a Scottish war. Stores were to be established at towns on the line of march north of Trent, and victuallers were to be honestly paid. All the soldiers in the King's army were to wear a white jacket with a cross of St George sewn on it, and those who wished to add some other badge might do so provided they wore the jacket of the arms of St George without change of colour. An enormous number of carts were to be collected at Newcastle. Scouts were to be 'continually and daily within the realm of Scotland', which, owing to the lawlessness along the Border, may have been easier than it sounds.

York offered 120 archers and a captain (Alderman Wrangwyshe). Gloucester had explained that the City was not so rich as formerly, and Edward accepted this and ordered that money was to be raised from the wealthy citizens and not from the poor. The soldiers were collected from each parish and paid for by the parish, and for the next few weeks there was much bustle equipping the soldiers and settling who should pay for what. On 4 July 1481 they were expecting to set forth at any moment, but by 21 July the expedition had been postponed and the

---

[8] Catherine Plantagenet was married in 1484 to William Herbert, Earl of Huntingdon (1455?–1491). He was the son of William Herbert, Earl of Pembroke, and had been married to Mary Woodville. It is not known what happened to either of Richard III's bastards after the accession of Henry VII.

money was being given back to the donors; on 25 July they were lending money to royal soldiers on their way to Newcastle, and on 8 September a new expedition was under discussion. In fact, it was a summer of false alarms and the only part of the 1481 invasion of Scotland which actually took place was a commando-type raid on the Firth of Forth made by Lord Howard, echoes of which appear in his accounts.

The 'household books' of Lord Howard, which were printed in 1844,[9] comprise two manuscript books and scraps of old accounts, and there are gaps and overlapping entries by different secretaries and occasional notes in his own hand. The main portion begins on 23 February 1481, and ends on 20 October 1483; there are also lists of the food in his store-room which he had written many years previously and Latin accounts by a secretary. Occasionally there are intriguing glimpses of his private life—he paid for several promising boys at Cambridge University; he had his own musicians and he welcomed touring companies of players maintained by other noblemen; besides his jester, 'Tom Fool', there was 'Richard the fool of the kitchen'; for his Christmas 'disguising' he bought gold and silver paper, glue, packthread, gold-foil, gold paint and gunpowder.

Lord Howard was getting on in years, but he had often in the past led naval forays, and it was probably the sort of occasion when experience was more valuable than youthful agility. The ships named on his list number fifteen: eight were to go to Scotland, and the rest were 'to keep the narrow sea'. The largest carried 500 men and the smallest forty. The total number of men was 3000, and they were engaged for six weeks. Among his captains was the Portuguese Jew, Edward Brampton, described in his indenture as a gentleman usher, but prepared to command the *Great Kerval of Portugal* 'if she be ready', with 400 men—160 sailors and 240 landsmen.

Howard's own ship was the *Mary Howard*, and the master was called Robert Michelson.[1] Amongst other equipment listed are four pairs of sheets for my Lord, four counterpanes of tapestry-work, a great basin of silver, a case with four goblets, a candlestick, a pissing basin of silver,

---

[9] *Household Books of John Howard, Duke of Norfolk* (Roxburghe Club, 1844).
[1] Presumably the Robert Michelson who had brought Edward from Flanders to Ravenspur in 1471.

a salt, two little salts of beryl, six silver spoons, two great pots of silver, a bag with gussets, a bag with chessman, some clothes of velvet, satin and cloth-of-gold, and fourteen French story-books, including *La Belle Dame Sans Merci*, He also took aboard a great quantity of wine, and ordered 4000 caltraps at 12 a penny.

About the middle of May 1481, Edward, accompanied by his eldest son, reviewed Howard's fleet at Sandwich. The Prince of Wales was now ten, and on the way through Canterbury the citizens celebrated his first appearance in their midst by presenting him with a silver-gilt box containing £20. Howard was off Harwich by 20 May; he then worked up the coast to the Firth of Fourth, where he captured eight ships and destroyed others. The land expedition which should have been co-ordinated with this raid had fallen through and by 17 August Lord Howard was back at Harwich. Needless to say, his account books do not reveal what this expedition cost him nor what he made out of it.

The war against Scotland then slackened off till the spring, though at some time during the winter Gloucester sent soldiers to Berwick and began a somewhat ineffectual siege of the town and castle.

1482, THE LAST YEAR OF EDWARD'S REIGN, was marked by several important events, and on 27 March 1482 the whole international situation was changed by the unexpected death of the young Duchess Mary of Burgundy as the result of a fall from her horse. Louis told Comines the news with delight; he was particularly pleased to hear that Mary's two children were in the hands of the people of Ghent, whom he knew to be selfish and short-sighted and always ready to make trouble for their ruling house. Burgundy had been held together by personal loyalty to Duchess Mary; Maximilian was young and a stranger, and Louis felt that Burgundy was at his mercy.

Edward, like Louis, was now a very sick man, and the only reason that this is known is because of one casual entry in the memorandum book of the cofferer (or treasurer) of the City of Canterbury.[2] The cofferer was naturally interested in what cost money, and for him the

---

[2] Historical MSS. Commission, 9th Report, Appendix, 1883. Records of the City of Canterbury, p. 145.

visits of important personages to the city meant, primarily, the cost of erecting a large marquee or temporary hall outside the town, and the bills for food and drink. In his account-book the City Council figure in no very heroic light and, in the words of the editor, 'The sundry expenses about this time consist in great part of treats of wine given to the Mayor and his brethren. In fact whenever there was a stir in the air, a revolution, a law-suit, or an expected invasion, the wines, red and white, sweet and dry, began to flow in gallons.' In the summer of 1482 the Mayor held a consultation with Hastings, who was presumably on his way to or from Calais, and he learnt that the King's health was not good and that another revolution was possible, which would mean that the City Council would have to go to the expense of purchasing a new charter—they were still sore from the losses they had incurred from backing Fauconberg.

Unfortunately we do not know from what Edward was suffering, how far he was affected physically or mentally, and when he had fallen ill: it is just possible that he had had a heart-attack at the beginning of April, when he heard of the death of Duchess Mary. He was certainly too ill to lead an army in the summer of 1482, and the command of the invasion of Scotland was given to Gloucester. The general plan now seems wild and foolish, but it was passed by Edward, Gloucester and the rest of the Council as being practicable. They realized that a pact made with James III would be of no value, because he had alienated so many of his nobles,[3] and they knew that his much more virile brother, Albany, was an exile in France, and Edward—or his advisors—conceived the notion that it would be possible to displace James and crown Albany who, they imagined, would be strong enough to hold down his nobles and grateful enough to do whatever the King of England requested.

Albany, a reckless character, accepted the offer and at the end of April 1482 he landed at Southampton, where he was welcomed with great effusiveness; by the middle of May he was at Fotheringhay, drawing up an agreement with Edward and the Duke of Gloucester. The latter had come down from the north where he had just made a tip-

[3] Eventually they murdered him.

and-run raid across the Border, burning Dumfries and any houses he had found on the way; the district had taken his fancy, and he asked for it to be his share of the plunder.[4]

Albany signed everything. The precise terms of the agreement did not much matter as no one knew how things would work out, and he glibly promised that when he was king of Scotland he would give Berwick to the English, break off the Scots alliance with France, do homage to Edward and, if he could get rid of his wives—he had a divorced one in Scotland and one in France—he would marry Princess Cecily.

Edward then returned to London while Gloucester and Albany went north together, and on 17 June the York City Council decreed that everyone of standing should turn out to welcome them; the Commoners were to be at Micklegate Bar at three o'clock in the morning in their best clothes, while the alderman dressed in scarlet and The Twenty four dressed in crimson were to be there at four o'clock. Absentees would be fined, and Gloucester and Albany should be presented with bread, ten gallons of wine, and fish.

Lord Stanley and the Earl of Northumberland joined Gloucester later, and Edward kept in touch with his army by means of relays of messengers whom he stationed at intervals of thirty miles along the route.[5] The siege of Berwick had now been going on for months and the new arrivals soon took the town, but the castle continued to hold out, so Lord Stanley was left to continue the siege while Gloucester, Albany and Northumberland marched into Scotland.

What had been happening over the Border is extremely obscure. The traditional story is that the gallant Scots nobles resented the King's low favourites, and in particular an architect called Cochrane, and that Archibald Earl of Angus (Archibald Bell-the-Cat) organized a rebellion, hanged Cochrane and other unworthy minions over the bridge at Lauder, imprisoned King James in Edinburgh Castle and mustered an

---

[4] There is no way of telling how savage these raids of Richard's were. One of his admirers says that he burned Dumfries 'and many a lesser town', but as Dumfries and Carlisle are only thirty-three miles apart it is unlikely that the towns he passed on his way were very numerous.

[5] This was in imitation of Louis, who had relays of messengers permanently stationed about his kingdom. They were effective but expensive, and Edward paid them off as soon as the Scottish expedition was over.

army which was cunningly held back while the English passed by. According to a modern historian[6] this story does not stand up to examination, but one thing is definite: no Scottish army blocked the advance of the English, and they soon covered the fifty-seven miles between Berwick and Edinburgh, Gloucester burning villages to his heart's content.

Edinburgh was entered without opposition. James had taken refuge in the Castle, and the whole English plan collapsed when Albany made up his quarrel with his brother and also disappeared into the Castle. Joint commands are awkward affairs, and Gloucester had inherited his father's tactlessness.

On 4 August 1482 the Provost and burghers of Edinburgh, acting on their own initiative, begged for mercy; they promised either to refund the dowry of Princess Cecily or to continue the engagement, to send Princess Margaret to marry Anthony—anything, anything, if only the English would go away. And the invaders had no reason for staying. A small army isolated in a hostile country, they could not besiege Edinburgh Castle, they had not the money for a long campaign, and they had no alternative but to retreat the way they had come, boasting that they had behaved nobly in not sacking Edinburgh.[7] When they reached Berwick they found Stanley still besieging the castle, but the defenders now surrendered and Berwick was once more an English town. Edward's relays of messengers appear to have got the news through to him in a couple of days, and he sent off a triumphant letter to the Pope, asking him incidentally to use his influence to restrain the Scots from raiding across the Border.

In Calais there had been bonfires and rejoicings at the news of the capture of Edinburgh, and when Berwick was regained the general public was satisfied that the expedition to Scotland had been a famous victory. The Croyland Continuator, looking back, took a contemptuous view. 'This trifling, I really know not whether to call it "gain" or "loss" (for the safe-keeping of Berwick each year swallows up ten thousand marks) at this period diminished the resources of the king and

---

[6] Rosalind Mitchison, *A History of Scotland* (Methuen, 1970).

[7] These amateur armies never seem to have got out of hand, and they only looted when they were encouraged to do so by their officers.

kingdom by more than a hundred thousand pounds. King Edward was vexed at this frivolous outlay of so much money, although the recovery of Berwick above mentioned in some degree alleviated his sorrow.'

THE MARTIAL VENTURES OF 1482 had kept the York City Council in a ferment. The Duke of Gloucester had asked them to contribute eighty men to his march on Dumfries in the spring, and each alderman had sponsored two soldiers and each of the Twenty-four one soldier. They had also promised 120 soldiers for the Edinburgh expedition, but when the time came they felt that they could only afford 100 and Gloucester accepted their apologies. The men were hired for twenty-eight days at sixpence a day plus twopence for horse-hire, and they were to be paid half their wages in advance and half later.

By 29 August the soldiers were home again and there were recriminations. When they had been about to set out, three men had incited the others to refuse to start unless they were paid all their wages in advance, and these three ringleaders were now brought before the Council and thrown into prison; but on 7 September they were released after promising to amend their ways. As there had been no fighting, the returning heroes were jeered at and brawls resulted, and on 30 December a man was accused of saying that the soldiers who went on the Scottish expedition had not earned their wages as they had done nothing but make whips of their bow-strings to drive carriages with, but he was able to extricate himself by explaining that what he had really said was that he had heard some soldiers say that they did nothing but wait on the ordnance and carriages, and that another soldier had said that he was so weary that he was fain to take the string of his bow to drive his horse with.

IF HASTINGS WAS TELLING STRAY acquaintances at Canterbury that Edward's health was precarious, the fact must have been well known at the Court and many men must have been wondering what would happen when his strong hand was removed. Small fry hoped to keep their jobs; great men got together and discussed how they could become still greater. It is easier to face death bravely than to live nobly, and with no dangers threatening from without and with everybody competing for jobs and aspiring to win worldly success the Court had split up into cliques and factions. The alignments and re-alignments that went on during these years of peace are unrecorded because no one who lived in high society wrote a chronicle, but an Italian, Dominic Mancini, put down what was being said in the summer of 1483 among the foreign merchants in Southwark.[8]

Mancini was an Italian who had gone to France to seek his fortune, and *The Usurpation* is addressed to another Italian, Archbishop Angelo Cato,[9] who had been a close confident of Louis XI. It was, as we have seen, extremely difficult for Louis to discover what was happening on the other side of the Channel, and the most obvious explanation of Mancini's visit to London is that after Edward's death he was sent over to collect information.[1] Presumably he could speak no English, but he was an intelligent and articulate man who knew French, Italian and Latin, and he could pick the brains of the regular French agents and bring back a lengthy verbal report to either Cato or Louis himself; it is quite conceivable that in the autumn of 1483, after Louis was dead, he wrote up the information he had collected—making a very readable little narrative—with the hope of attracting the attention of the new régime.

The first event which Mancini describes as though he had been an eye-witness was Richard's welcome to his soldiers from the north, which took place in the middle of June 1483 and as he states that he

[8] Dominic Mancini, *The Usurpation of Richard III*. From a Latin manuscript finished at Beaugency near Orleans on 1 December 1483, and discovered in 1934 in the archives of Lille.

Dominic Mancini (d. between 1494–1514) came of a good Roman family, and was a kind of cleric, a scholar and a man of letters. He lived mostly in Paris.

[9] Angelo Cato (d. 1496), Archbishop of Vienne. He came from southern Italy and was a physician, astrologer, politician, diplomat and scholar. He took an interest in history and it was at his suggestion that Comines wrote his memoirs. He had known Sixtus IV personally and had been physician to Duke Charles of Burgundy and, after his death, to Louis XI; and his diplomatic activities continued in the reign of Charles VIII. His appointment to the archbishopric of Vienne in July 1482 was much resented.

[1] The Editor assumes that Mancini had been in England since the previous autumn, but his account of Edward's reign has the marks of being a second-hand résumé—the chronology is vague and there is an absence of odd and unexpected detail.

was recalled by Archbishop Cato soon after Richard's coronation he cannot have stayed in England more than a few weeks, and because the whole point of his visit was that he should be able to get back to France quickly he took care to be unobtrusive and ventured out of the foreign ghetto but rarely. He described London as it would be seen from South-wark (which he said was a suburb remarkable for its streets and build-ings and which, if it were surrounded by walls, might be called another city). He noticed London Bridge, the warehouses and 'the numerous cranes of remarkable size' along the river, the Tower of London to the east and Westminster to the west, but he did not write as though he had actually landed at Westminster. He had, however, taken walks in the City and been impressed by the three main paved streets running parallel with the river, and the quantity and variety of merchandise in the shops and warehouses. He had also seen the young men of the town having sham fights in the streets on holidays, 'clashing on their shields with blunted swords or stout staves', and he had had a good look at Richard's soldiers who, he erroneously remembered, carried shields. The greatest value of Mancini's narrative is that he was a complete outsider with no prejudices in favour of anybody, and that he could put down just what his informants told him without fear of being prosecuted for treason. He did not embroider, because he wanted to produce an accu-rate report, and when he was wrong—as he often was—it was because he was misinformed or mistaken, not because he was deliberately inventing.

Mancini gives the story of Edward's marriage as it was told to him; it had become legend and had very little connection with reality. All the Woodvilles, of course, were *low*—particularly Elizabeth's son 'the Marquis'. The one exception was Anthony who, in the short time since his execution, had changed from a glamorous knight-errant into a kind of quaker: he was 'always considered a kind, serious and just man and one tested by every vicissitude of life'. Clarence, too, had become a martyred innocent, who had been murdered by the plots of the Queen and her family. Edward was a monster of lust. 'However, he took none by force. He overcame all by money and promises, and having con-quered them, he dismissed them.' He was also a glutton. 'It was his habit, as I have learned, to take an emetic for the delight of gorging his stomach once more.' (Mancini was a classical scholar, and had probably read about the customs of ancient Rome.) There was a deadly feud between 'the Marquis' and Hastings, which the French and Italians in Southwark naturally assumed was caused by quarrels over a mistress. About the Duke of Gloucester Mancini was told no legends; he had lived far away and the merchants in Southwark had never given him a thought until he usurped the throne and his nephews disappeared: they then knew just what sort of man he was—a wicked uncle.

Mancini was also told a certain amount in favour of Edward:

Edward was of a gentle nature and cheerful aspect; nevertheless, should he assume an angry countenance he could appear very terrible to beholders. He was easy of access to his friends and to others, even the least notable. Frequently he called to his side complete strangers, when he thought that they had come with the intention of addressing or beholding him more closely. He was wont to show himself to those who wished to watch him, and he seized any opportunity that the occasion offered of revealing his fine stature ... to on-lookers. He was so genial in his greeting that if he saw a newcomer bewildered at his appearance and royal magnificence he would give him courage to speak by laying a kindly hand upon his shoulder. To plaintiffs and to those who complained of injustice he lent a willing ear; charges against himself he contented with an excuse if he did not remove the cause. He was more favourable than other princes to foreigners who visited his realm for trade or any other reason. He very seldom showed munificence and then only in moderation, still, he was very grateful to those from whom he had received a favour. Though not rapacious of other men's goods he was yet so eager for money that in pursuing it he acquired a reputation for avarice.

Mancini enlarged on this theme and on the King's methods of extracting money from his subjects, but no one had told him that Edward had himself been a merchant, or—if he had been told—he had not taken it in because it did not fit in with his stereotype of how kings behaved.

There was undoubtedly a quarrel between Hastings and Dorset which divided the Court into two factions, and as it was owing to this quarrel that Gloucester was able to seize the throne it was an important quarrel, and one wonders what was the cause of it. They were so far apart in age that there seems no reason why they should have collided. Hastings had honours, wealth, power; Dorset was just a young courtier. Perhaps that was the trouble. Hastings was a busy man, constantly travelling here and there, and feeling old age beginning to creep on, while Dorset could stay at home and amuse his stepfather.

On 27 June 1481 Hastings made his will, and emphasized its solemnity by writing the last paragraph in his own hand. The King, he says, has given him permission to be buried in St George's Chapel, near his own tomb. He commands his son to serve the king faithfully and he begs the King to look after his widow and children. Hastings had worked and played with Edward for twenty years, and it is possible that he adored him and was wounded to the heart because Edward was invited to the merry evenings of the fashionable younger set and he was not.

By 1482 Hastings had ganged up with Lord Howard and his son, with Lord Stanley and his brother Sir William Stanley, and with the immensely rich young Duke of Buckingham—whose true motives may have changed from day to day and are unlikely ever to be revealed. Howard had an understanding with the Duke of Gloucester and appears to have conferred with him in south Wales in 1479; between them all, they could put a great many soldiers in the field. By comparison the Woodvilles were a very light-weight party and their natural leader, Anthony, was a lone knight and not an organizer.

Edward (always so alive to human relationships) must have been well aware that half his friends hated the other half, and that his Court was only held together by the force of his will and that, in the event of his death, it would be a bad look-out for his wife and children unless the most important peers agreed to form a council of regency. Meanwhile, he continued to travel about, though perhaps more slowly than formerly. In October he visited Norwich and Walsingham, and his last Christmas he spent at Westminster, where he acted the role of king with his usual panache. Even the Croyland Continuator could not help being impressed.

> King Edward kept the following feast of the Nativity at his palace at Westminster, frequently appearing dressed in a great variety of most costly garments of quite a different cut to those which had been hitherto seen in our kingdom. The sleeves of the robes were very full and hanging, greatly resembling a monk's frock, and lined within with most costly furs, and rolled over the shoulders, so as to give that prince a new and distinguished air to beholders, he being a person of most elegant appearance and remarkable beyond all others for the attractions of his person. You might have seen in those days the royal court presenting no other appearance than such as fully befits a most mighty kingdom, filled with riches and with people of all nations and (a point in which it excelled all others), boasting of those most sweet and beautiful children, the issue of his marriage with Queen Elizabeth.

Soon after Christmas, Edward received the news that Louis and

Maximilian had signed a treaty; Princess Elizabeth had been jilted and the Dauphin was now engaged to Maximilian's daughter, Margaret. Comines liked to think that the shock of this caused Edward's death, but as he must have been expecting something of the sort, and as he lived for another three months, there does not seem to be much connection between the treaty and his death.

Edward had survived worse setbacks, and when he surveyed his achievements there was much to make him feel complacent. He had brought his country from anarchy to order, from bankruptcy to solvency. He was an unbeaten general, and he had frightened the King of France into paying him an annual tribute. He had traded successfully. He was served by an excellent staff of officials; he was popular with his subjects. He had a faithful wife whom he had married for love, a fine family of sons and daughters; a delightful mistress. He had built St George's Chapel and Eltham Great Hall; he had collected a library of splendid picture books; he lived like a king, and had money in his coffers.

On the other hand his health was uncertain and his son was only a child.

XVI

Edward's Death April 1483

O N 20 JANUARY 1483, EDWARD OPENED HIS SIXTH AND LAST
Parliament; the Speaker was John Wode, a protégé of Gloucester, and supplies were voted for another invasion of Scotland. If Edward was now in bad health, it seems odd that he should have
wished to persevere with the Scottish war, but it may have been
that—like the dying Louis—he was determined to show that he was
still terrible: alternatively, he may have been talked into believing
that it was possible to obtain a quick victory and a firm peace, or he may
have been so ill that he was no longer in control of public affairs.

Gloucester at last obtained the prize which had been dangled in
front of him ever since the time when, as a boy, he had been sent to live
at Middleham Castle. In recognition of his raid on Dumfries in the
early summer of the previous year, he was made hereditary Warden of
the West Marches 'in as large wise as any Warden of the said Marches
hath had and reasonably used to have in times past'. His powers were
to be similar to those held by the Bishop of Durham. He was also given
the town and castle of Carlisle and any other estates held by the King in
the County of Cumberland, as well as whatever he could conquer on
the other side of the Border. These rewards were neither unprecedented nor unreasonable; in fact, he may have felt aggrieved that they

had not been given to him before. If Gloucester was to police the Border effectively, he had to have absolute authority in Cumberland and if he could capture and hold any fertile valleys in Dumfriesshire he was welcome to them.

In the course of this Parliament Edward agreed that his officials should not commandeer provisions for the royal household without paying for them, but the most interesting item in the Rolls is a protest against the use of machinery in the manufacture of hats. It was alleged that in the past hats, bonnets and caps had been made by men using hand and foot, but there was 'a subtle means found now of late, by reason of a fulling mill whereby more caps may be fulled and thicked in one day, than by the might and strength of twenty-four men by hand and foot may be fulled and thicked in the same day', and it was asked that fulling-mills should be forbidden. The King assented—'Le Roy le voet'—and the records are silent as to what happened afterwards.

There were also edicts to deal with common persons who were marking swans;[1] with Jews and Saracens who were importing silk goods to the detriment of the silk-weavers of London; with the price of bows—no long-bow of yew must cost more than three shillings and fourpence. Barrels of salmon, herrings or eels must not have good fish at the ends and inferior fish in the middle. To revive the battered town of Berwick, all goods from Scotland must pass through it (or Carlisle). Anyone who had a piece of private woodland in the King's forests and felled it under licence must fence it against animals so that trees could grow up again.

Short as the session was, the Lords and Commons found time to criticize each others' clothes and to tighten up the sumptuary laws. No one except the royal family could wear silk of purple colour; no one under a duke could wear cloth-of-gold tissue; no one under a lord could wear plain cloth-of-gold; no one under a knight could wear velvet. The clothes of the lower classes were regulated by price, and they must not wear hose which cost more than eighteen pence a pair. Women could wear what they liked—except for the wives of labourers. The very short tunics which the Parliament of 1463–5 had banned for

---

[1] The inhabitants of Croyland protested to the next Parliament that they caught swans for a living, and had always marked swans.

anyone under the rank of lord, squire or gentleman, were now forbidden to anybody under the rank of lord—though Edward insisted
that exception should be made for eight knights (Sir Thomas Montgomery, Sir Thomas Burgh, Sir Thomas Vaughan, Sir John Donne,
Sir William Parre, Sir Thomas St Leger, Sir Thomas Bourchier, Sir
Thomas Grey) and for three officials (his secretary, Dr Oliver King;
the Dean of his Chapel, Master Oliver Gunthorp; and the Treasurer of
his Household, Sir John Elrington).

Towards the end of March Edward fell ill. According to Mancini,
he caught a cold when he was fishing at Windsor, which seems probable enough and all the more so because a cold is a dull complaint
and not likely to have been invented by gossip. He returned to the
Palace of Westminster and here, on 9 April 1483, he died. He was aged
forty;[2] he had reigned, with one short break, for twenty-two years,
and he was the first English king to die solvent since Henry II's death
in 1189.

The Croyland Continuator (who may have been at Westminster
at the time) asserts that he had no symptoms and that the doctors could
not give a name to his illness; because he was so easy of access it was
rumoured that he had been poisoned, but this was not true. Smug prigs
liked to think that he had been worn out by debauchery, or that he had
died of a surfeit. Abroad they said, among other things, that he had
drunk too much of some wine which Louis had sent him. Looked at
coolly, there is nothing odd about Edward's death. A very fat man
carrying great responsibilities and leading an energetic life is ill for a
few days and dies. It is an ordinary occurrence. Heart? Pneumonia? A
stroke? Or some less common ailment which had not yet been
identified by the medical profession?[3]

The extraordinary thing was the behaviour of Edward's family.
Anthony was at Ludlow with Edward Prince of Wales; Richard Duke
of Gloucester was in Yorkshire; the Duke of Buckingham was at home

---

[2] Edward had been born on 28 April 1442.

[3] The only surviving book which Edward possessed when he was Earl of March happens to be a collection of medical treatises; his doctor became his private secretary, and he
seems to have had a great respect for doctors and a liking for their company. This may be
coincidence, or he may have suffered from some congenital weakness.

in his castle at Brecon; and all of them remained where they were. Even if there had not been time to summon them to his death-bed, the natural thing would have been for them to hurry to London for the funeral and for meetings of the Council: it was their plain duty to present the late king's eldest son to the people, and to crown him as soon as possible.

Lord Howard also was at home in the country. On 4 April he received a message from the Court, but it was not very urgent and he did not leave Stoke-by-Nayland until 7 April. Stopping a night on the way, he reached London on 9 April, the day Edward died. The following day he dined with Hastings, and tipped the cook.

Edward's funeral cost £1496 17s. 2d., a sum which was raised by the sale of some of his jewels, and an account of it has been left by a herald who complained that the ceremonies were not carried out absolutely correctly, but who was himself so careless that he misdated Edward's death 10 April and so was a day wrong throughout.[4]

First of all Edward lay in state for a short time, then he was embalmed and lay in the palace chapel till 16 April while priests eased his soul with appropriate dirges, requiems and masses—one might never have seen a picture of Edinburgh, or Paris or Rome but one knew exactly what the Day of Judgement would look like. Then his body was taken in procession to the Abbey, with most of the Court attending and Lord Howard leading the way with a banner. Next day the funeral cortège started for Windsor, the hearse bearing a life-sized figure of the late king wearing his crown and holding his sceptre and orb. At Sion Nunnery they stopped for the night, and at Eton there were fresh ceremonies; finally they crossed the bridge and arrived at Windsor Castle where they were met by the nobles who had ridden from London—Lord Howard was still well to the fore.[5] The coffin was carried into the Chapel of St George 'and there was a great watch that night'. Next day it was placed in the tomb which Edward had built for

---

[4] *Letters and Papers Illustrative of the Reigns of Richard III and Henry VII*, ed. J. Gairdner. Rolls Series 1861–3.

Some jinx seems to have muddled all the dates. The news of Edward's death is supposed to have reached Ludlow only on 14 April, which is quite incredible.

[5] Lord Howard's horse was shod at Maidenhead on 19 April.

himself, and which was near the place where his daughter Mary and his son George were already buried.

EDWARD'S TOMB WAS DESTROYED by the Roundheads, and St George's Chapel now hardly acknowledges the existence of its founder. The monument which bears his name, and which was put up in 1787, is dull, ugly and inconspicuous; his chantry was turned into a kind of opera box by Catherine of Aragon; the elaborate wrought-iron gates made to enclose his tomb by the Cornish craftsman, John Tresilian, have been moved to a place where they are flat against a wall; and it is doubtful if any of the Knights of the Garter, who proudly hang their banners in the Choir which he built, give a thought to a king called Edward IV.

Epilogue

WHEN EDWARD IV DIED IT WAS TAKEN FOR GRANTED THAT HE would be succeeded by his elder son, Edward Prince of Wales, and Edward V was proclaimed king on 11 April and his coronation fixed for 4 May. Edward V was twelve and a half; he would be a puppet king for several years to come and all power and patronage would be in the hands of whichever party held his person. Lord Hastings and Lord Stanley reckoned that they must physically get possession of the boy, edge out the Woodvilles and confirm themselves in the offices they already held; Lord Howard was their ally and so were Gloucester and Buckingham (the only two members of the royal family who were prepared to take an active part in public affairs).

It may have been the fault of Edward's domineering character or it may have been bad luck, but at the moment there were few authoritative figures in public life. The Earl of Essex had just died and the Archbishop of Canterbury had always been a straw in the wind and was now very old; the rest of the Bourchiers were ciphers, and so was the Duke of Suffolk. Salinger was only a knight, the Woodvilles had no royal blood in their veins, and the bishops were government officials whose political authority depended on the favour of the monarch.

The Queen and the Woodvilles were only too well aware that the richest men at the Court had ganged up against them, and they were as powerless as rabbits surrounded by a circle of stoats. Not one of them was capable of making a coherent plan, although they started with many advantages. Anthony was in actual possession of the new King in the family stronghold; the other little prince, Richard, was in London with his mother and five sisters; Dorset is said to have been guardian of the late king's treasure; Sir Edward Woodville was in command of a fleet of ships which had been mustered to defend Calais from a French attack which seemed imminent; and Lionel Woodville had recently been made Bishop of Salisbury. For once the rights of succession were perfectly plain and the country was behind the boy king, and yet by 6 July Edward V and his brother Richard had disappeared never to be seen again and their uncle, the Duke of Gloucester, was wearing the crown.

It is sometimes suggested that one thing led to another and that Richard III just drifted onto the throne, but today whenever a military coup is successfully brought off it has quite obviously been planned some time in advance, and there seems no reason why things should have been different in the fifteenth century. It would be amazing, in fact, if the events which led up to Richard's coronation had occurred by chance, and if there had not been one very clever and unscrupulous man in London who stood to win great things if Gloucester were substituted for the Prince of Wales.

The precise fate of the Little Princes is a mystery which has never been cleared up owing to lack of evidence. As several recent murder trials have demonstrated, in the absence of a corpse it is very difficult to convict a murderer although all the clues seem to point in one direction, and after nearly five hundred years the question of what happened to them is still hotly debated although it is only of academic interest. In 1483, when it was really important to know whether Edward V was alive or not, rumours spread rapidly; people immediately suspected the worst, and stories describing the exact manner of their death were soon invented.

FOR MANY DAYS ANTHONY HESITATED in Ludlow, but he had to emerge eventually, and about 24 April the new king, Edward V, started towards London escorted by his uncle Anthony, his half-brother Richard Grey, his old attendant Sir Thomas Vaughan, one of his Haute cousins and an armed guard that was too small to be effective. Immediately Gloucester in Yorkshire and Buckingham in Brecon—informed by a remarkably efficient system of messengers—set out also, and converged on the royal party at either Northampton or Stony Stratford. A day or two later Edward V, Gloucester and Buckingham continued towards London, while Anthony, Richard Grey, Thomas Vaughan and Haute were carried off prisoner to Yorkshire. The news of the kidnapping flew on ahead of the cavalcade and the Queen and her six children took refuge in Westminster Sanctuary.

Edward V reached London on 4 May; the coronation had been postponed, but he was welcomed like a king although he was not permitted to see his mother—indeed, he never saw her again. At first he was lodged in the palace of the Bishop of London, but some time between 9 May and 19 May he was moved to the Tower which, by tradition, was the palace where the kings of England spent the night before they were crowned.

THERE ARE SOME VERY PECULIAR entries in the account book of Lord Howard under the date of 21 May 1483. They come quite casually in the middle of ordinary domestic disbursements and they are bracketed together by the name 'Basley' written in the margin—Basley being a man who lived near Colchester and who sometimes performed odd jobs such as sending firewood to Lord Howard's town house.

> Item, paid to Basley that he paid at the Tower for 6 men for a day labour:

3d a man a day	summa 18d.
Item, paid to a carpenter for making of 3 beds	8d.
Item, for 100 foot of board and a quarter	2s. 11d.
Item, for 2 sacks lime	4d.
Item, for nails for the beds	3d.
Item, for his dinner	2d.

The Tower records for this period are missing, and it is obscure who actually was in charge of it in the summer of 1483. Old Lord Dudley was nominally Constable, and Lord Dacre had the reversion and Lord Howard had the reversion after Lord Dacre, but the officer who actually resided in the Tower and would be aware of what went on within its walls would be the Lieutenant, whose name is unknown. An obscure individual called Robert Brackenbury[1] became Constable on 17 July after Richard had been crowned, but by that time the Princes may have been dead. Expenses incurred by the Constable were normally entered in the Tower ledgers, and there are no other entries in Howard's account books which relate to the Tower. It is possible that the workmen thought their activities curious and that they gossiped afterwards, which would explain the spread of rumours that the Princes were smothered in their beds and that their bodies were walled up under a stair.

WHEN EDWARD IV FIRST DIED there were meetings of the Great Council to decide how the government should be carried on, and whether the Duke of Gloucester should be a solitary regent or merely the president of the Council—a position to which his rank certainly entitled him. It was alleged that Edward had left a will with a codicil which directed that Gloucester should be 'Protector', but as no copy of these documents survive it cannot be seen what Edward actually wrote. Mancini's informants were doubtful if such a codicil existed, but even if Edward had willed that Gloucester was to be Protector he cannot have intended that his sons should be condemned to perpetual imprisonment and that Richard should seize throne, lands, goods, everything.

Some time in May, Hastings and Stanley discovered to their horror that they had been fools as well as knaves and that—far from setting up a council of co-regents—Howard intended to liquidate Edward and his brother and to make Gloucester king. Hastings was appalled at the idea of murdering the sons of his old friend and perhaps drew the line at killing Anthony, Richard Grey, Thomas Vaughan and Haute, and he secretly got into communication with the Queen. Stanley shared his feelings but Buckingham's attitude is enigmatic: he may have been terrified of Howard, or he may have hoped that

---

[1] Sir Robert Brackenbury was killed at the Battle of Bosworth.

everyone who stood between himself and the throne would be eliminated. On 13 June there was a Council Meeting in the Tower; Gloucester accused Hastings of treason, and he was dragged out and executed then and there,[2] and Lord Stanley, Dr Morton (Bishop of Ely), and Rotherham (Archbishop of York and Chancellor) were arrested and imprisoned. These important personages would all have been attended by secretaries or chaplains, so there must have been a great many eye-witnesses of this dramatic scene and accounts of it are likely to be approximately true.

Meanwhile, Elizabeth Woodville was still in Westminster Sanctuary with her six children. Dorset had gone into hiding and eventually he reached the Continent; Edward Woodville had got safely to Brittany, supposedly with some of the royal treasure but with only two ships, the rest of his fleet having been captured by the brisk action of Howard's friend, the Portuguese Jew, Edward Brampton. On 16 June Gloucester, Lord Howard, his son Thomas and the Archbishop of Canterbury arrived at Westminster Sanctuary and persuaded, or forced, the Queen to deliver up her younger son, Richard Duke of York. Archbishop Bourchier was probably acting from stupidity or senility, or he may have shut his eyes out of cowardice and hoped for the best. Sir Thomas Howard conducted the child Richard down the river to the Tower. The Howard account books show that on that day they hired eight boats to go to Westminster and back, and eight boatloads of soldiers are a powerful argument.

On 25 June Anthony, Richard Grey, Sir Thomas Vaughan and Haute were executed without trial at Pontefract Castle.[3] Anthony and Hastings had been for twenty years the two most popular men in England, and their executions were a terrifying demonstration of the

[2] Gloucester was very ready to be conciliatory once Hastings was dead, and so he was buried in St George's Chapel as he had wished. His chantry, decorated with early Tudor paintings, is next to Edward's tomb.

[3] Anthony wrote his will at Sheriff Hutton two days before his death. It seems to have been scribbled off just as it came into his head. He was painfully anxious to pay all his debts, which he tried to remember and enumerate, and he begged Gloucester to have the decency to see that they were paid. His clothes and horse harness were to be sold to buy clothes for poor people. His Woodville property was to go to the next heir, his brother Richard (3rd and last Earl Rivers), and his Scales property to his youngest brother, Edward. *Excerpta Historica.*

power of the Duke of Gloucester. Letters expressing disapproval of the régime are naturally not to be met with, but one or two have survived which show how frightened people were, and there is a cryptic scribble among the Cely papers.[4] The Celys were a prosaic family of wool-merchants, who chiefly corresponded about business and their own private concerns, and there is no explanation of this scrap of paper.

'There is a great rumour in the realm. The Scots have done great [*gap*] in England. Chamberlain [Hastings] is deceased in trouble. The Chancellor [Rotherham] is dispossessed and not content the Bishop of Ely [Morton] is dead.[5] If the King, God save his life, were deceased, the Duke of Gloucester were in any peril, if my Lord the Prince [Richard Duke of York] who God defend were troubled, if my Lord of Northumberland were dead or greatly troubled, if my Lord Howard were slain . . .' Here the sheet is torn.

Among the Stonor papers[6] there are two relevant letters. They were written from London by Simon Stallworth, a cleric in the employment of John Russell, Bishop of Lincoln (who was now a rather unwilling Chancellor), and they were sent to Sir William Stonor, an Oxfordshire landowner who was a friend of Dorset's and had been one of the four knights who carried the canopy over Edward's bier. In the first, written on 9 June, Stallworth says that the Queen is still in sanctuary and so is her brother, the Bishop of Salisbury. Dorset's goods are confiscated wherever they can be found and the Prior of Westminster is in trouble for concealing them. The next was written a week after the execution of Hastings.

Worshipful Sir,
I commend me to you and for tidings I hold you happy that you are not of the press, for with us is much trouble, and every man doubts [each] other. As on Friday last was the Lord Chamberlain headed soon upon noon. On Monday last was at Westminster great plenty of harnessed men; there was the deliverance of the Duke of York to my Lord Cardinal, my Lord Chancellor, and other many Lords Temporal; and with him my Lord of Buckingham in the midst of the hall of Westminster; my Lord Protector receiving him at the Star-chamber door with many loving words; and so departed with my Lord Cardinal to the Tower, where he is, blessed be Jesus, merry. It is thought there shall be 20,000[7]

---

[4] *The Cely Papers* (Camden Society, 1900).
[5] Morton was alive and was sent to Buckingham's castle at Brecon.
[6] *Stonor Letters* (Camden Society, 1919).
[7] The Croyland Continuator says that Richard summoned armed men 'in fearful and unheard-of numbers'.

of my Lord Protector and my Lord of Buckingham men in London this week; to what intent I know not but to keep the peace. My Lord [Bishop Russell] has much business and more than he is content withal if any other ways would be taken. The Lord Archbishop of York, the Bishop of Ely are yet in the Tower with master Oliver King.[8] I suppose they shall come out nevertheless. [*This sentence is scored through.*] There are men in their places for sure keeping. And I suppose that there shall be sent men of my Lord[9] Protector to these Lords' places in the country. They are not like to come out of ward yet . . . Mistress Shore is in prison; what shall happen her I know not. I pray you pardon me of more writing, I am so sick that I may not well hold my pen. And Jesu preserve you.

From London the XXI day of June by the hands of your servant Simon Stallworth. All the Lord Chamberlain men become my Lord of Buckingham men.

Simon Stallworth was careful to say nothing that would incriminate him, but he showed that he thought anyone who was in prison was in a bad way. Mistress Shore was evidently well known and considered to be important. Gloucester made her walk through the streets of London in a white sheet carrying a candle, which turned her into a folk heroine. It was alleged that she became the mistress of both Dorset and Hastings, but outsiders could not know who in high society was sleeping with whom, and after Edward's death there was no leisure for amorous intrigues, although it is quite possible that she took refuge in the house of Hastings and was in touch with the Queen and Dorset. Gloucester could not forget her, and in a proclamation of 23 October 1483 he accused Dorset, who by this time was out of the country, of holding 'the unshameful and mischievous woman called Shore's wife in adultery' and there also exists a copy of an undated letter (probably written in 1484), about her. In this Gloucester tells his Chancellor, Bishop Russell, that he has heard that his Solicitor, Thomas Lyneham, is marvellously abused and blinded with the late wife of William Shore and intends to marry her. If Lyneham is determined on the marriage then she is to be released from Ludgate prison and put in the charge of her father or anyone else at Russell's discretion, but the marriage must be deferred till Richard comes to London.

Bishop Russell must have wished that Richard could make up his mind. Why did he not forbid Lyneham's marriage or else ignore it?

---

[8] Oliver King (d. 1503). After William Hatteclyffe's death he was chief private secretary to Edward IV. Henry VII reinstated him and he became Bishop of Bath and Wells and Register of the Order of the Garter. The Oliver King Chapel is in the south choir aisle of St George's Chapel.

[9] Up to this point the letter had been written in another hand.

Why did he not keep Mistress Shore in prison or else release her? Why persecute her at all?

Sir Thomas More, about 1513, was told that Mistress Shore was still alive and (inevitably) very poor and very ugly, but his gossip is worthless as he did not even know that she had married Thomas Lyneham.[1] Probably all that had happened was that she had left London and was living in bourgeois respectability in the west, as there was a Thomas Lyneham, gentleman, who sat on commissions in the Welsh marshes and was clerk controller to Arthur Prince of Wales in Ludlow Castle.

Effigy of Jane Shore in Hinxworth Church, Hertfordshire

PRINCE RICHARD HAD BEEN TAKEN TO THE Tower of London on Monday 16 June; the following Sunday, 22 June, a friar called Ralph Shaa preached a startling sermon at St Paul's Cross, announcing that Edward V had no right to the throne because the marriage of Edward IV had not been valid and all his children were bastards.[2] On Monday and Tuesday Buckingham made speeches to the same effect, and suggested that Gloucester should be crowned king. As far as can be gathered from vague reports, Shaa and Buckingham not only produced the totally new story that Edward had been secretly married to a widow called Eleanor Butler before he married Elizabeth, but they also revived the

---

[1] Elizabeth's father, John Lambert, died in 1487, and the executors of his will were one of his three sons and Thomas Lyneham. He left to his daughter, Elizabeth Lyneham, a bed of arras with a velour tester and curtains, and a stained cloth of Mary Magdalen and Martha. And to Julian Lyneham forty shillings. Elizabeth's mother, Amy Lambert, died next year and her residuary legatees were her sons (among whom she included Thomas Lyneham), and her daughter. (Nicolas Barker, 'The Real Jane Shore', *Etoniana* (4 June 1972).)

[2] Gloucester's own marriage was not strictly legal, but pots do not hesitate to call kettles black.

old scandal that Edward was himself a bastard, owing to the adultery of Duchess Cecily with the archer Blackburn, and as Clarence was the same physical type as Edward he too was a bastard and his children were out of the running. Gloucester, on the other hand, greatly resembled his father, the Duke of York and, what was more, he had been born in England—unlike Edward and Clarence.

On Wednesday 25 June there was a very large assembly at Westminster, which had much the appearance of a Parliament, although it was technically only a Council, and a long manifesto was produced and accepted. This put in writing Richard's claim to the throne. No copy of it survives, but it was probably nearly identical with the manifesto accepted by the Parliament of the following January.

In this no mention was made of the archer Blackburn, and Clarence's children were excluded on the grounds that he had been attainted. Edward's marriage was declared void for four reasons. Firstly, because it had been made without the assent of the Lords. Secondly, because it had been made by means of the sorcery and witchcraft of Elizabeth and her mother Jacquetta. Thirdly, because it had been made secretly, without banns. Fourthly, because Edward was already married to 'one Dame Eleanor Butler daughter of the old Earl of Shrewsbury'. There were no further details about this marriage, merely the assertion 'which premises being true, as in very truth they be true' and it will be noticed that as a reason for bastardizing Edward V it only takes fourth place.

When Friar Shaa first produced his revelation about Dame Eleanor Butler, very likely it was believed—we are all regrettably ready to give credence to scandalous stories about the great—but after the crowd had had time to talk it over they saw the flaw. Many people had had personal experience of litigation about an inheritance, and they knew that a man could not disinherit his nephews merely by announcing that his brother's marriage was not valid; there had to be proofs and witnesses. Edward's marriage to Elizabeth had always been considered valid, and it would remain valid until it was examined by an ecclesiastical court and found wanting and annulled by the Church authorities. No witnesses to Edward's other marriage ever came forward, no one suggested any details, any date, any place; and the crowd could see that if Gloucester had had a leg to stand on he would have got lawyers to make out a case, and Edward's children would have been disinherited in form.

Before leaving Dame Eleanor Butler, it should be mentioned that she was a real person although almost certainly not the daughter of the Earl of Shrewsbury. She was the sister of an unidentified Sir John Talbot, and she married Thomas Butler who died between 1450 and 1468, and who was the son and heir of old Lord Sudeley (d. 1473). Eleanor died before 30 June 1468, and presumably she was selected because all her relations were dead. In the absence of printed records, the public soon forgot why Edward V was supposed to be a bastard, and Mancini was told that Warwick had married Edward by proxy in France, while Sir Thomas More was under the impression that the woman in question was called Elizabeth Lucy.[3]

Comines is solely responsible for the legend that it was Bishop Stillington who alleged that Edward's marriage to Elizabeth Woodville was bigamous, and that he claimed to have performed a previous ceremony. English writers do not mention Stillington in this connection, nor did Richard, during his brief reign, show Stillington any marks of favour. Comines also tells the extraordinary story that Stillington had a bastard son whom Richard intended to marry to Princess Elizabeth on purpose to degrade her, but that he was captured at sea and taken to Paris and imprisoned in the Petit Chastellet where he died 'of hunger and poverty'. Comines was by this time no longer in the confidence of the French rulers and he was not meeting English courtiers, and there is no reason why he should ever have heard of Stillington unless he was involved in very important intrigues; his stories are third-hand and garbled but there is evidently *something* behind them.

At the time of the Battle of Bosworth, Stillington was living in Yorkshire, and five days after the battle, York Council received orders that they were to arrest him and send him to the king. It turned out that he had already been arrested and brought into the City but he was too ill to move further. Princess Elizabeth, incidentally, was also near York, at Sheriff Hutton. Stillington obtained a pardon from Henry VII's

---

[3] It has not yet been discovered whether Elizabeth Lucy existed, but Edward may have had a mistress of that name.

first Parliament, but he joined in Lambert Simnel's rebellion and spent the last four years of his life in prison at Windsor. He died in 1491.[4]

TO GO BACK TO JUNE 1483, London was thronged with soldiers. Mancini ventured out to Moorfields, a wide open space outside the walls of the City, and saw Richard welcome the large contingent which had come down from the north. He could see that Richard was bare-headed, but he was not near enough to be able to report on his appearance.

On 26 June it was announced that Richard was king, and on 28 June Lord Howard was created Duke of Norfolk and to those who remembered that the title already belonged to the younger of the Little Princes[5] it must have seemed proof that they were no longer alive. There were only two other Dukes, Buckingham and Suffolk; it had been a long haul for John Howard, but now he was on a par with the royal family. He was also made hereditary Earl Marshal,[6] an office which had been handed down in the Mowbray family, and he obtained the Mowbray lands which had formerly eluded him, and more than twenty manors belonging to Anthony. His son was created Earl of Surrey.

On 6 July 1483 the coronation of Richard III took place in Westminster Abbey. Anne Neville, the new queen, had come south for the ceremony, and was wearing sixteen yards of Venetian lace.[7] Cardinal Bourchier performed the ceremony, missing a great opportunity to make a heroic gesture at small personal risk. Richard's sister Elizabeth

[4] Other incidents in the mysterious Stillington saga are that he founded quite a large 'college' at Nethercaster near York, and this was in trouble in 1484 because, although some of the land with which it was endowed had belonged to Stillington's father, some of it was common land. (*P. Rolls*); and that on 5 August 1486 one Thomas Stillington received seventy-seven pieces of evidence, scrolls and muniments relating to Bishop Stillington. (*York Civic Records*)

[5] Little Prince Richard's title of Earl of Nottingham was at the same time given to Howard's cousin and co-heir, Lord Berkeley. He did not consider he had had his fair share and later joined Henry VII.

[6] His descendant, the 16th Duke of Norfolk, still holds the office of Earl Marshal.

[7] Richard Davey, *The Tower of London* (1910). Apparently the archives of the Frari reveal that sixteen yards of the finest lace of Venice from Burano had been ordered five months earlier for the coronation robes of Queen Anne of England. This is a very odd statement, and needs checking.

was there with her husband, and their eldest son, the Earl of Lincoln, played a conspicuous part in the pageant, but Duchess Cecily was absent and so was the Duchess of Buckingham, *née* Woodville. The crown was carried by the new Duke of Norfolk and the sword of state by the new Earl of Surrey: Richard could count on them for support, and also on Viscount Lovell,[8] but otherwise it was a sinister coronation. The Duke of Buckingham, who carried Richard's train, and Margaret Countess of Richmond who carried Anne's train, were both intending at the earliest possible moment to remove the crown from Richard's head and to place it on that of Henry Tudor. Lord Stanley and the Earl of Northumberland, both prominent in the procession, were proceeding with caution; Stanley had had a near shave when Hastings was murdered, but there was a good chance that Richard's reign would not last very long. Familiar faces were missing. Insignificant men filled the gaps.

WHEN LOUIS WAS TOLD THAT EDWARD HAD DIED 'he did not rejoice'. It was almost as though he *liked* Edward. Ill though he was, he was able to enjoy taking a high moral line when Richard usurped the throne,[9] and he refused to see the herald who brought him a formal announcement from the new king of England. According to Comines, Louis did not 'wish either to answer his letter nor hear his message and considered him very cruel and wicked'. The note he sent in reply was brief and perhaps accompanied by some verbal insult and Richard took umbrage. According to the terms of the Treaty of Picquigny, both the truce and the tribute should run for a year after the death of either king, and Richard was naturally more anxious than Louis was that this provision should be observed, but he was so angry that his reply to Louis was not likely to smooth things over; he had the shamelessness to refer

---

[8] Francis, 9th Baron, 1st Viscount Lovell (1455–87). On 13 August 1479 York Council were unwilling that Lovell should graze twenty cows and a bull on some common land, but on 15 September 1483, when Lovell had become Chamberlain to Richard III, he was given permission to do so.

[9] It is notorious that in prisons child-murderers have to be protected from the attacks of other criminals.

to 'the late king of most noble memory, my brother' and the offensive-ness to mention that the bearer was one of the grooms of his stable.

However, it did not matter. On 30 August 1483 Louis XI died at last. He was buried in a church he had built himself, the basilica of Notre Dame at Cléry near Orleans, and his tomb must have been uncommonly attractive.[1] He had directed a sculptor to make a life-sized statue of him in bronze, 'kneeling, his dog at his side, his hands clasped holding his hat, as handsome as possible, young-looking, not bald, hair rather long at the back, nose long, slightly arched'.

The new king of France, Charles VIII, was thirteen years of age when he succeeded and his eldest sister, Anne of Beaujeu, and her husband, conducted the affairs of the nation very competently until he was old enough to act for himself—proof, if any were needed, that a child-king is not a disaster if the regents are sensible and honourable.

Louis, on his death-bed, had sent for Charles whom he had hardly ever seen and had given him some excellent advice and, among other things, had warned him not to try to conquer Brittany until he had reached years of discretion. Accordingly, Charles waited till 1491, and then jilted Marguerite d'Autriche who had been living at the French Court as his queen ever since she had been a small child, and forced the Duchess of Brittany, Anne de Bretagne,[2] to marry him. Anne was already married by proxy to Maximilian (the father of Marguerite d'Autriche) but this was ignored. Charles VIII died in 1498 without leaving an heir, whereupon Anne married his successor and cousin, Louis XII, who for this purpose had to divorce his wife, the deformed younger daughter of Louis XI. No male heir survived Anne's second marriage, but she had two daughters and as the Salic Law did not apply to Brittany it was inherited by her daughter Claude. Claude married the next French king, François I, and at last Brittany and France were permanently united.

Burgundy was less fortunate. Philip the Fair, son of Mary and Maximilian, married a Spanish princess, and this eventually had the unforeseen and disastrous result that Holland and Flanders became part

---

[1] His tomb was destroyed in the next century, and again at the Revolution. The present tomb is a reconstruction.

[2] Her father, Duke Francis, had died impoverished and a physical wreck in 1488.

of the dominion of Spain, and years of misery were endured before they gained independence.

Margaret, Dowager Duchess of Burgundy, lived on at Malines till 1503. Her main occupations, besides good works, were keeping up her dignity and her income, assisting the children of Mary and Maximilian, and embarrassing Henry VII. She still had a soft spot for plausible young men, and she backed Lambert Simnel, Perkin Warbeck, the sons of the Duke of Suffolk and any other pretender to the English throne who solicited her aid. In Burgundy she was known as La Dame d'Angleterre or Marguerite d'Yorch; at the English Court she was called Juno because she made trouble in heaven and on earth.

AFTER HIS CORONATION, Richard III set out on a royal progress and reached the city of York towards the end of August. The aldermen had gone through an anxious time since the death of Edward IV.[3] They speedily decided to ask the Duke of Gloucester to use his influence with the boy-king to remit the fee-farm, and then four aldermen (including the egregious Wrangwyshe) had been declared members of Parliament, and it was agreed that they should go to London in good time to see the coronation and make useful contacts; but they had been thrown off-balance when, on 15 June 1483, they received a letter from the Duke of Gloucester, warning them of the apalling disasters that were impending and appealing to them to send soldiers to join the Earl of Northumberland's men and hurry to London to assist him against 'the Queen, her blood adherents and affinity, which have intended and daily do intend to murder and utterly destroy us and our cousin, the Duke of Buckingham and the old royal blood of this realm, and as it is now openly known, by their subtle and damnable ways forecasted the same, and also the final destruction and disinheritance of you and all the other

---

[3] According to the Record Book of the York Council, the news of Edward's death reached York on 6 April, three days before it occurred, and this has been explained in many ingenious ways. The simplest explanation is that the date is just an ordinary mistake, and that when the secretary came to write up the record book he looked at the wrong line of calendar—he was a very careless man, who was capable of calling Richard III 'Richard II' or 'Richard IV' or even 'Richard the furst'.

inheritors and men of honour, as well of the north parts as other countries that belong to us . . .' The messenger would tell them more.

The messenger was Sir Richard Ratcliffe ('the Rat') and his eloquence persuaded York to send three hundred soldiers under six officers (including Wrangwyshe) to protect the old royal blood. As far as they knew, Edward V was still King on 27 June when they agreed that John Harper, who had managed in the course of the vintners' pageant to obtain a vessel of white wine without paying for it, should be allowed to sell it for tenpence a gallon, and the Clerk wrote no more in the record book till '12 July 1 Richard III' when it was agreed that the mayor, four aldermen and 'as many of The Twenty-four as will' should ride to Middleham Castle to take Richard's son a present of wine, six cygnets, six herons and two dozen rabbits. (The horse of their cook died on the journey and next January he received thirteen and fourpence compensation.)

When Richard arrived in York, every effort was made to welcome him effusively. A king visiting a town for the first time expected a present, and all the Council contributed; Miles Metcalf topped the list with £100, and Wrangwyshe—who had more ambition than worldly wealth—came about the middle with £10. The Earl of Northumberland received the usual game and fish and John Kendall, Richard's personal secretary, was voted a scarlet gown or a chamlet gown.

It was Kendall who warned them in advance that they must show gladness and decorate the streets with cloth of arras and tapestry. The citizens of York were accustomed to mounting pageants and hardly needed this exhortation, but Kendall tried to spur them on to make unusual efforts by telling them of the pageants at other places and of the southern lords and men of worship who would be watching. Richard and his Queen walked through the streets of York with crowns on their heads and Edward their son was created Prince of Wales. On 17 September Richard graciously exempted the citizens of York from paying the fee-farm, but he needed the money and, try as they might, they never could get the exemption ratified.

Richard left Yorkshire in October and had reached Lincoln when he heard that rebellion had broken out in the south, and that the Duke of Buckingham—whom he imagined to be his warm supporter and on whom he had showered offices and estates—was among the rebels. There were risings in many places from Kent and Essex to Devon, but no clear-headed leader was in command. On 10 October the Duke of Norfolk wrote nonchalantly from London to Paston *minor* at Caister: 'It is so that the Kentishmen be up in the Weald and say that they will come and rob the City, which I shall lett if I may', and he asked Paston to bring six tall fellows in harness as soon as he could.

The Duke of Buckingham was in his castle at Brecon and Bishop Morton was his prisoner. Morton doubtless encouraged him in his determination to revolt against Richard, but the outline of the rebellion must have been arranged before he left London. Theoretically Buckingham could draw on practically the whole of Wales for men, but the Welsh disliked him and he had no organizing ability or flair for soldiering. He led an army out of Brecon, but it is not known which road he took and whether he intended to cross the Severn at Gloucester and meet Henry Tudor at some rendezvous on the south coast, or whether he meant to go north-east to Shrewsbury; he may even have been double-crossing Henry Tudor and have had a plan to seize the throne for himself. All that is certain is that before he had gone very far his army deserted—either because of his incompetence, or because it rained incessantly, or because the approaches to the bridge at Gloucester were flooded and impassable,[4] or because the Vaughans seized the opportunity to pursue a tribal feud and go raiding in his rear. Without meeting any opposing army, Buckingham was first a fugitive and then a prisoner and on 2 November he was beheaded at Salisbury.

Henry Tudor, who had hovered off the coast of Dorset, discovered that the rising had failed and, without landing, returned to Brittany; and it shows the feebleness of the Woodvilles that this very extensive rebellion collapsed without any fighting. Henry Tudor's mother was naturally suspected of being in league with the rebels but as she was the wife of Lord Stanley and it was very important to Richard that the Stanleys should remain on his side she was not punished except that her estates were given to her husband and her title of Countess of

[4] This happened from time to time until the 1950s when the level of the road was raised.

Richmond was taken from her. Salinger was executed at Exeter[5] and other rebels were executed here and there, but by and large pardons were given generously.

Contrary to popular legend, Richard III did his utmost to rule in a lenient and conciliatory manner. He was used to the responsibility of keeping order over a large tract of country, he was willing to apply himself to business, he longed to be loved and admired, and if he had acquired the throne in a normal manner he might have made a very passable king, although his tactlessness and indecision would always have been a liability. The government departments were running smoothly and he introduced some improvements; he set up the Council of the North which, under the chairmanship of the Earl of Lincoln, managed the matters which had formerly been controlled by the private Councils of himself and the Earl of Northumberland;[6] his only Parliament, which met on 23 January 1484, officially ratified the pronouncement of the quasi-Parliament of the preceding summer and recognized Richard as king and his son Edward as his heir; but he carried the stigma of being an usurper and a child-murderer, and although he spent large sums on rewarding his supporters he could not inspire confidence.

Richard was also short of money, although the French menace had receded after the death of Louis and it was found unnecessary to pursue the war with Scotland. At first he had been able to draw on the capital amassed by Edward,[7] but the subsidy from France had ceased and so had the income from Edward's trading ventures. Buckingham's rebellion had cost him a great deal of money, and he wanted his court to be splendid and to cut a fine figure as his brother had done. A military coup had placed him on the throne, but he could not afford to protect himself with a standing army. His reliable supporters were few, buying friends was expensive, and although he had grandly denounced 'benevolences' before very long he had recourse, as the Croyland Continuator

[5] Sir Thomas St Leger was buried in St George's Chapel, Windsor, in the chantry which he had built in 1481 in memory of his wife, Anne. His daughter married Sir George Manners, 12th Lord Roos, ancestor of the Dukes of Rutland, and it is now called the Rutland chapel.

[6] The Council of the North was not abolished until the 1640s.

[7] It is not known how large this was to start with, nor how much of it Richard was able to secure. Dorset and Edward Woodville may have been able to get some of it out o f the country and give it to Henry Tudor.

put it, 'to the modes of exaction which had been practised by King Edward and which he himself had condemned in full Parliament; these were the so-called "benevolences", a name detestable in every way'.

Ex-Queen Elizabeth stayed on in Westminster Sanctuary. She had gone through it all once before and ultimately had been rescued by her gallant husband, but now there was nobody to come to her aid. Richard had confiscated her lands and she had no source of income, and in March 1484 she gave up hope and made a pact with her brother-in-law, who had killed her three sons and her beloved brother Anthony, taken away her money, invalidated her marriage and bastardized her children. It was agreed that Richard should find her daughters respectable husbands, and that an official should be provided with funds to maintain her. Princess Elizabeth appeared at the Court, but it is not clear whether or not the Queen and her younger children remained in the Sanctuary.

On 9 April 1484 Richard's only legitimate son died and he was left without an heir. Characteristically, he havered. First of all he put forward Clarence's son, Edward Earl of Warwick,[8] but if Clarence's attainder were reversed Warwick would have a better right to the throne than Richard himself, and so John Earl of Lincoln was named as being next in the line of succession.

The thought of legitimizing his bastard son, John of Pontefract, may have passed through his mind and in the following year, on 11 March 1485, the vital post of Captain of Calais was bestowed on 'our dear son, our bastard John of Gloucester, whose quickness of mind, agility of body and inclination to all good customs gives us great hope of his good service for the future'. Lord Dynham was Lieutenant of Calais, and ever since the murder of his chief he had been acting as Deputy Captain;[9] whatever his political preferences, he could be trusted to defend Calais against the French and by appointing a child as honorary Captain Richard could keep the emoluments.

---

[8] Edward Earl of Warwick (1475–99). He was a prisoner for most of his life and, becoming involved with Perkin Warbeck, he was executed by Henry VII. His sister, Margaret Countess of Salisbury (1473–1541), was the last of the Plantagenets. She was executed by Henry VIII when she was nearly seventy.

[9] Lord Dynham became Treasurer of the Exchequer to Henry VII. His only legitimate son (educated at Winchester and Lincoln's Inn) died before he did and his three brothers left no heirs, so that when he died his estates were divided between his sisters, and the ancient family of Dynham of Hartland became extinct.

On 16 April 1485 Anne Neville died. Richard was now free to remarry and beget legitimate children—he was only thirty-two. The most important girl in England was Princess Elizabeth, and as nobody really believed that Edward's marriage was bigamous it was recognized that whoever married her would tremendously strengthen his claim to the throne. Illogically, he seems to have seriously contemplated marrying her himself, but he was dissuaded by his supporters, both because to recognize her claim would be to invalidate his own, and because the marriage of uncle and niece—although not unknown on the Continent—would shock English opinion. Richard officially denied that he intended to marry Princess Elizabeth and sent her up to Sheriff Hutton Castle in Yorkshire, where she probably found Clarence's children, Richard's bastards and other relations.

Émigrés of every party were now collecting in Brittany, and it was only a matter of time before Henry Tudor launched another attack. Posterity, poring over Henry's pedigree, does not find his claim very good, but his contemporaries knew little about pedigrees: all they knew was that he was descended from John of Gaunt, that he was a male of about the right age, and that it was said on the grape-vine that he was so astute that if he once got the crown he would be able to hold it, which was far more important than whether or not his great-grandfather was illegitimate. Furthermore, there was no other suitable candidate; he was first in field of one.

In the autumn of 1484 the Earl of Oxford, who had been a prisoner in the Castle of Hammes for ten years, persuaded the Governor of the Castle to go with him to join Henry Tudor, and the invasion force then had a commander who, even if he had never been successful in the past, at least knew how to make men follow him. By August 1485 arrangements were complete.

As usual, the man on the defensive was at a disadvantage. Henry might land anywhere along the south coast or in East Anglia or Wales, or even at Ravenspur; all Richard could do was to take up a central position in the Midlands and implore his supporters to stand in readiness.

Henry Tudor was now twenty-eight. Till he was fourteen he had lived entirely in South Wales, except for one fortnight's visit to London;

since then he had been a semi-prisoner in a rustic duchy. He had never been really free; he had never known his father, and he had seldom seen his mother; he had no natural charm or grace; he was unathletic and without experience of war; and his only true friend was his uncle, Jasper Tudor, who—like himself—was a homeless wanderer. Jasper was now about fifty-five, but quite ready to make another attempt to win England's crown for his relations. Pembrokeshire was the county he knew best and, in spite of previous disasters in the west, Pembrokeshire was chosen.

On 7 August 1485, Henry Tudor and his supporters landed in Milford Haven with a small army consisting mainly of French and Breton mercenaries. As they proceeded through Wales they were joined by a few Welsh chieftains, but their army remained small. The Earl of Oxford was in command. Henry had no pretensions to be a soldier but he had guts, and he agreed to throw subtlety to the winds and to march straight towards Richard and settle the question as to which of them was to be king in one deadly battle. They reached the Midlands unopposed, and here Henry managed to get in touch with the Stanleys and ascertained that they would join him when opportunity offered. At the moment Lord Stanley's hands were tied, because Richard was holding his son, Lord Strange, as a hostage (which, incidentally, was quite against the unwritten rules).

A curious thing about the Battle of Bosworth is that though Richard's military record was an unbroken series of victories, and Oxford and Jasper had been defeated again and again, Richard was not expected to win. As a matter of fact, he had never before directed a pitched battle. When very young he had fought at Barnet and Tewkesbury, but Edward had been the commander and he had merely led a wing. Since then he had rounded up rebels, done some Border raiding, ordered hangings and executions. His ambition to reopen the French war had not been gratified, his march to Edinburgh had been unopposed, his siege of Berwick had taken nine months, Buckingham's rebellion had collapsed without a fight. It is also possible that he was on the verge of a nervous breakdown and that this was common knowledge. According to More's story, he had become very jumpy, bit his lips, fidgeted with his dagger, and slept badly; and these symptoms all fit together and were the sort of thing that would have been noticed by his attendants. He was anyway in such mental confusion that he did not keep the Duke of Norfolk, the one magnate he could really trust, informed of his movements, and Norfolk wrote to Paston: 'Well-beloved friend, I commend me to you, letting you to understand that the King's enemies be a-land, and that the King would have set forth as upon Monday but only for Our Lady Day [Assumption, 15 August] but for certain he goes forward as upon Tuesday, for a servant of mine brought to me the certainty.' Norfolk went on to ask Paston to meet him at Bury St Edmunds on Tuesday, and to bring with him not only the soldiers he had promised to the King but also as many tall men as he could, at Norfolk's expense; if he provided them with jackets of Norfolk's livery they could settle up when they met. The letter was signed: 'Your lover, J. Norfolk'.

Paston *minor* was now a middle-aged man of property, living peacefully in Caister Castle with his wife and family, and he may have been amused by the affectionate way that he was addressed by his father's old enemy, John Howard, now Duke of Norfolk; however, it was no laughing matter, and he had to decide immediately whether he would go to Bury St Edmunds on Tuesday or stay at Caister. A month later Paston became Sheriff of Norfolk, and so it looks as though he decided to stay at Caister.

The Battle of Bosworth was fought on the morning of 22 August 1485, in open country in Leicestershire. As it marked the end of one epoch and the beginning of another, one feels that it should have been a stupendous conflict, but such evidence as there is points to its being a small, short battle with few casualties.

The Croyland Continuator, writing less than a year later, has the story that Richard's sleep was disturbed by nightmares, that his camp was disorganized, that there were no chaplains and that he got no breakfast. He looked ghastly, said that whoever won or lost the day it would be the end of England, and went into battle wearing a gold crown on his helmet.

Six distinct armies were involved—Richard's, the Duke of Norfolk's, the Earl of Northumberland's, Lord Stanley's, Sir William Stanley's, and Henry Tudor's—though how many of them actually took part is a moot point. It would seem that Richard and Norfolk drew up side by side on a ridge, with Northumberland immediately behind to form a reserve. It was a strong defensive position: to get to them, the enemy would have to skirt round marshy ground under fire from above, and attack uphill. The two Stanley armies are supposed to have been a short distance away on either side, but it is possible that Lord Stanley—who was naturally more interested in the life of his son than in the result of the battle—entirely removed his army.[1] Sir William was quite simply waiting to see who would win. Apparently he did not like either leader particularly; he referred to Richard III as 'Olde Dyk', and he was later executed by Henry VII for his activities during Perkin Warbeck's rebellion.[2]

Richard's army is said to have been the larger, but its size must have been a disappointment: for instance, the City of York, which had sent three hundred men to London at the beginning of his reign, now voted eighty and arranged that they did not arrive in time.[3] Perhaps his best chance would have been to take the initiative and to have rushed boldly down on the enemy, thus creating the impression that he was winning and bringing in Sir William Stanley on his side; instead, he waited and allowed Oxford, intrepid as ever, to march round the swamp and up the hill and, in the hand-to-hand fighting, Richard was killed.[4] One of the few things that is absolutely certain about the battle is that Northumberland pursued his usual policy of masterly inactivity and, instead of bringing up his reserve, kept right out of the fight—there was no reason why he should want to risk his life for either

[1] In January 1486 he testified that he first met Henry Tudor on 24 August, which was two days after the battle. *Calendar of Papal Registers* (1960), XIV 17.

[2] Sir William Stanley is generally represented as a calculating traitor, but he may merely have been a rich and stupid country gentleman who was out of his depth in high politics. The following jolly note was written to a Cheshire neighbour, Piers Warburton. 'Cousin Piers, I commend me unto you. I doubt not ye remember how I promised you to come unto your park and there to have killed a buck with my hounds, and it go so as now I am so busy with Old Dick I can have no leave thereunto. Notwithstanding if it please you to have my servant and my hounds, they be ready at your commandment. And Christ keep you. Written at Ridley the 6th day of September. W. Stanley, knt.' George Ormerod, *History of the Country Palatine and City of Chester*, II, 301 revised T. Selsby (1882).

[3] Alternatively, Richard may have failed to send them clear directions.

[4] If Richard had really said 'My kingdom for a horse' it would have been with the object of escaping but everyone seems to agree that he was killed fighting bravely.

Richard or Henry Tudor. Norfolk was killed, perhaps at the very beginning by an arrow or even a cannon-ball, and it is possible that his son, Surrey, who was wounded, surrendered his army, leaving Richard with no soldiers at all but his own contingent, who could not fail to appreciate that the battle was lost. The Earl of Lincoln, Viscount Lovell, Catesby and Ratcliffe were among those who managed to get back to their horses and escape.[5] But it was nobody's business to write an account of the battle, and there were quite a few people who were glad to forget precisely what had happened; the Earl of Oxford, who would appear to have been the hero of the day, had not got a faction to boost him, and so the myth-makers took over and turned the battle into an heroic one with the two kings engaging each other in single combat.

Richard's body was carried to Leicester and, after being exhibited to show that he really was dead, he was buried in the church of the Grey Friars. A tomb was later erected by Henry VII but—like so many other tombs—it was destroyed at the Reformation.

John Howard is chiefly remembered for the sinister couplet, 'Jockey of Norfolk, be not too bold, for Dickon thy master is bought and sold,' but it is he, rather than the Earl of Warwick, who should be known as the 'Last of the Barons'. Although so cunning, his ideas were out of date, and his grand design had the fatal flaw that in 1485 the country would not stand such methods. His son, the Earl of Surrey, was taken prisoner and, with that intelligent clemency that was such a feature of these family conflicts, his life was spared. He had always been completely overshadowed by his formidable father, and in the Tower he had leisure to reflect that the ambition of the Howards had brought about the deaths of his father, Richard III, the two Little Princes, Lord Hastings, Anthony, Sir Richard Grey, the Duke of Buckingham and many other men, and that the final result was that the outsider—Henry Tudor—had become King of England. For several years Henry VII was not absolutely certain whether Edward V and his brother were really dead, and he cautiously referred to them in vague terms, and it is quite

---

[5] Catesby was caught and executed three days later. Ratcliffe is said to have been killed in the battle, but a warrant was issued for his arrest, and he was exempted from a pardon on 24 September 1485. Sir Robert Brackenbury and Walter Devereux Lord Ferrers of Chartley, were among the supporters of Richard who were killed with him.

possible that not even Surrey knew precisely what had happened to them, but presently he and Henry came to an understanding and he returned to Court, and began working his way up the ladder again. In 1513, when he was seventy, he won the Battle of Flodden for Henry VIII, and the titles of Duke of Norfolk and Earl Marshal were restored to him. The Howards were again a powerful and dangerous family, and when the histories of Polydore Vergil and Sir Thomas More were first printed references to the part they played in the events of 1483 were toned down; subsequent editions, published when the Howards were in disgrace, were more outspoken, but by that time the legends had crystallized and their reputations were safe.

THE DEATH OF RICHARD CAUSED GREAT AMAZEMENT: kings were not usually killed in battle—it had not happened in England since the time of Harold.

When the first news of Bosworth reached York it came as a shock to the Council, and the clerk wrote: '. . . King Richard, late lawfully reigning over us, was through the great treason of the Duke of Norfolk [*sic*] and many other that turned against him, with many other lords and nobility of these North Parts, was piteously slain and murdered, to the great heaviness of the City . . .' And a humble letter was sent to the Earl of Northumberland (of all people) from the Mayor, aldermen, sheriffs, The Twenty-four and the whole Commonalty, asking him what they ought to do: had they got to accept this unknown foreigner as their king? The answer was in the affirmative, and they were soon begging Henry VII to be their good and gracious lord. They had invested a good deal of money in Richard III one way and another—there was even the 'nambling hors' they had given to his secretary—and now they were back at square one. Not that Richard's reign had been particularly peaceful in York: there had been riots when he had given some common land to a hospital, and Wrangwyshe had been mayor again and had thrown his weight about unduly. But Henry was an utter stranger. However, there were always small things to keep them busy. The soldiers who had been too late for Bosworth had only been away four and a half days, and they had had wages for ten days at a shilling a day; they kept wages for six days and returned the rest of the money to the parishes.

And then began the old game of trying to wheedle favours from the King without letting him interfere in their private concerns, and they successfully blocked all attempts by Henry to force his nominees into Council offices. Triumphant they may have felt as they flatly ignored his commands, but the remission of the fee-farm promised them by Richard had still not been ratified, there were more fish-garths on the river than ever, Miles Metcalf died and Alderman Wrangwyshe sank into obscurity.

JASPER TUDOR HAD NOW COME INTO HARBOUR and his years of strenuous adventure were rewarded; he was given the hand of a rich widow (Catherine *née* Woodville, relict of the Duke of Buckingham) and the illustrious title of Duke of Bedford.[6] Oxford was restored to his estates and, still in the prime of life, defeated Lambert Simnel and the Earl of Lincoln at the Battle of Stoke (1487) where, true to form, he and his division dashed on ahead of the rest of the army and were only reinforced in the nick of time. His wife, Margaret Neville, was also unbowed by her years of poverty and distress, and on 19 May 1486 she was ordering Paston in the King's name to catch Lord Lovell who was believed to be hiding in the Fens, and to watch all ports so that he should not escape abroad.[7]

Henry's mother did not even go through the form of renouncing her inheritance: a strong ruler was needed, and it was taken for granted that it should be he, not she, who was crowned. His supporters were determined that he should consolidate his position by marrying Princess Elizabeth, but years of captivity and danger had made him canny and he delayed his wedding to show that his right to the throne in no way depended on his wife. They were married by Cardinal Bourchier on

---

[6] Jasper died in 1495 leaving one illegitimate daughter. Catherine Woodville married thirdly) Sir Richard Wingfield (1469?–1525) a distinguished diplomat.

[7] Viscount Lovell is supposed to have hidden in his own house at Minster Lovell, Oxfordshire, and to have starved to death.

18 January 1486,[8] and the following 20 September she gave birth prematurely to a son and heir. Henry (who was half Welsh) insisted that she should lie in at Winchester, the old capital of England, and the baby was christened Arthur.

Elizabeth Woodville, after a life that was an extraordinary mixture of good fortune and tragedy, enjoyed an Indian summer. In spite of the appalling casualties among her nearest and dearest, her family had been so large to start with that she was still the centre of a circle of devoted relations.[9] Her eldest daughter was Queen, and when Prince Arthur was christened she was paid the compliment of being his sole godmother. The King's mother was an old friend of hers, and there is no reason to think that they did not all get on perfectly.[1]

At first Henry VII built up Elizabeth Woodville's estate to the sum of £400 a year; over seventy separate properties were needed to arrive at this total, and the list included such items as the right to feed pigs in Savernake Forest and to dredge for mussels in Tilbury Hope. In 1487 she exchanged her estates for an annuity and retired into Bermondsey Abbey which was just across the river from London. Catherine of France and the widow of the first Earl of Somerset had died there, and it was evidently regarded as a kind of royal nursing-home. She was not, however, a complete invalid, and the French ambassadors who visited the young Queen Elizabeth in Westminster Palace in 1489 were introduced to her. She died on 8 June 1492.

Elizabeth's will had been made on the previous 10 April and it was short, almost careless. She had explained her wishes to her family and she felt confident that they would divide her possessions amicably. She had, of course, no lands or money to bequeath, and she left her 'small stuff and goods' to pay her debts, or 'for the health of my soul', or for

---

[8] She was not crowned till 25 November 1487.

[9] All her brothers died before she did. Lionel Bishop of Salisbury died in 1484. Edward Woodville was killed in Brittany in 1488, engaged in a mad enterprise to help the Bretons. Richard, third and last Earl Rivers, died childless in 1491; he left his Grafton estate to his nephew, Dorset.

[1] The story that Elizabeth of York was downtrodden by her mother-in-law was started by Spanish diplomats, but as they also believed that Margaret had political influence—which she certainly had not—it seems that they were seeing the Court through Spanish spectacles.

her family to divide if they wanted to. She was quite unworried about the next world, and she asked to have a quiet funeral and to be buried with Edward at Windsor 'according to the will of my said Lord and mine'. She hoped that her son Dorset and her eldest daughter, the Queen, would see that her wishes were carried out. This will was witnessed by the Abbot of Bermondsey and her doctor, and the executors were the Prior of the Charter-house at Shene, her chaplain and another cleric.

Elizabeth's funeral was as quiet as was possible under the circumstances and a disappointed sightseer has left an account of it. There is no beginning or end to the letter, but for once we seem to have a woman writing to a woman and, judging by their extensive knowledge of the royal family going back to the days of Margaret of Anjou, they were wives of Windsor officials.

Late in the evening of Whit Sunday Elizabeth's coffin arrived at Windsor by water, accompanied only by her executors, one of the Haute cousins, 'Mistress Grace a bastard of King Edward', and another lady, and it was 'there privily through the little park conveyed into the Castle without ringing of any bells', and at about eleven o'clock at night it was put into Edward's tomb. Nothing much happened on Monday, but on Tuesday Elizabeth's three unmarried daughters—Anne, Catherine and Bridget—arrived by water, also Dorset's wife and daughter, two nieces and some other ladies. Dorset rode down with Viscount Welles (husband of Princess Cecily), Edmund of Suffolk and the Earl of Essex (nephews) and other fashionable gentlemen. The Queen was not present because she was shortly expecting a baby, and so the writer could not say what coloured mourning she wore, but it was probably blue which is what Queen Margaret had worn when her mother died. There were ceremonies in the Chapel both on Tuesday night and on Wednesday, but the whole thing was done very shabbily and cheaply, and there was nobody there except the Poor Knights of St George's and the Garter officials, the attendants, the servants and friends and relations.

Some Books

FOR REFERENCE

Cora L. Scofield, *The Life and Reign of Edward IV*, 2 vols (1923, reprinted 1967, Frank Cass & Co.).
No serious student of the period can avoid using this book though it is far from satisfactory.
E. F. Jacob, *The Fifteenth Century 1399–1485* (O.U.P., 1961). Here the reign of Edward IV is shown as part of the history of England. Comprehensive bibliography.
The Complete Peerage.
Much more reliable than the *Dictionary of National Biography* which is weak on the fifteenth century and also out of date.
English Historical Documents, vol. IV, *1327–1485*, ed. A. R. Myers (Eyre & Spottiswoode, 1969).

GENERAL READING

S. B. Chrimes, *Lancastrians, Yorkists and Henry VII* (Macmillan, 1964).
A very clear and readable run-through of the fortunes of the English Royal Family from the death of Edward III to Henry VII.

R. L. Storey, *The End of the House of Lancaster* (Barrie & Rockliff, 1966).
The years 1450–1460 as revealed by documents in the Public Record Office. The angle is unusual, and the sources are refreshingly authentic.

J. R. Lander, *The Wars of the Roses* (Secker & Warburg, 1965).
The story is told mainly by quotations from fifteenth-century writers. Modern spelling, and an interesting introduction.

Lt.-Col. Alfred H. Burne, *The Battlefields of England* (Methuen, 1950), and *More Battlefields of England* (Methuen, 1952).
Very entertaining and plausible, but Burne's range was too wide for him to be entirely correct about period details.

The Penguin Book of the Renaissance, ed. J. H. Plumb (1964).
Essays by different writers on various aspects of contemporary Italy.

J. Huizinga, *The Waning of the Middle Ages* (1924). Excellent translation by F. Hopman.
A fascinating picture of Burgundian culture. The people hardly seem to be living on the same planet as the Pastons.

ENGLISH FIFTEENTH-CENTURY CHRONICLES

Changes in the English language have built a formidable barrier between ourselves and our ancestors; moreover, the fifteenth-century English chroniclers were mostly ill-informed, ill-educated and writing after the passage of many years. *Warkworth's Chronicle* is often quoted because it contains chatty anecdotes, but it is particularly unreliable. *Pseudo-Gregory*, who gives a lively worm's-eye view of events, is semi-literate. The best is *Ingulph's Chronicle of the Abbey of Croyland*, translated from Latin by H. T. Riley, 1854. This contains the 'Third Continuation', which is the only English chronicle of the period written by an intelligent and moderately well-informed man. The original no longer exists, and anything may be an interpolation or a copyist's error, a mistranslation or a joke.

FOREIGN FIFTEENTH-CENTURY WRITERS

Memoirs of Philip de Comines.
French versions are not difficult to read. There is a modern translation by Michael Jones (Penguin, 1972).

Memoirs of a Renaissance Pope—The Commentaries of Pius II, abridged, trans. F. A. Gragg, ed. L. C. Gabel (George Allen & Unwin, 1960).
Entrancing passages compensate for the *longeurs*.
Calendar of State Papers and MSS. in the Archives and Collections of Milan, vol. 1, ed. A. B. Hinds (1912).
Disconnected letters. Some of them are amusing, and they are very well translated.
Dominic Mancini, *The Usurpation of Richard III* (1483). Trans. C. A. J. Armstrong (1936).
An intelligent Italian's attempt to write a short *Inside England* for French readers.

ENGLISH SIXTEENTH-CENTURY HISTORIANS

The three early Tudor historians who influenced subsequent writers were Robert Fabyan, Polydore Vergil and Sir Thomas More. They all wrote from hearsay, and none of them had access to any material which would be considered as genuine evidence if a later century were being examined. They could not consult the Rolls of Parliament or the Patent Rolls, or interview the surviving noble personages who had been involved in affairs of state, and all they had to build on was what their friends thought they remembered and scraps of illiterate chronicle which nameless Londoners had copied from one another.

Fabyan was a linen-draper, enterprising but not very intelligent, who could actually remember the reign of Edward IV. His history was first printed in 1516.

Polydore Vergil (1470?–1555?) was an Italian scholar who did not arrive in England till 1502. Henry VII commissioned him to write a history of England, and the first edition of his history was printed in 1534 by which time the reign of Edward IV had become a rather dim patch in the past.

Sir Thomas More (1477/8–1535), *The History of King Richard III*, ed. Richard S. Sylvester (Yale U. P., 1965).
More's history was very different from that of Fabyan and Vergil, as he intended to devote a whole book to the years 1483–1485. He worked at it from about 1514 to 1518, composed a Latin and an English version, and then stopped abruptly having got no further than September 1483. It was first printed, posthumously, in 1543.

More could remember his father telling him that Edward IV was dead, and he had grown up with the story of the wicked uncle who had murdered the two Little Princes in the Tower. The subject was dramatic, and he attempted to handle it in the manner of classical authors; what he produced is a reconstruction very similar to the semi-fictional histories which are so popular today. More lived among the professional classes, and although everyone a little older than himself had memories of Richard's reign they could not supply him with even such elementary facts as Edward's age, or the Christian name of Lord Hastings, though they knew the names of some minor government officials. When he was a boy, about 1490–2, he was a member of the household of Cardinal Morton, and so Morton figures more conspicuously in his narrative than he might otherwise have done, but naturally the aged Cardinal did not chatter about the recent past—which was still dynamite—and if More picked up any historical information when he was under Morton's roof it was from the other employees.

INDEX

Abergavenny, Edward Neville Lord, xxiii

Albany, Alexander Stuart Duke of, 266–8

Albergata, Cardinal, 54

Alcock, John Bishop, 181, 197, 215

Alfonso V, King of Aragon and Sicily, 61

Alfonso V, King of Portugal, 94, 208

Aliprando, Pietro, 208–9

Alyngton, William, Speaker, 236

Angus, Archibald 'Bell-the-Cat' Douglas 5th Earl of, 267

Angus, George Douglas 4th Earl of, 86

Anjou, Margaret of, see Margaret of Anjou

Anjou, René Count of, King of Sicily and Naples, xxvi, xxvii, 46, 61, 82, 186–7, 229

Anne, d. of Edward IV, 240, 243, 306

Anne of Beaujeu, d. of Louis XI, 292

Anne de Bretagne, d. of Duke of Brittany, 241, 292

Anne of Caux, nurse of Edward IV, xxxi

Anne Duchess of Exeter, sister of Edward IV, xxxv, 65, 93, 107, 121, 204, 296

Antioch, Patriarch of, 118

Antoinette de Villequier, 59

Aragon, John II, King of, 61

Arrivall, The, chronicle, 161–84

Arthur Plantagenet, Viscount Lisle, bastard s. of Edward IV, 96

Arundel, William Fitzalan Earl of, 145, 214

Atclif, William, see Hatteclyffe, William

Audley, James Tuchet 5th Lord, xl

Audley, John Tuchet 6th Lord, 12, 13, 34, 137

Bacon, Francis, 249

Baker, William, painter of Eton murals, 247

Balowe, William, heretic, 250–1

Balue, Cardinal, 256–7

Barnet, Battle of, 169–72

Basley, dealer, 282

Bastard of Brittany, 161

Bastard of Burgundy, Antoine, 121–2, 124–5, 130–1, 230–1

Beauchamp, Richard, Bishop of Salisbury, 45, 122–3, 130, 215, 246

Beaufort, Cardinal, xxiv, xxv, 14, 96

Beaufort, Joan, Queen of Scotland, m. James I, 29, 57

Beaufort, Joan, m. Earl of Westmorland, xxi, xxiii, xxiv

Beaufort, John, 94, 175, 180–1

Beaufort, Margaret, Countess of Devon, 29

Beaufort, Margaret, d. of 2nd Duke of Somerset, 114, 238

Beaufort, Margaret, Countess of Richmond, d. of 1st Duke of Somerset, xxx, xxii, 72–3, 107, 157, 192, 245, 253, 291, 295, 304–5

Index

Index

Somerset, Eleanor Beauchamp Duchess of, m. 2nd Duke, xxviii
Somerset, Margaret Beauchamp of Bletsoe, Duchess of, m. 1st Duke, 73
Somerset, Edmund 2nd Duke, xxviii, xxx, xxxi, xxxiv, xxv, xxxvii, xxxviii, xxxix
Somerset, Edmund, 4th Duke, 94, 116, 131, 154, 175, 179–81, 238
Somerset, Henry 3rd Duke, xxxv, 5, 6, 12–14, 24, 26–9, 39, 46–9
Somerset, John 1st Duke, xxi, xxx, 14, 29, 72–3
Sorel, Agnes, mistress of Charles VII, 83
Stacy, John, 235–6
Stafford, Henry, s. of Duke of Buckingham, 73
Stafford, Humphrey of Southwick, Earl of Devon, 12, 13, 34, 51, 134, 137, 143–4
Stallworth, Simon, 285–6
Stanley, Thomas Lord, Earl of Derby, 73, 166, 192, 216, 220, 262, 267–8, 273, 280, 283–4, 291, 295, 299–301
Stanley, Sir William, 127, 165, 273, 299–301
Stillington, Robert, Bishop of Bath and Wells, 24, 108; Chancellor, 124, 128, 157, 165, 175–6; dismissed, 192, 239, 289, 290; bastard son, 289
Stillington, Thomas, 290
Stonor, Sir Thomas, 96
Stonor, Sir William, 133, 285
Stonor Papers, 31
Strange, Lord, 299, 301
Strangways, Sir James, Speaker, 78–9
Sturgeon, John, Master of the Ordnance, 216, 217
Sudeley, Ralph Butler Lord, 96, 168, 289
Suffolk, Alice Chaucer Duchess of, m. 1st Duke, xxvi, xxvii, 187, 228
Suffolk, Elizabeth Plantagenet Duchess of, m. 2nd Duke, 65, 243, 290
Suffolk, Edmund de la Pole 3rd Duke, 306

Suffolk, John de la Pole 2nd Duke, 65, 72, 93, 145, 216, 243, 280, 290–1, 293
Suffolk, William de la Pole 1st Duke of, xxvi–xxx, xxxv, 72, 93, 96, 246
Surrey, Henry Earl of, poet, 243

Talbot, Sir John, 289
Tetzel, Gabriel, of Nuremburg, 117–19
Tewkesbury, Abbot of, 237
Tewkesbury, Battle of, 177–80
Thomas, William ap, of Raglan, Mon., 4
Thomas of Woodstock, 22
Thursby, John, 235
Tiptoft, John Earl of Worcester, 79–81, 85, 87, 89, 121–2, 127, 147, 152, 157
Torre, Antonio de la, 29
Towton, Battle of, 46–9
Tresilian, John, master smith of St George's Chapel, 279
Trollope, Sir Andrew, 4–7, 12–14, 24, 26–8, 39–41, 45–6, 49
Tucotes, Sir Roger, 235
Tudor, Edmund, xxxii, xxxiii, 72–3
Tudor, Jasper, see Jasper Tudor
Tudor, Owen, xxxii, 35–6
Tunstall, Richard, xxx
Twynho, Ankarette, 234–7, 239
Twynho, Roger, 234–5

Vaughan, Sir Thomas, 123, 204, 277, 283–4
Vaughan family, 295
Vaux, Catherine, 181, 187, 229
Vere, de, bros, of Earl of Oxford, 81, 171, 194, 244
Vergil, Polydore, 138, 209, 239, 303, 309
Vernon, Henry, of Haddon, Derby., 166, 181

Wakefield, Battle of, 27–8
Walpole, Horace, 73
Warbeck, Perkin, 293, 297, 301
Warkworth, John, chronicler, 156, 193, 205

321

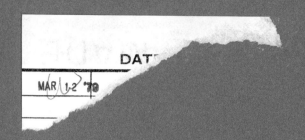

Clive, Lady Mary.
This sun of York; a biography of Edward IV ₁by₁ Mary Clive. ₁London, New York₁ Macmillan ₁1973₁

xiii, 323 p. illus.. geneal. table, maps, ports. 22 cm. £4.25
GB•••

Includes bibliographical references and index.

1. Edward IV, King of England, 1442–1483. 2. Great Britain—History—Edward IV, 1461–1483. I. Title.

DA258.C5 1973   942.04′4′0924   73–175045
ISBN 0–333–14752–9   [B]   MARC

Library of Congress   73 ₁4₁